CHANGING GEARS

Bicycling America's Perimeter

BY

JANE SCHNELL

MILNER PRESS
Atlanta, Georgia

Published by Milner Press, Atlanta, Georgia.

Manufactured in the United States of America.

International Standard Book Number 0-9626112-0-4

First printing
5   4   3   2   1

Edited by Georgie Meuth Mundell and Phyllis Mueller
Editorial assistants: Lisa Barnard and Laura Segraves
Photographs by Jane Schnell unless otherwise noted

Library of Congress Cataloging-in-Publication Data:

Schnell, Jane, 1930
    Changing gears : bicycling America's perimeter / by Jane
    Schnell.
        p.   cm.
    ISBN 0-9626112-0-4 : $19.95
    1. Bicycle touring—United States. 2. Schnell, Jane, 1930-
-Journeys—United States. 3. United States—Description
and travel—1981- I. Title.

GV1045.S3   1990
796.6'4'0973—dc20   90-36250
                                                            CIP

CONTENTS

Introduction

Summer on the Canadian Border
1 Life on the Road in Lower Michigan   2
2 Upper Michigan Beckons Us West   17
3 Voyageurs Come Alive in Minnesota   33
4 Grains and Grasshoppers in North Dakota   44
5 Wind-cycling Eastern Montana   63
6 Mountain Montana Hospitality   85
7 Panhandling Idaho   102
8 Cascading through Washington State   106

Down The Pacific Coast
9 Washington Dikes and Ferry Hopping   128
10 Fog and Cold in Craggy Oregon   146
11 Getting South to California Sun   157

Winter on the Mexican Border
12 Changes in Southern California   190
13 Rolling Free in Arizona and New Mexico   211
14 The Rio Grande Valley of Decisions   235

Spring Along the Gulf Coast
15 Texas Turning Points   274
16 Deltas, Bayous, and Sugar Sand   289
17 Beached on the Spanish Main Panhandle   304

Discovering the Thirteen Colonies
18 Atlantic Marshscapes   326
19 Skylines to Treelines   350

Back to the Beginning
20 To Square One   374

Epilogue   394
Appendix   396
Index   398

INTRODUCTION

I wrote this book to share my American bicycling adventure, my tour around the perimeter of the United States. I did the trip because I wanted to, although when I started I wasn't sure why.

For the occasions when people asked why I was doing such a thing, I had prepared a few half-baked replies: "to collect photos, to get in shape, to live outdoors, to get away from air conditioning." All of these were true, though frequently I forgot to take photos or didn't stop to take them. My aerobic condition improved, but I didn't lose weight. I did a lot of camping, but I also stayed in motels and with friends.

I added, "to prove an old lady can do it, and to escape routine and responsibility." I celebrated my fifty-sixth and fifty-seventh birthdays on the road. The trip itself, like life, quickly became routine. I didn't escape responsibility; it follows you no matter where you go. Finally, I realized I didn't need to know why I was doing the trip; I just really wanted to do it. And I did.

Eight and a half months were spent actually bicycling, although my trip, including vacations from bicycling, covered thirteen months. The actual bicycle mileage on the perimeter was between 11,500 and 12,000 miles. I traveled 700 miles in other vehicles and took a few excursions off the perimeter, including Bicycle Ride Across Georgia and pedaling in the San Juan Islands.

There were times when I read the mileage off the map because my cyclometer wasn't working, and there were other times when I forgot to recalibrate when I changed the front tire size. Often, when I traveled with a companion, our recorded mileage did not agree. Allowing for errors, I've determined the trip mileage to be over 12,000 miles, though I'm not sure what difference it makes to know exactly.

The exact mileage would matter if I wanted to join Richard De Bernardis in the *Guinness Book of World Records*. He took 180 days to pedal America's perimeter, 12,093 miles in 1978-79, when he was twenty-two. Dwight Smith and Bill Horne have completed longer perimeter bicycle tours, but no female is known to have done it. For me, competing with myself, finishing the journey, mattered more than the miles.

To prepare, I bicycled as much and as often as possible on

club rides that presented a challenge to me. I rode with better riders when I could and tried to learn their techniques. I read about bicycle theory and training.

I pedaled about eight hundred miles the month before I began and five hundred miles per month for two months before that. During the trip, I expected to ride an average of a thousand miles a month.

Frequently, I was asked who sponsored me. When I answered, "Me" people wanted to know why. I did not want to take the time or assume the obligations to obtain sponsorship, so I paid for the trip myself.

To meet expenses on the road, I bought traveler's checks and left them with my mother. When Mom forwarded my mail, she sent a few traveler's checks as well. Quickly, I learned denominations over twenty dollars often presented a problem at small town stores. Sometimes the clerk had never seen a traveler's check and had to consult someone. Larger checks required a trip to the local bank.

Credit cards were used whenever possible. In small towns there were no automatic teller machines; the national systems were confined to larger metropolitan areas, which I avoided. I packaged cash, traveler's checks, personal checks, and several identity documents in reclosable plastic bags, carried on my person and in several places on the bike. The checks were handy for self-registering at campgrounds. I had an AT&T card for charging telephone calls.

I kept going because the trip continued to be fun and challenging. Although I pedaled the bicycle and then the computer with my own feet and hands and I am responsible, the trip and this book are the work of many.

I cannot count the ways I am indebted to people I encountered on the road. They are the story. Where known, their names are mentioned in the text. In some cases, I changed a name or omitted part of a name for the sake of privacy, or obscured the location of a home. You will recognize yourselves.

I called the companion with whom I began the trip "Bea," but that is not her real name and she is slightly fictionalized, again to protect her privacy. Her contribution was significant and appreciated. Had she not encouraged the idea through her participation, there would have been no trip. I learned a great deal from her about camping and birdwatching, and I learned from her stories and her experiences. Our conversations are written as I remember them, not necessarily as they were spoken.

Over a hundred friends and family members provided oral and written feedback from the letters they received from me during the trip. These "pedalgrams," as I came to call them, were dispatched for me by Julia Samson or sent from roadside copy machines. Several recipients sent me postage. Others wrote letters, asked questions, left messages—feedback that kept me going. You and I know who you are and I thank you.

I also thank my editors. Georgie Meuth Mundell patiently extracted meaning out of confusion, untangled my imaginative spelling, and turned monologue into proper English. She and her husband, Ken, encouraged me with cheer and many lunches. Phyllis Mueller shaped my experiences into the story in your hands with perception, skill, and artistry.

I cannot forget Willie T. Weathers, who never let me get away with carelessness and encouraged my desired to write, and the many other students, teachers, and administrators at Randolph-Macon Woman's College, where I was offered more opportunity than I accepted. I'm grateful for the support of my mother, Ruth Schnell, and my good friends Tom and Septima Murray and Frances H. Porcher.

I am grateful to the League of American Wheelman (LAW), the national organization of bicyclists, for its advocacy, consumer affairs, and education programs that benefit all bicyclists. LAW celebrates its 110th anniversary this year.

Mistakes in this book are my own. I used the spelling from AAA maps and cross-checked my notes, memory, and photographs in an effort to recreate the trip's images accurately. I would appreciate having mixups called to my attention.

At times on the road, I was ready for the trip to end, but I was never ready to stop bicycle touring. It was the experience of a lifetime!

Jane Schnell
February 20, 1990
Washington, D.C.

SUMMER ON THE CANADIAN BORDER

CHAPTER ONE

Life on the Road
in Lower Michigan

Detroit, Michigan, Thursday, July 10

At the Metropolitan Airport terminal, waiting for Bea's plane to land, I felt foolish. I had walked through the airport wearing skin-fitting blue iridescent tights, bicycle touring shoes, and a jersey with brilliant, diagonal, five-color stripes. It was an odd getup for a fifty-five-year-old woman with graying hair. Awaiting luggage, I didn't blend into the swirl of young men in business suits and young women with attache' cases.

Months ago, glad my thirty years in the workplace was over, I stood on the top step of the rest of my life and decided to go vagabonding on a bicycle. To see the country I served would satisfy my yearning to do something really different, really free. I wanted to live outdoors instead of in an office that reminded me of an oversized safe deposit box. I wanted to meet other Americans, people who had not submitted to detailed investigations and polygraph tests, people who had not been trained to control their thoughts and feelings for fear of revealing a state secret, people who lived beyond city centers, suburbs, and interstate highways. I wanted a vacation from life as I knew it.

I decided as a parting gift for thirty years' commitment to the United States of America I would give myself one year of freedom from schedules, regulations, or responsibility — one year to do anything I chose. I wanted to see what this country looked like, felt like, smelled like, and sounded like. Freedom was a privilege, a "gold watch" I gave myself, a retirement present from me to me.

I wanted to wander but felt constrained by a socially-ingrained conviction that it was not a wise thing for a lone woman to do. I had not been afraid on vacations to walk alone in Nepal, Pakistan, and India or travel across Laos, Cambodia, and Indonesia. I had not been afraid to float down the Irrawaddy River on a paddle steamer. Yet, I felt I should not bicycle alone, so I found a companion. I met Bea in Homestead, Florida, when I participated in the Dr. Paul Dudley White 20th Wheelmen's Winter Rendezvous during the first week of March. On one of our rides together, she talked about her interest in bird-watching and her great desire to make a long bike tour. Then she added, "But I can't go alone. It's so hard to find someone to ride with, especially for a trip like that. Most sixty-one-year-olds can't ride that far." I wondered if, at fifty-five, I could. I knew I could ride across the country, but I did not know how fast I could go. Bea sounded like me.

Before the rally in Homestead ended, Bea sought me out to talk further about touring. Since neither of us thought we could tour alone, we agreed to accompany each other. Bea was committed to tour England with a group of bicyclists in June. The first day we could meet to begin our trip was July tenth.

The tour Bea and I anticipated would be self-contained. We would carry everything we needed to camp, cook, and travel. We wanted to go around the perimeter of the United States, following the international borders of the forty-eight states south of Canada. Most bicyclists crossing the United States, over ten thousand a year, travel from west to east to maximize the advantage of the wind at their backs. Our route would take us into the wind some of the time.

In July and August, we wanted to pedal along the Canadian border, and we needed to cross the Rocky Mountains before early September snows. A travel estimate of fifty miles per day, five days a week indicated that we would have to begin our trip in the Great Lakes region. I picked the Detroit Metropolitan Airport as the place to meet. We would begin by pedaling north, toward Canada, then continue west counterclockwise around the borderlands and coastlines, cutting off the tips of Florida and Maine, useing ferries along the coasts and avoiding population and traffic centers. I estimated the trip at twelve thousand miles and thought a year should be time enough. Bea, before leaving for England, agreed with the general plan and happily left the details to me. As I planned the route I came to think of myself as the leader.

And here I was, bicycle box reclaimed and unpacked,

impatient to begin. I decided to weigh the bicycle with my luggage in saddlebags called panniers. The bicycle, its load, and I weighed 280 pounds. I weighed 165 pounds — too much, I felt for my five-foot five-inch height.

Bea triumphantly glided down the escalator. Her bike bag appeared on the turntable. We unpacked it, turned the handlebars, screwed in the pedals, attached the wheels, and hung on her panniers.

My trip to discover the United States on a bicycle started when my right foot activated the treadle at the exit. The airport terminal doors opened to America! After rolling my heavy bicycle into the street, I straddled it, looking over my shoulder. Bea followed. I had my left foot on the pedal and my right toe on the curb. I pushed the pedal. The bike moved ahead. I could barely keep my balance. The headset, joining the front wheel and frame, felt as if it would explode. My bike wobbled uncontrollably, its tail and nose trying but failing to swim like a fish through the Michigan sunshine.

"Now I know why I never before loaded the bicycle and tried to ride it," I said to myself. "I would have abandoned this whole idea. Home, however, is too far away now." Pedaling on, I tried to gain a little speed and stability. Certain that the bicycle frame was about to dismember, I finally stopped and, standing over the bike, turned around to see what Bea was doing.

"I can't ride this thing," I shouted over the airplane engine noises. She wobbled closer. Her reply was ringing laughter. We walked the rest of the way to the entrance of the building where a post office was located.

Bea watched the bicycles while I found one box near a trash bin and obtained another from a ticket clerk. When I returned to Bea and our bicycles, she was pulling my clothes out of my panniers!

"What are you doing?" I asked, shocked.

"You brought too much. There's just too much stuff." We filled the two boxes with our excess items, including my duffel bag and Bea's bike bag. We then taped, addressed, and mailed the boxes home.

I was dripping with sweat despite a mid-seventies breeze, but the temperature was still a welcome change from the ninety-degree weather I'd had in Washington early that morning. Our bikes probably were neither a lot safer nor more stable now, but I felt better about them. By mid-afternoon, we rolled out of the airport into unknown Michigan.

Bea had never commuted to work on a bicycle, as I had in downtown Washington, D.C. Her riding, more extensive than mine over a longer term, had been more rural. I led, zigzagging our way west and north for about forty miles that afternoon, avoiding major towns. I had never been to Michigan, but my well-studied maps were easy to follow.

Ten miles, over an hour, into the afternoon, still insecure upon our mounts, we stopped at a busy intersection. Our rear-view mirrors were not helping. We could not balance the bikes well enough in traffic to turn our heads, and the noise made it impossible to hear our shouts to each other.

I had brought voice-activated, two-mile range walkie-talkie sets, and now we put them on, stuffing the aerials through the holes in our helmets and clipping the batteries to our collars. I thought these communicators would be great in noisy traffic and, perhaps, out on the road when we were within sight but out of each other's hearing. At GEAR (Great Eastern (Bicycle) Rally) in Buffalo, a pair of ride leaders used this equipment with great success at the head and tail of a group of twenty or thirty bikers. Our experience, however, was disappointing, and we took our sets off. One unit was defective and would not broadcast. I decided to send them both home from the next post office.

At a red light, we stopped side by side. A man in a car in the next lane shouted, "How far are you going?"

"Around the U.S.A.'s perimeter," I said.

"The what?"

"All around the edges of the lower forty-eight."

"How long will that take?"

"Over a year."

"That's great! Can I go with you?" he grinned.

"Sure, you carry the stuff in your car, and we'll pedal the bicycles." We all laughed, while the light turned green and horns honked. We wobbled uncertainly through a left hand turn which soon led us into farmland.

After forty miles of bicycling, about seven miles north of Ann Arbor, we turned into the Lakes Motel at Whitmore Lake. We needed food, sleep, another reorganization of our saddle-bags, and a fresh start. Camping could wait.

Whitmore Lake, Friday, July 11

I peeped out the window early. There was a light rain. Bea was lying in bed, hands in the air, massaging her wrists. My shoulders were sore. Balancing loaded bicycles had stressed the upper parts of our bodies.

When we stopped for the evening, my bicycles frame still felt loose-jointed, but the feeling that the bike would come apart had dissipated. I knew I had a good bike. I remembered a conversation with Floyd Hartman, a friend from my home bicycle club, when I was in Homestead, Florida. Encouraging me to undertake this trip, he said, "There is only one bicycle designed and built for such a tour. They're not made anymore. World Bicycles, the shop helping sponsor our rally, had one in my size, and I bought it today. They have your size, too."

"But my Fuji America is a touring bike. Why should I buy another one?" I asked.

"The Centurion Pro Tour 15 has a sealed headset, bottom bracket, and hubs. That means that you won't have to repack the bearings during a twelve-thousand-mile trip. It means you won't have to worry about riding in the rain. In addition, it has heavier tires to carry the load, and the rear wheel has forty spokes instead of the usual thirty-six. You probably won't have any broken spokes to repair. You've had your Fuji three years, but it was designed about five years ago and has none of these features. Although it was one of the first touring bikes, it was not designed as a true touring bike; the manufacturer just stretched the derailleurs and gears to capacity and called it a touring bicycle. The Centurion Pro Tour 15 was designed specifically for what you propose to do. It has never been sold widely on the East Coast, but this shop has one in your size for four hundred fifty dollars. It is well worth that price." Convinced, I bought the bike.

Because of the light rain, we took our time, packing two more small boxes of less-than-essentials to mail home from the local post office. After breakfast, I completely repacked the contents of all four of my panniers inside plastic bags, putting heavier items over the rear wheel to relieve the strain on the headset, where the fork that holds the front wheel joins the rest of the bicycle frame.

About twenty miles down the road, as we headed north, we stopped to eat. There were no sandwiches. Bea had discarded the bread bag containing them. I was hungry, tired, and exasperated. It began to rain and, putting on my raincoat, I began to cry. Bea had no way of knowing that I had eaten lightly at breakfast, intending to snack on the peanut butter sandwiches or have them for lunch. She felt hurt, and I was angry at myself for being so upset over the loss of a little food. In the next store, I chose bread sticks to go with my milk, and Bea ate Twinkies with hers. The day was gray and the rain intermittent as we rode on. We often paused to put on or take off shirts or jackets. Bea was hungry, so we stopped for lunch. I ordered a bowl of chili and a decaffeinated diet Coke. The chili tasted good, but later I felt sick from eating too much. I rode better on an empty stomach, doing ten to twenty miles before breakfast, and then having no more than one egg and one piece of toast. I also rode better after a light lunch. Bea ate a large breakfast and a fast food snack every two hours thereafter. Both of us liked a good dinner to end the day. We differed, too, in our bicycle riding styles. Bea liked to ride fast and stop frequently. I liked to begin the day slowly and halt infrequently.

My legs, in short pants, were cold and wet. Bea had sent my long warm pants to her daughter in one of the parcels. Cold, wet calf muscles did not make me feel charitable. Tired, damp, and disgruntled, we halted at Welcome Inn across from the Owosso Airport. Bea called her daughter, Beth, and then fell asleep. I called Beth back and asked her to send my long pants that also functioned as pajama bottoms to General Delivery in St. Ignace in northern Michigan. Then I studied maps and wrote notes to friends — to get rid of the paper!

Owosso, Saturday, July 12

After consulting with our waitress at breakfast, I decided on a route change. A man at another table heard us, said he was a bicyclist, and suggested we use a different road. Bicyclists give the best information, but their advice needs to be understood in relation to how they ride. That bicyclist's directions resulted in a good day.

We came upon our first country store by mid-morning. Still acting with my big city mindset, I stayed outside with the bikes while Bea went into Chapin General Store. I marveled at the old red-white-and-blue letter box on a post. It was genuine antique, street furniture. Three antique cars drove up: a 1928 Oldsmobile, an old Lincoln, and a Ford. The occupants and I took pictures of each other. "We're just driving around on this lovely Saturday," Carl and Mary Goldman told me. "It's so wonderful to be out in the country!"

A woman standing in front of the store who said she was seventy-four gave me accurate instructions on the route, and said she had a pacemaker. Everyone thought our retiring and circling the United States on bicycles was a splendid idea. They wanted to go with us.

Bea said, "The more you tell them how nice they are, the nicer they get." I felt the same way about trust. Everyone has some fear of strangers, but usually the more you trust people the more they wish to be worthy of trust. Aloud, I said, "If they all came with us, we'd really have a gang!"

Bea responded, "Talking to a dozen people around the store is like throwing a stone in a pond. You don't know what the effect of the ripples is going to be."

We were in a part of Michigan where paved farm roads ran mostly at right angles. On the road, I looked down, watchful of hazards: gravel, sand, water, glass, holes, cracks, debris, and dogs. When I looked up, I saw wheat and corn fields along a flat, straight road. A motorcyclist approached and gave thumbs up.

We had travelled twenty-five miles northwest when we stopped at the Marion Springs Country Store. Fresh baked bread, still warm, was for sale. The storekeeper would not sell us a quarter pound of butter, so we bought a pound of margarine sticks and gave three of them to the girls selling the homemade bread to help fund a festival. We also had a half-gallon of orange juice, cheese, molasses cookies, and two bananas for lunch. While we ate, we sat on the grass outside the store, watching swallows swoop over the closely cut grass and goldfinches and robins flit and hop. Bea described the nearby corn as soldiers standing at attention, green bayonets raised.

Later, riding among fields of wheat in the bright sun, we sang "America the Beautiful" at the top of our lungs and pedaled as hard as we could. Then, gasping, we sang alternately, yelling out the phrases.

Miles further, at another country store, we drank orange juice and filled our water bottles. We chewed dried figs all day, because I refused to send them home and they were heavy. Bea, who was born in southwestern Michigan, told me she really liked this black, flat earth.

We rode from nine to five, covering sixty-five miles,

stopping at several country stores, and halting before it rained again at Flats Campground on Sanford Lake. Getting in was like registering at a motel, except that I received a map and a receipt with the site number "for display on your windshield" instead of a key. I hung the receipt on my bike. The shower stalls were spacious and clean and the hot water plentiful.

Bea had the tent up and was opening a can for part of supper when I returned from the nearby wash house. There were few campers. I thought being outdoors all day was grand!

As Bea continued her food preparation, I began maintenance on my bike chain. I was taking the chain apart to remove it from my bike, clean it, and then relubricate it by boiling it in hot paraffin. I prefer using paraffin, even though I knew I'd have to recoat the chain every time it rained. Bea used WD40 on her chain and usually had "chain leg," a greasy imprint on the back of her right leg. A dirty chain also leads to greasy hands, face, and clothes.

I started to twist the chain tool to push the rivet through three of the four sides of a chain link. At the critical moment, I lost my concentration and pushed the rivet too far so that it fell out. Once the rivet is totally out, most people think it cannot be put back. I have put them back, two or three times, but it takes about twenty minutes and is a terribly frustrating task. I decided not to try to replace the rivet after cooking the chain in the hot paraffin. Instead, I replaced the whole link with an extra one from my one-inch-square tool box. I threw away a lot of frustration with the old link.

Soon after we ate, it began to rain. Quickly we covered the bikes with plastic and put our panniers in large plastic bags under the picnic table. We crawled into our tent, and Bea fell asleep. I was chilly but finally slept, too.

Sanford Lake, Sunday, July 13

Going to bed at sundown had us up at dawn. The day was sunny, warm, and crisp like early fall. We drank coffee while oatmeal cooked and were ready to roll in two hours. Our route led us north on M18, then through Beaverton, Gladwin, and Skeels. I took a few photos of a stone house and barn and then stopped again by a field to photograph hay bales I named "jelly rolls." Far ahead when I stopped, Bea rode out of sight. The land undulated gently up and down as I rode along, watching the kingbirds, goldfinches, red-winged blackbirds, robins, and sparrows. In mid-afternoon, we stopped at Pruden-ville for spaghetti, meatballs, and salad.

Expecting to continue about twenty more miles, we then rode between Houghton and Higgins Lakes. I adored peeping between the houses along the shore to see the boats, yards, and flowers. I watched the people, glad I wasn't taking out the garbage, painting the house, digging in the garden, or cutting the grass. I was delighted to be smoothly pedaling along on my bike, humming to myself.

Along Old Route 27, we came to the Fawn Motel. Bea was tired and wanted to stop instead of proceeding another five-and-a-half miles to the campground. We turned into the driveway.

near Higgins Lake, Monday, July 14

Dawn came — sunny, cool, and windless. Bea phoned her daughter, while I pumped the tires and repacked my panniers. Dodging the potholes, threading our way around glass, gravel, and other dangers to bicyclists, we rolled down the road to breakfast. My attention faded as my legs became chilled. I hoped for warmer weather until we reached St. Ignace three days hence and the long pants Beth was sending. We stopped at The Hut for breakfast, then cycled into a beautiful day, riding through Au Sable Forest under large, white, puffy clouds.

I decided Michigan was a good place to begin a bicycle tour. Traffic along these thin map lines was light. The land was flat, allowing us to acclimate to daily riding on a loaded bicycle. Campgrounds and grocery stores were plentiful.

I plotted our route all the way to Mt. Vernon, Washing-ton, using AAA and state-issued maps. For the first month, I made a list of potential campgrounds for each night. Then, depending on where we halted each night, I revised. Four days' experience on Michigan roads provided confidence and feed-back for future decisions.

In Gaylord, a sister city to Pontresina, Switzerland, an Alpenfest was underway. I stood still a moment, lost in remem-brances of my first ski vacation at Pontresina, of the glittery, pale blue eyes of our ski instructor, of my parents and my joy at leaving war-ravaged Berlin for a week in a country where there was glass in the windows. For a few days, there had been no beggars, and I had not had to close the shutters before turning on the dining room light to avoid a hungry audience at meals. Mostly, however, I remembered the snowy hillsides of Pontresina and the joy of being out in the sun all day in the mountains. Pontresina was a prelude to many ski vacations following my year as a student in Switzerland.

"They've got it together," Bea pronounced.

"Yes, the Swiss have," my mind responded, before I realized she was talking about Gaylord. A carnival atmosphere permeated the town.

We rode north on Old 27 through green land worthy of all I had heard about Ireland. Riding an old road which was superseded by an interstate proved pleasing. We pedaled past black farmland under wonderful trees. Though the temperature was in the seventies, the wind carried a chill. We had yet to see the Great Lakes, and only had whiffed their influence. Last evening, I read that one could stand anywhere in Michigan and be within six miles of inland water and that Michigan has eleven thousand lakes. We seldom had been out of sight of one.

In mid-afternoon, we entered Vanderbilt, named for Cornelius, who donated land for the town. After lunch, I sent home another box containing my spare shoes, the Walkman, and four 120-minute music tapes. Bea's butterfly and flower books were sent, too. Perhaps because I felt the weight difference, I rode buoyantly over gentle hills and through woods where the sun streamed down in spotlights to the clean forest floor. Up and down we went, happily, until Bea's chain came off. It was not broken, and she got it back on easily. Looking at her black, greasy hands and leg, I was relieved to have paraffin on my chain. We turned at Thumb Lake into Boyne City Road and stopped for a banana split at about five o'clock with twenty miles to go.

Later we paused at a house with a large yard. Bea had spotted a pair of killdeer with a lot of babies just out of the nest and running along the ground. They hid in a wood pile and nearby tall grass as we watched. Seeing us, two small children came out of the garage and ran toward us, passing the killdeer. We stood still. The adult killdeer skillfully swooped and called, leading the children away from the baby birds, who were running from grass tuft to grass tuft not twenty-five yards away. Slowly, we walked our bikes along the roadside away from the nestlings. We left quietly, turning our pedals gently on the descending slope.

With the sun shining and the road smooth, I sailed down hills with the wind screaming through my helmet at about thirty miles per hour, reminding me of five summers spent sailing and racing a small boat on the rivers feeding the Chesapeake Bay. Today, the breeze with its watery smell made our bicycling seem like sailing; only the salt was missing. Beautiful cattails flew past in the ditch; beyond them was grass, cattle, or woods of maple, birch, hemlock, aspen, spruce, and fir trees. I was surprised to find aspen, which I had seen only in Colorado.

Houses here were interesting, too. As I rode beside the Erie Canal from Buffalo to Albany in preparation for this journey, New Yorkers called my attention to the rock masonry in homes and barns. Here in Michigan were similar structures with the best stones on the front, and less-exactly matched stones along the sides and rear. Glaciers of the last Ice Age polished and deposited stones in both New York and Michigan.

Bea stopped to observe swans and Canada geese. I pulled out my binoculars and looked, too. She was teaching me to be a bird watcher. We saw a red-headed woodpecker, a bird I had not seen since leaving my home state of Georgia when I was eleven.

We rolled into our campsite at Young's State Park about seven o'clock, not really exhausted but tired of being on our bicycles nearly twelve hours. My cyclometer registered 77.6 miles. I set up the tent while Bea heated water for coffee. She observed, "I've worked all my life so I could have a car, a house. Then I abandon them to go around the country on a bicycle."

I joined the game, "We have a fine tent, self-inflating mattresses, a lot of elaborate gear to get away from all the elaborate gear." We were both laughing.

Boyne City, Tuesday, July 15

I was elated by speeding downhill, descending the escarpment into Petroskey. We spent another marvelous morning spinning past beautiful homes overlooking Little Traverse Bay and through Bay View, where the homes and the road followed a high bluff above the water. We looked out toward Lake Michigan and continued pedaling until our arrival in Harbor Springs brought us to a halt. Like squirrels eyeing nuts, we spotted homemade cookie samples on a sidewalk table and stopped to taste them. The town was charming, its Main Street restored as a shoppers' outdoor and indoor mall, and just waking for the day. We ate, drank, and photographed.

Then, we rode out of town, continuing thirteen miles along a high bluff overlooking Lake Michigan and through green forests of pine and leaf-waving aspen, birch, and maple whose branches met over the country road. Here and there the sun penetrated, unexpectedly changing the green tunnel to gold. Buoyantly, lightly, I felt propelled by the champagne air gently wafting from the lake. We shouted back and forth about birds, trees, views; we sang at the top of our voices. I remember not a single interruption by an automobile.

I shall always be grateful to the Michigan bicyclists I consulted at the Buffalo GEAR before our trip, who advised me to use Route 119 no matter where else we might ride in lower Michigan. As we spun through those few miles in about an hour, I sensed something special.

At Good Hart we realized we were famished. At the combination store and post office, I bought a loaf of homemade bread and asked that it be made into two sandwiches for our lunch and then that the rest be buttered. While we ate, we talked excitedly with other bicyclists sharing the picnic tables outside. They advised us to continue along the coast, and we did.

The bluff rubbed down to sand dunes. We rode between them and the lake shore. I laughed at myself for being astonished that Canada geese drank the water as they waddled along. Then I shook my head and thought, "It's not salty, dummy!"

Turning inland, we pedaled the last miles of the day. The twin towers of the bridge across the Straits of Mackinac, between Lakes Huron and Michigan, tugged us toward Mackinaw City where I phoned for a ride across the five-mile bridge. Then we sat at the roadside "Bicycle Waiting Area" until the truck appeared. Rested now and getting cool, we paid a dollar each, climbed in the back of the pickup with our bicycles, and looked up at the bridge and across the strait separating Lakes Michigan and Huron. The bridge was called the Mighty Mac before newer bridges dwarfed its status as an engineering first. There was as much history on the other side of the Mac Bridge as on this side. Without realizing it, I set a policy for the rest of the trip. We would never *go back*. Going back to see something missed would not be a choice. Perhaps I could come again.

Soon, encamped at Straits State Park in St. Ignace, we each phoned home and went to sleep looking forward to two days of rest.

St. Ignace, Wednesday, July 16

In the morning, I was tired and vowed not to ride six days again without a rest day. We hung around the camp site, wrote letters, washed clothes, cleaned our bikes, and watched birds. At dinner time, we went to the nearby Northern Lights Restaurant where local whitefish and vegetables revived us further. Back at our campsite, surrounded on three sides by cedar and pine trees, we had dessert of fresh-washed Michigan cherries and peaches. During the night it stormed, but I awoke only momentarily, realizing the tent interior was dry and comfortable despite thunder, lightning, and rain.

St. Ignace, Thursday, July 17

Morning dampness discouraged us from cooking. We went back to try a Northern Lights breakfast, then on to the post office where we retrieved a package sent by Bea's daughter that contained my warm pants! Right there in the post office, I pulled them on over my bicycling shorts.

I had planned fifty miles a day, five days a week. We had cycled six straight days, covering 391 miles, averaging sixty-five miles a day on loaded bikes. We were exhausted. I chalked up the extra mileage to initial enthusiasm. Certainly, we had earned three nights and two rest days at Straits State Park. Bicycle travel was much more fun than I expected.

During breakfast, we decided to cram the long hours of daylight with activity. Before and after taking the ferry to Mackinac Island, we explored St. Ignace.

Father Jacques Marquette, a Jesuit missionary, was thirty-four years old when he established the mission of St. Ignace to bring the Christian message to the Indians. In 1673, he journeyed to the Mississippi Valley with Louis Joliet. He never returned alive, but his bones were reburied here beneath the chapel altar.

Archaeologists and students from Michigan State University were excavating the old mission. We watched them work and listened to one person who explained some of the finds. In the mission church built in 1830s, now a museum, we saw artifacts.

We boarded the ferry to Mackinac Island, rode through a fog into sunshine, and felt that we disembarked a hundred and fifty years ago. On this very day, July seventeenth, in 1812, Redcoats and Indians surprised the American garrison at Fort Mackinac and again raised the British flag. The United States got the fort back as a result of the Treaty of Ghent in 1814. The military remained here almost until 1954 when the old fort became a state park.

I was busy taking photographs, listening to the commentaries of a guide, and admiring the views when Bea called my attention to swallows feeding their young under the eaves of the West Blockhouse, constructed in 1798. Then we watched the fife-and-drum and musket-shooting demonstrations on the parade ground. When I looked over the parapet, I saw a flock of cedar waxwings in a large tree below. Beyond them was the Strait. Imagine paddling a canoe out there!

It was on Mackinac Island that John Jacob Astor, who had arrived in America a penniless German immigrant, founded the American Fur Company after the War of 1812. Mink, muskrat, otter, and beaver pelts were sorted and processed on Mackinac Island. Pressed into bales of fur worth millions, they were floated across the Great Lakes and on through the Erie Canal or the St. Lawrence River to New York and London. We ended our walk down from the fort with a look inside the reconstructed missionary chapel made of bark.

We rode down Huron Street toward Mission Point, then back past magnificent hotels and restored homes. I marveled at the displays of colonial life and the realistic-looking Victorian homes, shops, and quarters. There were also horsedrawn carriages, with horses shod in rubber or plastic to prevent slipping and noise. I had walked through real, lived-in towns in northern Kashmir, where people live like the colonists did in the 1700s. Here, though, the smells were missing and utility wires evident.

After lunch, we bicycled slowly along Lake Shore Road and returned to the ferry landing for a hydroplane trip. On our way back to Straits State Park in the sun-washed afternoon, we bought local fish and, while preparing and eating supper, watched a gray jay near our campsite.

When I was planning our trip, I thought about immigrants traveling west through the Erie Canal, then onward by water. Now, here we were, bicycling west along the immigrant routes, moving about the same as boat speed, and twice as fast as horses. While theoretically we were without a schedule, we needed to get over the Rockies before the snows flew. Although retired almost a year, my addiction to schedules, clocks, and goals had not changed much. My businesslike attitude chafed Bea, who was already adjusted to retirement.

Our first week had been completed. Uncertainties about road selections, pedaling a loaded bicycle, and camping had rolled under our wheels. We had worked hard at smoothing over the threat of trouble between us triggered by stresses of hunger, fatigue, and twenty-four hour proximity.

I knew I would find it difficult to adjust to being with another person day in and day out for months on end. I have been called a loner, but I prefer to think of myself as an "only." I was an only child and never married. Though quite independent, I highly value friendships. Bea, widowed after twenty-six years of marriage, the mother of two girls and a boy, had probably never spent much time alone. As we got to know each other, I began to suspect we had only two things in common. We adored riding bicycles on this dream-of-a-lifetime trip, and neither of us believed she could take a long tour alone. Our first week confirmed that our perimeter tour was a realistic goal.

CHAPTER TWO

Upper Michigan
Beckons Us West

St. Ignace, Michigan, Friday, July 18

We packed quickly for the road, breakfasted once more at the Northern Lights Restaurant, and set off to cross Michigan's Upper Peninsula. From the hilltop above St. Ignace, we rolled down past the closed post office, the excavations, and museum on to Mackinac Trail Road. While Bea found a battery for her watch at the Ace Hardware Store, I watched the bicycles and thought how facile travel in the United States was compared to my journeys on four walking vacations in the Himalayas. Here I knew it was safe to drink the water.

We pedaled through a warm, humid morning. The waitress at breakfast complained of the heat, but I was glad not to be cold. "Hot" to me meant high humidity and temperatures at least twenty degrees more than anything we had experienced so far in Michigan. I've found that when I spend all day out in the weather, my body adjusts naturally to the temperature. There is no time to adjust when one is running in and out of air conditioned cars and buildings all day. A big benefit of retirement was life without air conditioners.

When we reached Moran, I mailed home another package containing the fifty-millimeter lens, filters, a bathrobe, extra underwear, and papers and guidebooks for places behind us. A man talking to the postmistress wanted to know how far we were going. I said, "Seattle."

Incredulous, he said, "That's a long way to pedal." He told me the forecast was for three more days of hot, humid weather.

I wanted to say, "Good!" but smiled instead.

We rode out of town on M123, flanked by daisies, black-eyed susans, and blue common chicory. Last week, we had mostly seen sweetpeas, the wonderful Michigan lily, New England asters, fringed gentians, and Houghton's goldenrod. The road was nice and smooth, first flat and then gently rolling. We rode as usual, about fifty to one hundred yards apart, with Bea in front except on downhills or when there were many turns or route markers to find. We turned west on Worth Road and pedaled through planted forests of jack and red pine not yet as tall as the utility wires. Milkweed flowered along the road's edges. We continued at about eleven to fifteen miles per hour with no sign of habitation nearby. Only two cars passed in half an hour.

As we turned into Route 2 just west of Brevort and along Lake Michigan, civilization returned in the form of light traffic. Now we were on a Bikecentennial Bicycle Route. We stopped near New Cut River Bridge to pump water by hand to fill our bottles. I drank a whole quart, cool and sweet, and filled the bottle again.

Not far away, in Epoufette, we paused for lunch, and I saw two great blue herons flying. Later, I saw buffalo in a field, but told myself, "Of course they aren't buffalo! They must be some type of cattle." A half-mile further was a sign, "Oldson's Buffalo."

At Naubinway it began to rain, providing a wonderful excuse to stop for fruit and yogurt at a grocery. Then, since the rain continued to pelt down, we sampled pasties with gravy in a restaurant across the street. "Pasties," the waitress explained, "are a kind of meat pie originally made by the Welsh to take in their pockets for lunch in the mines."

Continuing to Gould City, Curtis, and Helmer, Bea led, setting a fast pace. She protested she did not want to stop about two o'clock after a "mere" fifty miles, but when we reached Luce County Park after seventy-six miles, she was tired.

Since we had run out of cook-stove fuel, I asked a family camped nearby to sell me some from their gallon can. For a dollar, I refilled our bottle. With three water bottle cages on my bike, I carried the stove fuel in a quart metal container in the lower cage. Two water bottles were enough for me.

While we ate, an extra-long motor home pulled into a site on a flat area between us and the lake. We watched with some amusement as it backed and pulled, straightened and leveled. Bea said it looked like a whale out of water. The people who emerged from the giant motor home were large, too. Henceforth, we referred to RVs as whales.

Immediately after supper, Bea went to sleep. I looked out from the trees, across the sloping grassy area at North Manistique Lake. Between me and the lake were several campers, a few tents, and whales. This was our first campground without a shower, and children were swimming in the lake. The air was much too cool for me to contemplate swimming, yet I felt hot and clammy. I went to the lake, removed my shoes, and waded in knee-deep, dangling my arms in water to the elbows to cool off. Tired, but relaxed, I was asleep before the sun set.

Helmer, Saturday, July 19

Dawn was foggy and, therefore, very quiet. Bea was still sleeping when, determined to have a bath, I crawled out of the tent. With a bar of soap, clean clothes, and my towel in hand, I went to the lake. The water was covered by fog. At one edge of the campground, I stepped below the bank and bathed, completely out of sight. Chilly but clean, I found Bea up and packing. No one else was stirring as we pushed our bikes quietly through the fog about nine o'clock. I was a bit surprised at how late people slept at campgrounds.

Rain began. Forty-five minutes later, we reached McMillan and a restaurant breakfast. I ordered the house specialty, the largest, fluffiest cinnamon bun I had ever seen. Inside, the cafe was warm and comfortable and friendly. A woman was selling raspberries for $1.25 a quart. Unable to eat another bite, we bought a quart and a cinnamon bun to eat later. Walking out from breakfast, a couple asked where we were from, where we were going, and if we were afraid. The man told Bea all the places to see in one direction, and the woman told me what not to miss in the other direction. As we talked, the rain stopped. By eleven o'clock we had covered all of six miles.

An hour of steady riding took us through wilderness marsh to the historical museum at Seney. A man inside asked Bea, "How far do you average every day?"

She replied, "We're trying to average seventy miles." It was a surprise to me.

I bought a paperback, *The Dark Peninsula,* by John J.

Riordan. It is a book of stories about people who lived in the lumber boom town of Seney about 1885. I read it during the next few days.

After leaving Seney, we covered a long stretch of flat road where we were just grinding off the miles. It was hot and, as traffic picked up, we rode with concentration in single file on a two-foot shoulder. When Bea got hungry, we stopped for the cinnamon roll and raspberries. The berries were beginning to mold in the heat and, while we ate the good ones, flies and mosquitoes ate us. We paused to see evening grosbeaks and to watch a ruff-legged hawk sitting on a dead branch overlooking a flat marshy area.

While riding into a headwind, we were passed by three bicyclists who commented favorably on our bright, high-visibility jerseys. Later, at Wandering Wheels Campground, two of these bikers came to talk while we set up our tent. They were traveling in a group of five bicyclists with a station wagon to sag for them. ("Sag" refers to a motor vehicle that supports bicyclists, for example, carrying clothes, tents, and equipment, in contrast to "self-contained" touring as we were doing with all our belongings hanging on our bicycles.) The riders took turns having a day off the bike to drive the car. Slim Kauczka, a member of the Middletown Connecticut Cycling Club who had been at the Buffalo GEAR, said he planned to go to Homestead next year. He had ridden on the West Coast and told us about his trip there.

They asked if we had been harassed by a truck driver who, apparently intentionally, tried to run them off the road. Bea felt she, too, had been run off the road. I had not.

They checked Bea's tires and concurred that one tire had been about four years old when she bought it, for it was cracked around the casing. They advised her to buy a new tire at the next opportunity.

I soon left the group and took a shower, put on my bathing suit, and lay on the warm concrete at the pool in the sun. No way was I going into that cold pool water! It was fun to talk with the bicyclists. Had I not been so tired, I would have enjoyed a longer conversation.

Wetmore, Sunday, July 20

I awoke on my fifty-sixth birthday to the buzzing of

mosquitoes. Fully awake, I realized they were all outside the tent — splendid.

During the morning, when we stopped to eat, I phoned the ferry office and the park ranger at Isle Royale. I learned that, although bicycles were not allowed, we could take ours if we left them on the ferry landing where they should be locked to the railing. The exception was permitted because we would be taking one-way ferry rides from Michigan to Isle Royale National Park, then on to Grand Portage, Minnesota. Transit of the park was allowed but not encouraged. We, however, would have to board at Copper Harbor rather than at Houghton, fifty miles nearer. I needed to call the next day to make reservations.

For the first hour of riding, I was so tired I did not want to continue, but, after coffee, juice, and a short rest where we observed a yellow-bellied woodpecker and a hummingbird, I pedaled slowly for a while and gradually began to feel normal.

It was fifty-eight degrees, and there was a slight breeze. I had put a wool shirt over my polyester jersey but was not warm enough. Reversing them, putting the wool shirt next to my skin, improved things. I also wore wool bicycling shorts and my warm tights. I put on and took off my windbreaker jacket several times. It is made of paper and has *The Washington Post* written in small letters all over it except on the broad, orange horizontal stripe. It weighs only a couple of ounces. Bea had one, too. Since we were riding many roads where drivers might not expect bicyclists, we wanted them to be able to see us as soon as possible.

In Harvey, we stopped at an A&W restaurant. After lunch, we rode through Marquette, "Tree City, U.S.A." Every town has some special claim to fame. I wondered if there is a list of them all somewhere.

Along the bike path, we stopped to eat our fill of wild berries. Thimbleberries, which I had never seen or eaten before, taste similar to raspberries but are more delicate in flavor. On the way out of town, a camper passed so close to me that I wobbled from the wind blast. Most drivers of large vehicles were wary of us, perhaps even more afraid of us than we of them. We stopped at Van Riper State Park about seven o'clock, showered, bought wood, and prepared supper. Bea built a splendid campfire.

Champion, Monday, July 21

Bea was still sleeping, so I remained quietly in the tent and read Michigan lore for about an hour. The Algonquians called this area Mischiganong, "The Great Lake." Chippewa, Ottawa, Potawatomi, Wyandot, Miami, and Menominee, as well as French missionaries and fur trappers, lived here until 1763 when this area was ceded to the British after the French and Indian Wars. Michigan was ceded to the United States in the Treaty of Paris in 1783, and became our twenty-sixth state in 1837.

Perhaps we were fortunate to begin our trip on the flat tableland in the state boasting more campsites than any other. I was delighted by how much I learned about places from reading the free brochures, advertising papers, booklets, signs, and schedules.

After breakfast, I phoned Isle Royale and the ferry offices to confirm our schedule for the coming week. Meanwhile, Bea washed clothes, transcribed her notes, and drafted portions of the joint letter we decided to send friends. I liked Bea's ability to summarize and appreciated her sense of humor. Bea was chief proofreader; I financed the project. Julia Samson, who operates a computer software company in Florida, printed and mailed them for us. It was a way to communicate with friends during a year when I could not write them individually.

About one-thirty, we rode four miles to Nettelon's Cafe for lunch and then on to Champion. During the day, we met three bicyclists who were coming from Seattle accompanied by a sag. We felt rather smug about our decision to travel self-contained. Carrying all our camping gear gave us freedom to act according to weather, inclinations, or interests. We did not have to meet anyone anywhere, and a vehicle driver did not have to crawl along with or behind us. Long distance riders and racers, such as those in the Race Across America (RAAM), require sag support, particularly for night riding. We had no intention of riding at night and carried no lights. In rain or fog, we wore our brightest jackets. Our helmets, panniers, and some clothing were festooned with reflectors.

In camp again, we watched sparrows feeding a nestling, and Bea called my attention to purple finches, a myrtle warbler, and a black and white warbler. There were what I called chipmunks and Bea called seven-line ground squirrels hungry for a handout. Every day, I learned something new about camping. Most of all, I was surprised by the scope of the camping sub-culture in America. There were unwritten rules to learn, such as never walking through an occupied site whether people were there or not. The evening stroll custom, perhaps an American version of the Spanish promenade around the city park at dusk or after dinner, provided a time for meeting fellow campers. I had not learned how to cook when camping. Bea seemed to enjoy cooking as much as I liked eating, and her lovely supper, interrupted by a few sprinkles, was enhanced by a rainbow.

Champion, Tuesday, July 22

For a change, I prepared the morning coffee and oatmeal. About an hour along the road posted with Lake Superior Circle Tour signs, we went through the community of Three Lakes. I saw Lake George and Lake Ruth but saw no sign for a third one. We stopped to identify the flowers: Queen Anne's lace, wild roses, water lilies, evening primroses, and marsh marigolds. Later with "Wildflowers of Michigan" in hand, we identified pitcher's thistle and fireweed.

Out on the road day after day, I relied on my ears to detect traffic. Drivers did not seem to realize that we bicyclists could often hear them long before they saw us. We heard engines, wind noises, wind whistling through certain car grilles, and, of course, the blasts of horns that said, "Get off my road!" The more numerous, friendly toots cheered me almost as much as an arm stuck out in the rain to give the thumbs-up signal. Wind displacement blasts against the road told me the size and speed of approaching vehicles long before I saw them in my rear view mirror. I appreciated fast vehicles passing as far from us as possible since bicycles are so affected by windshear. Commercial truck drivers appeared to know this and seemed courteous on the road. I felt my responsibility was to anticipate conditions and get out of their way when the drivers had no choice. I had heard bicyclists complain about truck drivers, but my experience had been positive. When two large trucks had to pass right where I was, I would swerve to the sand, grass, or un-rideable shoulder. Perhaps five years of racing small boats had given me an edge in judging vehicle convergence.

Near Canon Falls, there was enough downgrade so that pedaling normally I reached twenty-two miles per hour. I adore speed.

When we reached the roadside park, Bea noticed a bulge in her tire. She let the air out, pumped it up again, and pronounced it better. I was grateful for Michigan's conveniently located roadside parks with picnic tables, pit toilets, and water pumps. When we stopped I usually lay on a bench or the picnic table and pulled my legs up to my chin to rest and flatten my lower back.

About eleven, when we left the park, the sun was out, the sky cloudless. It was a beautiful day that I intended to savor. The hills were gentle, long and gradual, so that I could go up them at about twelve miles an hour and down at about thirty miles an hour.

As I rode, I often dictated observations into my microcassette recorder. Today, when I picked it up, the back fell off and the batteries tumbled to the ground. I stopped, reinserted the batteries and the back, and taped it shut with electrical tape. Bea said she had the same problem with her "dictator," and I taped hers, too. I carried duct tape and electrical tape wrapped around the handle of my bicycle pump which was stored under a bungee holding the sleeping bag and tent on top of the rack over the rear wheel. On my small bicycle, a nineteen-inch frame, a pump does not fit under the top tube without interfering with the gear shift levers.

After thirty-seven miles, we entered the crowded Hilltop Restaurant in L'Anse and shared a table with a woman named Theresa, her daughter, and two younger children. The six-year-old girl had a bicycle, and I tried to answer her questions in terms she would understand. The homemade bread was wonderful, and we could not get over having it in a restaurant. We later bought raspberries in the parking lot.

A few more miles took us from L'Anse to Baraga State Park Campground. There, I caught Bea's excitement about the birds, as we saw a white-breasted nuthatch, evening grosbeaks, cedar waxwings, and my first American redstart. Bea saw a grebe and two of her young, and finally, her favorite bird, the loon with its laughing cry. There were four of them in the bay.

We walked across the street to Irene's Pizza Restaurant for supper and watched Canada geese and grebes while we ate at the water's edge of L'Anse Bay. Walking back through the nature trail behind the campground, we were chewed up by flies and mosquitoes.

At our tent site, we talked with neighbors Janet and

Ronnie Leech from Marion, Indiana. Bea told me that the stove was not working very well. I looked at it and saw a hole for oil, but we had none.

I asked Ronnie if he had a drop of oil to spare. "I could give you a drop off the dip stick from the car," he responded cheerfully. After that, the stove worked well.

From reading the tourist information I collected in L'Anse, I learned we had ridden all day along the stagecoach route which opened in 1865 to supplement water travel from Marquette to Baraga. Named for Father Frederic Baraga, it was located on the site of an Indian community where he founded a mission in 1843. Today it is part of the L'Anse Indian Reservation.

Baraga, Wednesday, July 23

We set off, intent on riding the full hundred-mile length of Keweenaw Peninsula that juts into Lake Superior during the next two days in order to reach the ferry for our trip to Isle Royale. I was exhilarated by the ride along the Keweenaw waterway to Lake Superior and F. J. McLain State Park. The park was almost full, and we were lucky to have arrived early enough to claim a place on the bluff overlooking Lake Superior.

We set up the tent and watched a black storm blow in from the lake, retreating into the tent when the first raindrops reached us. The tent also gave us relief from swarms of flies and mosquitoes, but it was hot inside until the storm lowered the temperature. When the rain stopped, we emerged into a fine, cool evening.

Except for the bluff-side view of the lake, the campground was unappealing. It was the first really full camp we encountered and it reminded me of Saturday afternoon in a small town — adults promenading, children bicycling or running in every direction, teenagers giggling everywhere, radios and TVs audible. The noise and activity of the evening contrasted with the serenity of cycling through beautiful countryside resplendent with wildflowers and thimbleberries.

F. J. McLain State Park, Thursday, July 24

Our morning tasks had become a shared routine: lighting the stove, cooking, taking down the tent, and rolling up the mattresses and sleeping bags, wrapping them in plastic to keep them dry. Fed, washed, and dressed in freshly laundered, slightly damp clothes, we pedaled out of the park.

We traveled eight miles of flat road to Calumet. As the first few raindrops hit the street, we were looking at delightful Italian Renaissance buildings and at the restored Calumet Theatre where Lillian Russell, Douglas Fairbanks, and Sarah Bernhardt performed. Rain continued to threaten, and we sought shelter. The cafe we chose had no windows low enough for us to see our bicycles, and Bea was worried about locking them. I thought locking the bikes was pointless because all the valuables were stored in easily-opened bags. I handed her the lock, however, and then rolled my bike into a nearby gutted garage. My theory was, if you do not see it, you do not know it is there. She argued that the dark corner provided cover for anyone to steal individual items or even, perhaps, load the entire bike into a truck. I said a prayer for my possessions.

People ask if I am afraid. Of what? I'm more afraid of the paralysis caused by fear itself than anything else. My overriding concern, however, was not bike security. I wanted to keep the chain dry so that I would not have to stop during the day to cook it or spray it with lubricant.

With my bike hidden in the garage and Bea's locked in front, we ducked into John's Family Restaurant for breakfast. As the door shut behind us, sheets of rain descended, thunder clapped and lightning crackled. When we finished eating, the thunderstorm was still raging overhead, shaking the restaurant ceiling and blinking the lights. We ordered more toast and waited. When the rain stopped, we crossed Main Street to the bakery, selected sweet rolls and cookies for snacks, rolled our bikes into the street, and headed for Copper Harbor.

The road was being prepared for resurfacing and was quite rough. Red rock dust, freshly soaked by rain, made it unpleasant for a few miles. I had to concentrate to avoid rocks, holes, cracks, debris, and slippery spots.

The sky seemed to have wiped its eyes as our wheels rolled toward Mohawk. We found the post office open but without power as a result of the storm. Mail was being sorted by flashlight. I obtained a box and filled it with everything I thought I could do without. I crammed maps and papers describing the places behind us into the box, and off it went. The modern post office building, with its windows which could not be opened and an air conditioner which was without power, made me appreciate living outdoors even more. I breathed deeply as we left.

On we rode through Cliff and Phoenix, turning left off Route 41 on to Route 26, a good two-lane pavement with little traffic. Down a small hill we flew to a one-lane bridge where Bea and I squeezed our brakes to a stop midway to look at a small dam and lovely waterfall.

As we moved on, I saw a sign that said "The Jam Lady" in front of a house that included a small post office. This was too good a photo to pass up and, after I took the picture, we went in. I bought a jar of thimbleberry jam.

Florence Mihelcich, the postmistress, picks the berries, makes the jam, sells it, and also deals in used books — quite an industrious woman! With governmental permission, she converted her sun porch into a post office to avoid trekking to work in severe winter weather. We understood. Earlier in the day, we passed a snow-depth marker showing a record snowfall of 394.6 inches. The Keweenaw County average is between 200 and 250 inches each winter.

Approaching Eagle Harbor, we rode a wonderful forested road with high-bluff views of Lake Superior. It was my favorite kind of ride — the momentum of one downhill swoop propelling me up the next rise. For miles, the road wound along the cliffs overlooking Lake Superior past occasional cottages and through evergreen forests. Wild thimbleberries were everywhere.

Eagle Harbor proved large enough to have a cafe. When we walked in, we were greeted like old friends by Ken and Barb Robinson who had been in the same campground at Baraga. We shared a table and, as we ate, asked each other John Bunyan's universal questions about where we had been and what had occurred on the way.

With farewells, we were off again, skimming up and down the slightly hilly and curving road, Lake Superior expanding out of sight on our left and Lake Bailey on our right. Whenever we stopped riding during the afternoon, the flies were biting so fiercely that we set off again to create a breeze. Stopping for thimbleberries, historical markers, and ducks was not worth the fly bites.

On we went, in and out of light rain which, once we were wet, made no difference. In a mid-afternoon darkened by clouds which soon blew away, we arrived in Copper Harbor. Since it was too cold and wet to tent we decided on a warm room, a hot shower, a desk to write on, and the absence of flies at the Brockway Inn Motel. We took turns showering and then bought a gallon of stove fuel, washed our clothes, completed our second joint letter, sorted our gear to prepare for an early start the next day, and cleaned our bicycles with the extra stove fuel so that we would not have to carry more than the new full gallon. Our chores completed, we pedaled off to visit Fort Wilkins before dark.

Surrounded by Canada geese in the middle of the road, Bea chatted with Worth and Walter Johnson and their wives, who were from Tennessee. We six looked at Fort Wilkins, built in 1844 during the Indian Wars and now restored.

On our return to town, Bea and I found out exactly where to catch the ferry in the morning. We ate sandwiches and bought supplies for the next two days on Isle Royale. It was about ten o'clock and getting dark when we tumbled into our motel beds. I looked forward to restful ferry rides and a couple of days off the bicycle.

Copper Harbor, Friday, July 25

Isle Royale is actually an archipelago made up of more than two-hundred islands in the northern part of Lake Superior. On the main island, the largest in the world on a freshwater lake, is most of Isle Royale National Park, accessible only by seaplane or boat. It is a wilderness formed ages ago of lava, sandstone, basalt, and conglomerate. Today, its unspoiled shores and forests are home to many species of wild flowers, including twenty-eight kinds of orchids, wolves, waterfowl, including loons, and the largest herd of moose in the United States.

Until 1843, Isle Royale was considered Chippewa Territory. During the latter half of the nineteenth century, mining, commercial fishing, and logging industries led to the development of settlements. Early in the twentieth century, Isle Royale began to attract tourists, some of whom built summer homes. The National Park, established in 1940, offers thirty-six campgrounds near some of the seventy lakes, a lodge, cottages, and hiking trails. Rules prohibiting wheeled vehicles and pets help maintain the ecological balance as well as the primeval feeling of the area.

While waiting in great anticipation to board the ferry, I overheard a child asking, "Why does the water pile up?" pointing to the waves rolling in off Lake Superior. I could not hear the answer, but hoped it was worthy of a thoughtful question from someone under two feet high.

Bea and I took Antivert pills and stayed on deck in the open air during the voyage aboard the *Ranger III*. Lake Superior was glassy smooth, but both of us are prone to seasickness. Since wheeled vehicles are not permitted at Isle Royale, other passengers asked questions about our bikes. I explained that they would be locked to the dock on arrival, and we were only bringing them because we were in transit to Minnesota. The fresh, sunny air felt restful during our four-and-a-half hour passage.

At Rock Harbor, just before one o'clock, we stepped ashore hungry and cross. We locked our bikes to the rail and went to find food, a campsite permit, and a canoe. When we had piled our bags and panniers into the boat, we shoved off into the glorious day. Bea wanted to paddle stern, so I put my forty-pound-heavier body in the bow. We began canoeing already tired. We chose water travel instead of hiking since we had no backpacks or shoes suitable for walking distances over rocks. We paddled past Park Headquarters and an ancient lighthouse. We paddled until our arms ached and still paddled on, stopping occasionally to rest and look at ducks. On a bicycle eight miles does not seem nearly so far as in a canoe, we discovered, before we stepped ashore on the Daisy Farm dock.

Our campsite was a ten-by-sixteen foot wooden house screened on one side. Our southeast view across the inlet and through the rocks to Lake Superior was magnificent, well worth the long paddle. We tied our canoe to the dock, carried our gear to the house, and attached our Back Country Use Permit to the door handle. The free camping site already felt like home.

Bea soon had spaghetti water boiling since we were starving again. In her haste, Bea poured the spaghetti out with the boiling water, into the grass. Laughter dissipated the stress. Having no more to cook, we returned the spilled spaghetti to the pot, picked out the grass, and reboiled it for good measure. Soon the loons joined our laughter. Once more, we went to sleep before the sun had vanished.

Daisy Farm, Isle Royale, Saturday, July 26

Twelve hours of rest and breakfast with a breathtaking view of Lake Superior recharged us. We walked along the trail toward Greenstone Ridge with renewed spirits. Spider webs sprinkled with dew glittered. We picked and ate a few berries, admired the flowers, and froze to watch a snowshoe rabbit.

Walking along a wooded trail, we heard a crashing and thrashing just ahead. Then all was quiet. We crept forward and saw two moose thirty feet away looking over their shoulders at us through the thickets. We watched one another until the spell was broken by my camera click. Hiking joyfully to the top of the ridge, I was so elated that I was not aware of climbing the slope.

Returning to our cabin, we packed up and carried everything to the canoe. This time, I stepped into the rear. We had a beautiful two and a half hours on the water. Shortly before we reached Rock Harbor, two common loons flew right over us squawking their heads off. I thought Bea, thrilled and excited to see and hear them so close, would fall right out of the canoe! Ashore, we claimed another shelter and hurried off to the dining room next to the small store. I bought groceries for supper and took a nap.

Still tired, I wandered back to the lodge, observing magnolia warblers, mallards, grebes, and woodpeckers on the way and watched sport fishermen cleaning their catch. They had so many lake trout that I could not resist asking if I could buy one. They told me it was against the law to sell fish caught with a sporting license. I wandered back to the dock to watch *Voyager II* bringing in a load of passengers and goods. We would be on it in the morning.

Back at our cabin, I wrote some notes and began to think about a hot shower.

Rock Harbor, Isle Royale, Sunday, July 27

During the night, Bea awoke sick to her stomach. I felt so cold that I got up at half past six, packed everything, and carried it all to the boat. While Bea continued to rest, I went to breakfast. I ate with several people who had been with us aboard *Ranger III*. Since we had all visited Singapore's Raffles Hotel, we compared our visits there. I recounted the thrill of seeing W. Somerset Maugham in the Raffles lobby during his last trip to the Far East. As we discussed roads in Minnesota, I learned we would have a shoulder along the highway for the first thirty-five miles ashore. They also said that Route 1 was flatter and had less traffic but that Route 11 was more scenic and that, after Lake of the Woods, there would be almost no traffic.

It was almost time to catch the ferry to Grand Portage, Minnesota. I dashed back to get Bea. She ate one cracker and a piece of cake and took an Antivert. When she got on the small boat, she looked pale and sick. Our bikes were handed to the top of the deckhouse.

Heavy clouds hung over the smooth water as we motored down the inland passage where we had canoed and out into the lake through Midland Passage. Our boat made a quick stop at Chippewa Harbor to put off and pick up canoeists. Rain began to fall as we squeezed through the narrow strait between orange lichen-covered rocks and continued parallel to the coast of Isle Royale National Park. Bea appeared to be asleep, but I checked on her frequently.

Other passengers brought out lunch sacks. We had none and had eaten all our reserve food. I talked with a man who had just completed a week-long canoe trip, and we agreed on the desirability of carrying equipment by canoe instead of on one's back. He, too, seemed to have no lunch. I had not realized this would be a six-hour trip with no food service.

Visibility narrowed as the rain increased. For a time, I could hardly see the bikes, shrouded and washed by slanting rain. I decided we should go to a motel since Bea was sick and the weather was foul. From other passengers, I learned a lot of people at the lodge yesterday had gotten intestinal flu. Except for Bea's sandwich, we had eaten the same foods and had drunk water from the same sources. I suspected the sandwich. It rained all the way across Lake Superior, clearing at three-fifteen just as we landed at Hat Point in Grand Portage, Minnesota.

The family running the Voyageur Marina had three motel rooms attached to their house, and I rented the last one. Drew, a young man of nineteen, and his recently widowed grandfather, Herb Melby, ran the motel, marina, and restaurant for four months of the year. Drew let me put the bikes in a shed with the lawn mowers and brought me a sandwich and milk, even though the cafe was closed on Sunday. Bea, who could hardly walk, had gone to bed. She had a fever and seemed really sick.

In the night, I had a dream, and I awoke afraid. Had the trip ended? I had rearranged my life for this trip, but was it worth it? Should I have been home instead? Was I learning enough? Perhaps it was a mistake for two people our age to be attempting such a trip. "No," I decided, "What happens is not important, but how I react to it is important. For now, I'll keep pedaling and hope for the best." From the window, I looked at the sunset behind the mountains. "Perhaps," I thought, "freedom is only an abstract idea, an attitude." I tallied up the figures: 12 biking days, 6 rest days, 63 miles per biking day, 42 miles a day overall, 757 total miles. The tally did not tell our story.

I went outside and walked among the dry-docked boats parked on trailers to the pier. There it was lovely, quiet, lonely, and wild. Soothed, I returned to our room to sleep.

CHAPTER THREE

Voyageurs Come Alive in Minnesota

Grand Portage, Minnesota, Monday, July 28

When I awoke after a long, good sleep, Bea was starving. "Good," I thought, "Bea feels better."

"The cafe opens at seven a.m.," I said.

Dressing involved changing to short cycling pants underneath and deciding what layering of my shirts was suitable to the weather. When we were in a motel, Bea got her weather information from TV; I sniffed out the door for mine. The clouds over the lake were blowing east; it would be a fine day. I felt fit and ready to ride.

I had scheduled us to ride forty miles before stopping at a state park along the lake near Schroeder. I wondered if Bea could ride that far.

We were waiting at the cafe door when Herb Melby opened it. This wonderful grandfather served us each two eggs, bacon, juice, and, when we complimented his "home-made" bread, he held up the wrapper for "English Muffin Bread." While we ate, feeling better with each bite, Herb was chatting outside. He came and asked us if we wanted a ride with the Olsens. "They are towing their twenty foot boat which could easily carry the bikes, and you could ride in the carryall with the family."

"When will they leave?" was my follow-up question.

"As soon as you are ready, but no hurry about finishing your breakfast." We hurried anyway. Bea was out the door to get the bicycles. I paid and thanked Herb. I carried all our money, and paid all the expenses. Periodically, I totaled and divided the balance, and then Bea wrote me a check.

Outside, Gary Olsen and his son were lifting our bikes and panniers into the boat. The six of us climbed into the car, started from the lake shore up to the road, and turned south on Highway 61. I noticed from road signs that we were on the Lake Superior Circle Tour route, a 1300-mile route through Canada, Minnesota, Wisconsin, and Michigan. Judging by the parts I'd seen so far, it would make a great bicycle tour. I watched a reconstructed fort and Ojibwa exhibits flick past the car window. The road was perfect and the shoulder fine for bicycling.

Driving with the Olsens, I realized that I was missing a lot on this trip by associating only with Bea. They bubbled over with joy, telling us about skiing, snowmobiling, hiking to waterfalls, hunting, and sailing here in their state. What a wonderful family! They are the people I worked thirty years in the C.I.A. to protect. For them, it was worth getting up when the phone rang at three a.m. and going to work for fifteen hours. I asked, "Would it be too much trouble to halt a moment at the post office in Schroeder?"

The Olsens laughed, "We were planning to stop next door at the bakery, the best anywhere in this part of Minnesota. We always stop there and hoped you'd not mind the delay."

"Does a horse mind being delayed by oats?" I asked.

Bea picked up our mail while I went into the bakery — she could sign, and I had the money!

As we continued, Gary showed us the Sawtooth Mountains. The Olsens told of family outings along the Gunflint Trail, sixty-three miles of blacktop from Grand Marais to the Canadian Border. It sounded like another fine bike trip, but we had to get over the Rockies before snow began. I'd have to come back to Minnesota. Rolling through Tofte and Lutsen, we were told about fishing and boating wonders and the 2,200-foot Alpine Slide for special toboggans. Maybe I should return in winter with my skis.

At the junction where Route 6 turned north, we disembarked about ten-thirty. Despite the sunny, clear sky, sixty-five degree temperature, and a smooth road, I was reluctant to leave. Our road went uphill at once. After three miles, when I had to slow down to avoid overtaking Bea, I saw how weak she was from eating almost nothing for three days. This hill was the steepest one yet. We stopped to observe a flock of evening grosbeaks. There were so many of them so close I could see them in great detail with my 9x25 Nikon miniature binoculars.

Four more miles brought us to Finland, settled in the 1800s by guess who. I was out of water. As we were leaving town, I waved at a man in his yard and asked if we might have some drinking water. Axel Peterson invited us into the house where he and his wife, Joyce, fixed large glasses of ice water.

Joyce filled our bottles with the tepid water we preferred for glugging along our way as Axel told us of a moose looking in their kitchen window one winter morning. Another day, there were wolves in the back yard.

"Wild ones?" Bea asked incredulously.

"Every January, the four-hundred-mile dog sled races begin in Duluth and finish in Finland," Axel said, pulling out his snapshots. I remembered seeing excerpts of the races on TV; next January, I'd certainly be watching again.

As we rode on, I remembered reading that "Minnesota" comes from a Dakota Indian word meaning "sky-tinted waters." State pride is fierce in Minnesota, not unlike national pride in Europe. Having lived abroad from as a teenager and young adult, I've naturally put country first. In my adulthood in the District of Columbia, I never considered "state" and "county." Out here, every county line is marked on the highway, and maps and guides are often by county. People often tell you what county, rather than what town, they live in.

About an hour and a half after leaving Finland, climbing uphill through the forest, I was hungry and Bea was tired. I got out a mattress for her to lie on while I sauteed fresh fish fillets the Olsens had given us. Bea ate nothing. I had no trouble eating all the fish. Then, while the stove was still going, I cooked my chain and put it back on my bike. I read my mail. When Bea awoke, I packed up, knocking over her bike and breaking the rear view mirror in the process.

Another half-mile brought us to the Wildhurst Campground where, at two-thirty, we quit for the day. When camp was set up, Bea took another nap while I wandered around. I talked with the woman who ran the campground and learned we could get supper at the bar. After showering, I sat at the bar talking with the few people present.

Bea joined us. From behind the counter, our hostess mentioned it was difficult to run the bar and restaurant, and keep all the grass cut to maintain the campground. Her husband was in Colorado, and she had been quite worried because she hadn't heard from him for two weeks. His last letter had said he missed her cooking. She was hurt he hadn't missed her.

After dinner, we ate fresh wild raspberries and watched "Wheel of Fortune."

Finland State Forest, Tuesday, July 29

Up before the sun, we packed and left the campground as quietly as possible, trying not to awaken the dogs near the restaurant. They barked politely — once. In the mud at the side of the road, we saw fresh tracks of deer and moose. Evening grosbeaks were everywhere. Bea said they were nighthawks, but they sounded awfully chattery to me. Rested and back to normal, we spun happily down the road through Finland State Forest.

Near Isabella, we found a cafe and went in for breakfast. I was amazed to find a lone woman running the restaurant and a gas station grocery a hundred yards away. She did it all — cooking, pumping gas, selling groceries. No wonder it took so long between coffee and toast. Her husband wasn't up yet; he did the late night shift alone. Incredible.

We continued riding through forest over roads that dipped and swooped, through tunnels of trees with rays of sun spotlighting our way. On mile after mile of my favorite type of terrain I pedaled, crouched down over the bars then standing on the pedals to crank over the next crest, through the range of fifteen gears.

Bea motioned me to come alongside; we hadn't spoken for over an hour. Just as I came abreast of her, a big black bear ran across the road not thirty yards ahead of us.

"Let's get out of here," Bea yelled, standing on her pedals. A mile or so later, I caught up with her, now easing along after a bout of furious pedaling. Whatever made the bear run so fast had made us quite safe. The animal reacted to us first and was long gone almost before we realized its presence. Imagine seeing a wild bear not thirty feet away! Never getting off the bikes, adrenalin at full flow, we continued our swooping ride, right through the Bear Island State Forest into Ely, completing fifty-six miles before noon and acquiring a bear-like hunger.

I leaned my bike against the post office building and sat down on the steps to enjoy the flowers and catch my breath. Bea went to find a hardware store and a mirror to replace the one I had broken and temporarily repaired.

When she returned, I went to Wavin Enterprises where Bobby Johns gave me a box and tape at no charge. After I packed and mailed the box home, we met two women who wanted to know about our trip and asked permission to notify the local paper.

I cautioned, "We haven't done anything yet, only two weeks of riding. They wouldn't be interested until we've done something." I couldn't object to their suggestion that they walk around the corner to the newspaper office and ask. When they returned, Angie Fredrickson and Mattilda Blanche introduced themselves and asked us to come and meet Anne Wognum at the newspaper.

We were astonished by people's interest in what we were doing, and by their pride that we would come to their town. They fingered our sleeping bag and remarked on the plastic bags of grapes and potatoes held atop it with a bungee cord. Angie, writing about our discarding desks for bicycles, closed her story with, "It was hard not to envy them."

Rested and fed, we cycled until we saw a historical marker. We learned that the Old Vermilion Trail, our route, had been built during 1865 and 1866 by mining company employees who were looking for gold. The eighty-five-mile-long road stretched north from Duluth to Lake Vermilion. Nearby, the miners, including Civil War veterans, had built Winston City. Very little gold had been found, and Winston City became Vermilion Range's first ghost town.

We continued a hot ride to Tower where, tired and thirsty, we stopped at a filling station to ask directions to the Hoo Doo Campground. While we drank water and Coke as fast as we could, a man gave us clear directions. After Bea bought WD40 for her chain, we rolled to the bottom of the hill to see the railroad station and train exhibit, and we then headed for camp.

Our marvelous site was on a small, sandy knoll right on the edge of Lake Vermilion. Shaded by small trees was a picnic table and space for the tent. Kinglets fed their babies nearby.

Two women bicycle tourists wheeled into the campsite next to ours. Carol Reddy and her friend were part of the National Nuclear Power Plant Protest group making their way across the country to have their say in Washington, D.C. I began to ask questions and admired the quality of their replies, although I did not agree with their opinions. Who was I to criticize? One of the things I had worked to protect in our country was freedom of expression.

Tower, Wednesday, July 30

Our campsite neighbors came into the Tower Cafe while we were eating breakfast. As we said goodby, Carol asked to take our picture. I'll always remember her explaining why she spent so much money for a hand-carved, made-to-her-measure canoe paddle with a twist at the paddle end. She said the paddle felt like an extension of her arm. I laughed when I first heard there were special shoes for bicycling. Now, I always wear special shoes for bicycling.

Finally, we rode out of town. After only a few miles, Bea noticed the bulge on her tire again. She tried to fix it, couldn't, and asked for the spare. She had trouble mounting the old tire made of kevlar on the rim.

We reached Orr about one-thirty, just as a severe thunderstorm was collecting itself overhead. Both of us were tired. At Motel Alexander, Bea drafted our third joint letter and I phoned Mom, asking her to send the extra tires I had prepared.

Orr, Thursday, July 31

When we ventured outside the motel, we found the storm-washed morning fresh, cool, and clear. We pedaled up a rise out of Orr into an area with forests on both sides of the road and cattails in the ditches. With a ten-foot road shoulder, we rode side by side, talking and joking. Bea created the humor, telling me Minnesota dealerships sold cars with the canoe already attached and pickup trucks that came with dogs. The buyers choose the color of the canoe or the breed of dog! We took breaks every twenty miles to eat fruit and wash it down with water. Both of us preferred a very short break to a long one. Once our old legs stopped, they didn't want to go again.

At Cold Springs Deer Farm, we paused for coffee, apple turnovers, and a look at the deer. Bea bought a sweatshirt and had the shop send it home. We filled our water bottles, ate a peach and a banana, and rode into a stiff headwind, through three miles of construction.

We stopped at the Voyageurs National Park Information Center and looked at the replicas of a voyageur's canoe and clothing, listened to a tape of loons, and read about exhibits. I was fascinated by voyageurs and I realized that we had paralleled the voyageurs' route as closely as anyone could on a bicycle. We would continue to do so through most of Minnesota.

We ate, checked into International Falls Motor Lodge, denuded our bicycles, and wheeled back downtown to look at the wood processing plant and the excellent Koochiching County Museum. Back at the motel, we worked on letters, showered, transcribed our taped notes and washed clothes. I also studied maps for the next two days' journeys.

International Falls, Friday, August 1

Following the voyageurs route west along Highway 11, we continued out of International Falls upstream along the Rainy River, moving along on a bluff with small peepholes among the trees marching past on our right and broad vistas of Rainy River. At the top of my lungs, in French, I sang the French folk songs I learned as a teenager.

Rainy River must have been named for a reason. Not unexpectedly, the sun slid out of sight as we rode further and further. As we passed under a mountain of black clouds, I stopped to put on my jacket. We pedaled right into, then through, a gray-green wall of water. The voyageurs, singing in unison, must have paddled through vertical curtains of rain, too.

We rode all morning against the wind and through two or three more showers, arriving at a restaurant in Baudette. Tired from the wind, hungry and cold, we hurried to remove our raingear, frustrated by damp clothing that clung to our arms and legs. We leaned the bikes, draped with rain suits, against a handrail. People watching from inside the Ranch House Restaurant greeted us as we entered.

"How far have you come?"

"How do you like our weather?"

"It is supposed to clear soon."

And we responded wearily, "Two coffees. We don't mind the rain. It's the wind, riding into the wind that makes it so hard."

One man said, "Normally, the west wind begins to blow about nine in the morning and continues until dark."

Another laughed, "But you can't count on it."

I was content to smile and listen to their banter, too tired to care that the place was busy and the service slow. After eating, resting, and getting warm, we were still reluctant to depart.

The clouds continued dripping intermittently and, outside again, we saw the Baudette Motel next door. Nodding our heads in agreement, we entered.

Should we ride from five to nine in the morning and as long thereafter as we could? Could we ride at night? What could we do about the wind? No wonder so many bicyclists fly to Seattle to ride cross country west to east. I had planned our trip counterclockwise to avoid the desert in summer. Since our route circled the country, we had to travel east to west somewhere at sometime. We kept riding against the wind.

Bicyclists counteract a head wind by "drafting." One cyclist rides inches behind the other. It takes practice. The front rider breaks the wind for the second rider, creating a vacuum which pulls the second rider along. Taking turns being the first rider, bicyclists can go two to five miles per hour faster. Of course, the faster and closer you ride the greater the benefits of drafting. I wanted to and did practice drafting. I found it didn't really help a lot, given our slow speeds and the amount of concentration required. It was a variation from mental to physical effort, concentrating or pedaling harder to achieve the same pace. When I was tired and needed a pull, I couldn't concentrate as well. Racers in pace lines draft so much they hardly notice the concentration. It becomes automatic, like balancing the bike.

Baudette, Saturday, August 2

Out for breakfast at six-thirty the next morning, we pedaled along, motivated to reach the Warroad Post Office before it closed, presumably about noon. It seemed forever since we had received mail, and we were both expecting packages from home containing accumulated letters culled by Bea's daughter Beth and my mother. We went as fast as possible before the wind picked up at nine o'clock. You could set your watch by it. After only another sunny hour of pedal pressing, we halted at the Warroad Post Office. Our thirty-seven grueling miles quickly forgotten, we sat on the grass and read our letters.

"Where you from?" came the familiar question. We really wanted to read our mail. "Where you from?" the voice was more plaintive. I looked up into the face of a two-foot-high, smiling boy, holding his mother's hand.

"Detroit," I said, putting my head down, trying to read. There was a long silence from the young mother.

"Where you going?"

I answered, "Seattle."

A full minute of wide-eyed silence permitted the mother to digest this information without taking her eyes off of us. Then she said, "I seen your bicycles and knowed you was from some place."

Neither of us lifted our heads as she ambled away. I've always been sorry that I wasn't polite to one of the most ingenuously interested people I met on the trip. We began interrupting each other to share our news from home, oblivious to the procession of staring people collecting their mail.

Next door to the post office, I ate fried rice, and Bea a ham and cheese omelet before we bicycled out to the edge of Lake of the Woods to camp two nights at Warroad City Park. It took three minutes to set up the tent with its waterproof cover. Then we emptied two panniers and, leaving everything else in the tent, pedaled off to the grocery.

I stopped to read the historical marker along our route. Bea came back to read it too. It said that Sioux, traveling by way of the Red and Roseau Rivers, invaded the Chippewa villages located on Lake of the Woods. The Indians fought over the wild-rice-growing areas. Warroad, a former Chippewa village, had been aptly named.

For Saturday and Sunday meals, we bought chicken thighs, sirloin steaks, one onion, one quart of wild blueberries, nectarines, one green pepper, bananas, grapes, tomatoes, doughnuts, and milk. When we got home to our tent, the blueberries disappeared first.

That afternoon, we walked over to the Lake of the Woods water's edge to watch birds. On the way, we saw a flock of yellow-headed blackbirds hopping about in low bushes and freshly cut grass. Far out over the lake were several flocks of snow geese in flight. Closer were osprey, Canada geese, and Wilson's warblers.

I returned to the tent to rest. The muscles in my upper thighs hurt when I touched them. I was not hungry and was sure that I was over-fatigued, for my body had begun to bloat. I lay down, too tired to read.

Bea burst into the tent. She had seen an adult eastern kingbird place a dragonfly sideways into the gaping mouth of a fat offspring. The baby had been unable to choke down the dragonfly. The adult had pulled the insect out by the tail and had poked it into the mouth of a second squalling youngster who had blinked, gulped, and finally swallowed it. This baby then hopped to another branch, preened momentarily, closed its eyes, and fell fast asleep. The first baby continued to clamor for food. Birds were beginning to catch my interest, too.

Bea expended the rest of her energy preparing supper and building a fire. It was all I could do to praise and eat the results and fall asleep as though I, too, had eaten a dragonfly.

Warroad, August 3

On rest day, Bea bounded out of the tent, built a fire, ate, and went off to birdwatch. I crawled out, blinked, took a shower, wrote postcards, and returned to bed to read. There I remained all day, quiet. I also did my homework, reading the free papers and pamphlets I recently picked up.

Although water flows from Minnesota in three directions, to Hudson Bay, the Atlantic Ocean and the Gulf of Mexico, no water flows into the state. Near the geographic center of North America, the northernmost point of the continental United States, the Northwest Angle of Minnesota is about six miles north of where our tent sat.

I called my mom and learned she had just sent an order for twenty copies of my booklet on Tibetan Rugs to Stockholm. Mom was fine. She was approaching her eightieth birthday, and I couldn't keep up with her.

Periodically, Bea interrupted her birdwatching to stick her head into the tent, incredulous that I would spend a wonderfully clear, sunny day inside. I was glad that, several months ago, I selected this campground for its birdwatching potential. I hadn't realized I would find it so peaceful and comfortable. "I'm worried about your energy running out," Bea told me. "Why don't you rent a car? Then you could stay with me and rest at the same time. That way the trip could continue."

Her suggestion annoyed me. I took a deep breath, but Bea went off to call her daughter. She told me her daughter was ill and was going for tests tomorrow. Bea was worried.

I wondered whether either of us could have found a traveling companion any more different from herself. I wondered, too, how much of the conviction that I couldn't travel alone was American cultural baggage.

Warroad, Monday, August 4

In early morning light, we rolled up the tent, packed our panniers, and pedaled to Reed's Landing Restaurant for breakfast overlooking Lake of the Woods.

I was sorry to have missed a ten-dollar seaplane ride over the lake, but yesterday's solitude was necessary. I had needed to stay in one place for a few hours.

During the morning, we cycled past butterscotch wheat fields under a rainbow. There were no more evergreens, just farmlands as far as we could see. We stopped a moment outside Greenbush to photograph thousands of red-wattled white turkeys raising an awful racket at our passage.

Every time I seriously doubted the sense of continuing as far as Seattle, I got another dose of patience. I did not want to abandon this trip.

Lake Bronson, Tuesday, August 5

I struck the tent and packed it away while Bea took care of the kitchen. She finished her coffee and fruit, while I ate blueberries and drank water.

We headed for the town of Lake Bronson, where I sat on the curb while Bea tried to reach her daughter, by phone — no result.

In about an hour, we had pedaled to Hallock where I had my favorite breakfast of one egg and wheat toast. Bea pronounced the French toast excellent, "the best I ever had," which she said almost every day. Continuing at a fast pace, I drafted most of the time, except when a slight tailwind pushed us.

CHAPTER FOUR

Grains and Grasshoppers
in North Dakota

Cavalier, North Dakota, Tuesday, August 5

We crossed the Red River and arrived in Cavalier, North Dakota, for mid-morning lunch. Between Cavalier and Langdon, we changed gears and pedaled up a steep escarpment to the prairie plateau. Thus, we entered what nineteenth-century maps called the Great American Desert, the Plains States. The perimeter along the Canadian border is quite different from the North Woods. We felt the open space and dry air in our throats at once. I felt as though the Red River had cut off the woods and raised us up to a new level, closer to the sky.

Nearby were two U.S. Army fenced facilities, one with a drive-through bunkered building and another with a lot of white masts and two small towers. The only missile sites I had ever seen were in pictures. It felt strange to see a real one in the United States. As the sun moved higher and we rolled along a road beautified by blooming sunflowers that covered the gently rolling farmland in all directions.

Langdon, our first prairie town, was clean and small. We camped at the city park for three dollars. There were toilets, wash basins with cold water, and shelters and picnic tables for campers, as well as children's slides, swings, and climbing equipment. There were also two hook-ups for RVs. It was a splendid place to relax shaded by small trees after eighty-five miles of travel.

The park attendant suggested we go to the swimming pool and ask the lifeguard's permission to shower there. The ladies' locker room was open to the sun, and the cold water dispensed a bit more vigor than I wanted.

We were pleasantly surprised by North Dakota so far. We had expected stark, flat, wind-blown, boring terrain. Instead, the houses were trim and neat, the lawns carefully tended, the flowers brilliant — a Scandinavian attention to detail, I thought.

People saw us but no one spoke unless we did. Too tired to grocery shop and cook, we went into town for supper in a restaurant. On the way home, we bought fruit, milk, and orange juice for breakfast. I frequently thought about recording the weight of the fresh fruit we consumed every day. It would have been interesting to know, but I never remembered to do it.

Langdon, Wednesday, August 6

Early morning found us again on Route 5, headed west across the beautiful prairie of North Dakota less than twenty miles south of the Canadian border. The Bikecentennial Trail followed Route 2, a busier highway to the south of us. On our road, we met people who had not talked to cross-country bicyclists for the past ten years. We were also north of the voyageurs' water route and the wagon routes of the Oregon Trail.

Grain, brushed and rippled by the wind, stood waving green, yellow, gold. The harvest was in process. There wasn't much corn, the only grain I could identify. I was pleased to be able to recognize the sunflowers. As we swooped downhill to a stream and then pedaled up the other side, we saw a vast field that looked like a blue lake. I knew it wasn't string beans. There were low bushes with small wonderful blue flowers. Later we learned we probably had seen flax in bloom.

We arrived after twenty-five miles at the turnoff to Clyde, half a mile away. Thirsty, we followed the dirt road to town. It was a difficult ride on my inch-and-a quarter tires and worse for Bea on one-inch tires.

At the end of town stood Nick and Helen's Bar. Helen was making something for dinner that smelled deliciously Italian. Nick could offer us only beer, Coke, and microwaved sandwiches. With filled waterbottles we returned to Route 5 for a seventeen-mile pedal to Rock Lake and a cafe. When I could see the Rock Lake water tower and grain elevator, I drained my last water bottle. We entered town, crossing rail-road tracks, and found ourselves on Main Street.

I wonder if motorists think bicyclists crossing railroad tracks are suddenly drunk. The only safe way to cross is at right angles, but the tracks are seldom at right angles to the highway. Bicyclists moving steadily along the edge of a road make odd zigzags to ensure their tires cross the tracks at ninety-degree angles.

We joined the rest of town in the Community Coffee Shop for delicious chicken fried steak and real mashed pota-toes with gravy. A farmer and his son invited us to sit with them.

All spring and summer, we had been reading about farm foreclosures, mostly in Iowa. Now we asked for a North Dakotan's opinion. We ate and listened — it was a great monologue. Our table-mate felt that the government had tricked the farmers into getting into debt over their heads by offering low interest rates. Borrowing was encouraged; then the prices of grain went down so farmers couldn't pay their loans no matter how good the harvest.

During the eighteen-mile ride to Rolla, we were es-corted by jet fighters, apparently flying practice runs between Route 5 and the border. I thought it was great fun when one after another roared along right overhead, and I enjoyed watching them fly in formation, one to the right, one to the left. They reversed direction far away, out of sight, and then sud-denly roared overhead again, all turning to the same side.

We set up camp at the Rolla City Park. With use of the swimming pool shower and a fine cement platform with two roofed picnic tables, we didn't mind the absence of trees.

I went to find the post office, stopping on Route 5, now Main Street, to ask a red-headed teenager on a bicycle where it was. He grinned and said, "I'll show you. Follow me." At the post office, I thanked him and answered his questions about the trip. He said he used his bike for transportation around town and to school, but he liked just to ride it. As I came out of the post office, an older man spoke to me. Wishing to compli-ment his town, I said how helpful the red-haired boy had been. I headed for the grocery and was taking out the lock for my bike when the red-head approached and said, "You don't have to lock your bike in our town." Since I didn't want to insult anyone, I put the lock away. At the store entrance, the boy spoke again, "Thanks for telling my grandfather that I'm a nice person."

On four hiking treks in the Himalayas, I had grown accustomed to being a novelty in mountain villages accessible only on foot. Here, in the United States, I was growing fond of small towns. When I spoke, people were friendly; when I didn't speak, they politely left me alone. Everyone seemed to know I was here and a stranger.

Dakota is the Sioux word for "friend." Mr. Grandfather had asked whether or not we were going to International Peace Garden, a place that celebrates friendship between nations. We hadn't planned to, since it was off our route. Even the waitress at the North 40 Restaurant wanted to know not whether but *when* we were going. "You really shouldn't miss it," she urged. "North Dakota even has the words 'Peace Garden' stamped on its license plates."

Rolla, Thursday, August 7

In the morning, we were reluctant to ride off into a strong wind from the west. Bea said that she would like to put her clothes in a machine since hand-washing was making them dingy. All of our clothes combined would make a small load at the Laundromat but, if we washed everything, what could we wear? We donned our rain gear and washed everything else, including our shoes, and carried them "home" wet in our panniers. We hung them up around the picnic tables to dry in the wind. It was cold barefoot, but our shoes had been dirtiest of all.

We had stopped twice at the post office to retrieve our mail. The workers there became interested in our trip and repeatedly insisted that we go to Peace Gardens. They gave us directions for a short cut, which I wrote down and studied on the map. It seemed that we had to go through the Turtle Mountains to get there. When we mailed our letters on the way out of town, we conceded. We would go to Peace Gardens. When our clothes were dry, we packed up and set out in early afternoon, straight into the wind.

By two o'clock, we had covered the six miles to Belcourt, the Turtle Mountain Indian Reservation town. We were saddened by the obvious poverty of our first large Indian reservation. As instructed, we turned near the monument with four arrows, on a concrete strip called Jack Rabbit Road.

Appropriately, it went up and down, up and down. It seemed that each up was two-thirds further than each down. The hills drained our energy, and we drained our waterbottles. About to despair, we reached Highway 281 and continued north.

Finally, on a graded road not nearly so steep, we paused to question a farmer who was towing a hay-roll maker. He estimated we had about three more miles to go. To our delight, half of the distance was a long descent right into International Peace Garden.

International Peace Garden was dedicated in July 1932, a joint venture celebrating peace between Canada and the United States. It is a place for conferences, musical events, and all sorts of public get-togethers. Cannas, bush clematis, hundreds of orange and yellow Asiatic lilies, and lavender lythrum were blooming. Bea was impressed by the eighteen-foot floral clock donated by the Bulova company. Much of the basic structure of the garden was built by the Civilian Conservation Corps. The Corps work has endured. My father was employed by the CCC, and I remember visiting him at work in North Georgia when I was a small child.

Getting to the campground required pedaling another couple of miles around the tourist route. As I hammered in the last tent peg, Bea returned from the shower, exclaiming, "There's lots of hot water!" When I returned after dark from my shower and a long telephone conversation with a friend from Belgium who was visiting the States, Bea had a roaring blaze going. Of all the people I have ever met, Bea was the best camper, especially when we wanted a fire. She always found wood somewhere.

International Peace Garden, Friday, August 8

There had been no trees under which to camp, and there was dew on the tent when we awoke. After breakfast, we poured as much fuel as possible into the stove and our fuel bottle and discarded the rest in the gallon can we bought in Copper Harbor. Although I got rid of the fuel can, I added the stove to my baggage.

We surprised several white-tailed deer on the way to the customs house. There, Bea talked with the inspector about jogging, and I asked about the route. "Route 43," he told me, "is quite rolling and Route 5 quite flat."

From Peace Gardens south to Route 5 was mostly downhill. There were no stores or towns where we could buy food. Invigorated by the chill morning air, we covered ten miles quickly. In Dunseith at the Route 5 junction, a truck-stop restaurant beckoned.

We dived into breakfast. Between mouthfuls we told our story to two men at the next table. One of them went around the restaurant, telling other diners that we had "paddled them sickles" all the way from "Deetroit." He turned his hands in front of his face as though he were pedaling.

When we reached Bottineau, the next town, we were hungry again and found a bakery-restaurant on Main Street. I opened the door marked "restroom" and found myself in the kitchen, where I stared in disbelief at two people covered with flour as they kneaded dough. They looked like ghosts. One nodded, the other waved a flour-coated finger to my right. Through the storage room, around another corner, and into a closet, I went. Trying to keep a very straight face when I returned to the table, I said, "It's a nice restroom."

"Thanks, but I don't need it."

"Go anyway," I suggested, and she knew something was up.

Bea came back with a big grin. "Thanks, I wouldn't have missed that for anything!"

In the street, a woman was standing by our bikes. She introduced herself as Sandi Bates and said she wanted to photograph us for the local paper. At the same time, a couple came along and asked me where we were from. I quickly said, "I'm from Washington and she's from Ohio. Where are you from?"

"Boulder, Colorado. I'm Diane Norman, and this is my husband, Arlan."

"I know it's far-fetched but I can't resist asking. Do you happen to know Bill and Pat Johnson?"

The man and woman looked at each other. Arlan replied incredulously, "We live next door." We chatted gaily about how I had known Bill and Pat when they lived in Washington, but missed them greatly since they returned to Bill's home state, Colorado.

I glanced over at Bea, who was eloquently explaining our trip to Sandi Bates. I continued talking with the Normans. Arlan was born in Bottineau, and he and Diane had come to visit his parents. They would be back in Boulder soon and would tell Bill and Pat about our meeting. When Sandi came to get me for a photograph, our Main Street encounter ended.

We rode out of town headed for Mohall. On the way, there was only one store for food and water. There was no wind, but it was hot and the sun was burning my left leg. A car came alongside, honked, and stopped ahead of us. It was the Normans, who wanted a picture of us riding along the road. They left us in the grain fields, alone but for the grasshoppers everywhere. By the time we reached the store, we were hot and had empty water bottles. After quenching our thirsts and refilling our bottles, we continued enjoying the afternoon ride.

On the outskirts of Mohall, we passed the fairgrounds, which looked bleak, and an RV camping area without a tree or a blade of grass. We decided, in spite of having traveled over eighty miles already, to proceed to town. We hoped for a nice city park with grass and a tree to camp under.

As the houses became closer together, we pedaled slowly, looking down each cross street until we saw a park. A couple of blocks brought us to the swimming pool surrounded by trees, grass, and picnic tables. It looked great, so we got off our bikes to rest and inquire about camping. We hailed a passing police car, and the officer, Jeanne Thomas, said we were not permitted to camp in this park. She concurred with our reasons for rejecting the RV park and informed us there was no water at the fairgrounds. She asked more about our trip, and then offered us her back yard for camping. We accepted.

Jeanne went about her patrol. Sitting at the picnic table, we discussed the advisability of staying here a little while to write up our notes before joining the family at Jeanne's house.

A car drove up and a smiling woman got out and walked toward us, carrying a steno pad and pen. Gloria Abrahamson said her husband had seen us riding into town and had phoned her. He had been a grocer-butcher but when he couldn't lift those whole sides beef any more, he sold the business and bought the *Renville County Farmer*, a weekly newspaper. She thought maybe other people in Mohall might like to know about us. We agreed to be photographed and interviewed. Discovering our camping plight, she invited us to stay at her house, but we had already accepted Jeanne Thomas' invitation. Gloria suggested we might like a shower at her house, and we accepted. She drove, and we followed. There we met her husband who invited us to their club for dinner.

We were thrilled but concerned about what to wear. I wore my blue, long-sleeved T-shirt that advertised white-water rafting on the Chattooga River in Georgia and black velvet-looking pants, actually my pajamas. Bea wore her long, black cycling pants and a bright t-shirt. We were not dressed for dinner at anyone's club, but they politely said we looked fine.

I reminded myself of my aunt's advice. When her husband was economic advisor to the Federal Reserve Board, she bought many of her dresses at thrift shops for only a few dollars. It isn't *what* you wear but *how* you wear it. Without benefit of her lifetime of ballet training, I threw my shoulders back, put my head up, laughed, and climbed in the Abrahamsons' car.

It occurred to me we were equally glad to share an evening with new acquaintances. The meal was delicious. It was my first meal ordered by a professional butcher.

In another part of the room, the Friday night Bingo game got underway. "Blackjack, Bingo, and Pull Tabs are the only gambling permitted in North Dakota. They provide a lot of public revenue," our host explained. "A high proportion of the take must be spent on charitable projects." Never having heard of Pull Tabs, we were presented with ten to pull apart to see if we won anything. We didn't.

During dessert, the Abrahamsons asked if there was anything particular we wanted to know or see. We had ridden past many farms, but we had never visited one or talked with a farmer. We would like to know what all those metal buildings contained and how they were used. I had read North Dakota is the most agricultural state in America. We would never have a better chance to learn about it. We were soon in the car and headed east.

We met Carolyn and Marlo Brackelsberg and their children Kari and Chad, who together farm three thousand acres. Their land has been in their family since it was homesteaded. In this part of North Dakota, neither the Brackelsbergs or the Abrahamsons knew of any foreclosures. Chad, about fourteen, went to a quonset-type building, and shoved open the forty-eight foot doors. "A Piper Cub only has a forty-foot wing span so we could use this building as a hangar. It will be full to the rafters with grain next week," said Marlo, as Chad drove the big new tractor out for us to see.

"The wheels are taller than me!" exclaimed Bea as the tractor rolled to a halt. We climbed in, and Bea, under Chad's guidance, drove it around in a circle while I watched. The controls were complicated.

"Strange," I thought, "a young boy can drive this hundred-and-forty-thousand-dollar vehicle all day but isn't allowed to take a car on a public road."

"That's the cost without any attachments," Marlo continued as I was climbing down. "A combine costs about the same." I thought that their disbelief at our ignorance must be as great as our joy in learning. Marlo explained how, with the grain dryer, it didn't matter so much if the harvest got wet. It could just be run through the dryer and augered into the correct conical-shaped storage bin.

Marlo showed us how they test the grain and talked about marketing. He told us how to tell the difference between barley and wheat in the fields (barley has long whiskers). Then he showed us the grains, and we chewed some. He hoped to sell to Anheuser Busch or some other big brewing company.

I told him that a farmer in Rock Lake said he has had to sell crops for less than it cost to grow them, and that is why farmers are failing. Marlo's opinion was the North Dakota farmers who were failing were poor managers. He uses a computer to keep track of planting, fertilizing, rain, and the grain tests. He said that the reason we had seen a lot of grain piled along the railroad tracks, on the ground next to the grain elevators, was that the government had filled all its storage. As soon as the government begins to ship grain, there will be room for the new harvest. Obviously, a lot is going on in these quiet fields.

Raising grain in the summer permitted the Brackelsbergs to travel and enjoy winter sports, unlike cattle ranching which was a year-round responsibility. They did keep a horse to ride, and had snowmobiles for winter.

In the house, Bea and the others drank a glass of wine, and I almost fell asleep over my ice water. It was after ten o'clock. Why did everything interesting seem to come on the same day? On the way back to town, the Abrahamsons told us we had visited not the richest farmer in the area, but one who is very well educated and whose income is above average.

When we arrived at the Thomases' and our tent, it looked like rain. We dug out our toothbrushes and went into the house where the family was gathered around the kitchen table eating supper. What a warm atmosphere we sensed as we met Bob Thomas, the town sheriff, and the children. We felt like members of the family everywhere in Mohall; the people were so kind and friendly.

As the first drops of rain began, we stowed the bicycles in the garage and fell asleep almost before getting into the tent.

Mohall, Saturday, August 9

The next thing I knew, it was almost six in the morning, and I was starving. I crept out of the tent and rummaged through the panniers for peanut butter, bread, and jelly. It must have rained hard during the night, for there were leaves and branches down and the grass was very wet. I was glad my bike was in the garage, and I wouldn't have to cook the chain.

Later, I woke Bea, and we packed up after washing in the house. The family wasn't up, but they had told us the doors would not be locked, and that we could come in to the bathroom. We rode our bare bikes downtown to the Paragon Cafe for Saturday breakfast. Marlo greeted us when we came in and brought his coffee to our table. Another man greeted us. "I was the Bingo caller," he explained. They talked with us while we all ate and, without our realizing it, Marlo picked up our check and paid it while we were still eating. We thanked him and went back to the Thomases'.

The family was still asleep. Jeanne had patrolled until one a.m. when the bars closed. We rolled up our tent, packed our bikes and headed for Main Street. We had planned this to be a rest day but there wasn't anywhere in town we could answer our mail. Our chores were not nearly as interesting as Mohall, the largest town we'd seen for a while, and its people, all 1049 of them! Turning west into Main Street, Route 5, we waved at Marlo, coffee cup in hand as he talked to someone in a pickup.

We decided to go to Flaxton or Columbus, both of which have city park campgrounds with showers. It took us three-and-a-half hours to grind twenty-five miles into the wind, normally a two-hour ride, including stops. Yesterday had been fantastic, and we needed time to rest and assimilate our experiences.

The scenery was marvelous. We crossed the Mouse River (the Souris River according to the map — a little French helps). Its western portion flows south through Minot and its eastern loop, which we crossed yesterday, flows north into Canada. Passing through the Upper Souris National Wildlife Refuge, there were hawks and birds a-plenty to watch while riding. Exhausted, we waited half an hour at the junction of Routes 5 and 52 for a lift in a pickup. The wind was debilitating; I didn't know whether I could continue. I felt better after a rest. We had no luck hitching a ride, so we pedaled two more hours, ten more miles, into Bowbells.

A sign indicated camping was allowed, but first, we needed the cafe. We ate vegetable soup, roast, potatoes, corn, bread, and pudding. The waitress had told us they would be closed for dinner. We went back to ask about the camping at the park, and found it was free, and we could shower at the swimming pool. We put the tent up beside one leg of the water tower, where it was shielded by a hedge on two sides from the rest of the park and the pool.

I assumed everything would be closed tomorrow, Sunday, and planned to stay here two nights. Again, we had traveled six days without a rest day. We had made our longest ride of the trip, eighty-eight miles, but thirty-six miles against the wind had been tougher. We dumped the loads out of a couple of panniers and biked off to the grocery store for a long list of supplies.

At "home" Bea said she would be sick if she didn't sleep and crawled into the tent. We were both exhausted, but I didn't like to sleep in the daytime. I puttered around a bit, then walked to the petting zoo at the other end of the park. People packing up the zoo equipment told me this was a special holiday weekend, because Bowbells was celebrating the new paving of Main Street. There had been a parade this morning, and a free dinner would be served at the fire hall from four-thirty to six.

While I was taking my shower, a little girl asked me if I was going swimming. Afterwards, I met her mother who said she and her husband raise cattle and grain on a small farm of eight quarters, some of which are not suitable for crops. Later, I figured out there are one-hundred sixty acres to a quarter and four quarters in a section. She invited us to visit the farm, but, since gravel roads were involved, I declined. I questioned her about how much the "jelly roll" hay stacks weighed. We had guessed about three-hundred pounds, but she thought six- to eight-hundred pounds was closer. The little girl, impatient for a promised Tastee Freeze, tugged at her mother's hand.

About five, I woke Bea to go to the supper in town. At the hall, we received a good roast beef sandwich, baked beans, chips, mints, and Coke or coffee. Holding a plate full of food, I looked around and finally asked where to pay. "It's free," they said. "You are a guest of our town! We're celebrating paving the street and all-new sidewalks!" The swimming pool usually cost a dollar fifty; today, it had been free. I wondered if Pull Tabs and Bingo had financed the celebration.

Apparently the only pay phone was in the lobby of the hotel across town from our park. After eating, we went there, and I called my mom, who was visiting a high school friend. I had to cut our conversation short because other people were waiting.

While Bea talked, I learned that the three people waiting were members of Loners on Wheels, as my mom's friend had been. They had parked their whale and smaller RV on the other side of the water tower from our tent. They introduced themselves as Pat, Dottie, and Hank and said they left Detroit the day after we had. We thought it was pretty funny for two bicyclists to be travelling faster than two RVs. They said they had spent a lot of time birding, parking their RVs and using a car to enter small places in the wildlife reserves and to conserve gas. When Bea finished her call, we agreed to meet tomorrow.

On the way back, we stopped by the fire house again and weighed on their scales. Each of us had lost five pounds. Once settled in the tent, Bea went to sleep. There was a street dance at the other end of town, but here it was quiet except for the sound of an occasional car. Because of our public location, we had put all the food, cameras, tape recorders, books, and clothes in the tent. Outside were the panniers, helmets, and water bottles, stuffed in a large extra-heavy garbage bag. The bikes were locked to one leg of the water tower. A misty rain fell intermittently, and, when it got too dark to write inside the tent, I went to sleep.

Bowbells, Sunday August 10

When I awoke, it was in the forties and I found myself lying flat, very flat on the ground. My air mattress had deflated again during the night. We'd both had this problem, and Bea's mattress was older than mine. We had used them long and hard. Mine had insulated me at over fifteen-thousand feet on a bed of scree in the Himalayas as well as in the sun on the beach. Today I would check again for leaks.

I also decided to buy another sleeping bag or have one sent. At night, summer was over. Using one bag as a blanket was no longer satisfactory. We gathered bowls, spoons, milk, Raisin Bran, and bananas for breakfast inside the tent. For warmth, we kept our legs covered by the sleeping-bag blanket. A cold cereal breakfast was a special treat; now it was cool enough to keep milk overnight. When we crawled out of the tent, Bea poured orange juice and boiled water for coffee and rice.

There was not a cloud in the sky and not a zephyr of breeze. I couldn't help wondering why our rest days often seemed to be windless. "I wouldn't pedal that bike today if the road were downhill for eighty miles," I thought, drinking a second cup of orange juice.

We each chose a picnic table to use as a desk, and Bea transcribed her notes from the microcassette recorder. I decided to file my tapes and not use up today listening to yesterday. I tested the mattresses in the wading pool, thoroughly, both sides. No bubbles. I blew them up as tightly as I could and tested them again, but I could find nothing to patch. Perhaps they were worn out. Well, they would just have to serve until we reached a camping store.

Next, I turned my attention to maps and campground guides to plot our overnight stops for Montana. I made a pile of maps, guides, and receipts from North Dakota for sending home.

Dottie and Hank Hull came to find us at our picnic desks. We talked about birds and the joys of wandering. Hank brought some brochures and maps to help my planning. I had asked Mom to send the Montana maps to the post office in Plentywood, the first town in Montana, but we weren't there yet. The Hulls invited us to dinner in their whale and then left for a day of birding with Pat.

After lunch, I overcame the urge to sleep by taking a shower at the pool. Although the water was cold in the middle of the day, it was not frigid. After each shower, we grumbled about the pull chain to make the water come out. It is rather difficult to soap, scrub your back, rinse, and pull a chain for water at the same time. I had taken along a bungee and managed to hook it to a pipe, but it only kept the water half-on. Later, in campground pull-chain showers, I took two or three bungees. Once I managed to keep the water running by holding a bungee with my foot. Another time, I succeeded in hooking it over the door.

We'd gained enough altitude so that, even though it was August, we were sure it wouldn't get warmer. As we ascended the prairie toward the Rockies, we talked about the necessity for getting warmer clothes sent.

By the end of the day, we were still tired. My legs ached and I just didn't have any spunk. Nevertheless, we'd rather push on to Plentywood and the mail than rest another day. Bea went to the tent to nap. I inspected my bicycle, cleaned it, and paraffined the chain.

We knocked on the whale door at the appointed time for dinner. Hank and Dottie ushered us into a luxurious living room. I had never seen the inside of a modern RV and couldn't believe my eyes. Rugs, plush sofa, TV, bookcases, and drinks with ice made it a real home. Pat Barth joined us, and we listened as they all bubbled over describing a successful and interesting birding day. I decided to take a birding class at the local Audubon Society when I got home.

They carried special wines and offered us our choice of drinks. I tried to hold out for ice water and did for a time. When we sat down to the beautifully set table with crystal goblets and bone china plates and silver cutlery, my reserve crumpled. I really adore good wine, but it makes me feel weak and tired the next day, especially since I'm not expert at sipping half a glass.

Each of us was served cornish hen stuffed with cabbage, carrots, cauliflower, rice, and lentils. Dessert was a fantastic apple-cranberry betty with granola sprinkled on top. I probably gained back my whole five pounds at one meal. It was a special treat.

We learned that Hank's first wife was killed by a hit-and-run driver while she was bicycling. He and Dottie had met during Loners on Wheels RV rallies which Dottie and Pat attended together. Dottie has multiple sclerosis and she can't walk far, even with her cane. She could get around inside the RV since there was always something to hold for support. After they married, Dottie and Hank both sold their homes and bought this RV as well as a car equipped with hand controls that Dottie could drive. They lived on the road all year long and adored it. Among RV people, they were "full-timers."

We even found we had mutual acquaintances in Washington, D.C. and talked of spending more time together in Plentywood or meeting on the West Coast. They told us how to contact them, and we provided the phone number of my friends in Mt. Vernon, Washington, where we would stay a while to rest and break the trip. Bea and I vowed that no one around us would ever claim whale people to be unfriendly and get away with it.

After dinner, we reconvened at the hotel telephone booth. The hotel looked more like something from the movies than from real life. It was a two-story brick building on the corner next to the grain elevator.

At home under the water tower, we packed the panniers for an early morning departure. Our new friends, Pat,
Dottie, and Hank, would be leaving several hours later in the
morning and would pass us on the road.

Bowbells, Monday, August 11

We waved goodbye to the water tower and wheeled
down Main Street to the cafe. On our way out of town, as we
passed the post office, I suggested, "Why don't you see if it's
open so you can mail your package?"

"No way any post office will be open at seven-thirty,"
Bea said, dismounting and giving me her bike to hold. She
found a cleaning woman and asked, "Is the post office open?"

The cleaner replied, "Alma, can you open up? Here are
two bikers who need to mail a package." Alma, smiling, came
to the counter.

When we passed butterscotch-colored wheat fields,
some with oil wells or fenced missile sites, I thought how
advantageous it must be to have grain above and oil or missiles
below; in case the price of one fails the others are sure to
produce. We passed so many oil wells that morning we could
smell them. I succeeded in getting a missile site, an oil well, and
the grain all in the same photograph.

On the outskirts of Columbus, we could see a green
water tower, a tower for radio or TV, at least two grain elevators, and a church steeple. There were a few buildings on the
highway, but most were about a half-mile away. The water
tower was about twice as large as the one in Bowbells, so
perhaps there were twice as many people. Some isolated farm
houses caught our eyes because of the trees planted near them.

Our breeze became a crosswind, slowing us less than a
headwind would have. Two red-tailed hawks sailed above us.
Lower down was a fine crop of grasshoppers, occasionally
hitching a ride by landing on my bicycle. More often, they
jumped, pinging into my spokes. I hit a bump, and a big guy on
my front pannier decided the ride was over and jumped away.
I was really enjoying pedaling today.

We stopped one mile from Columbus. We were hungry,
and it was a good time to get rid of our large, heavy can of fruit
cocktail. While I was looking for the can opener, our mobile

home friends overtook us and pulled off the road. We chatted, thanked them again for the dinner, and waved, expecting to see them in Plentywood tomorrow.

Seeing stubble in the fields reminded me that Marlo Brackelsberg told us he cuts the grain about eight inches above the ground and plows back the stubble to fertilize the soil. Beautiful fields of sunflowers lay ahead. Marlo said he hadn't planted them this year, and that the bottom had dropped out of the market. I watched a dust devil make its way across a recently plowed field. It was almost as high as the utility pole, but, when it reached the highway, it disappeared.

We had been fifty-one miles and, while passing a field where workers were using a combine, we spotted the grain elevators of Crosby in the distance. Marlo said that this was right in the middle of the harvest season, the very best time to visit this part of North Dakota. Hundreds of squawking red-winged and yellow-headed blackbirds seemed to know that, too. Their shiny, black feathers contrasted brilliantly with their flashes of red, orange, yellow, and white.

Daily, it became drier, and I was out of water again and hungry, too. We turned off Route 5 and, to my relief, saw a sign saying, "Crosby Loves Visitors, One-Fourth Mile." There were also symbols for sleeping, tenting, golf, eating, picnicking, gas, and swimming.

On Main Street, we entered Bakkes Chat and Chew Cafe. I saw a man sipping an old-fashioned milkshake. It looked so good that I ordered strawberry, and Bea followed with chocolate. The milkshakes cooled and satisfied us until lunch arrived. For dessert, we got another milkshake with two glasses.

Near the Pioneer Village, which was closed, were camp sites with electricity for RVs but no toilet facilities or water. In a lovely garden park, the man mowing the grass told us to go to the fairgrounds for camping, on the other side of town. There we found camp sites all right, but there were no trees, and the grass, which hadn't been cut all summer, harbored swarms of grasshoppers. There was a picnic table, but there were no other people. We didn't like the looks of things but were too tired to go further. I decided to check the shower, and, when I turned on the tap, plenty of hot water sprayed forth. We put up the tent, but it was too hot to stay inside and there were too many grasshoppers outside.

We had heard other bicyclists extol the value of libraries. After we located the one in Crosby, Bea went to sleep on a sofa, and I nodded over a book. I read that the eight North

Dakota counties on the Canadian border have a semi-arid environment because the Rocky Mountains divert rain from the area. Crosby's climate is affected by this "rain shadow." Forty percent of the drainage water from North Dakota eventually empties into Hudson Bay and sixty percent flows by way of the Missouri and Mississippi Rivers into the Gulf of Mexico.

Assiniboin Indians lived in northern North Dakota and Montana. In the mid-1800s, most of Montana was inhabited by Sioux and Crow. I was reminded of Africa, where the borders bore no relation to the people living in the areas at the time the maps were drawn. To this day, there is only one nation in all Africa that contains one ethnic group, Somalis, who also spill into Ethiopia and Kenya. Probably the same geographers cut up western North America!

The librarian told us she was the landlady of a young man who worked at the local paper. She called, and he made an appointment to come see us at the campground at seven-thirty. We had showered, had put all our stuff in the tent, and were battling the grasshoppers and mosquitoes when he arrived.

Kevin Brooke, the reporter, became so interested in our conversation that we thought he wouldn't leave in time for us to cook and eat supper before dark. He took an excellent photograph of us but reversed our ages, causing merriment among our close friends.

Sunset and the mosquitoes shortened dinner preparation and hastened us into the tent to eat. Finally, I could lie on my back with my knees drawn up to rest my lower back. We resolved, henceforth, to do only one interview per state.

Crosby, Tuesday, August 12

Hordes of mosquitoes attacked us when we came out of the tent, so we packed frantically. Once out of the high grass and rolling, we were free of them. The sunrise was marvelous as we traversed Crosby to reach the Chat and Chew Cafe. It was filled with men. We took a booth next to Karen McFarlin, the only other woman. She was dressed for business, we for bicycling. Some contrast! The men all knew each other and were noisy. Cowboy boots shared equal time with work boots, and jeans were a synonym for trousers. As we moved west, T-shirts were giving way to sweat shirts, jean jackets, and vests.

In larger towns, we selected the cafe with the most

pickup trucks in front. When our first meal was good at a cafe, we never sought another in that town. Many places that opened early closed early, but we preferred supper outdoors at our camp. Once halted, we were reluctant to move again. The pattern of evening inertia had become a habit.

Turning our bikes from Main Street into the highway, a man we recognized from the Chat and Chew offered us a ride to Plentywood. We thanked him. Since it was a lovely morning, we were eager to cycle.

I concentrated on the road. My position on the bicycle changed slightly and pleasantly on such terrain. There was a mild tailwind, and it was quiet on the road, so quiet that I could hear cars coming miles away. The fields smelled good. A few miles east of Fortuna, I stopped to photograph a patch of grain where there were small signs telling what each section contained.

At Lee's Highway Service Station at Fortuna, I bought some milk, ate a bowl of cereal, and then drank the rest of the milk. Gradually, I've weaned myself from caffeine drinks, and I even talk about omitting sugar and salt. I was pleased to find a packet of unsalted peanuts. Bea consumed a quart of orange juice, pie, and doughnuts.

A little after ten, we were spinning along the road toward Plentywood, about forty miles away, where our mail awaited. Westby, Montana, was only twelve miles ahead. Almost to the state border, I noticed that my front derailleur, the gear changer that controls the chain, needed adjustment and cleaning. I also knew that I needed to rotate the tires and cook the chain. Suddenly, I felt tired, desirous of *being* somewhere. This floating lifestyle was beginning to pall.

As I came over a rise, I saw what appeared to be a mirage. Certainly there were no frozen lakes out here in August! The impression was so startling that I stopped to take a picture of the alkali lakes.

After a few more miles, we crossed into Montana at the town of Westby. I was dragging. We had changed time zones and gained an hour. On we went, enjoying the meadowlarks, past a "Warning Crude Pipeline" sign. Sky and dry earth prevailed. Color changed. Nothing was green. All the golden grain had been cut and the land plowed. The "big sky" and earth held dominion. I began to count the rolls of hay on trucks. One was loaded with twelve rolls, eight on the bottom and four on top.

My Avocet mileage indicator was recording inaccurately. Bea's had recorded about three miles more every fifty, and now it was five in forty. A sign indicated eleven miles to Plentywood. I was running out of energy, and Bea had to wait for me at the top of each knoll. I had rubbed Ben Gay on my knees so that the sun could intensify the ointment's effect. I was overdue for rest. At last we were on a rise overlooking all the barren, gray, stony landscape.

"Jane, we're out West!" shouted Bea.

It was bleak. We stopped briefly to rest and eat a peach. I was ready to sit out this dance. Grasshoppers were everywhere, supplying the music. We rode on through masses of them. They whirred past our ears, stuck to our clothes, banged against our arms and legs, and covered the road. As they flew, they pinged against the spokes of our bicycle wheels.

It was funny watching the scattering 'hoppers tumble over and over when they hit the ground. Others would catch a breeze with wings a-whir and sail across the highway, across the ditch, across the bank, and into a field before lighting on a swaying weed or stubble stalk. "There are so many grasshoppers," Bea said, "it's like bicycling through a popcorn popper." As we rode, we heard whir-whir, crunch, crunch, ping-a-ping, ping-a-ping.

Then, with the wind whistling through my helmet, I sailed downhill into the Big Muddy Creek Valley and collapsed in a motel in Plentywood, Montana.

As the trip proceeded, the question, "Where did you like best?" was often posed. I was tempted to say, "North Dakota." Instead, I usually replied, "Wherever I am."

CHAPTER FIVE

Wind-cycling Eastern Montana

Plentywood, Montana, Tuesday, August 12

We had picked up our mail and looked over the camping choices before we checked into the Plains Motel. None of the campgrounds had showers, and there was no evidence of Pat and the Hulls. It was hot. We opted for comfort and convenience at the motel which had a cafe and grocery store within walking distance.

Wearing bicycle touring shoes, with bottom ridges that prevent sliding off the pedals, decreases my idea of "walking distance" to across the street. The shoes that I prefer, sold by Performance, are wide enough to accommodate my bunions and short enough to fit properly into the toe clips on my bike pedals. Bea had encouraged me not to wear socks, and I became accustomed to omitting them. In my mail, a package contained wool socks, so that I had one pair for riding, and one pair for sleeping. Bea joked that she carried half as many.

We ventured on our bikes to a downtown restaurant for dinner. A young woman on the sidewalk stopped us and asked the usual questions. After we had each responded, she looked first into my face, then into Bea's and remarked, "Gutsy." Thereafter, we referred to her as "the gutsy girl." We fled into the restaurant. Each time the waitress came by, there was another question about our trip. Instead of the joy and thrill provoked by the interest people took in our retirement project, we had become interview-shy. We feared that someone would notify the newspaper. Our wariness mounted when a waitress, not our own, filled our water glasses and deftly slid in a question. We asked to keep the water pitcher and replied in undertones to her question, for we had noticed adjacent dinners listening. Gulping final glasses of water, we left without dessert.

Plentywood, Wednesday, August 13

On our rest day, we gobbled the remaining grapes and walked to the nearby cafe for breakfast. When we returned to our room, we read our mail for the umpteenth time, wrote letters and notes, and washed clothes.

Then it was time to attend to the bicycles. Bea cleaned the kitchen pannier entirely and washed all the utensils in hot, soapy water. I asked the motel cleaning woman for some rags, and, delighted by a quantity of old towels, we began to clean our bikes. Bea sprayed hers with WD40, then wiped it off. She soaked her chain in stove fuel, rattling it around in the aluminum cake pan, then brushed it with a toothbrush, wiped it, and again sprayed it liberally.

Chain and freewheel wear together, and both work better when the chain always runs in the same direction. I punched out a rivet toward me, so that I could punch it back away from me, keeping the chain and freewheel mated and the chain always turning in the same direction. I used stove fuel as a cleaner, then heated the chain and paraffin together, stirring chain with the pliers handle to ensure the wax got into the joints where it needed to be. Next, I removed the hot chain, careful not to drip on anything wax would damage, and wiped all four sides as well as I could before the wax cooled. I wanted to keep the wax only in the joints of the chain, not on the exterior. I then hung it to cool thoroughly so that I could put it back on the bike without burning my hands.

My Avocet wasn't working well, and I couldn't seem to discover why. After cleaning parts, testing connections, and adjusting the rear derailleur slightly with a screw driver, I pronounced the problem a mystery. I had exhausted my maintenance abilities and closed my bike shop for the day.

Fatigued by our labor, we consumed blueberries and milk with Raisin Bran and extra raisins. I then worked with the Montana map and campground book until Bea announced that she was starving for a salad-bar lunch.

Across the street from the cafe, we noticed a beauty parlor, and we ambled over to see how busy they were. Bea's wispy, fine, blond hair had grown so long it stuck through the holes in her helmet. My thick brown haircut, ultra-short when I left home but now shaggy, was usually matted by sweat inside my helmet. We got good washes and cuts and soon came outside into the dry air for a Montana sun-dried special. I felt like a new person without what Bea termed "helmet hair."

Black clouds and lightning threatened rain as we strolled the hundred yards back to our room. Bea fell asleep, and I continued reading the maps and booklets about Montana. We entered Montana in Missouri River country, the northeast corner, where the great river sets a unifying theme for the entire landscape. Here everything is big: the prairie stretches from horizon to horizon; ranches measure in miles; and waterfowl take to the big sky by the millions. But they had forgotten to mention the hot sun and the dust. I relished the sun, and dry heat felt splendid to me.

Late in the afternoon, we rode across town to the museum which proved to be a treasured collection of everyday items from the times of cowboys and homesteaders. Several items reminded Bea of things she had heard about from older siblings or her mother.

Bea began to tell me about her mother's youth homesteading in Montana somewhere near Cut Bank. What a privilege, coming to visit these places with a descendant of a homesteader! The people I met in the street were probably descendants of trappers, homesteaders, or railroad people — everyone interesting to know if I just had more time. Life is frustrating. I just couldn't do it all, see it all, learn it all.

Plentywood, Thursday, August 14

During our second breakfast in Plentywood, we discussed whether or not to stay all day. Our aching hands had not fully recovered but our legs were fine. Each of us had awakened during the past few nights with arm pains caused by leaning on the handlebars. A discomfort common to bicyclists, frequent exercise and shaking the hands can minimize it. I really wanted another day of reading and rest, but Bea didn't, and we decided to resume our trip.

The morning was cool, dry, and clear as we rode though Plentywood, passed the museum, and continued south. Our route paralleled the Big Muddy River which cut through a wide valley leaving an escarpment on both sides. Many of the fields along the valley floor contained hay stacks which resembled freshly-baked loaves of bread two stories high. Some fields contained jelly rolls. The road, elevated on one side of the valley, provided us with a sweeping view across the river, railroad, and farms.

Plentywood, just over two thousand feet in elevation, was a thousand feet above our camp at Warroad on Lake of the Woods. The Rockies were on the other side of Montana, about seven hundred miles ahead.

In a field parallel to us, some ponies ran alongside with their manes and tails flying. It was so beautiful with the river and escarpment in the background. I mentally positioned Indians upon the ponies, one hand grasping the mane and the other carrying a feathered weapon overhead. I imagined the riders whooping and hollering, as I felt like doing.

Soon, we entered the town of Medicine Lake and found it an exceptionally neat, quiet village. When we went to mail a package, a woman in the post office asked if we had motors on our bicycles. She thought the two water bottles and the shiny stove-fuel bottle were my motor. Another person asked if we pedaled "under our own steam."

A woman followed us out of the post office. She had not seen toe clips before. I explained that, although designed for racers, they held our feet on the pedals, helping us to pull up as well as push down and giving us more power with each stroke of the pedals. I sometimes pulled the straps tight when going uphill, but it was safer to ride with them loose. If you stopped in a hurry and couldn't get your feet off the pedals, it was easy to fall. Such tumbles didn't hurt but were disconcerting to both bicyclists and motorists in traffic.

Laden with milk and orange juice from the grocery, we sat in a little park under a "Welcome to our little Town" sign to eat Raisin Bran and bananas. The town of about two-hundred people contained neatly-painted houses surrounded by innumerable petunias in well-tended yards. North Dakota gardening seemed more meticulous, but there was less rain here, and wind was a menace. Perhaps it was the unpretentious attitude of the town that appealed to me. Welcome signs in other towns seemed to brag.

A mile or so down the road at Medicine Lake Wildlife Refuge, white pelicans were feeding. Flapping awkwardly for take-off, they spread long wings once aloft and spiraled upward in a tight circle, following one another closely as though ascending an unseen smokestack. We watched them through our binoculars for a long time.

Over twenty-five thousand ducks are born at Medicine Lake annually, so it was not unusual that we saw a few. We also watched a Swainson's hawk soaring as we rode and passed two or three deer and a man fishing for northern pike.

We met two bicyclists out on a day trip. They warned us not to stay overnight on any Indian reservation. The poverty was so extreme that the motels built there were soon vandalized. Going through in the daytime was all right, but we should watch our bikes and never leave them unattended.

We had headwinds the rest of the way to Culbertson and had to climb up an escarpment before reaching a rolling terrain. The last ten miles were long, gentle climbs into the wind with short descents where the wind held us back better than gravity pulled us down.

We reached town about noon, completely exhausted. Spaghetti and blueberry pie at the Wild West Diner helped. After lunch, we felt so drowsy that we went to the motel next door and slept all afternoon.

It was the first day of the Roosevelt County Fair, which, when we awoke late in the afternoon, was going full tilt. We watched youngsters grooming their sheep, cattle, and ponies, and carefully inspected some chickens with feathers on their legs. There was a huge room full of handmade items of every description, from decorated plates, to cookies, to sewing displays. We decided the fair was mostly for the children. I had lost my taste for cotton candy.

"The latchstring is always out in Culbertson, Montana," I read in the town brochure. North Dakota isn't the only place advertising friendliness.

Culbertson, Friday, August 15

We left the diner still talking about the man who was eating a pancake so large it hung over the edges of a serving platter. We put on our helmets and imagined the cook substituting a shovel for his pancake turner. "Not only the sky is big out here," I mused.

Brockton, the next town, lay twenty miles ahead. As we climbed away from low hills along the Missouri River bank, I could see, by looking at the trees, where the water wound its course. Most of the ride seemed uphill until we coasted down to cross the Big Muddy River. I wondered how I was keeping up with Bea on the hills. It took no extra pedaling effort, but I needed to relax my hunched shoulders, wring my hands out, and stay loose on the bike.

On Route 2 now, we were riding along the Bikecentennial Route. The highway, designated the "Old West Trail," included parts used by the Pony Express. In the valley behind the trees shading the Missouri River, ghosts of the Lewis and Clark Expedition hovered.

We rode through the Fort Peck Indian Reservation, home of the Assiniboin and Sioux Tribes. The Reservation's foothills appeared like a rumpled, olive-green, quilted coverlet pushed up along the edge of the river valley. I passed eight trees, riding in the shade for the first time in many days. Eight trees — count them, and they are past. Glorious shade for seconds!

We rolled up and down, and I wasn't sure whether it was three-fourths or two-thirds up. Enjoying the morning ride, I wondered whether I would ever want to pedal out and back or around in a circle again without going somewhere. Down the railroad tracks near us came an orange pickup truck fitted with metal wheels to keep it on the tracks. "Practical," I thought, though I had never seen a pickup riding the rails.

Along the roadside, we saw an olive-colored bush I called sage, often bleached silver. Here, as at our last Indian reservation in the Turtle Mountains, there were bright blue houses. Did Indian culture place a different value on colors? Was blue symbolic?

In Brockton, the home of Badlands Singers, a small Indian boy stood on the sidewalk wearing a broken fan-belt necklace. His broad smile revealed several missing front teeth. "Where are you fellahs going?" he shouted.

I waved and replied, "Out West." He waved but apparently didn't realize we were women. This mistake was made so frequently that I grew to consider it a safety factor. So why would a woman have any problems bicycling alone?

After drinking a pint of orange juice at the store and refilling the water bottles, I got the Avocet working properly. The sensor had been too far away from the wheel hub piece. Once I squeezed them together and held them with a wire, the sensor worked perfectly. Now all I had to do was remember to set the stop watch on zero at noon, and timing would be fine too. I wear a wristwatch but prefer to take it off while cycling and use the Avocet. We moved along the road again toward Poplar, thirteen miles away.

We had full lane-width shoulders, and it was splendid to ride side by side to talk without yelling. A train rumbled past with the engineer waving and the men in the caboose, too. Between their greetings were lumber cars, coal cars, boxcars, tank cars — all freight. As we rode, there were fewer grasshoppers and an occasional cricket. None of the people seemed the slightest bit interested in our trip. Bicyclists traveling this route for over ten years had made us commonplace.

Poplar, with its two water towers, lay ahead between the highway and the railroad tracks. In town was the Fort Peck Tribal Headquarters and Indian Agency. We visited the Indian Arts and Crafts Museum, begun in 1980 as the only tribally-owned and operated museum in the state of Montana. It displays the history of the Assiniboin and Sioux Tribes from about 1820. Craftspeople exhibit in rotating shows.

We ate some soup in a cafe and learned that it was now late in the season for bicyclists. Only three had gone through last week. Soon the skiers would be coming here, our waitress told us, to the ski capital of eastern Montana.

We moved out of Poplar into a ten-to-fifteen mile-per-hour crosswind. A passenger train went by and, later, a mile-long sea/land, containerized-shipping freight train passed us. Most of its cargo was big boxes, like those carried by eighteen-wheel trucks. The wind made it hard to ride in a straight line at only eight or nine miles an hour. We tried riding side by side so one of us was shielded from the wind, but it didn't help much. Finally a curve put the wind behind us for a short period and pushed our speed up to twelve miles. I could think of nothing but getting there. I was hot, tired, and hungry, for the wind and sun had sapped my strength. I sank as low over the bike as I could and concentrated on pressing the pedals.

In Wolf Point, we checked into the Sherman Motor Inn, then dumped our bikes in the room and ourselves in the restaurant. A town of thirty-five-hundred residents, Wolf Point is the Roosevelt County Seat and is located on the main line of the Burlington Northern Railroad, now Amtrak. The railroad came in the late 1880s, replacing the river boats that were the principal mode of travel in the 1860s and '70s.

I leaned back on my pillow, closed my eyes, and remembered the five days I spent floating lazily down the Irrawaddy River in northern Burma on a riverboat, hearing the shouts that meant "mark twain" in Burmese. I joined this experience with today's views of the Missouri River, and then mentally exchanged the piles of cargo and ballot boxes on the

Burmese sand-banks into piles of furs. Thus, I experienced a picture of Wolf Point before the Fort Peck Indian Reservation was opened to homesteaders and the town moved from the river bank to the railroad tracks.

Wolf Point, Saturday, August 16

After breakfast at Stockman's Cafe, we departed about eight. I was still tired, and Glasgow was almost fifty miles west. A historic marker told me that Lewis and Clark had passed here in 1805 on their way west.

Out on the road, we at last had a tailwind! We spun along at twenty miles an hour, shouting and joyous. Cattle looked up to stare as we passed. Our plan was to do our miles and quit for the rest of the day. I squared my shoulders, guided the handlebars with the tips of my fingers, and held my head up and back to catch as much wind as possible. Pedaling was a breeze! I wanted to skedaddle as far as possible while this tailwind lasted.

We rode side by side, Bea telling me that in the Wolf Point Museum she had seen a photograph of people standing outside the railroad beaneries. Her mother had worked in one, and she remembered hearing about it, so the picture fleshed out her memory. We stayed together the first hour, and then I began to drag.

As we sped through Frazer, I noticed the Red Bottom Indian Celebration Grounds were overgrown by weeds, and the store and trading post were boarded up. Near Little Porcupine Creek, a crosswind reduced our speed to about twelve miles an hour. Then it became a headwind, and I dropped to eight. A movement caught my eye. It was a train in the distance. I counted over forty-five cars but I never heard a sound. It was eerie not to hear anything when I could see so far and so clearly. Wind blocks smell as well as sound. Now I understood how an attack from downwind could succeed.

Passing Nashua with fourteen miles to go, I felt I was getting a sore throat. We needed a rest day. We checked into Rustic Lodge, bought fruit, cereal, yogurt, and milk, and spent the afternoon with ABC's "Wide World of Sports." Pizza Hut provided supper, and tomorrow we didn't have to go anywhere!

Glasgow, Sunday, August 17

On rest day, we spent hours at the Pioneer Museum. It was just what we needed and particularly poignant for Bea who connected more scraps of homestead life she had heard about from her mother. The museum booklets and displays described the lives of the eighty thousand homesteaders who filed land claims in eastern Montana between 1900 and 1917. Sheltered by primitive dugouts or sod shanties, they began new lives on the treeless prairie.

Bea remembered that her mother lived in a sod home. In the Glasgow area, one-room tar-papered shacks were prevalent. The Great Northern Railroad brought the lumber. I studied sample rooms from all types of homes in detail. Many people lived as we camped, without hot water or food from a convenient grocery store.

In some ways, I identified more with the pioneers than with people who asked whether or not we were afraid. I found it pathetic to realize that, among the masses of our country, fear has replaced the homesteaders' courage, their dreams of success, and their great and boundless belief in the future. They were, as we are now, mixed in nationalities, seeking better lives, encouraged by rewards, and delighted with small joys like hearing rain on the roof or seeing the first meadowlark.

Was I really living only in the past century on this bicycle trip? Small-town America was certainly a different place from the ultra-large cities where I'd spent my adult life. My neighborhood in the District of Columbia is not unlike a town of five hundred, except another five hundred live in the next few blocks instead of fifty miles away.

The early schoolroom was nostalgic for me. There were the same style desks, the same maps, and the same Gilbert Stuart unfinished portrait of George. We had entered several working post offices not larger or vastly different from the Lustre, Montana Post Office in the museum. Bea was particularly interested in the homesteader doctor's office and I rather liked the barber shop. Somehow a jump from the cowboys' chuckwagon to modern tailgate picnics wasn't too far-fetched. (I recalled the friend whose date had turned to her at a Virginia Hunt Cup to inquire what all the horses were doing at the cocktail party.) The sheepwagon, containing a bed and kitchen, certainly could be dubbed the first RV, although following sheep all day was hardly recreation.

Upon the Pioneer Museum walls were mounted heads of buffalo, deer, elk, antelope, bobcat, moose, owl, coyote, golden eagle, wolverine, and mink. I wondered whether I would see these animals in the wild.

One of the last real elk-hide tepees and its contents caught my attention. It was made of twenty-three tanned and handsewn hides. Its floor was carpeted with buffalo, mountain lion, bear, and beaver pelts, and its pine lodgepole was eighteen feet high. Looking into this tent reminded me of a wonderful day high in the Kashkar mountains when I visited a family of nomads camped for the summer in an alpine valley of Kashmir in northern India. They had invited me into their canvas tent, its floor covered with animal skins, and I had stuck my head into their kitchen, a tepee of evergreen boughs over the cooking area. We hikers were shown around their summer home, a tent village for a dozen or so people, all related. A cow had been brought off the mountain, and we were presented with fresh warm milk. "Similar," I thought, "must have been the hospitality of the Indians, the people who made this tepee."

I found a list that helped me understand how events had unfolded: before the 1870s there were buffalo and Indians, in the 1880s sheep and cattle, 1887 was railroad year, and the homesteaders came beginning in 1900. I wondered how many people who rode the Erie Canal boats got this far. One of the brochures stated, "From buffalo bones to sonic boom, that's Glasgow, the Queen of the Plains." Both the skeletons and the noise referred to U.S. Government policies. The buffalo provided the staples of tribal life: its flesh was the Indians' basic food, and its hide was used for both clothing and shelter. Skins taken in January or February had the best hair — thick, fluffed-out, and silky. Indians only killed buffalo as needed, and no part of the animal was wasted. It was a matter of survival, not savagery. Even the hides were sometimes eaten; hide scrapings which had been dried could be boiled and eaten in emergencies. Killing the buffalo was part of a government policy to dispose of the Indian problem.

A different exhibit brought us back to the present, where cows in the pasture hear sonic booms. We were impressed to see photographs from the SR-71 spy plane whose pilot had come from Montana. It was something of a novelty for me to stand before these pictures. They were similar to thousands I had seen during my government career, where I had, for a time, helped send requirements of what to photograph with cameras in those planes.

Footsore after many hours, but sure that we had missed important exhibits, we left the museum. We spent the rest of the day writing letters, phoning family, and watching the Sunday television specials. My sore throat had developed into what seemed to be a sinus infection. I took a few aspirin, drank a lot of water, and went to sleep early.

Glasgow, Monday, August 18

By morning, I had sweated out the fever and knew I had hit bottom and begun to bounce back. We mounted our bikes and headed down the road — it was go-to-work time for the pedals. We hoped that our next stop would be a recreation area and hot springs on the other side of Saco. Luxurious green trees bordered the valley floor along the Milk River a mile away.

Route 2 led us westward through a landscape bleached to sameness. Even our shoes were the color of earth. I felt that we blended with everything else. While my sore throat abated and the fever had broken, a cough persisted and the wind soon blew away every vestige of energy. Bea told me she watched me lurch and wobble down the road as the wind attempted to push me backward.

At Hinsdale, we entered the Double D Cafe and ordered breakfast. Doug, the owner, informed us he invented the four-teen-inch pancake complete with blueberry, strawberry or whipped-cream topping. "All the other places are imitations," he claimed. His all-you-can-eat breakfast was a novelty; if you ate it all in an hour, it was free. He said, "No one ever suc-ceeded."

We returned to Highway 2, a through-the-state truck route referred to locally as the Hi-Line to set it apart from more southerly cross-state routes. Another water-bottle-draining stint on the road brought us to Saco where we leaned our bikes against the wall of a typical cafe. We entered and removed our gloves and helmets. Bea said she felt everyone was watching her.

Eventually the question came: "Where are you from?" Once the ice was broken, the atmosphere was transformed and everyone within earshot joined the conversation, firing ques-tions faster than we could answer. Their genuine interest and concern were heartwarming.

On our way again, we stopped to watch bales of hay

being compressed near the roadside. A large tractor with an enclosed cabin pulled what resembled an extra-tall, two-horse trailer with a chute the width of the tractor in front of it. The hay went up the chute and into the trailer. When full, its top compressed the loaded hay. We discovered the tractor was operated by two boys about eleven and fourteen years old. They stopped in front of us. Wordlessly and competently, the boys pulled ropes and cranked handles, causing motors to whir. The trailer disgorged a shaggy, twelve foot-high loaf of golden hay, made by two kids while two city slickers gawked. They acknowledged our presence with a carefree wave and resumed driving the tractor.

We continued to ride, pressed on by the hope of getting over the Rockies and out from under their rain shadow. Though desperately tired, I couldn't rest. When there were camp-grounds, they were treeless and dusty. Usually they were in the wrong towns for our schedule, or we didn't know about them. We also had tired of motels and moaned over our dependency upon them, but hot showers seemed to be the only thing that revived us.

Our water bottles were dry again, but we could see the water tower and grain elevator of Malta in the distance. Des-perately thirsty, I held Bea's bike while she walked up to a house to ask for water. No one was around, but she used the hose to fill her bottle. I still had half a bottle which I drank while waiting for her.

We pedaled another couple of miles and found that the first building in town of any interest to us was a Dairy Queen. I staggered in and ordered an ice cream soda. Apparently perceiving my condition correctly, the girl promptly gave me a large cup with the lid on and a straw protruding. I took a big pull on the straw just as Bea reached the counter and I told her, "This is terrible! It's tasteless! Don't order a soda." Then I took off the lid, discovered ice water, and swilled the contents until my head ached. I was unaccustomed to ice.

Everyone behind the counter laughed. Chagrined, I apologized as the same girl handed me the soda and refilled the water cup. The sodas were superb, too. Thus strengthened, we entered town, found a motel, and collapsed for the rest of the day.

Malta, Tuesday, August 19

Looking for a breakfast cafe, we emerged from Mann's Motel in Malta, a town founded in 1887 when the Great Northern Railroad had built a siding here. Bea adamantly refused to let me use the stove in a motel, even in the shower stall and with the window open. She was convinced it was too dangerous. We ate cardboard pancakes and soggy toast.

We headed for Harlem. I was still feeling lousy, and I wanted to get a ride in a truck. Bea said, "No way. If you hitch, you go alone. This is a bicycle trip."

"It's so dry and hot, and I'm just not up to it, I'm really tired, bone tired, and I want to stop," I whined, but there was no decent place to halt. To myself I continued to moan, "I don't want to stay here any longer—not anywhere in this scorched country." Bea rode behind me, except on the hills, when she waited on top. We rested on a bridge. In three hours we had ridden only twenty-seven miles into the wind. A fifteen-minute rest revived me, and we began again.

Half an hour later, the wind picked up, but I churned my pedals for another forty-five minutes. We met a bicyclist riding from Seattle to Boston. He had shipped his clothes and books for school and was transporting himself to college. He encouraged us when he said that the Going-to-the-Sun Road, which he had just come over, would be less steep for us than for him. "Highway 20 through Washington is great; it goes all along the river valleys. You can swim in the rivers when you get too hot. You've got a great ride ahead, a great ride. Idaho only takes one day and it's quite flat." He had a tailwind of about twenty miles per hour, and we had the headwind. He had been doing long days of around a hundred miles, sometimes more. His longest day was one-hundred-forty miles, but he had been assisted by a downhill slope and tailwind. All three of us were too far from anywhere to spend more time talking.

I could hardly budge, but finally achieved some momentum and kept moving. About a mile short of Harlem, an eighteen-wheeler went by, and Bea fell off her bike because of the wind blast. I almost lost my balance, too. Bea was furious and stood shaking her fist and shouting after the truck

One more mile of fuming brought Bea, with me trailing, to Deb's Diner. Everything was home cooked and the soup, Swedish meatballs, and salad were delicious. The diner was clearly in a class with the North 40 Restaurant we liked so much in Rolla, North Dakota. After a chocolate shake for dessert, Bea calmed down, but she was not ready to think about hitching a truck ride to Chinook. We talked about waiting for a wind change in late afternoon or trying to get a truck ride or, since this was such a good place to eat, staying at the R&R Motel next door.

Harlem, Wednesday, August 20

We were up at five-thirty. I sniffed the chilly air, and put on socks, my long "blue legs," lycra tights, orange shirt, *Washington Post* jacket, a green, flannel-lined, windproof jacket, and gloves. Admiring the full moon about to set behind the Bear Claw Mountains south of the highway, we left the motel.

When the diner opened at six, we were the third and fourth customers to enter. The others coming in were men. The waitresses greeted us warmly, recognizing us since we had eaten both lunch and supper here yesterday. I watched the morning cafe ritual unfold: the first two men sat at the largest table in the center of the dining area. After the waitresses greeted us, the men said good morning. Perhaps they had seen us before also — on the road from their pickups or in the cafe. These men met here daily to swap stories and weather tips. I noted that each new arrival spoke to the others by first name. It was the custom to serve your own coffee. I heard no orders, and assumed the waitress served them the same food each day. There was a round table group and a square table group who seemed to know each other but were not, I deduced, of the same "club." I had eaten my egg and toast. It was time to go, but I felt I was walking out in the middle of a play where I heard the voices but understood no words. I found scenes of the same drama reenacted all over America.

Just the other side of Havre, we stopped to read a signpost listing cattle branding marks, like Two Pole Pumpkin, U Lazy J, and Circle Diamond. Today's cattle sport large colorful identification tags in their ears. There was no wind, and I rode as hard as I could, drafting so as not to lag behind. We paused for a second breakfast at Havre and then proceeded to Inverness where we ate lunch in a quasi-ghost town. By three-thirty, we arrived in Chester, having ridden one-hundred-five miles. I felt wonderfully elated and wanted to continue, but didn't say so. What an exhilarating day it had been, with no wind in the morning and steady tail winds from ten to three-thirty.

From the names of the towns on our hundred-mile journey, it appeared we had been all over the world. We had seen Harlem, Zurich, Havre, Fresno, Kremlin, Inverness, and Chester!

After checking into the MX Motel, we visited a Chester grocery where we met an exuberant young man whose wife had just presented him with a son. Bea congratulated him adding, "You know, I'm going to have a baby, too." He smiled when she explained she was anticipating a grandchild.

Supper consisted of granola and milk with extra raisins and fresh grapes added. We completed writing our joint letter and fired off other correspondence in all directions.

Chester, Thursday, August 21

At five in the morning, I awoke feeling healthy, raring to go. I read, wrote, washed, and dressed and, by six-fifteen, roused Bea. We left the motel at the same time as three men with new Schwinn Voyager bikes and identical new Tailwind panniers. All three wore grey wind pants and tops. It would be utterly impossible to see them on the road, I thought. Everything they had or wore was low visibility. They probably thought our international orange shirts were garish. They said that yesterday's headwinds had held them to sixty miles. We were impressed. The men had left Olympia, Washington two weeks ago and were headed east

Gray-black clouds threatened rain, and headwinds and crosswinds pummeled our progress. By ten o'clock, we had covered twenty-five miles before the headwind began to freshen. We proceeded more slowly, especially up long rises or short hills. There was little flat terrain though views from the rises made the land in the distance look level.

We headed for Shelby. Our goal was Cut Bank, some sixty miles ahead. After about eleven miles, I saw a fox cross the road. I yelled at Bea, and she saw it, too. We stopped and focused our binoculars on the fox as it ran through a field and right past a pronghorn antelope. What a thrill! The fox's white-tipped tail was flying, and its black-socked feet were stepping lively. The animals avoided each other and after they were both out of sight behind a hillock, we stowed away our binoculars and moved on. Half a mile down the road, I again caught sight of the fox, far away, trotting across a field of grain stubble. When people ask if it is boring out on the flat, empty road, I think of the fox and antelope, and answer, "No."

I could hardly pedal seven miles an hour, a speed at which Bea could barely balance her bicycle. Still racked by a dry cough, I began to wonder whether I could make the nine or ten miles to Shelby. I made a prayer of thanks for the assistance of the wind yesterday, and asked for help today. I felt so bad that I decided that, no matter what Bea did, I would ride in a truck. None came. There was no traffic except for an occasional car. Bea decided we would halt overnight in Shelby, take another day to reach Cut Bank, and another day to St. Mary at the foot of the mountains. We would have to travel from Cut Bank uphill to St. Mary in one day because the entire fifty-five miles was within the Blackfeet Indian Reservation. We had been repeatedly warned not to stop overnight along that route. I wanted desperately to be done with eastern Montana. The wind continued to cost us extra days of struggle.

On the Hi-Line, I wobbled into the wind. A truck with a hardtop over the pickup section passed us. I wanted to signal, but it took all my strength to raise my eyes enough to see the driver look into his rear view mirror and wave. His brake lights went on. He pulled off the road, turned around, and came back, stopping on the other side of the road just ahead of us. My heart leaped. He was going to offer us a ride, and I was going to accept. I didn't care what Bea did. He got out of the truck and smiled. "Would you like a lift? That wind is pretty strong."

"Yes, thank you. You bet!" I was already off my bike. To Bea, "Please come. I've got to do it." She came.

The pickup was new, empty, and stood high off the ground. We loaded the bikes and panniers in no time. I was afraid Bea would want to get out of the truck at Shelby or Cut Bank.

"Where are you going?" I asked the driver.

"Up to Duck Lake, fishing. Where are you going?" He had a nice voice.

"We're headed for Cut Bank and St. Mary."

"I can take you there," he said as he snapped the cover, shutting our bicycles into the truck. We entered the spacious cab.

Thus, Tom Durand, a Sioux Indian who lived in Havre and worked for the railroad, drove us along the Hi-Line.

Instead of three days, it took less than two hours to reach St. Mary. We stopped twice, once for gas and once in Browning for our mail. Bea said she was satisfied to see Cut Bank from the truck. On this overcast and chilly day, we traveled thirty-two miles by bicycle and eighty-nine miles via pickup.

Tom answered the questions that had accumulated during our pedal along the Hi-Line. He seemed to know all the people along both the highway and the railroad. We asked about a man we saw riding a rail car, and Tom said that was common now. If they were careful, there was no problem, and he wouldn't bother them, although railroad policy was to chase them off. He felt work was hard to find, and people often needed to travel to find work.

We recounted our wonderful lunch in Inverness. He was amazed we found the cafe, a great favorite with the train people and the truck drivers who know about it. Inverness is a town of old people, he told us. Their children live elsewhere and return about three months per year to grow crops on the family land, one month in spring to plant and two months in summer to harvest. The rest of the time it is almost a ghost town.

We asked a lot of questions about Indians. Tom's father leased his land to others and took his family to live off the reservation. Tom worked his way through college, got a railroad job, and went into the Army. Later he returned to the railroad. Now he worries about how the government will screw up his retirement.

Most of his close relatives live off the reservation. He laughed, saying that his family often accuses him of behaving and thinking too much like a white man. He lived in Kentucky and worked for the Southern Railroad, but he prefers it here. He can't stay in the mountains too long, he said, for he likes space. Tom expressed my feelings in reverse — I adore spaciousness but am now ready for the closeness and comfort of mountains.

On the street of Browning, Tom called our attention to a man staggering drunk although it was early in the day. "If he had to work he wouldn't do that," Tom commented. He said all his nieces and nephews, ten to twenty of them, got grant money from the government to go to college. They went and partied. No one graduated, and it was a waste. I was surprised when Tom advocated the government should do away with reservations. He saw no reason to subsidize people who thought they didn't have to work. "Feeling useless is what makes them drunk and rowdy," he said. He showed us the wreck of a Best Western Motel which had closed two years after it was built. Of all the

Indian reservation towns we had seen, Browning appeared to be in the poorest condition. We were overjoyed not to bicycle through the area and to have this opportunity to listen to an Indian talk. He offered to wait for us to visit the museum, but we declined, explaining truthfully that we were too tired to absorb anything more.

We tried to buy the gas and offered to take Tom to lunch, but he said there was no need. "Please don't be trying to buy something all the time," Tom told me. He only needed nine gallons of gas. His pickup had two extra-large tanks and he kept them full. I would, too, in this country. We got out and hung the panniers on our bicycles at the junction in St. Mary. We waved goodby and wished Tom a good catch of trout. The most interesting places seem to be those where we spent time listening to someone who lives there. How rested I felt!

In the information office, I decided on Johnson's Red Eagle Motel on a rise overlooking the valley. We ate bowls of chili at The Post Cafe then pedaled up to register at the motel. We lay on our beds and talked about how we did not want to do anything until we were completely rested. We would stay until we were no longer content to look at the Rocky Mountains on the other side of the window panes.

We ate a turkey dinner and then read in bed, falling asleep early. I awoke at two a.m., dreaming about talking on the phone with my friend, Betty Woodsend, who was in Kathmandu. I could neither remember what we talked about nor return to sleep. My legs were hurting, and I soaked them in a tub of hot water. Still not sleepy, I closed the door to prevent the light from waking Bea, sat on the closed toilet lid, and wrote notes on the tank top. It was a pretty good desk!

Eastern Montana was behind us.

St. Mary, Friday, August 22

We ate at Johnson's Cafe. Johnson's also had a campground, but the nights were cold and rainy when we first arrived. We were too tired to even think about camping. Outside our motel window, in front of a rocky backdrop, the valley spread.

In 1932, Glacier National Park in the United States and Waterton Lakes National Park in Canada were joined to form the first international peace park in the world. The park, like the

Peace Gardens in North Dakota, symbolizes bonds of peace and friendship between the people of the United States and Canada. While studying a map, I discovered a number of peace gardens and parks along the longest unarmed border in the world.

A trip to Park Headquarters provided us with the rules for bicycling the Going-to-the-Sun Road, the fifty-mile route from St. Mary over the Continental Divide at Logan Pass. A schedule of activities and lectures mentioned a movie, "Bears and Man." Although we had seen no more bears since Michigan, we were in bear country, and decided to attend.

We cleaned ourselves and our bikes, emptied and repacked the panniers, read and replied to our mail, read copies of *Montana Magazine* and the tourist folders, and wrote a joint letter. We were so busy during rest days that it seemed riding the bicycles was the vacation portion of our odyssey. There was so much to see and do in this area we knew we could happily camp here for weeks. But the park was closing for the season in a few days, and we really needed to be on the other side of that beautiful rock wall outside our window.

After hearing so much about the Going-to-the-Sun Road, we didn't want to attempt it until we were able to enjoy the experience. I had not yet fully recovered from my cough and tired easily.

On each visit to Park Headquarters, I asked more questions about bicycling in the park, the campgrounds on the other side, and facilities at the top. In addition, I spoke with bicyclists, some of whom had brought their bikes by car and ridden without loads for a day trip. I learned that the rangers who worked at Logan Pass each day drove up early in the morning from St. Mary where they lived. They were not allowed to carry passengers, but probably there was no specific rule to prohibit their carrying a knapsack containing our lunch. My plan congealed. I learned what time the rangers departed and where to find them. Our "lunch" would consist of all of our panniers, or the heaviest ones. We would keep only tire and tube repair equipment, cameras, film, and our jackets.

I relished becoming acquainted with the rangers and telling them about our trip. Since it was the end of the season and tourists were fewer, they had time for conversation. Although accustomed to bicyclists, they apparently found two old ladies riding across the United States, camping without a support vehicle a novelty.

St. Mary, Saturday, August 23

By our second full day of rest we were beginning to calm down. I was not stalking in and out of the room, but spent more time reading, washing clothes, or answering mail. We were not yet ready to clean bicycles or buy food in preparation for getting on the road again.

We liked this Johnson family; every member we met was an interesting, industrious individual. I read and reread "How the Johnson Family Started in the Restaurant Business" printed on the placemats. It was a universal American story of family cooperation, long hours, and hard work yielding a better start for each generation.

At the telephone booth in St. Mary I called Celia Chandler in Mt. Vernon, Washington and learned they had moved, but were expecting us to stay with them. The new house has a guest house, not furnished, no water, but a comfortable room. We could stay there or in the main house. I chose the guest house, so that neither child would have to give up a room. I insisted furniture was unnecessary as we were in our own beds every night with our sleeping bags and mattresses. She gave me permission to use her address for mail. Celia had married and had two children since she lived with my mother while studying at Catholic University after the death of her first husband. We had seen each other rarely, yet she seemed so pleased that we were coming and I would have a chance to know her children.

I called my mother, who recounted problems with the temporary tenants in my house in Washington. Mom received our fourth joint letter and would include a copy in my mail to Whitefish. She seemed in good spirits and health. Mom encouraged me at every call, insisting that were she younger she would have come too. Bicycling was prohibited to young ladies when she grew up, so she had learned to ride secretly, falling off her big brother's bike until she learned to ride it.

On my way back to the motel I stopped in the filling station to see about some stove fuel. They didn't have any gallon cans to sell but told me that Coleman fuel is the same as kerosene but with additives. They had kerosene, but I wasn't sure the stove would burn as flawlessly without the additives to make it cleaner. When he discovered I wanted less than a quart, he sold it to me out of his Coleman can for a dollar.

When I returned to the room, Bea was washing the tent

floor in the bathtub. I reinspected the air mattresses for leaks when she finished with the water. Finding none, I took the mattresses outside to dry.

I read an article in *Montana Magazine* much of which was excerpted from Dr. Stephen Herrero's book, *Bear Attacks*, based on seventeen years of study and research on grizzly and black bears. I also read the National Park Service information and saw two informative movies about bears. I felt prepared and unafraid. We had no chance of seeing a grizzly while bicycling along a road. Any black bear, less dangerous, would probably see us first and depart. Our experience so far underscored these statements. Should we have a confrontation, we should not look into the bear's eyes, or make any sudden movements. We were to stand still or back away slowly. In no case should we allow ourselves to get between a mother and cubs. Food should be stored on bear poles or away from a sleeping tent. We should not sleep outside the tent, eat in the tent, or place the tent near cooking or eating areas. Above all, we should not panic if we saw a bear.

We had crossed North Dakota and eastern Montana visiting only two cities of over a thousand people.

St. Mary, Sunday, August 24

On Sunday, we were feeling much better. I read about trail rides in Glacier Park, and wondered where I would find the energy to ride a horse, even one of those tourist nags that only walks. I was determined to ride a horse somewhere during this trip. But rest days were for rest and quiet activities like reading.

I wrote down the pass elevations, the miles from below to the top of the passes, for the seven passes between us and Mt. Vernon, Washington. Combining that data with the town populations, I planned our stops for the rest of the trip and located alternate campgrounds when they were available. I had learned enough now to correlate facilities to town populations. Along the way I sought information about groceries, cafes, motels, and campgrounds in advance. People along the road knew what was open and closed and, frequently, I got excellent subtle advice about places to avoid.

We cleaned and readied the bikes, went to park headquarters to see the movie about grizzlies, and walked around the Johnsons' nice campground. We had made a good decision to remain in the motel. I still had my cough occasionally, and we enjoyed the weekend TV programs. Besides, the wind was blowing, and it was chilly at night. Anyway, we had been too lazy to move, and there would probably be fine camping every night from now on.

I had told Celia that we expected to arrive September 10 at their home in Mt. Vernon. We didn't have to rush, but I wasn't sure how to estimate mountain pedaling. We had not yet climbed any mountains.

Tomorrow, Logan Pass at 6,646 feet would be the highest. From St. Mary, a little over 4,500 feet, we would be climbing 2,100 feet in twenty miles, not a particularly steep ride. I knew the road ahead was well graded. I also knew we would encounter three passes over 5,000 feet and three over 4,000 feet and that we would go through the lowest point in Montana, at 1,820 feet, just before entering Idaho. I felt apprehensive about tomorrow and the Going-to-the-Sun Road, our first real mountain ride.

We remained at Red Eagle three-and-a-half days. So far, I had not been able to stay anywhere long enough.

CHAPTER SIX

Mountain Montana Hospitality

St. Mary, Montana, Monday, August 25

Early in the morning, we looked out our hilltop window to the cloud-covered Red Eagle Valley. The Rocky Mountains were blotted out. Walking to breakfast, we could barely see the Glacier National Park entrance, a mile away. Bea, depressed by the weather, was anxious to get started but asked, "What can we see on the way?"

"Let's see what happens while we're eating," I replied. I thought if the clouds were this low, it was probably splendid above them. Besides, TV weather predicted clearing today. Mornings had been cloudier than afternoons; this morning was worse, but there was a breeze.

During breakfast, Mr. Johnson, patriarch of the Johnson clan, answered our questions about the antique tools hanging on the walls. The hay cutter was used to slice bales into bite-sized pieces for feeding animals. There was an ancient waffle iron for use over a wood fire — imagine carrying that on our bicycles, or on a horse! He commented on a photo of his grandson riding a sheep, "He doesn't like it so much now that he's older." He recounted tales of the saws, skins, photos, and taxidermy hung on the cafe walls, and I realized we needed at least another full day just to listen to his stories.

During breakfast, I thought this was the first day in a long time that I felt normal. Looking back over my calendar, I realized it was the first time in over a month that we had rested more than a day and a half at one time. We had not been sticking to a ride-five-days-and-rest-two plan.

As we mounted our bikes, Bea noticed a flat tire. Afraid we would miss the ranger's departure, I piled all the panniers and luggage on my bike and coasted downhill. Bea yelled. I had forgotten to give her the tire irons. I put my bike down and walked them to her. Then I rolled rather precariously to the Park entrance while Bea repaired the flat. There I met our angel for the day, Ranger Eleanor Guerin from Otter Lake Conservation School at Greenfield, New Hampshire. She stowed the sleeping bags, tent, and panniers in the back of her vehicle and drove away. I never had met anyone who went to a conservation school and hoped to chat with her further. While waiting for Bea I learned from the other young rangers that they would be going back to school within a week. One of them had grown up here. Her parents, with the Justice Department, work at the border.

Bea and I each had kept one saddlebag containing warm clothes, sandwiches, water, cameras, and spare tubes. When Bea arrived, I looked at the contents of her pannier while she told me about repairing the tire. Then I asked, "Where's the pump?" I wondered if she had wrapped it in the mattress which was lashed to her rack.

"Oh, I left it on the bed!" She wasn't pleased to pedal the two miles up and back to retrieve it.

I sat down to wait and watched the clouds continue to lift. They were lighter than the near-black masses of early morning. I decided it would be a magnificent day. There was no surface breeze, and perhaps we would have a day without headwind. It was about nine o'clock, but there was no particular hurry since we had fewer than twenty miles to ride uphill. We would not be permitted to go down the other side until four p.m. because bicycles had to stay off the road between ten and four, the high-traffic times. On the other side of the pass, the road was narrow and the curves were tight.

Bea returned, upset. A few drops of rain had fallen on her, and she was convinced we wouldn't see anything. Her handlebars kept twisting. She tightened them. We had hardly pedaled a mile into Glacier National Park before I realized my bottom bracket was loose. I got off and tightened it as much as possible by hand. Then, using a screwdriver and a rock, I tapped it really tight. A few miles along, Bea became concerned that she had not put enough air in her front tire, and we stopped to goose it a few squirts with the pump. I hoped to reach Whitefish tomorrow, where we could have the tire repaired.

For almost ten miles, our route ran along the edge of St. Mary Lake, a narrow finger of water that crooked toward the pass. I looked over the valley and the lake. On the other side of the road, dense evergreens pranced up the mountainside. Above, large patches of blue were expanding and the clouds clustered into ever-whiter popcorn, clearly reflected in St. Mary Lake. From the end of the lake, we climbed through the tree line and rode along the edge of a giant glacier-dug bowl of exquisitely colored and striated rocks. The six-mile climb above the lake was warm, pleasant, and not nearly so difficult as I had feared.

Here in the park more people seemed to wave. One car full of people stuck their hands out the windows, smiling and waving. They even looked out the rear window, still waving. I was further encouraged by the views and by seeing the Visitor Center long before our arrival there. We passed small water-falls and a vast variety of wildflowers blooming among the rocks as we crept slowly upward. By the time we reached the Visitor Center and walked up the ramp to the terrace, it was almost noon, and there was not a whip of cloud left anywhere.

We sat in the sun on a rock under a "Do Not Feed the Animals" sign, eating our sandwiches. Gray Columbian ground squirrels about a foot long sat on their haunches, watching hungrily. We were intentionally careless about crumbs, which they nabbed before they touched the ground. These burrowers help create porous soil, allowing rain to soak into the ground instead of running off.

Thus refreshed, I notified Ranger Eleanor of our arrival and intent to walk in the meadow during the afternoon. She said I could leave our gear in her car until we returned.

We walked up the three-mile round-trip boardwalk trail. The wooden walkway helps control random movement of people over the alpine meadow; hardy tundra plants are easily damaged by feet. If destroyed, some areas could require hundreds of years to rebuild to a natural and persistent ecosystem. I could see that sloping meadows, rocky ledges, and moraines were drained by a network of streamlets and creeks fed by receding snowfields. Along these water paths grew a profusion of colorful flowers, including purple aster and yellow St. Johnswort. At timberline, we passed the last *kummholz* groves of trees on the boardwalk. *Kummholz* is a German word meaning "elfin timber" or "crooked wood." The subalpine firs so characterized are shrubby and dense, becoming more twisted and contorted as a result of snow and the desiccating force of the wind. I sympathized.

Further along, only about half of the ground had plant growth. This was an intermediary growth, between the lichen-covered slopes of Clements Mountain in front of us and the plant-filled alpine meadows. Here I looked at yellow scrubby cinquefoil, pink moss campion, and alpine willows only two inches tall. Bea frequently reversed her binoculars to study the lichens growing on the wind-abraded rock surfaces. I tried it, too. It was fascinating.

Looking around at the moraine, I took a deep breath, and was suddenly transported in memory to Kashmir, to Pakistan, to Nepal where I had slipped and slid about at high altitude on vacation hikes. I looked up from my feet out over the space left between the mountain walls by the carving of glaciers, sniffed the clear air, and marveled at the optical illusions of proximity to the green lake below and the peak opposite. I took a deep breath of what I call champagne air, unexpected at such a low altitude.

Near Hidden Lake, Bea called my attention to several hoary marmots and a mountain goat. A man came along the trail and asked what I was looking at through my binoculars. "Mountain goat," I said without moving.

"Well, if you'd like to see one better, there's one about a hundred yards along the trail, and you don't need the binoculars."

"What? Thank you." We walked along cautiously, afraid of frightening the animal. No chance — there were nanny and baby goat posing between nibbles of turf for the lenses of fifteen photographers and as many watchers.

By the time we returned to the Visitor Center, I realized neither of us was as rested and fit as we thought. Bea tired easily and my cough had returned. We retrieved our possessions and packed our bikes. The last tourist bus to Lake MacDonald Restaurant and Lodge departed from Logan Pass at three-thirty. Its driver, Joe Chamberlain, agreed to carry our panniers down in his bus and leave them at the lodge for us. Although we didn't need help as much as we had coming up, it would certainly save wear on our brakes.

It was pure joy to soar and swoop effortlessly past the changing scenes, golden in the afternoon sun. I leaned into the curves as cooling wind whistled through the holes in my helmet. We glided into the forest, burned, re-grown, thick, and young. I should have stopped for pictures, but couldn't break the spell. Avoiding rocks in the road, whizzing around curves, I was astonished how seldom brakes were needed. I vaguely remembered a principle of physics about a maximum speed for a falling object. For me it seemed to be thirty to thirty-three miles per hour.

Hating to stop but knowing Bea would want me to wait for her, I talked with a couple at a turnout. They had just come from Winthrop, Washington, and recommended eating at the Duck Brand. Bea pulled up, breathless. We admired the view and continued. Bea noted there was no guard rail — only yawning chasms awaiting the luckless cyclist. Large stones along the side of the twisting road left ample room for a laden bicycle to hurtle into eternity. Bea crept down the mountainside, dry-mouthed. No way did she dare go near the edge for a view. Long afterward, Bea told me that it made her palms sweat to think of that descent.

Near the bottom, while paralleling a swift creek, I heard a splash. A black bear stood midstream. I squeezed the brakes hard and ripped out my camera for one quick shot as the bear walked over to the rocks on the opposite bank. Where was Bea? I looked back, but there was no sign of her.

Jeeps, cars, tour busses, mobile homes and pickups slammed on their brakes, creating a "bear jam." The bear walked into the bushes. I scanned the opposite bank of the stream and saw the bear's eyes, yellow-green circles shining through a bush. As quickly as they had come, the vehicles were gone. Soon the bear emerged, looked at the audience remaining along the road, and ambled down the stream bed into another clump of bushes. One car remained while a young man with a long-lens camera sat on the stone wall overlooking the McDonald Creek.

When Bea came, I told her about the bear and suggested we ride slowly, for it might come out again downstream. Half-a-mile further along, we did see the bear, as it glanced at us over one shoulder and ducked into the bushes.

I had to stop to tighten my bottom bracket two more times. I wasn't able to tighten it completely, but it held together. Perhaps I could find a strong man at the campground to pull it tight.

Continuing to roll downhill slightly and pedaling furiously, I rounded a bend and saw a ranger's car parked. I quit pedaling and slowed, wondering why the ranger was sitting there. I looked at the creek and observed a black bear with three cubs. As I reached for my brakes, the ranger motioned me on and said to keep rolling, not to stop. We did, slowly, but we had a good look at the bears.

We collected our panniers at the McDonald Lodge First Aid Station porch. Then, hungry, we took time to look inside the wonderful old building which reminded me of another of the same era at Mt. Rainier National Park.

We ate chicken soup and salad in the restaurant, and I just couldn't get enough water. Over blueberry pie we met Tom, a bicyclist from Kalispell, who had ridden up from the campground to eat supper. He told us that Sprague Creek Campground wasn't far and invited us to stop there. Although headed for Apgar, we were ready to halt and couldn't resist the prospect of meeting other bicyclists. Tom preceded us.

The road twisted mile after beautiful mile with trees on the left and the rushing stream on the right, ever gently downward. Yelling to each other as we rode, half coasting along, Bea said, "Look at the water. It's so clear!"

I responded, "Yes, if you're fishing you can even see where to throw the hook."

"That's how you catch them!" came a fisherman's cry from the bank as our bikes sped by.

Two spaces at Sprague Creek Campground were reserved for bicyclists. One of these spots had been usurped by two women touring in their car. We had no other place to go and it was almost dark. Out west, campground managers understand that bicycles can't go another twenty miles when a place is full, but the women probably didn't realize this. Tom and three other cyclists were sharing the remaining site and, as the two women looked on silently, the bicyclists invited us to join them. This was the first time in two weeks we were able to camp. To have the company of cyclists who shared our joys, difficulties, and deprivations was a real source of comfort.

Tom introduced us to Maureen and Russ Bishop, who were riding back home to North Hollywood via Seattle from their cross-country trip to the east coast. The men looked at my bottom bracket and agreed that I had no major problem. Using their tools and mine, they tightened it as hard as they could and assured me I would be able to get to the bike shop in Whitefish. Dick and Marilyn Williams came in about that time on a motorcycle and joined our group.

The eight of us cooked and ate our dinner on the same table. It was a bit crowded, but the company was friendly. Although all of us were tired, we were exhilarated by the companionship. We set up the tent before dark, ate, and hung our remaining food on the bear pole. Then we sat around the picnic table "yarning" in the dark.

The Williamses had the top-of-the-line Gull Wing from Honda, a motorcycle that makes less noise than our bicycles. I had always thought motorcycle people were rowdy and not very well educated. It just doesn't make sense to hold a prejudice. I had never met anyone touring on a motorcycle, and doubted I would ever meet people nicer, or more interesting.

Maureen, who told my favorite story of the evening, prefaced her tale by describing cyclists' clothing. Bicyclists often wear black or brilliant colored-tights, causing them to resemble ballerinas without a tutu. Bike shoes with cleats to grip the pedals cause a person to tiptoe when walking, and they sound like tap shoes. Cycling gloves have only half-length fingers with satin or crocheted backs. Maureen recounted the lunch time when she and her husband and two male bicyclists clad in tights, helmets, and brilliant-colored jerseys tiptoed into a remote, dreary, unpainted cafe filled with ranchers in cowboy boots, hats, jeans, and huge belt buckles. As the ranchers gaped in disbelief, the intimidated bicyclists bolted their food without removing their gloves and fled. Maureen had the feeling the ranchers weren't too sure she was the only woman.

Late that evening, two of the bicyclists followed us, continuing to talk animatedly. We fell exhausted into our tent. Bea and I crawled under our sleeping bag blanket and, though half-asleep, stuck our heads out the door to continue conversation with our newly-found friends. Finally, they crawled into their tents and quiet descended. The bears were elsewhere.

Exhausted, yet wide awake, Bea confessed to having a headache from stress and fear. She explained how much and how long she dreaded the descent. She thanked me over and over for getting the baggage taken not only up but down.

For me, it has been a wonderful, very special day, one of the best of the whole trip, capped by the camaraderie of the people who scooped us into their campsite. I realized we both eagerly visited with the others because we were tired of each other's non-stop, twenty-four-hour company day after day.

Lake McDonald, Tuesday, August 26

With the other campers and the sun, I was up at five, although I had a headache. Bea cooked rice and added a tin of beef to it for breakfast. Hidden Lake overlook, where we had walked from Logan Pass, was at about seven thousand feet and our present campsite was on a bluff above Lake McDonald at about thirty-two hundred feet. We had climbed and descended nearly four thousand feet yesterday. My lack of appetite last night and a headache were both mild symptoms of altitude sickness, to which I am sensitive. We discussed taking a half-day off and going for a horseback ride. Bea wasn't interested, and I didn't have enough energy. We didn't hurry our showers or packing, but left by midmorning.

Gliding down the hill past Lake McDonald, we stopped for lunch in West Glacier, negotiated some road construction through Hungry Horse, refilled our water bottles and enjoyed a cold root beer at Columbia Falls, and reached Whitefish by midafternoon.

I found the bicycle shop, and the mechanic tightened my bottom bracket, adjusted the brakes, and tested my computer, which had consistently under-recorded our distance. The sensors were not close enough together because of my faulty installation. The repair forced the sensors closer together and stabilized the one on the frame.

Later, I realized the Avocet had never worked so well. Although I always recorded two to three miles in fifty less than Bea, I insisted that I was accurate according to the road signs and maps. I also insisted that we use the lower mileage as the "official" trip mileage so as not to exaggerate how far we had gone. Well, by now the official distance was at least a hundred miles short of what we had actually traveled.

Bea had her wheels trued and bought two new tires and tubes. I stayed out of the shop while she was making these arrangements. It was her business. Shortly after leaving the shop, a block away, her rear tire was flat. Back at the shop, they inserted a new tube. The next day, while we were in town, we had to return again to the shop because of another flat. The situation was worse than before. There was another flat before we left the area.

These flats were fixed or the tubes replaced without further charge. Since we rode about town without our loads, repairing a flat was no big problem; anyhow, the shop did it. I wondered whether anyone had thought to fix the cause of Bea's flat tires instead of just replacing the tubes.

While Bea had her turn with the mechanic, I went to the sporting goods store next door and bought a gallon of stove fuel. When Bea joined me, we bought two new three-quarter-length Therm-a-rest mattresses, the ultra-lightweight new models. Not certain why our old mattresses had deflated before morning ever since North Dakota, I decided to mail them to Celia's address in Mt. Vernon. They were made in Seattle, so I thought we could investigate the problem when we got there.

We needed new mattresses for softness and insulation since it was getting colder. One sleeping bag used as a blanket was no longer sufficient, and, since the shop had a good sale, I bought a new bag, adding two pounds to my load.

The Glacier Cycle people recommended camping at Whitefish Lake, about five miles out of town, and told us how to get there. Camp was lovely, right on the lake, but we hadn't noticed that the Canadian Pacific main line ran past it. In the middle of the night, the trains roared through, sounding as if they were over the tent. I awoke for one or two trains; then, realizing what the noise was, slept through all the rest. The next morning, another camper told us he had counted eighteen trains.

Whitefish, Wednesday, August 27

After breakfast at Buffalo Cafe, we picked up the mail and returned to our lovely wooded camp to read and answer it. Late in the afternoon, we headed for town. I had to go back to the bike shop because I had carried off all parts to the charge slip. We also needed to mail our letters and the package of mattresses. Bea bought a new pair of tennis shoes and threw her old shoes in the trash. I bought a pair of cotton shorts to replace the pair I left somewhere. The shorts and a T-shirt were my pajamas.

Wandering around the shops, we decided on a splendid restaurant dinner. As we ate, we started out talking and wound up fussing with each other. Being with Bea was increasingly less fun. I considered ending the trip in Seattle. If it wasn't fun, why do it?

When we returned to the campground I tried to concentrate on the maps, for Bea had told her daughter to send mail to both Newport and Colville. With Labor Day weekend coming up, I was having trouble getting us to both places when the post office would be open.

At another table, Bea read a newspaper, wrote, dictated into her machine, and finally went into the tent and fell asleep. I felt recovered from my cough. It was almost dark now, and I ate some granola and a peanut butter sandwich. Since I couldn't see and it was getting chilly, I lit a fire and burned our paper trash. I then went over to the edge of the lake. It was quiet and peaceful as I sat there watching the last darkening rays of evening.

Mentally, I felt free of Bea's presence. The trip was still paramount, and I didn't want either of us to abandon it. I still didn't think that I could or would enjoy bicycle touring alone. When I stumbled through the underbrush to the tent, the last train I heard that evening rumbled past slowly, shaking the ground as I lay down. Rumbling rhythm pulled sleep over my head.

Whitefish, Thursday, August 28

We rode out of the campground along Route 93 toward Eureka. About an hour later, Bea said, "Let's not spoil this lovely day." I said nothing. The morning was lovely, and there was nothing wrong with my day.

Another hour of pedaling went by with Bea riding behind me. I rode like a demon, observing the scenery and waiting at the tops of hills for her. She said, "Don't wait for me," so I let her go by and didn't catch up with her again for awhile. When I did, I passed her.

In silence in a Eureka cafe, I ate a milkshake and salad and she a cheese sandwich. There were two elderly ladies in a booth, a waitress, and the cook. The cook asked where we came from, and, when I answered, she exclaimed, "Wow! Golly! Gee, and where are you going? By which route?" They thought we were taking Route 37, but I had planned to take 508 by way of Yaak. They extolled the road to Libby — downhill all the way. They said the Libby route was faster, the road straight, and the downward slopes beautiful along the lake. They thought of the Yaak road as very hilly. I mentioned the route via Libby was twenty-five miles further, and they protested it was downhill and not so curvy. Curves don't bother bikers. The mechanic in the bike shop had suggested the Yaak route as having no traffic and being a favorite among cyclists. He had told of twelve miles of uphill grade, but had said the views and camping were well worth it, and the distance to Idaho was shorter.

I cashed a travelers check at the bank, and Bea mailed a package to her daughter, Meg, in Kansas. At the grocery we bought carrots and fruit before pedaling the seven miles out of Rexford to the campground.

We pitched our tent near where the Tobacco River runs into Lake Koocanusa behind the Libby Dam. There were no showers, so we paddled around the swimming area in our clothes, washing everything at once, rinsing by swimming. I even washed my shoes. Back at the campsite, Bea scavenged wood and built a fire. Supper somewhat smoothed over our moods. During the day, I had decided to get to Seattle as fast as possible and then go home. I've never seen the Pacific Coast, however, and wanted to bicycle it. Perhaps I would be able to find another partner.

near Rexford, Friday, August 29

Friday morning, as we ate breakfast, the lure of the land and the promise of freedom continued to beckon. Grapes, nectarines, and peaches were stowed in our pockets or our front bags where they were easily accessible. I washed my eyes, plastic and real, and teeth, plastic and real. We packed up and rolled out on Route 37, headed downhill for the bridge.

It was a lovely ride, with marvelous views of the long, skinny reservoir. We crossed the bridge, took a few photographs, watched the boats and ducks, and proceeded uphill toward Yaak.

Ascent began at the bridge and would continue for about twelve miles, but the rest would be down, all the way to Route 2. I knew it was through the Kootenai National Forest, the sparsely traveled Yaak Ranger District. A few miles uphill on a curve with the reservoir in the background, Bea had a flat. She removed both panniers and her sleeping bag and mattress while I got out the tools and a new tube. It was the second new tube the shop had put in that tire. Bea replaced it, pumped it up, then replaced her saddlebags, and we proceeded.

About three miles further along, we realized why this route was considered difficult. The roads were not graded to the same specifications as highways with greater use. Bea had another flat.

We removed all the gear this time, and, while she inspected the tube, I inspected the rim, and covered all the spoke holes near the punctures with duct tape.

All the tube holes were inside. Bea decided that they had incorrectly trued her wheel and that the spokes were punching into the tubes. I thought the tubes might be the problem. They were less than half the weight of the tubes she had used previously. The patch she applied to the flat three miles ago had not held and another hole developed. After patching them both, she pumped up the tube, but it went down. She couldn't find the leak.

I tried. Eventually, by pumping it up, feeling, and listening, I discovered that the valve stem was bent and slightly cracked. We threw it deep into the woods. Finally, Bea was ready for the road. We inspected the remaining tubes and found another with a slit valve. I took the tent to help lighten her load. Already I was carrying the fourteen-pound gallon of stove fuel, some food, both mattresses, my sleeping bag, all the spare tires and tubes, all the bike tools, my cameras, and personal belongings.

We rode up and up and up all day long.

Sometimes we got so hot and tired that we walked and pushed the bikes. Bea, tired of waiting for me, offered to push mine and let me push hers. After a few hundred yards, I took it back. We went up about three thousand feet, crossing the pass at Dodge Summit, 5,230 feet. There we put down our bikes, drank our last water, ate a fruit snack (also our last), admired the view, and congratulated each other on getting there. We were nowhere.

For the next twenty miles, we coasted down through forest. More than ever, I realized that lumbering is an industry like farming. The trees are planted, tended, inspected, counted, measured, cut, and shipped just as though they were vegetables. I had never before considered trees a crop like corn. Some forests had been burned and replanted, while others were densely green and growing. Only growing time seemed to separate farming from forestry. It was beautiful and I loved it.

Bea appeared more content in the woods than anywhere else. Trouble with flat tires had served to wash away our petty wrangling. Isolation and adversity had forced us to cooperate. Going over the Yaak became an even greater treasure. We pedaled along, hungry, tired, hot, thirsty. We passed one or two deserted cabins. Had I counted the vehicles other than an occasional logging truck, there would not have been ten all day. Although it was getting cooler, our tongues felt as if we had doused them with the medicated powder we carried for heat rash (seldom needed) or to put on the tubes whenever we changed them (too often of late).

If and when another car came, I would ask where we were and how far it was to Yaak. I heard one, got off my bike, and waved it to a stop. Inside was a college girl who was working for the National Forest Service for the summer, studying grizzly bear habitat. She said she had only seen two at a great distance. We didn't need to worry about bears here. She gave us the last water from her jug and told us she had been drinking out of the creeks in this valley all summer and had never gotten sick. Yaak was about five or six miles further. I thanked her, longing to be somewhere.

Another mile brought us to a creek. We each drank about a quart of water, then refilled our bottles. All that water was gone when we reached the Yaak Mercantile, a gas station and country store with a big front porch. There was one phone booth. We bought two giant turkey sandwiches for supper, a can of hash, a can of peaches, a box of raisins, some chips, and two quarts of milk, one to drink in the store and another to take with us.

A call to my mom developed into a long consultation about my tenants. She had also visited the cabin I was having built in the north Georgia mountains, and the builder wanted me to call him. I called Celia and talked with her husband, Jerome, who said they were looking forward to our arrival. I couldn't get a third call to go through. The operator came on, saying "I can't hear you at all. There must be something wrong. You'd better use another phone." Since no one could hear me, I only agitated myself by shouting, "There isn't another phone for over fifty miles, thank you!" I flung the phone on its cradle. Bea called my attention to the other building in town, the Dirty Shame Saloon, as we rolled downstream beside the Yaak River.

About three miles later, we came to a water junction at the Pete Creek Campground. There were large trees, fewer than a hundred yards of dirt road, pit toilets, and a pump with delicious-tasting water. Several people were camped in mini-whales. We pitched our tent on the edge of the creek and I was thrilled when Bea suggested that we stay here tomorrow, too. With the tent up and the mattresses and sleeping bags inside, home was ready. We sat at the picnic table and ate our sandwiches, enjoying the forest sounds.

Just finishing the other quart of milk, we looked up and saw a woman coming through the bushes from the next site with a pot of hot coffee. Earlier, she had introduced herself as Jean Peters, and I had asked her advice about storing food overnight and what kind of animals to expect. She recommended that I read the campground bulletin board. It was blank. For overnight storage, we put the food in the tent and were not bothered except by a skunk sniffing the paper in our fire ring.

We had done the two highest passes and had only five lower ones between us and the Pacific Ocean! I smiled and fell asleep.

Pete Creek, Saturday, August 30

During the night I awoke several times to eat cookies or bread and drink water. It was raining hard. By morning, my feet were wet because I had failed to tension the tent properly. Although the rain had stopped, the trees were still dripping. We had aches in our arms and shoulders.

Bea got up and made coffee. She cut her finger on the hash can top and called for help. I clambered out of the tent with our first aid kit which contained merthiolate, Band-Aids, and aspirin. Still hungry after eating the hash, we devoured a half can of peaches. Bea went for a walk in the woods, and I lay down in the tent to write.

Jean Peters invited us for coffee and doughnuts. Bea stuck her head into the tent and said, "Come on. It's real coffee, not that instant excuse." We joined Jim and Jean Peters around the table in their mini-whale. The coffee was excellent. Jean's daughter had lived for a time at Medicine Lake which she said "used to be a nice little town," but the population had been dwindling. Jim said he liked trout fishing — casting flies, not wading. Jim had emphysema, but he had stopped smoking; now he was trying to stop chewing tobacco.

They asked if we were frightened by the thunder and lightning last night. Bea hadn't known it rained, and I heard nothing except when I was hungry. They were amazed. We also hadn't heard the police come to quiet down some campers in another part of the campground. We thanked them for the company and coffee, and they soon departed for their day of fishing and sightseeing.

We had to pedal up to the Yaak store, for we were out of food. We bought apple juice, chicken, milk, Rice-a-Roni, a loaf of seven grain bread, and homemade cookies from the Saturday morning bake sale. I tried to phone, but the operator still couldn't hear me.

We returned to camp and put the chicken, milk, and juice in the creek to keep cool. I then found an isolated part of the creek in which to bathe and wash clothes. This bath certainly contrasted with the steamy hot showers and shampoos we had taken at the Downtowner Motel and Health Club in Whitefish. In the past three days, we had luxuriated in the facilities of the elegant club, simultaneously washed ourselves and our clothes while swimming in a reservoir, and now I was standing in an isolated part of a swift and rocky creek.

For me, the frequency of bathing was more important than the source or temperature of the water. Here, in the creek, the trick was to not get too cold or too public. I took my soapy clothes, put a large rock inside each item, and threw them into the current to rinse. Later, I hung them on bushes, sorry that I had not kept a long piece of line. Parachute cord would have been perfect. I moved the clothes during the day so that they stayed in the sun. The tent dried too, and I repacked my panniers.

We decided to gather wood for a fire. I found a dead tree but couldn't move it without help. I intended to burn it in half, then in quarters to make it smaller, but first I had to move it to the fire ring. I asked a woman sitting in a nearby pickup, "Do you have an ax or a hatchet that I could borrow for a few minutes?"

Climbing out of the truck, she introduced herself as Jan Hilmes and said, "Just take some wood, we have plenty." She came over with an ax and began deftly splitting a large chunk into kindling. I split another log, but not so expertly. She said, "I've been coming here since I was a kid." Her father had come here to fish and trap in winter when there were only logging roads. He told the kids there was gold here, but he wouldn't tell anyone else. Now it was mined and the trees were farmed. Jan liked to pick huckleberries. "Bears are no problem. Moose are more dangerous here," she continued. Bea had joined us and was listening, too. "Black bears won't bother you; I've picked berries on one side of a patch while a bear ate on the other side."

We asked about elk and moose droppings since we had seen some on the road. She said moose droppings are like those of a cow, only smaller, but elk droppings are like a rabbit's, only larger. We had seen moose prints in the mud and a lot of droppings. "Bear droppings are full of berry seeds," she added. Jan told us they had been at Glacier and were meeting some of her kids and family here for the weekend. "There are seven adults and four kids," only a small group, she laughed. We thanked her for the wood and returned to our site.

Jan's husband arrived, bringing vegetables from a friend's garden. She brought us tomatoes and a cucumber. Later she came back with four rainbow trout, cleaned and ready to cook, a frying pan, oil, and flour. They were leaving for a high place where she thought there would still be huckleberries. She said it is unusually warm here now for this time of the year. According to Jan, winter snow could come in a week and wouldn't be unusual now. I decided we should go as far as possible tomorrow, and travel at least half a day on Labor Day.

Bea built a grand fire while I cut up tomatoes, onion, and cucumber. We ate salad with herbs and then fried our trout. Fish had never tasted better, and I even crunched the tails. Then Bea built up the fire. A box of stuff we could do without was ready to send to Mt. Vernon; the fry pan was washed and returned. We were ready for a quick start tomorrow.

Pete Creek, Sunday August 31

I stuck my head out of the tent into chilly fog. I packed while Bea prepared breakfast. After eating, I washed hurriedly and put in my contact lenses, careful not to drop them in the creek as I stood unsteadily on two stones.

We rolled our bikes quietly past the Peters' RV, stopping momentarily to put our plastic garbage bag on their doorstep. "The Coffee Lady" repeatedly asked what they could do for us. Since she wouldn't come along and make coffee for us the rest of the trip, I had suggested they carry out our garbage bag. It presented no difficulty for them and was a great help to us. I stood quietly looking over this comfortable camp and silently saying goodby to our friends there. I could feel the pull of gravity and the weight of extra baggage combining to speed me along. Bea really had to pedal to match my pace. We looked for moose in all the marshes but saw none. Wisps of fog hung only in the hollows, but mist dampened the road. An early morning spin on my bike was a treasure.

We glided quietly almost twenty miles downhill before slowing at the tiny settlement of Sylvanite, an old silver mine where I sensed the bygone days of miners and loggers. The town seemed deserted this morning as we rolled past the Golden Nugget Cafe and Bar, a frame building from the 1800s. Next door was a trailer made into four "motel" rooms, each with a girl's name. We passed a few shacks, one-room size, each with a front porch, and we once more were in the forest.

The road changed from narrow, pot-holed 92 to wide, smooth, graded 508, and five more miles brought us to Yaak

Falls. A six-mile ride along the Yaak River's best trout-fishing waters led us to Route 2, where we turned right and headed westward. We were over the Yaak, and a treasured experience in Montana had ended. I wondered why it was called "Yaak," a word I associate with the "buffalo" of the Himalayas. Rolling past the "Lowest Point in Montana" sign at 1,820 feet, we entered Idaho.

Bea said I'd been doing some fine riding. Clearly, my strength and ability were increasing. She got tired about the same time or even before I did — the reverse of the trip's beginning. She hadn't hassled me recently about whether or not I could make it to the West Coast.

CHAPTER   SEVEN

Panhandling Idaho

Sandpoint, Idaho, Monday, September 1

Labor Day dawned cloudy and with rain. Expecting traffic, I intended a short bicycling day across Idaho's narrow panhandle to an overnight stop in Newport, Washington.

Bea insisted on riding behind. I wanted her to ride ahead, in case of more tire trouble. She kept saying, "Don't wait for me." Since I was tired, I was glad we expected to travel fewer than thirty miles. I liked to stay off the roads on weekends and holiday afternoons, for protection from good-time or drunk drivers.

On a long downhill bordering the Pend Oreille River, I let my bike have its way. Rain began to pour down but, enjoying the coasting, I continued until the road flattened about two miles outside of Priest River. I stopped, put on my rain jacket, and waited — no sign of Bea.

I stood at the roadside in the rain for a long time. To myself I said, "Even with her brakes on and a stop to dig out her rain coat, she couldn't have taken this long." I turned and began to pedal back, rounded a curve after a mile, and saw Bea slogging along the roadside, pushing her bike, and being splashed by every car and truck. I felt sorry for her. Another flat tire, the same one as last time, had put her afoot. Since I was usually last, I carried all the tools.

Wordlessly, she worked on her tire. Rain still descended, not hard, just constantly. Neither of us spoke beyond the necessities of, "Hold this," "Where are the tire irons?" and "I'm ready for the tube now." We were both tired.

Mounted again, we continued into the town of Priest

River. On the uphill grade was a motel with a cafe nearby. We turned in about one o'clock, glad to get out of the rain.

Bea began ransacking every pocket and container in her panniers in a state of panic. "I've lost my thyroid pills! The doctor told me I must take them every day, and I haven't been able to find them since we were camped at Pete Creek. Will you please help me look? I've looked everywhere. It's hopeless."

I began looking in her front bag where they were supposed to be. It was an old habit. At work, I had learned the first place to look for what the boss couldn't find was on his own desk. The pills were in the handlebar bag where they belonged.

We talked about a possible cause for her repeated flat tires. She thought it was the spokes, because the bike shop trued the wheels after putting on new tires and tubes. The small adjustment of truing her wheel wouldn't, shouldn't cause all this trouble. Granted, all the punctures were on the insides of the tubes. It didn't look as though she had replaced the rim tape. With the one inch rims and their shape, there was a close tolerance around the valve and, sometimes, the tires didn't seem to fit, but what could cause holes inside the tubes? I hoped this tube would hold. Perhaps, I told myself, a sunny day tomorrow, mail from her family at Newport, taking her pills, and no more flats would make this trip fun again. During the evening, we read and watched a lot of TV.

Priest River, Tuesday, September 2

On the way to Newport and the state border, we stopped at the Albeni Falls Dam, where we learned about hydro-electric power. Water that has produced electrical energy at the dam flows down the Pend Oreille River and then into the Columbia River.

We would cross the Columbia following the Pend Oreille River by road. Far north of the Lewis and Clark route, in what was British Columbia for many years, our route was used by early pioneers. We were now in the Columbia River basin, and I began to realize that we were much further west than I had ever been before. Oh, sure, I had flown to San Francisco on the way to Asia but when flying, each place is an isolated pocket. Proceeding by bicycle along a route that followed water courses and adhered closely to the periphery of the contiguous United States showed me history, geography, and biography.

After thirty years of daily international relations con-
cerns, history, for me, had centered much less around dates and
places than around people, their personalities, desires, and
effects upon each other. At bottom, even their capabilities took
a back seat to their thoughts. What a leader thinks isn't easy to
learn, even by inference, but it is the key to action. What I think
makes me the person I am becoming.

From my bike seat, I looked over this great country,
thankful in previous lives I earned birth here, hopeful I would
never take it for granted. When I returned from two years in
Europe as a teenager, someone asked me what country I
learned the most about over there. Automatically I said,
"America," astonished by the truth that came out of my mouth.

Newport, Washington, Wednesday, September 3

Since the Newport Post Office would not open for
another hour, we stopped at an American-Chinese cafe for
breakfast. While we were removing our helmets, gloves, and
jackets, a young man, Joel Jacobsen, introduced himself and
asked to speak with us about our panniers. He said he was
interested in designing and marketing panniers. He was thinking of making hard-sided, aerodynamic ones that would be
fully waterproof. We insisted they should be bright-colored, no
matter what marketing said would sell. The safety of bright
international orange or golf ball green panniers should be
stressed. Aerodynamic design was offered only in gray, black,
or blue. He said that all designs had reflective stripes.

"How many people who tour ride at night?" I asked.
Then, warming to my subject, I answered myself, "Probably
only those who misjudge the distance, or occasionally, those
who want to avoid wind. Anyway very few." I stopped for
breath. "Yes, commuters often use panniers and ride in the
dark. Is the market for panniers tourists and commuters?
Reflective material helps some in rain if cars have their lights
on. Blue and gray blend into the color of the road surface. Black
and white, not being colors in nature, are better than blue, but
bright is best!"

On the question of hard sides, we split. Soft sides allow
packing a multitude of shapes, but hard sides offer more
protection. "How about a plastic hard-top curved to cause
water to roll off and soft, water-repellent sides?" The aerody-

namic shape might help on the front wheels, but touring bicyclists rarely go at the speeds of racers, and probably don't travel fast enough to make aerodynamics a major consideration. We suggested that he write *BikeReport*, *Bicycle USA*, and *Bicycling* for articles and current opinions.

At the post office, Bea picked up a delightful food package from her daughter, Meg, and a letter from her daughter, Beth, who was now recovered from her health problems.

We traveled the rest of the day along the Pend Oreille River. I reveled in the experience, recalling our wonderful ride along the voyageurs' route in Minnesota. Fittingly, we entered Washington State between Oldtown and Newport. We could hardly believe it—only seven hundred fifty miles to the Pacific!

CHAPTER EIGHT

Cascading through
Washington State

Newport, Washington, Wednesday, September 3

Well into Washington, we stopped at Outpost for potato soup and raspberry milk shakes. "We crossed Idaho, and never saw a potato growing!" I said to myself, spooning soup. Idaho's fertile southern valleys are home to the russet Burbank potato which also is grown in Washington.

Fortified by soup, we pedaled along the Pend Oreille River bank to Blueslide, named for a sliding, blue-clay mountainside that had hampered building the original railroad through this valley. We continued our lovely ride into Tiger, a left turn around a few small, wooden buildings leading to a climb into the hills. Seven or eight miles of ascent brought us into a meadow, which we crossed before climbing again through the forest.

The entrance road to Lake Leo Campground led downhill and was a gravel surface, difficult for our bikes. We stopped. I couldn't see how far it was to the tent sites. The next campground was only three miles further, but it also could have a gravel entry. We were tired. I headed down the gravel road.

The camp was less than a quarter mile, on small Lake Leo. There was no one visible. We had seen moose droppings all afternoon, and the lake's marsh was ideal for moose. Along the campground road, I saw bear droppings. I said nothing, hoping Bea wouldn't notice. I selected site one, while Bea discovered site two had a pile of wood. We moved ourselves instead of the wood. Bea went off to explore.

As I began to unpack and set up the tent, two whales from California drove in. One driver told me someone just saw a bear in the campground. The RVs parked nearby, and Bea returned and built a huge roaring blaze which soon crackled gently. We dragged in fallen branches from the nearby woods and snapped them across our knees. We consumed every bite of the tuna stroganoff we cooked and then stored all our food supplies in an empty garbage can and put the lid on tightly. I took my bare bike for a ride to see how large the campground was, while Bea explored the lakeside.

On my ride, I met the couple who had seen the bear, and I heard what had happened. "Last night a bear dumped all the garbage cans in this camp. The rangers cleaned up this morning. As campers came in, we noted a man in a black shirt. It turned out to be a big black bear. A man in another camper took a photo before the bear departed. Tomorrow is the first day of bear hunting season."

That news made me feel great. If bears know as well as deer when hunting season begins, we need not worry. They would vanish. I returned to our site, and we sat around our fire. Before dusk, the squirrels serenaded us, chattering back and forth, running up and down the nearby trees. We weren't often awake after dark, but dark came earlier now. We saw the vivid, glittery stars above while the golden sparks of our fire drifted into the blackness.

Ann Brendel from California wanted to take our photograph to include in her travel journal. We were more impressed that she wanted our picture than that her husband Frank won an Oscar for special earthquake effects in movies. They could watch the whales (real ones!) from their home in Mexico, she recounted to Bea's delight. I arranged with them to keep our food inside overnight. The RV would certainly be safer than the garbage can. Frank said he was always up early, and a light tap on the door would signal him to hand us our food pannier.

After dark, it got colder, and we stood around the fire.

Lake Leo, Wednesday, September 3

We got up early. Bea built a fire, made coffee, and heated the can of beef stew. We cleaned our bikes, using at least a quart of stove fuel. I got our fruit from Frank Brendel and ate grapes while completing my bike maintenance.

We divided up the contents of the package Bea received from her daughter, Meg. In front of the post office, we drank much of the juice, which is heavy, and ate handfuls of macadamia nuts. Now, we ate the chocolate covered cherries, and burned the box. We wrapped the shampoo, one-ounce liquor bottles, and other heavy things for mailing to Bea in Mt. Vernon. We took turns washing in the lake, one keeping lookout while the other bathed. Our fire still going, we wrote thank-you notes to people we met at Pete Creek Campground.

By mid-morning we rolled, mostly downhill, until Bea had a flat. She fixed it, patching the tube. I calculated that she had averaged a flat every day-and-a-half since we left Whitefish, traveling only about seventy miles per tube. We now had three multi-patched tubes and were almost out of patches.

At Beaver Campground, Bea had coffee and I drank a soda. As we rode off, I heard a yell and looked back to see the owner holding my helmet. I rode back to get it while Bea waited. When I reached the porch, he said, "I'll trade you. You pay for your soda, and I'll give you your helmet." I thought Bea had paid for both drinks. I've learned storekeepers don't expect two women to pay together, or one to pay for the other. At eleven-thirty, we entered the Rustic Inn in Park Rapids. As we ate, the owner answered my questions. "Where you see pilings in the rivers, there probably had been an old saw mill. The pilings were used to anchor logs that had been floated downstream."

Soon after we left, Bea had another flat. We laughed. She fixed it and was pumping it up when she realized the valve stem was cracked and air wouldn't go in. She put in another tube, pumped it up, and we headed straight for Clarke's All-Sport Shop. I stayed outside while she wheeled the bike through the doorway. I heard the store clerk ask about her problem.

Bea replied, "My wheel needs trueing," before the door shut. I sat down on the curb in the sun beside my bicycle. Soon, Bea came out, rolling her bike. "He doesn't have anything I need. He doesn't know anything. He can't fix my bike. We'll have to stay here until I order what I need." She was angry.

Rising slowly, I took a deep breath and asked if she minded if I talked with him. She nodded and sat down on the curb.

Inside, I consulted with the man. He had one tube with a "French valve." Not knowing what that was I looked at it — whee, a presta valve on a heavy butyl tube — the cheap kind Bea used during the early part of the trip. I bought it. He asked whether or not I needed rim tape. "Blessings, for I would not have thought of it," I said aloud. Equipped with rim tape, the new tube, and another patch kit, I thanked him, paid, and departed. Fortunately, Bea cooled off just as fast as she heated up.

While she checked the post office for mail, I inspected the remaining tubes and found another broken stem. I discarded both tubes with cracked stems. She now had two tubes, one in the tire and the new one, as well as another patch kit.

When Bea returned, we started to ride toward Kettle Falls, eight miles away. It had a campground overlooking Roosevelt Lake. We were beyond Kettle Falls and headed downhill for the campground when her tire spewed air again. We rolled the bikes into a picnic area at a junction. A fellow with a bicycle came up and asked us how far we rode in a day and I snapped, "It depends on how many flat tires we get."

Bea began to cry, but she persisted in changing her tire. The fellow continued talking about bicycling, and I tried to listen rather than make Bea more nervous by watching her. I knew she was frustrated, too. She started to put the new rim tape on, and said that she couldn't because there was no hole for the valve stem. As she handed the tape to me, the light caught the punched hole edges, I pushed the circle of rubber out, and handed it back.

Finally, she got the tire together and the bike reloaded for our remaining mile to the campground. Bea cried the whole way. I left her alone, set up the tent, and fixed supper. Bea didn't want to eat and sat looking out at the water. I built a fire, washed myself and my clothes, and explored the lovely site. The sunset was beautiful, but Bea remained out of sorts.

She slept outside the tent, and cried some more. Inside was hot, and outside was the domain of noisy, dive-bombing mosquitoes. There was a lot of truck noise from the bridge. I thrashed around and kept reviewing our problems in my mind. Bea had thoroughbred, one-inch racing rims and was trying to use them as a pack horse with all the weight on the rear. I didn't want to ride down the whole California Coast dealing with these same difficulties.

Perhaps I should just go home. I didn't *have* to do this bicycle trip. I had said all along I wasn't going to do it unless it was fun. Perhaps we could get to San Diego and end the trip there. I could go to Florida in March and ride up the East Coast, which I know quite well, and pedal the southern segment another time. Unable to reach a conclusion, I eventually slept.

Kettle Falls, Thursday, September 4

When I awoke, there was just enough light to read the folder about Kettle Falls. Yesterday, I had smiled at the sign, "Home of 1234 Friendly People and One Grouch." The flyer said that Kettle Falls has its own, very official Grouch who is elected every year by local residents. This morning, I felt over-qualified for the job.

Kettle Falls is located on Lake Roosevelt, formed in 1941 when the Grand Coulee Dam was built across the Columbia River. The present town was built on high ground, replacing the old town that lies beneath the lake. Seventy-five miles south is Spokane, and thirty-two miles north is the Canadian border.

Wouldn't it be fine to stay here a few days and go for a horseback ride and a sail! I put the flyer away, crawled out of the tent, and walked along the bluff overlooking Lake Roosevelt and the sailboat basin. This bike tour could take five years instead of one, and still there would not be enough time to savor this wonderful country. Rays of sun shot over the mountain. I walked back to the tent, ate the leftover cold rice from supper, and took the tent down. Bea was stirring. After I sponged in cold water, we rolled our bikes out to the road.

I was tired and concerned about this morning's route, which would take us from Kettle Falls, at about sixteen hundred feet, over Sherman Pass at about fifty-six hundred feet. The next town, Republic, was about forty miles, and the top of the pass seemed a little over half way.

Log trucks, loaded and unloaded, had been whizzing past us for a week. Half a mile down the road, Bea stopped to observe double-trailer log trucks unloading. A huge three-fingered fork lift machine lifted the whole truckload of forty-foot logs to an adjacent pile. Another fingered monster sorted the truckloads into piles. Sprinklers constantly swished water over the sorted heaps of logs as though they were a golf course. We had been told the sprinklers prevent the logs from splitting and catching fire.

We cycled to the end of the bridge across Lake Roosevelt where we ate a restaurant breakfast. Then we began pumping up the road beside Sherman Creek through Colville National Forest. The forest was dense, and we wound our pedals slowly up the mountain for several hours. I got quite tired and out of breath several times.

A white truck coming toward us stopped, and the

driver leaned his head out the window to warn, "There is a bear with two cubs just around the bend about a half mile up the road. Please be alert. Don't let yourselves get between the mother and her cubs." We thanked him.

"You go first," ordered Bea. I pedaled on, assuming the bear had gone, but keeping a sharp eye. A couple of hundred yards ahead, the bear crossed the road into the woods. I saw no cubs and silently thanked the man for warning us. I stopped. Bea stopped far behind me. I kept quiet, took out my camera, and attached my longest lens, 135mm, which was too short. Bea came up closer, and we waited in the middle of the road. The bear returned, also to the middle, and stood looking at us. We stood looking at her. I took a photo, knowing the distance was too great for a good picture. The bear began to walk toward me. I stood still. She was far away, but I kept thinking that she could run at thirty miles an hour and I couldn't go that fast here, only downhill. We were in a rather flat place. The bear looked back into the woods. I waited. She took one last look at us, turned, and ambled back to where she first came from. I assumed she wouldn't risk bringing the cubs across the road at this time or at this place.

I decided to wait ten minutes before proceeding, or until a car came past. No car came and my feet got tired. I got on my bike. Bea did nothing. I rode quite slowly, just fast enough to keep my balance. In my rear view mirror, I saw Bea still standing in the middle of the road. I kept looking ahead and at the roadside where the bear had gone until I was well beyond that place. Once on her bike, Bea pedaled fast, passing me, and we continued uphill.

Half an hour later, I rounded a curve and saw Bea standing on the roadside. When I got there, she stammered, "A bear came out of those bushes, looked at me, turned, and retreated into the woods, right there." The hand that pointed was shaking. "I heard it walk away." We laughed, drank some water, and proceeded, reaching Sherman Pass Campground about one-thirty. There we stopped to rest, eat the rest of our peanut butter sandwiches, and fill our water bottles from the pump.

During the next hour, we glided seventeen miles of wonderful downhill road to Republic. When rolling, I never exceeded thirty-three miles an hour. I lifted my head, caused wind to catch and fill my helmet, and slowed myself one or two miles an hour. I raised my shoulders and trunk to slow still more. I did anything to avoid using the brakes, and experimented with body movements to change speeds. It was wonderful fun. Going down was like skiing when you let the skis run. I let the wheels roll freely. When I wanted to stop, I pulled both brakes at increasing pressure, released them, and let the wheels spin to cool, then pulled again, continuing until I stopped.

We pedaled up a short hill into the town of Republic. I was very tired. We registered at the Klondike Motel, ate a meal on Main Street, and bought fresh fruit for the next day before retreating to hot showers, television, and a long sleep.

Republic, Washington, Friday, September 5

While I was mailing a postcard after breakfast, a woman told me the cafe we hadn't gone to had the best coffee in Washington State, we should see the deer near the grocery, and we must not miss the lovely lake only six miles off the highway. I thanked her kindly, and we pedaled out of town on Route 20. The day was beautiful, and I was going to enjoy it.

We reached the top of Wauconda Pass about ten-thirty and began to roll down the other side, stopping at the "town," one building containing a grocery, post office, cafe, and dining room. After eating, we continued gradually downhill for the rest of the day. We rode beside Bonaparte Creek amid arid, barren hills dotted with cattle and horses, realizing we'd left the forest behind us.

Our dry, hot throats called for sodas in Tonasket, at an elevation of nine hundred feet, and then we pedaled down the Okanogan River Valley, site of the Caribou Cattle Trail. With a tailwind out of Canada, we rolled past irrigated orchards, past Omak into Okanogan, towns at the crossroads of three major state highways. Only fourteen of our seventy-four miles had been uphill and green.

The exhilarating day's journey ended at the Okanogan Motel. Showered and refreshed, we took ourselves out to dinner at the Apple Valley Inn and ate the bicyclist's favorite food: pasta. The inn was a former movie house and contained old gas pumps and rides for children. Back in our room, we watched television until Bea fell asleep; then I turned it off and read until my mind relaxed.

Okanogan, Saturday, September 6

We rode our bare bikes back into town for a great breakfast at the Sawtooth Cafe. There was something I really liked about Okanogan. It has a dry climate, and it is tucked into soft "teddy-bear-fur" hills similar to those near Livermore, California. I liked the attitude depicted by a sign at the Okanogan Senior Service Center: "If the elevator to success is broken, take the stairs."

We began the day with a long climb to Loop Loop Pass, passing irrigated pear trees, miles of irrigated apple orchards, and ranches with irrigated pasture. I had never realized that my favorite Washington apples grew in irrigated orchards.

The road wasn't steep except for short distances in a few places, and we arrived about noon, after eighteen miles, at Loop Loop Campground. The campground was so nice that we decided to cook lunch among the fir trees. While cooking, we decided to stay for the rest of the day. We ate hot Lipton's mushroom noodles and drank coffee. I asked some people in a nearby trailer if they would sell me half a loaf of bread to go with our peanut butter and honey mixture. They gave us the bread. Juncos, Steller's jays, and a chipmunk-like creature made away with our crumbs. I took photographs while Bea wrote and napped. I cleaned and cooked my chain, then dumped the wax. If it rained during the next four days to Mt. Vernon, I'd oil the chain with WD40.

It was a lovely, relaxed afternoon with the sun's rays filtering through the trees. When Bea awoke, she went off to birdwatch and gather wood. Not having planned this overnight stop, we cooked and ate our emergency rations: beef stroganoff and a can of chicken mixed with boiled rice. I drank instant hot cider and Bea had coffee as we built up the fire and watched the sunset. Ending a quite evening in the fir tree forest, we read aloud to each other by the firelight.

In the middle of the night at our highest camp, four thousand twenty feet in the Okanogan National Forest, Bea shook me awake, "Listen!"

"What?" I asked sleepily.

I listened. There was silence, except for the wind soothing the trees. Bea sat upright, not knowing if she was dreaming or in mortal danger. In a few moments, a cacophony of wails, yip-yips, and yodels blended to form a chorus of coyotes. They were far, far away. A barred owl grumpily hooted, "Who cooks for you?" while we sat huddled in our sleeping bags, under brilliant stars, thrilling to the music of these unseen performers. "Thank you for waking me," I said sliding back to sleep.

Loop Loop, Sunday, September 7

It was thirty-eight degrees when we struck the tent packed the bikes. Bea built a small fire to warm us while we stomped around drinking coffee and eating a mixture of rice and raisins. Chipmunks, juncos, and four gray jays hovered nearby.

We turned out of the campground road into Route 20 and rolled downhill about twelve miles. There were no cars, and we had a whole smoothly-paved, well-graded lane to ourselves. Farms and mountains whizzed past. It was a glorious way to start a day! After gliding down, we came to a valley and the town of Twisp at an elevation of less than two thousand feet. Here we had breakfast, and then Bea headed for the launderette and showers while I went to the phone booth.

I called Mom, who had scheduled her bridge group at her house so she wouldn't miss my call. There were still problems with the temporary tenants in my house. The meeting and lecture I wanted to attend at home would be held October fourth. I would get there for a few days by plane, and Bea might or might not come with me. I made other calls, and then took a shower. Bea had met a woman from South Carolina who was in St. Mary a day or so ago when it snowed there. Apparently, we were just ahead of the snow, and I hoped we stayed ahead of it. For the next two or three days, the forecast was clear. We expected to reach Celia's house in Mt. Vernon in three more days, before clouds and precipitation descended for the winter.

We gathered up our laundry, and pedaled through the valley, arriving at Winthrop a little after one p.m. Winthrop is a western-movie-set-type town, where automobiles, pickups, and motor homes look out of character. Behind the old-looking facades are fine shops. In 1972, when Highway 20 was nearing completion over the North Cascades, several business people underwrote the frontier-village renovation which now makes the town so attractive.

We went to the Duck Brand for a splendid lunch, following the suggestion of the people I met descending the Going-to-the-Sun Road. Waiting for the food to arrive, I drank glass after glass of water and read about Winthrop. There were no white settlers until 1883. Somehow the idea that a place has no history until whites arrive recalled colonialism. I thought of Mt. Everest which had both Tibetan and Sherpa names before it was renamed by the English and Indians.

Before leaving, we watched a spinning demonstration and admired handcrafts. We sensed winter whistling at our heels as we rode up the Methow Valley, surrounded by national forest. The heavy black undersides of the clouds threatened rain as we turned toward Washington Pass and continued climbing.

We reached the turn-off to Klipchuck Campground, descended to Early Winters Creek, then climbed up a road so steep that we had to walk. I could harly push my bike. I had felt tired all afternoon, and I guessed there just wasn't enough energy to digest a large lunch and pedal uphill at the same time. After a light supper, Bea gathered wood, and I mixed peanut butter and honey together in a plastic container. I put the empty peanut butter jar on the ground to keep the chipmunks off the table. Watching the chipmunks lick the jar clean was a grand dinner theater.

The gnats were so bothersome we had to retreat into the tent. I had pitched the tent so that we could watch the dying fire through its net doorway. It felt good to flatten my back and elevate my legs. We were at a lower altitude in a sheltered valley, so it was much warmer than last night. I soon fell soundly asleep.

Klipchuck, Monday, September 8

We agreed to stay here for a rest day. We weren't expected in Mt. Vernon until September tenth, and this campground appealed to us. During the morning, I put the peanut butter jar out again for the chipmunks. This time I put it in a good light, and watched them lick as I occasionally took pictures.

We rode down to Mazama Country Inn for lunch, but it was closed for the season. At a nearby store, we ate ice cream and drank orange juice before carrying Spam and eggs back to camp. The best part of the thirteen-mile round trip was watching a downy woodpecker feed on a roadside thistle.

For lunch, Bea scrambled six eggs, Spam, and some cheese into a delicious main dish. We spent the rest of the afternoon sitting at the picnic table writing as clouds rolled over and the sun sparkled through them, alternately chilling and warming us. While we were fixing supper, a mule deer wandered up, trailed by last year's and this year's offspring who were a bit less brave. Mom mule deer wanted something to eat, but it wasn't the carrot we offered. Beas said deer like bread and, holding out a piece, was thrilled to pet the deer between the ears while it ate.

The Thorntons, mini-whale travelers from Gaithersburg, Maryland, came over with their cameras. The deer and the people stalked and ambled among one another in friendly fashion. We were not supposed to feed the animals, and we had only enough bread for lunch tomorrow, so Bea parceled out one slice in very small pieces. When the bread was gone, the party was over. All departed. We rolled up in our sleeping bags and watched the fire flicker and crackle until it went out. Only later did we admit to each other that we wondered whether we had enough strength for tomorrow's trip through Washington Pass at almost fifty-five hundred feet and Rainy Pass, a thousand feet lower. Our reserve energy had ebbed.

Klipchuck, Tuesday, September 9

Morning dawned brilliantly clear. Bea built a fire and began cooking a breakfast of our last emergency food, spaghetti with mushroom sauce. I made all the bread and peanut-butter-honey mixture into sandwiches, sprinkled them liberally with raisins, and packed them away for lunch. Our commissary was never permitted to run out of raisins; each of us carried a plastic bag full of them.

I had grown fond of camping and touring. I enjoy the uncertainty of travel itself. I like being titillated by ever-changing unknowns. Touring is a private joy. I was ready for a respite and needed to go home briefly, but I wanted to complete the perimeter tour. I could not imagine continuing alone.

About seven forty-five, we rode and pushed our bikes back to Highway 20. The fourteen-mile route undulated upward. Each long gradual climb ended at a hairpin turn and led to another long climb. Views of the Silver Star and Liberty Bell

Mountains rotated slowly as we pedaled.

Bea used less breath pedaling than in exclaiming over the crystalline water of Silver Star Creek, the towering Needles, and black, thorny spines of trees reaching for the cloudless, ultra-blue sky. It was what, years ago, skiing in Switzerland, I had termed a "postcard sky." Cutthroat Creek was filled with huge boulders, and pockets of ice clung to shady spots. Buoyed by Bea's enthusiasm and amused by the names of the creeks and peaks, I wished I had begun a list of every river and creek that we had crossed, or a count of bridges.

Several deer interrupted my musing but not my pedaling as they scampered across the road ahead and leapt the guard rail, looking over their shoulders at us and springing up the rock bank into the trees.

I chose this route on the recommendation of a fellow at the Department of Energy who had grown up in Washington State. Mentally, I thanked him, for I was not disappointed. There had been a magic about our bicycling route ever since we entered The Cascade Loop at Twisp. I would like to bike the whole loop around Washington State sometime.

After one last hairpin curve, we looked back. Looking down made our accomplishment seem more difficult than it had been. Shading our eyes, we watched cars that looked like toys crawling silently up the mountain. We stopped in the pass for photos and drinks of water. I was exhausted, exhilarated, and exuberant. The last great barrier to the Pacific Coast had been breached.

I expected to cover eighty miles today, now mostly downhill. Our last pass, though a thousand feet lower, was still five miles ahead. We stopped where the Pacific Crest Trail crossed our road. Having read of its difficulty, I was thrilled to stand upon the trail. We rode into the parking and picnic area at Rainy Pass to find the water had been cut off for the season. Thirst could be worse than snow. I had only half a bottle of water left, and could easily have drunk two bottles. Bea had almost a whole bottle. What to do? We explored the area and biked the mile to Rainy Lake.

I was entranced by the rainforest vegetation along the trail, paved so that people in wheelchairs could enjoy it. We emerged at the bottom edge of a large rocky mixing bowl filled with water so clear could watch the rainbow trout swim. In a split second, we were off our bikes, had unrolled the sandwiches, and were sitting on the stone wall over looking the lake. "Do you believe this?" questioned Bea. "Who would believe today? I wouldn't." She was looking at the waterfall cascading from high among the rocks and bouncing a thin stream of water off several ledges on its way to the lake. It stretched like a long spider web, glittering in the sunlight until it disappeared into spray.

"Stop it!" yelled Bea as a gray jay made off with a piece of her sandwich. Gray jays and one Clark's jay surrounded us. They tugged at our clothes, pulled, screamed, begged, cursed, and flew about our ears with soft whirs. One perched on Bea's knee, and she felt the jay's claws through her winter cycling pants. I tried to focus and shoot pictures during the mass conflutter. One jay even lit on the camera lens. When we stuffed the sandwiches into our mouths, the birds retreated.

My mouth gummy with peanut butter, I finished the remaining water and needed more. We retreated through the rain forest while fingerlets of sun pointed to a monstrous tree, now fallen and clad in brilliant green moss and tall ferns.

Holding my water bottle, I knocked on the door of a trailer in the parking area. Until I saw the woman's puzzled face, I didn't realize how strange I must look in my black tights and a vivid jersey. I had left my bike and helmet leaning against the restroom building. Thinking she might be frightened, I quickly stated, "The water has been turned off for the season. Would you be able to spare some drinking water from your tank?" She didn't look happy, but she took my bottle, filled it, and handed it back. "Thank you," I said, slinking away instead of draining it and requesting a refill. Our next town was forty miles away, the state park at Rockport about sixty miles. Too far before dark, unless it really was all downhill.

About twelve-thirty, with both food and water depleted, we began to roll. After a few miles, I knew that the speed I expected to attain riding downhill would be cut in half by strong headwinds. In fact, when the slope was gentle, I had to pedal just to keep moving. On the steeper sections, instead of coasting at thirty to thirty-five miles an hour I had to pedal to keep moving at fifteen. On certain curves there were cross-winds that turned natural balance into precarious effort.

Nevertheless, the views were glorious. My eyes flitted back and forth from inspecting the road for pebbles, cracks, sticks, and curves to absorbing the ever-moving panorama.

Somewhere overlooking the vast expanse of Lake Ross, we stopped for the view. Some Dutch tourists invited us to join their picnic. They shared their homemade fruit bread with us and when we asked about water, they said they had been drinking from the streams. Our mouths were like cotton and our bottles dry. I had read about the parasite giardia and had suffered with it too often in Asia. I also knew a sip was as lethal as a bottleful, if the stream was contaminated. I prayed it was safe, drank deeply, and filled my bottles.

After thanks and farewells we proceeded, refreshed and rested, to pedal into the strengthening headwind. Since the day was slipping away, we stopped only briefly to admire the incredible green of Lake Diablo. Battered by increasingly strong winds as we reached the Diablo Dam area, we pedaled harder.

Clouds followed the wind as we entered the gorge of the Skagit River and struggled on to the campground at Newhalem. Although we arrived after five p.m., we found the grocery was still open but learned that the campground was closed for the season. We bought red and green grapes, peaches and pears and, sitting outside, ate them all. I then looked for a ride to Rockport, twenty miles away.

From the east came two people in an empty pickup truck. They stopped at the store, and when they came out a few moments later, I asked, "How would you like a couple of hitch-hikers with bikes?" They agreed to give us a ride, and we began taking the panniers off our bikes and hoisting them into the truck. In a flurry, we added the bikes and sleeping bags. As we climbed in, two young men with large backpacks asked it they could also squeeze in. I intended to move our stuff and make room, but the driver said the truck was full. Turning to me, he asked where we wanted to go. I replied, "Rockport." He was going all the way to Route 5, only five miles from Mt. Vernon. As we passed through the canyon, I thought about extending our ride. Since it was cold in the pickup, we kept our helmets on and layered on all the shirts we could reach.

I studied the sky. Rain was imminent. Bea refused to consider proceeding by truck past the state park campground in Rockport. As our benefactors let us out, they again offered to take us further. Bea's mind was made up. Since we had no food and the weather was getting worse, I thought we should continue, stay in a motel overnight, and bicycle the five miles the next day. Our drivers made one last comment. "You've seen the pretty part. The rest of the way to Mt. Vernon is not so lovely."

The campsite was hollowed out of the rain forest. After showering, we rode to town, expecting to eat a hot meal, but everything was closed. We returned to camp. Bea rummaged through our baggage for something to eat. Fortunately, we still had oatmeal. While she prepared it, I found a phone booth and talked with Celia in Mt. Vernon. She said if it rained tomorrow, we should call and she would come get us in their pickup. "No way," I said to myself. I wanted to end this portion of our journey on my bike. In the long run, I was glad we camped.

Before going to sleep, we talked about how we liked this campground, where each site had been chopped out of the ferns and moss. The massive tangle of greenery was overhung by Douglas fir trees. I felt we were in a jungle.

Rockport State Park, Wednesday, September 10

During the night, despite our shelter of dense vegetation, I heard the cadence of heavy rain. It was barely daylight when we got up and put on rain jackets and pants. After we carried everything to one of the sheltered picnic table areas, Bea made coffee while I took down the wet tent and packed our sodden laundry. We had washed our clothes in the shower and hung them on the picnic table where, instead of drying, they had been thoroughly rinsed. Celia wasn't expecting us until after lunch, and we had to ride only forty miles downstream along the Skagit River. I was somewhat reluctant to bring this section of the trip to a close. We joked about learning first hand the meaning of "rain forest" as we departed. I wouldn't have missed staying there for anything

I stopped to pick and eat blackberries along the road. The clouds lifted above the Skagit River Valley, then blew over the moutain, and patches of sunny sky expanded. As the road dried, the world would have looked brighter has it not been so obvious that we were rolling out of the wilds of nature into the wilds of humanity.

At a cafe in Sedro Woolley, we ate, warmed up, and dried out before leaving for Mt. Vernon. I made several wrong turns and learned the town better than we intended. In early afternoon, we found Celia and Jerome's house.

Celia met us with open arms and led us to hot showers and their guest house. We were its first residents. Although the little house possessed no hot water or heat, it did have a rug, sofa, lamp, and a large window with a high-hillside view of Skagit Valley. There were stacks of mail and boxes of real clothes which made us feel like kids on Christmas morning.

After a hot shower, I found real socks, tennis shoes, roomy jeans, and a soft sweatshirt -- a wonderful relief from cycling clothes. It was good to get out of uniform.

I opened all the mail, but I was too excited and tired to read it. Fidgety, I talked with Celia, Jerome, and the children, Paul and Anne. We transferred our already damp clothes from pannier to washer to dryer. We unloaded the bikes, spread the tent over a fence to dry in the sun, and moved into our house, a spacious, dry "tent" with a reading lamp!

Skagit Valley, September 11-19

Our first morning in Mt. Vernon we were up for breakfast with the family. Jerome, a science teacher, and the children left for school. Celia's music students came to the house. Bea spent the morning reading and sleeping. I spent it on the telephone, straightening out my late insurance payment, consulting with Norwood Griffin, designer and builder of my new house in Clayton, Georgia, and calling 800 numbers to request maps for the next segments of the trip. We divided the rest of the day between business and recreation.

On Friday Celia arranged her schedule for a visit to Seattle. My, what we accomplished: finding maps for the Pacific Coast bike ride, ferry information for the San Juan Islands, and data on the World's Fair at Vancouver. After lunch at the Seattle World's Fair Center, we had ample time at REI to inspect all the light tents. They repaired Bea's tent-door zipper which had broken a few days earlier. We found no better tent that weighed significantly less. Each of us bought bicycling Gore-tex raincoats. I bought a fuel bottle and a Whisperlight stove which weighed less than Bea's older model.

For the first two days we slept and ate with our guardian-angel family, unable to even look at the bicycles. As I rested, I became aware of how tired I had been. Exhaustion is insidious.

By the morning of our third day, I emerged, blinked at the sunlight, and felt alive. Vicki Archer, Paul's violin teacher and founder of the local symphony, came on her "clunker" bicycle to lead us on a ride through Skagit Valley to Conway and La Conner and back. This twenty-six mile tour, she said, was her long ride for the week. We could hardly keep up with her. Vicki's reward for doing this exercise was Saturday breakfast at Calico Cupboard Bakery and Cafe. The notice in the restroom amused us: "No smoking here, please. If we catch you, we will assume that you are on fire and take appropriate action."

Vicki told us about the early Dutch settlers who diked the river floodplains, creating rich farmland. I smelled the humid, freshly plowed black soil and saw fields of cabbages, carrots, raspberries, peaches, and pears. Apparently more tulip bulbs are produced for sale here than in the Netherlands.

In Conway, Vicki introduced us to high school friends who own the store and tavern, and to Floyd, elderly caretaker of the town dump. He was angular, taciturn, and thoughtful. He had recently undergone laser treatment to correct his greatly impaired vision, and he took off his glasses so that we might see the reults of "razor" surgery. When he had first seen Vicki after the surgery, he announced, "You're a beautiful little thing." Everyone laughed and agreed Floyd had his eyesight back.

We learned that, in the early 1980s, La Conner became such a popular destination for tourists that shop restrooms suffered overcrowding. "Get-a-Head Day" began in 1982, when waterfront shops, cafes, restaurants, and The Tillinghast Seed House joined with the Chamber of Commerce to build a public facility. Named for toilet-spearheader Bud Moore, "One Moore Outhouse" annual fund-raising festival, referred to locally as "Potty Day," was today. Because of threatening rain, we missed the "Potty Parade," and the coronation of "King John," "Queen Latrine," and "Princess Tinkle." This frivolity raised four thousand dollars for the annual upkeep of the necessary.

Late Sunday afternoon, we helped Celia get ready for her dinner party. She had invited friends who had cycled in the United States and the Netherlands, a man who worked in the logging industry, and a college student who spent the summer fishing for salmon and would bring a whole fish for dinner. The international company and rapid leaps of discussion from subject to subject were stimulating. I enjoyed every individual, frustrated not to have more time with each one. I also realized since I was tired of telling about our own trip, I had become a better listener.

I decided to try to ride with Vicki daily, to keep in some sort of condition. She set a steady, fast pace, and I thoroughly enjoyed her company. Since she sat all day to teach, Vicki pedaled her clunker bike as fast as possible, never changing gears, every weekday morning on this twelve-mile round trip. She rode against the clock, allowing time to shower, dress, and arrive at the music academy before her first student. Her good humor was contagious.

On the return ride, I met Bea for breakfast. We discussed questions that appeared most frequently in our mail and decided to reply to them in joint letter. We had no trouble agreeing on the most-asked questions, but decided to give individual answers.

To "Why are you traveling the perimeter of the U.S.A.?" I answered: "I wanted to see the country I've served and to live outdoors in fresh air. Exploring this country on a bicycle achieves both of those goals and provides exercise to help overcome lengthy imprisonment in a desk chair. It also provides transition time for me to decide how I want to spend the next twenty or so years."

"What do you do when it rains?" was another question. My reply: "I get wet. Regardless of what you wear, if it rains hard enough, you get wet. The idea is to keep warm and as dry as possible. It didn't rain much east of the Rockies and Cascades in July and August, and the raincoats we carried were so hot they were worse than the rain. I dried off quickly when showers stopped, and pedaling usually kept me warm enough. Fog, mist, and heavy rain in Washington encouraged us to buy new windbreaker jackets, which provide both warmth and protection from dampness. Although we each have wind- or water-repellent pants, I find them slick to sit on and uncomfortable for pedaling. I still prefer to let my legs get wet, then dry when the rain stops. Our gear in the panniers is wrapped in plastic bags, but I have to be careful with my cameras in order to avoid condensation which is just as bad for them as rain. I am installing generator-operated lights, and I lubricate my bike more often in damp weather."

People always wanted to know "What unfortunate experiences occurred?" I think they were surprised when I said, "I expect to find America at its best and have not been disappointed."

Part of an afternoon was spent at the bike shop where I had my bottom bracket tightened and wheels trued. I also bought new tires. I was advised that I could ride about five hundred more miles on one tire, but I decided to change them both. There might be no bike shop in five hundred miles and this shop had the Specialized X-touring, one-and-a-quarter inch tires I preferred. I'd rather carry the new tire on the wheel than in a pannier until it was needed. I kept the same tubes, original with the bike and as yet un-patched. Since I didn't feel like working on the bike myself, I had the tires and my new generator lights installed by the shop.

Supper with Celia's family was great fun. Everything was cooked according to Celia's Atlanta upbringing and was definitely to my taste. After dinner, there was a family concert, with Paul playing the violin, Anne the cello, a piano duet, solos by Celia, and Jerome's songs which brought tears of laughter. Then, it was bedtime. I was always ready before the children's "pumpkin hour."

The next morning I met Vicki and cycled with her to Conway. We drank steaming cups of coffee in the tavern and then returned, pedaling furiously. I was drawn into the mist, brilliance, color, and contrast of the Skagit valley. The climate dramatized each day with light and shadow, blue skies and sunshine following banks of morning fog. The local people said, "You should see it when the flowers are in bloom!" How could even flowers improve upon the tawny fields, the tingling leafsmoke, and apple scent?

On Thursday, Bea and I went to EXPO in Canada. When we returned, Celia told us that the newspaper people wanted an interview tomorrow during our ride with Vicki and would meet us along the way.

Bea went to bed. I got into the hot tub to soak. I reveled in the hot water, unwinding my tourist feet and leg muscles. I sank deeper into the hot water, up over my ears.

Mt. Vernon, Friday, September 19

In the morning, Vicki was waiting at the railroad tracks as we raced down the hill blindly through the fog. It was a straight shot to Conway, except for a curve at the edge of town where we often saw a great blue heron in the creek.

Right behind us, the car with Scott Terrell and Gale Fiege from the *Skagit Valley Herald* bounced over the tracks into Conway. They interviewed and photographed us under the grocery store overhang. We had pedaled far enough through fog to become mistily damp. "The article will be in today's paper. We'd like to visit, but we have another appointment," they sang out as the doors slammed and they drove away. Vicki couldn't keep her student waiting, so we got on our bikes and whirred back.

Celia had prepared breakfast for us and arranged her day so she could take us to Seattle. Bea and I spent a thoroughly relaxed and interesting time in the aquarium while Celia did her errands at the music store. All three of us then walked up to The Pike Place, a seven- acre market. Our trip purse took us all to lunch at the market which overlooked the glorious sunny harbor. I was smitten by Seattle, the Skagit Valley, and Washington State. We stopped at the Science Center where we enjoyed many hands-on exhibits and learned something about Chief Scow's home and the Kwakiutl life. I fell asleep on the drive home. I still didn't seem to be getting enough rest.

Celia stopped in town to pick up a paper so we could read about ourselves. We couldn't believe we were pictured in the center of the front page! Headlined "Long-haul Bicyclists Pedal Past" the article opened: "Being at the west end of Highway 20, Skagit County welcomes its share of cross-country bicyclists. The popular route offers a scenic and less-traveled way to ride, cyclists say." I felt satisfied to have completed a significant portion of the journey. Somehow, I would complete the whole trip.

DOWN
THE
PACIFIC
COAST

CHAPTER NINE

Washington Dikes and Ferry Hopping

Mt. Vernon, Washington, Saturday, September 20

I began to prepare for our seven-day trip to San Juan County, which is nestled near Puget Sound between the western coast of Washington and Vancouver Island, British Columbia. Pedaling to Anacortes to catch the ferry was part of our perimeter tour, and so were the San Juans. After exploring the islands, we planned to leave our bicycles in Port Angeles while we flew home for brief visits before resuming our journey.

We caught the ferry to the town of Friday Harbor on San Juan Island at one-ten p.m. on a beautifully clear and sunny fall day. I enjoyed the sea air and read about the area in *Ebb Tide*, a free paper. Two hours splashed by as the sturdy ferry plowed through the water.

Friday Harbor welcomed us to San Juan Island, which is fifteen miles long and seven miles wide with seventy miles of waterfront. There are 450 islands in the San Juan Archipelago. Of those, 172 are above water at high tide. Only ten are inhabited. I scanned the harbor, breathed lungs full of salt air, and thought longingly of my sailboat racing days. With my sailor's eye, I saw I was someplace special. We rolled our bikes off the ferry and leaned them against the entrance to Downrigger's Restaurant, where we ate soup, salad, and all the fresh bread the waitress would bring. I was enraptured by the view of the harbor and the sailboat marina.

After riding around, I went in the National Park Information Office while Bea stayed outside. The woman at the desk gave me suggestions on camping and sightseeing and sent me out the door at a run to the Whale Museum, scheduled to close in ten minutes. There I found information on where to see whales and confirmed the museum hours for a return visit. The sun was sinking we rode out the Roche Harbor Road to Lakedale Campground. At site twelve, a glorious spot on Neva Lake, we unpacked.

San Juan Island, Sunday, September 21

Sunday morning was foggy, cold, and overcast, not conducive to getting out of bed. Bea built a fire, and I fried red snapper for breakfast. We had burned all the wood by the time the fog lifted enough for us to see across the lake. We each packed a pannier of lunch supplies and tucked everything else into the tent. At the campground store, we saw Jane Hathaway and her RV traveling companions whom I met yesterday on the ferry. Jane invited us to visit her in Denver where, she said, "I have a big house, three cats, and the children are gone. I thanked her, but reminded her Colorado, though a great place for bicycling, was a bit off the perimeter. Our enthusiasm for our tour returned in full force as we explained our adventure.

At English Camp, the park ranger, a watercolorist and jack-of-many-trades who had lived on San Juan for nine years, told us San Juan Island lay between two straits resulting a border dispute between England and America over which way the 49th parallel should zigzag to determine ownership of the island. Both countries claimed it under the 1846 Oregon Treaty. Neither side recognized authority of the other. Tempers were short, and it took little to produce a crisis in 1859. An American settler, Lyman Cutlar, shot and killed a Hudson's Bay Company pig that was rooting in his garden. When Canadian authorities threatened to arrest Cutlar, Americans drew up a petition requesting U.S. military protection. Because of the "Pig War," British and American forces placed the island under joint military occupation for the next twelve years. In 1872, San Juan Island became an American possession. The only casualty of this international military confrontation was the pig.

We intended to spend the day whale-watching at Lime Kiln Point State Park. The park ranger said, "A lot of bikers go that way in spite of the gravel road." We discovered its entrance after a mile and a half of most difficult road. There was gravel, all right: hard-packed gravel, gravel ground into ruts by vehicle tires, and, worst of all, new, loose gravel. The terrain was steep and frequently curved. We wobbled, swerved, and sometimes had to walk.

Finally, we arrived at a picnic table overlooking the sea. Hungry again, we hauled out the stove and food. While Bea scrambled happily over the rocks, I cut potatoes, onion, carrots, and broccoli for stew. Glancing seaward, I then cracked six eggs into a bowl, added herbs, and beat them. Bea put them in the frying pan and set it on the stove. I noticed the stove was atilt under the big pan. Bea moved to straighten it, and knocked over the whole thing. We stood mesmerized as the eggs slurped through the crack in the picnic table, leaving only a damp place below on the sand. We laughed until our eyes filled with tears.

Forlornly, we ate vegetables until Bea shouted, "Whale! She had heard the long blowing as the whale surfaced. Our lost omelet was forgotten as we peered through binoculars. It was a Minke, shining black, the dorsal fin far back almost to the tail. Whales seen from here are considered residents of the Greater Puget Sound area. They do not migrate great distances but spend their entire lives in these waters.

Since the sun was sinking and the whale had disappeared, we headed for Friday Harbor, arriving too late for the Whale Museum but in time to buy food and pedal hurriedly to our tent before dark. The days were getting noticeably shorter.

San Juan Island, Monday, September 22

The morning was shrouded by fog, quiet, and dampness, but our fire and stove produced warmth. I rehung last night's laundry on rocks near the fire, since the clothes seemed wetter than ever. By eight-thirty, our wood supply was used up, and I had finished my notes. Since Bea was still writing, I began packing.

We left in an hour and reached the Whale Museum door just as it opened. Once inside, I barely resisted the opportunity to "adopt an orca." I wanted to contribute to everything and to buy every T-shirt or sweatshirt design that supported a cause. Best of all, I liked the sounds of the whales we heard in the exhibit area. I learned that every orca can be identified by the shape and composition of its saddle patch and dorsal fin. Orcas live at least fifty years, travel in pods, and are the top predators in the world's oceans.

On the way to the ferry landing, we chose our carry-out lunch from a crowded bakery. As we sat on the dock and ate, we watched the approach of the huge showcase ferry that would take us to Orcas Island.

When viewed head-on as it came in for a landing, the ferry had the largest whale mouth of all. We could see all the way through a monstrous tunnel and out the tail of the four-story ship. Nothing appeared too large for this behemoth: Bea watched in amazement as oil trucks, garbage trucks, RVs and countless cars were disgorged and consumed. Two trucks filled with bleating sheep were scarcely a mouthful. Bicyclists, back-packers, kayakers, and canoeists boarded — there seemed to be no end. As a truck laden with forty-foot logs backed into the throat of the ferry, Bea grabbed my arm, "Will it sink?"

"No," I said, remembering my train trip from Bonn to Copenhagen, when the whole train was carried by ferry. "I've come a long way since those four days," I smiled to myself. On that trip, in addition to visiting Denmark, I forced myself to eat in a restaurant at least once a day, in a country where I could not speak the language. I had hoped to defuse my fears of eating alone in restaurants and of traveling in a country where I was unable to communicate easily. Thinking of it reminded me that my unwillingness to ride a bicycle alone in my own country made no sense.

We pushed our bikes aboard the ferry. Leaving Friday Harbor, I observed glaucous and herring gulls, cormorants, and grebes. Bea's bird-watching was rubbing off on me. She carried the book and made the identifications. Gradually, I began to borrow her book and read about the birds we had seen.

The ferry ride confirmed our agreement that the San Juans merit their reputation as some of the world's most beau-tiful islands. Geologically, they are the topmost peaks of eroded and glacier-carved mountains, often with steep drops to the sea.

We walked ashore at the village of Orcas, hardly larger than the ferry we were riding, overseen by the historic Orcas Hotel. From a storekeeper I learned that we could buy groceries across the island at Eastsound before reaching Moran State Park Campground. He also told me that Jack Gardner, a friend of mine from work who had retired here, still operated a bookstore in his home overlooking Back Bay near Olga.

We decided to leave our bikes here, take the bus from the Sidney ferry landing to Victoria, and really be tourists, not bicyclists, for a day or two. Coming back, we could jump off the ferry long enough to reclaim the bikes and reboard for Anacortes. I studied the schedules carefully. The idea was practical, but it would have to be implemented precisely according to the ferry schedule. We would have to pack accordingly and carry one pannier each as overnight baggage to Victoria. The woman in the liquor store offered to store our bikes in their shed.

We set about bicycling across the Orcas Island. What a jewel it was! We stopped to pick and eat ripe blackberries, and to look over the fence at the Charolais cattle, imported from France. Just before we entered Eastsound, we sighted mule deer scampering across the road and up a rock face. We decided to stay an extra day in Orcas so we could see more. I called the Gardners from the grocery. Jack answered the phone. He remembered me! He graciously invited us to stay with them, but we really liked camping, and I didn't feel I knew them well enough. He seemed pleased that we would call on them tomorrow.

We bought food supplies for two days and pushed our bikes out to the road for the long uphill climb to the campground. It was almost dusk, but I didn't feel like biking anymore, especially uphill with heavy groceries. Luckily, I spotted an empty, red pickup stopped at a traffic light. "Are you going toward Moran State Park? Would you give us a lift?" I asked the driver.

He had a pleasant face. "Sure," he grinned. We clambered the bikes aboard and joined our host in the cab. Our driver told us he had retired from teaching. He had come to teach for one year and had remained for twenty-four. Before that, he went to Bavaria to teach one year and remained six, teaching science and math. He let us out at his turn-off to the condo community at Rosario.

Back on our bikes, we coasted downhill into the park, picked a campsite, and set up between the road and Cascade Lake. Bea gathered a large pile of wood while I fixed supper. Using butter pats from recent restaurant visits, I sauteed potatoes, onion, green pepper, and mushrooms sprinkled with herbs and, while we ate that, added more butter and sauteed two whole rainbow trout. After supper, we erected the tent under giant evergreens.

As the sun was setting across the lake, we finished writing our notes. When it was dark and our fire was burning beautifully, Bea invited the bicycling couple at a nearby site to join us. Barbara and Mike Minor stowed their things in their tent and came over. They were very nice, low-key people on vacation from their jobs as engineers for Union Carbide.

A great clatter erupted from their campsite. We ran over, flashlights ablaze, to see a raccoon climbing a tree at the water's edge. There was no way down except past us or into the lake. We shone our lights on the raccoon who stared nervously at us. We watched and took flash photos. When we retreated enough for him to reach the ground, the whole camp suddenly came alive with raccoons. At our fireside, there were five sitting around, squalling at each other. With Barbara and Mike, we stood by the blazing fire, turning ourselves as on a spit, occasionally shining our flashlights at the army of raccoons circling and squabbling in the darkness.

What to do? Barbara and Mike had hung all their food and put their other possessions in their tent. Bea stayed near the tent while I carried our panniers containing food into the women's cement-block bath house. We left only clothes and cameras in the tent. The fire burnt down to cinders and there was no more wood. We zipped ourselves into the tent. The raccoons continued their racket even after it began to rain. During the night, Bea heard them on our picnic table. It was several days before we missed the aluminum wind-screen for our stove and assumed the raccoons dragged it off.

Orcas Island, Tuesday, September 23

It was still raining in the morning and our food and pans were in the rest room, so we cooked there. We set up the stove on the floor and I sat cooking and drinking coffee as campers washed and chatted. Barbara told us Mike found a splendid stone shelter with picnic tables and a large fireplace. She asked if we would like to share the shelter for the rest of the day and tonight.

Leaping upon the idea, we hastily packed our bikes and rode through the drizzle to the end of the lake where our soggy belongings filled the shelter. It had a fireplace eight feet long with a mound of dry wood at one side, a sink with running water, and a large trash can.

We built a roaring fire to warm our new home. Everything was hung out to dry. Two tents hung from rafters like large yellow kites, and every available spot was festooned with damp clothing. Over the "No Camping" sign hung a big blue sleeping bag.

Late in the morning, Bea and I rode four miles to visit the Gardners. Jane and Jack Gardner welcomed us so warmly that we felt like family. Their shop and home had an admirable view of Buck Bay. After a short visit, they took us to Cafe Olga for mushroom strudel and shrimp salad. After lunch the rain stopped, and Jack ushered us into his station wagon to show us Orcas Island.

The clouds at sea level had lifted but not enough for us to see the top of 2,409-foot Mt. Constitution. "You can't tell from down here whether the peak is out in the sun or not. We have to go up," explained Jack as he twisted the car back and forth along the steep road. It was grand to see the route and the park. "Last night's downpour was unusual," he told us, "for September is one of the best months of the year. Rainfall here is less than half that of Seattle. The Olympic and Vancouver Island mountains form a rain shadow protecting our islands from southwestern and western weather systems that dump rain on the other side of the ridges. So the islands are dry and sunny.

"People choose to live here because they aren't interested in the flash and splash of urban America, or they have earned their escape from modern stresses. Here we do things easily, without pretense. People's homes are set back and blend in. Their cars and trucks are old. Their dress is casual and comfortable."

Jack continued, "Their boats are practical. Wildlife protection and preservation are important. Past accomplishments, often formidable, are not relevant and are rarely mentioned. A decision to come here is not for everyone. It is a decision to get off the beaten path into a world many never want to leave. Many of our family members now live or vacation here, and we are hoping our East Coast child will eventually move in this direction."

Jack seemed disappointed that we weren't staying longer and wanted to take us to their house for dinner and the night. We declined, feeling a bond with Barbara and Mike and wanting to get "home" to our camp. Jack departed, saying he would appear at eight-fifteen to drive us to the ferry. He couldn't imagine that we would want to begin pedaling early enough to reach the ferry in time — besides, it might rain again.

At camp, Bea and Barbara went for a walk and Mike for a shower while I packed gear for our Victoria trip. Back together, we all gathered wood since the night promised to be cold and perhaps wet. Mike and I had identical bicycles, except for the size. I had never met anyone else touring with this bike, so there was much shop talk. Barbara had a Trek.

By five o'clock it was almost bright, almost sunny over the lake. We shared a bottle of wine. They marveled at our cuisine and dishes, while we marveled at their clothing. They had North Face rain hats, the best we had ever seen for bicycling. We talked for an hour about stoves. Mike summarized, "Now we only buy quality. It's cheaper in the long run."

Bicycling was the perfect counterbalance to their high-pressure, mechanical engineer careers, they felt. I was surprised to learn from Mike that more bicycles are sold in a year than automobiles and that more women buy bicycles than men.

We pooled our food to create a feast and drew the picnic table close to the fire to escape the cold, damp, penetrating air. After dinner, the wood pile was almost gone. I saw a log four feet long and eighteen inches in diameter that would last the night and discourage the 'coons, but it was heavy and big. I decided to try to move it. Bea, Barb, and Mike watched incredulously while I lifted one end off the ground until the log was upended. I pushed it so it fell over in the direction of our shelter. Repeating the process several times, the log and I approached the parking area thud by thud. Mike helped me roll it across the parking lot, then we continued upending and plopping it right into the fireplace and were showered by sparks. Mike stuck a stone under the log to prevent it rolling. From then on Barbara and Mike referred to me as "Jane Bond."

With food hanging among the rafters in case the raccoons revisited, we placed our sleeping bags near the crackling logs. Once settled we continued to talk. Suddenly, Mike bolted out of his bag shouting, "Here they come!" The 'coons lurked in the shadows, prowling like huge, masked, house cats under the picnic table. They stood on hind legs and jumped on the benches to search the table tops. As I fell asleep, I heard Mike's battle cry one last time, "Git out of here - GIT!"

Orcas Island, Wednesday, September 24

I awoke late and realized Jack would be here in an hour. We had to scurry. I stood up and looked across the lake. There was soft ground mist, but the sky looked clear, and there was no wind. We had been up and down during the night because of our raccoon visitors and the discomfort of sleeping on a stone floor. Anyone who got up had stirred the fire to keep it going.

Now we stoked the fire and fired up our stoves for breakfast. Mike and Barbara were packing, too, although they were leaving later. Bea and I, tired from a restless night, were glad to see Jack. When he opened the car door, I smelled shaving cream and soap. He must have smelt wood smoke and damp, dirty people, or even raccoon! We wrung Mike's and Barbara's hands saying goodby.

At the ferry landing, I stored our bikes in the liquor store shed and paid for our tickets to Sidney, the ferry-port for Victoria. I then called Mom from the phone booth and told her our plans. We waved goodby to Jack, who had driven a forty-mile round-trip to bring us to the ferry. What great hosts he and Jane had been!

The ferry route to Sidney took us through the narrow Wasp passage under a cool, sunny sky full of large popcorn clouds. Disembarking, I realized that I had left my passport in Mt. Vernon after carrying it all the way across the country! Fortunately, I had my driver's license for identification. The ride to Sidney took only forty-five minutes; then we caught a bus to Victoria.

We had no idea where to stay. It occurred to me that in the British-influenced areas of Singapore and Hong Kong, the YWCA had been a great place to stay. I jumped up and asked the bus driver whether we were near the YWCA. Pulling to a stop, he directed us to a building two blocks away. There we found a clean, pleasant double room with two beds, two desks, and two closets. Hot showers were down the hall. We were right downtown and could walk everywhere. We booked two nights.

After showers, we were off to a bicycle shop. Bea bought a red Cat Eye battery rear light which she needed for riding early in the morning, late in the afternoon, and in coastal fog. In bad weather or at twilight, I had been riding behind her. My generator rear light was excellent.

Victoria is said to be Canada's most beautiful capital city, but it was the Provincial Museum that made the whole trip worthwhile. We spent over two hours there absorbing the rich natural history and native heritage.

After dinner, footsore and with aching legs, we returned to the Y for a quiet evening. I was itchy to get on our bikes and be on the road again.

Victoria, Canada, Friday, September 26

While awaiting the bus to the ferry landing, we briefly encountered Barbara and Mike who were enjoying their day in Victoria. Sorry not to have more time together, waving and yelling farewells, we boarded our bus.

At the ferry landing, the sun, cool air, and view from a bench were fine. There was just time at Friday Harbor for me to phone Celia, while Bea fetched delicious turkey sandwiches from The Donut Shop. We boarded the ferry. At Orcas Island we reclaimed our bicycles and gear from Margaret Russell's liquor store shed. There were no clouds until after dark as we approached Anacortes, where Celia met and drove us home.

Mt. Vernon, Washington, Saturday, September 27

The Chandlers departed for a day at EXPO and left us the keys to their truck. We spent most of the day phoning friends and reading and answering mail. My letter from Jo Whiteley, who was driving west from Virginia, proclaimed: "What a glorious great big country this is! If you look at it with the eyes of a Third Worlder, how obscenely rich it is. All that firewood, greenness, open space no one is using. A look at our poverty areas would make them say, 'I'll take it.'"

Mt. Vernon, Sunday, September 28

Dottie and Hank Hull and Pat, whom we had seen in Bowbells, North Dakota, were camped nearby and wanted to meet us in town. Delighted, we raced down to Main Street. One cafe was open and, over coffee and pie, we shared tales of the road. When they asked how we got along, I laughed comfortably and explained: "I have never married, have no siblings, and habitually live alone. I need space. And I lack diplomacy. Bea was married over twenty-six years, has reared three children, and needs company as much as I need space. I think it's a tribute to us that we get along at all. It's also a measure of how much we want to continue this trip. It's the trip that holds us together, for neither of us can conceive of continuing it alone."

Before we departed, I wrote down a number to call and

dates when we might find them in Oregon. We parted, hoping to meet again soon.

Mt. Vernon, Monday, September 29

We were ready to leave for Port Angeles. Celia drove us by way of Discovery Point to within a few miles of the ferry. On Wednesday we would return by ferry to Anacortes where she would meet us. We would fly east on Thursday.

As we pedaled to Sequim, the Olympic Mountains, peeping in and out of black clouds, were on the left. To our right through the trees or beyond fields spread the ocean, glittering in the sunlight. Overhead were ragged clouds. We pedaled in their shadows, through spotlights of sun rays, among drops of sporadic rain. All afternoon sun and clouds, light and shadow created a kaleidoscope of color reflected in the water against a backdrop of evergreens, mountains, and fields. The day ended in heavy rain, and after a Chinese meal we spent the night at the Sundowner Motel.

Sequim, Tuesday, September 30

In the morning, we cycled the Old Olympic Highway from Sequim through the Dungeness Valley down Voice of America Road to Dungeness Spit and the Natural Wildlife Refuge. Locking our bikes, we followed a shaded path among towering trees to a cliff high above the Strait of Juan de Fuca and Dungeness Bay where we peered along the longest natural sand spit known. Waves crashed ashore, and the narrow beach was littered with logs, limbs, and trees polished white by the sun and surf. Many stranded tree trunks were so large we were unable to clamber over them. We had seen numerous sea ducks, and found the white-winged scoter here. There were black and surf scoter, too. Among the evergreens, I got my best-ever view of a red-breasted nuthatch.

Hunger drove us back to our bikes where we lunched on apple halves spread with peanut butter and raisins. We then rode to Port Angeles along the shores of the Strait of Juan de Fuca, which connects the Pacific Ocean with Puget Sound. White clouds in round balls circled the dark green necks of the mountains like strands of pearls.

Once the bikes were safely stored in the Budget-Rent-a-Car garage, we decided to take the ferry that was ready to depart for Victoria and see Port Angeles when we returned. The ferry crossed in cloud-filtered light, golden in the sunset, to Victoria where we got the last double room at the Y. We walked around that wondrous city as the lights came on.

Victoria, Canada, Wednesday, October 1

In Victoria, breakfast and Smithy's Pancake House became synonymous. Afterward, we walked to Beacon Hill Park, set aside in the 1850s by the Hudson's Bay Company. At Goodacre Lake Wildfowl Sanctuary, I particularly enjoyed the widgeons. We marveled at one of the world's tallest totem poles and the site of an ancient Indian village. On top of Beacon Hill, we found the zero milestone for the Trans-Canada Highway. Down the cliff, on the beach, I spoke with a woman gathering seaweed to make soup. "Only the black is good. Green not good," she proclaimed. I wanted to know how to make the soup. "Chop it up well, wash, boil for over an hour in water, put in pork," was her recipe.

A bus took us to the ferry landing where we sat overlooking the water and watching western grebes, coots, and a seal. Mt. Baker towered above the clouds in one direction, and the Olympics were silhouetted by the setting sun which gilded Mt. Baker.

Mt. Vernon, Washington, Thursday, October 2

Back again at Celia's in Mt. Vernon, we were joined for breakfast by my friend Jo Whiteley, on the way from Virginia to visit her daughter in California. Having not seen the sun since she left the East Coast, Jo told us, "I got snowbound in Jackson Hole. You barely missed the snow. With your letters and phone calls I followed you closely. Snow, floods, and other bad weather were a week or less behind you from the Rockies through the Cascades."

Bea and I showed Jo around Mt. Vernon as proudly as though we lived there ourselves. Then we went to lunch in La Conner where, without our bicycles, we were free to wander the shops. Jo and I spent most of our time in The Wood

Merchant. I bought a chair which she had room to take home for me in her car. Jo had done what I claimed I wanted to do. She had taken shop lessons and carpentry classes and has been building things and remodeling her house. Having spent all the time we could in La Conner, Jo drove us to the Seattle airport before settling in a motel.

While waiting to board our plane home to the other Washington, I walked to the gate where we would, on return, catch our plane for Port Angeles. I selected a place to meet Celia and then called to tell her. When we landed in Washington, a friend met us and took us to my house. Bea went to sleep and I took my camera, broken from a fall to the pavement earlier that week, to the repair shop. I had to change clothes since it was in the eighties, twenty degrees warmer than in Washington State. I spent four days problem solving, visiting, and consulting with friends and family. Our all-night return flight was draining because I was so tired when it began, and the planes were late.

Celia met us for breakfast between planes. The clouds lifted for our flight to Port Angeles, and I relished seeing from the air the area we cycled, especially Sequim, the Dungeness Spit, and Hurricane Ridge. In a motel, I went bed early in the afternoon and slept straight through until five the next morning.

Port Angeles, Thursday, October 9

At the Olympic Park Visitor's Center, I overheard a man talking to the hostess. He planned to drive up to Hurricane Ridge. "How would you like some company?" I asked the man, who introduced himself as Don Shaw. "We're bicycling and don't really have the time or inclination to pedal up."

"Sure, but I'm going up, look around rather quickly, and come right back down."

"Perfect." Bea came, and got in the back seat. I enjoyed the drive and the views, and seeing a black-tailed deer on the way.

We retrieved our bikes, loaded them, and pedaled west toward Neah Bay. In several places the road was very close to the water. The scenery was stunning. We alternately traveled through sun and mist and arrived at Clallam Bay.

Bea pleaded, "I have to eat, NOW." By this time, I knew

hunger panics were partly a result of her thyroid medicine. We entered Smuggler s Inn. While eating, we decided to stay at the motel for two nights. Tomorrow we could ride a round trip on bare bikes. I was still tired.

Clallam Bay, Friday, October 10

We rode off. At every overlook, the shining sea was pristine. Bea stopped to see a sawmill, then turned off at the museum, and I continued straight toward Cape Flattery. I rode on and on, over ten miles through wilderness, much of the way on hardpacked, unpaved roads.

I walked out to the northwestern-most point of the forty-eight states. What a grand view I had of the lighthouse on Tatoosh Island and the Pacific Ocean. There were caves carved in the cliffs by waves. I trod the path along the water's edge among gnarled rain forest trees. I had set a goal and achieved it. I had reached the Pacific Ocean and the northwest extreme of our contiguous land mass.

On the way back, I scrutinized the contents of The Makah Museum, a small treasure house. Operated by the Makah Indian Nation, it preserves the legacy of the coastal village of Ozette. The museum is the repository for what may be the most significant archeological find in North America. In 1970, a tidal erosion exposed a group of five-hundred-year-old homes, perfectly preserved in an ancient mud slide. Thus, thousands of artifacts were discovered that have helped re-create the Makahs' rich history as whalers, sealers, fishers, hunters, craftsmen, and warriors. I particularly enjoyed the full-scale replica of a fifteenth-century Indian long-house and its early clapboard construction.

Rested and restored, I gloried in a fast ride home. I bought some fruit, cereal, and milk and went to the room. Bea was there. I ate while she went to the library. I showered and washed clothes while she went for a walk.

On returning, Bea told me about seeing a coyote, turned on the TV, and went to sleep. I turned it off, and began writing.

Clallam Bay, Saturday, October 11

From Clallam Bay we headed south for the first time, pedaling through scattered white scarves of ground fog, and past hillsides of giant cedar stumps charred by logging trash burned to promote new growth. Douglas firs, hemlock, cedar, broad leafed maple, and alder predominated. The maple leaves were fire red and the alders brilliant yellow. When we stopped at Forks, a maple leaf fluttered down and landed on Bea's new front bag. She exclaimed, "Winter's coming — better get south!"

We pedaled all day through clear, cloudless sunshine. We rode solo, in sight but widely separated, all the way to the Ruby Beach overlook bluff where Bea saw the Pacific Ocean for the first time. She was excited, and we shared our feelings of accomplishment. Near the sign about Destruction Island, we ate apples and spent almost an hour looking at the Pacific. Most of the western shoreline of Washington State is now national park, wildlife refuge, or Indian reservation.

We continued along the sparsely traveled road not far apart, commenting as we went. Kalaloch Campground was right on the beach. We picked a site, rode a few miles to a grocery, and returned supplied. Bea gathered wood. I never stopped being amazed how she could find it. After a satisfying supper, we set up the tent, hung out our laundry still damp from yesterday, and went to walk on the beach. Bea asked, "Are you as excited as I am to see the Pacific Ocean, to be here?" I smiled and nodded.

Back at our picnic table, I calculated we had ridden about three thousand miles. Our fire burned and crackled. I went into the tent, crawled into my bag, and wrote. From the tent door, on the other side of the fire, I could see the beach and the Pacific Ocean. Surf thundered against the shore. Although there were many campers, they were quiet, and their tents and vehicles were hidden by the thick, aromatic forest.

Unaccustomed to the pounding waves, we awoke frequently during the night. I put on socks and another shirt, but adding clothes all night failed to keep the damp cold from waking me. Sleeping was impossible.

Earlier than usual, Bea got up and quickly built a fire. I took out the new stove to boil some water for coffee, but I couldn't get it lit. Trying to clean it, I unscrewed the top of the fuel bottle without first releasing the pressure, spraying my head, face, shoulders and half of the picnic table with cooking fuel. Luckily, I was wearing glasses instead of contacts! My hands and fingers were numb and covered with soot. I couldn't find the stove directions, had taken apart the wrong pieces, and couldn't get them back together. Coffee took an hour-and-a-half. I pedaled out of camp in a sweat of frustration that combined with the smells of stove fuel and wood smoke.

Tired from cold and lack of sleep, I rode for fifteen minutes with tears and rain streaming down my face. Steller's jays in their ultramarine feathers romped among the trees along the highway, upgrading my mood.

Bea was half-a-mile ahead of me when two mongrel dogs ran out of an Indian reservation trailer home. I continued pedaling, not looking at the dogs so as not to challenge them, confident they would desist at the border of their territory. Pursuing me, they continued to bark. Since I was ahead, there was no danger of their running under my front wheel and causing a wreck. They gained on me and began barking and snapping at my panniers. There was no paved shoulder, and logging trucks were passing at high speeds every few moments on my left. Both dogs moved to my right. I rode on the white line at the edge of the highway to avoid dropping off into the gravel on one side or wobbling into the trucks on the other. There were only a few inches of space to absorb the windshear as each truck passed.

Now both dogs ran one behind the other on my right side. First one dog seemed to rest its voice then the other, but they showed no signs of tiring. My legs began to ache as I tried to spin my feet faster to keep ahead of the dogs. I talked to myself: "Keep your eyes on the line far ahead. If you look too close, you'll wobble." I tracked the dogs out of the corners of my eyes and the trucks with my ears.

There was a slight rise coming up at the curve ahead. I flicked up one gear, stood on the pedals when there was no truck close, and powered up the rise. I flicked up a couple more gears, using momentum and the very gradual but long descent to leave the dogs behind. I had hoped to get close enough to Bea to yell at her to slow down and hand me her Halt.

Halt, a tear-gas-like substance used by mail carriers, temporarily creates a burning sensation in a dog's eyes. Bea always had some handy. This time, luckily, the terrain was in my favor. At Amanda Park, we turned in for soup and salad.

The afternoon was warm enough for us to ride in shorts for the first time in quite a while. I felt too hot going uphill, so I unzipped the neck and pushed up the sleeves of my jersey. We sped along for about twenty miles in the sun. Bea had ridden through some spider webs that trailed several yards behind her like long silver threads glittering in the sun. As we rode through the town of Humptulips, I smiled and pedaled in the rhythm of "Tiptoe through the Tulips."

After two-and-a-half hours, we reached Hoquiam and dumped the bikes in a motel. At dinner, we stuffed ourselves with spaghetti.

Hoquiam, Monday October 13

The next morning, I wanted to stay in the motel, read, and rest until checkout time but we were out the door for breakfast by seven. Bea wanted to get south. It was damp, overcast, and in the forties as we rode through Hoquiam into Aberdeen. Crossing two large bridges was fun. We pedaled over rolling hills, reaching the attractive town of Raymond where one high-tech sawmill replaced the twenty or so that had been along the Willapa River in 1900. When we stopped for lunch, we realized how tired we were. We went to a motel for the rest of the day to work on our letters, read, and relax. Nights along the Pacific Coast were too long, damp, and cold for camping.

Raymond, Tuesday, October 14

I felt at home pedaling along the Willapa River, oyster capital of the west, and along the banks of Willapa Bay. The smells and sights here felt comfortable. The area recalled my five years of racing a sixteen-and-a-half-foot Windmill in the tidal rivers near Annapolis, Maryland, among the last sailing oyster fleet in America. Watching ducks fly, bob, and feed, I found observing them more interesting than identifying them. Cranberries were totally unexpected. I thought they all grew in plastic bags, or perhaps in New England! We passed extensive bogs between Seaview and Ilwaco. Although most of the day had been sunny and pleasant, mist and fog rolled in as we approached the coast and the day waned. I was cold when we reached Ilwaco. Darkness would come soon; visibility was already occluded. I found a motel, but we had to haul our bikes and panniers up to the second floor. Having showered and changed clothes, we headed for a hot meal at Red's Family

Restaurant.

After supper, the temperature dropped, and our walk to the end of town ended when we detoured, shivering, into our motel room. I read about American widgeons and soon fell asleep.

Ilwaco, Wednesday, October 15

It was still dark when we walked to breakfast at seven-thirty. At the restaurant, two women about our ages sat in the next booth. Judging by their attire and briefcases, I assumed them to be professionals. As I got up to pay our bill, one woman looked at my legs. Then she put on her glasses and inspected my cycling shoes, tights, yellow and red wool bicycling jersey, and red and black cycling jacket. I thought the cashier would never come to take my money. Finally, flashing my finest smile at my inspector, I fled out the door.

Expecting mail in Astoria, we were tugged along south to Fort Columbia on the north bank of the river. It was too foggy to see the view, so we picked wild blackberry snacks. Refreshed, we coasted downhill to the highway, pressed a button which turned on a caution light alerting motorists that cyclists were in the tunnel, and proceeded to the nearby Lewis and Clark campsite, now a picnic area, next to a wonderful old wooden church. As we pedaled up to the bridge entrance, we noticed white winged and sea scoters. The span over the Columbia River seemed to end in fog midway across the water. Beyond the fog, on the other side of the bridge, was Oregon.

CHAPTER TEN

Fog and Cold
in Craggy Oregon

Astoria, Oregon, Wednesday, October 15

Pedaling the four-mile bridge over the Columbia River, I saw sunlight on the causeway a few hundred yards ahead. By mid-river, my rear view mirror was filled by fog. The salt air blowing in from the Pacific expanded my lungs, and the fog bank appeared to loft gently ahead as I rode across the causeway portion of the bridge. As I approached, the two-hundred-seventeen-foot hump in the bridge seemed to rise higher as the last feather wisps of fog faded. I shifted to a low gear and began to climb. Washington State disappeared from my rear view mirror. At the bridge crest, Astoria, Oregon stretched below along the river bank in the morning sun.

Our first stop was the post office where Bea received a large package of food from her daughter. While eating the macadamia nuts, we noted our departure from Washington in our joint letter and mailed it.

We felt like eating seafood and had a splendid lunch. While Bea read her letters, I read about Oregon. In October, along the coast, we could expect twelve days of sun, six inches of rain, and average high temperatures of fifty-four degrees. Our guidebook, *Bicycling the Pacific Coast* by Tom Kirkendall and Vicky Spring, told me to expect "384.2 miles of spectacular ocean views, long beaches, and sandy dunes, along with quiet farmlands and deep forests." I could expect heavy rain and winds gusting over sixty miles an hour. The State Highway Department provided wider shoulders in narrow places going south than traveling north since bicyclists usually journey north to south to take advantage of the prevailing winds. We were a month too late for the tourist season and helpful winds.

Astoria was named for the fort built by John Jacob Astor's Pacific Fur Company in 1811. The town contains several fine museums and is a showcase for Victorian homes. I liked the town, and was most anxious to visit the museums. It reminded me of Annapolis. When we walked out of the cafe, the midday sun was shining. I hated to forfeit the museums, but I hated more to miss an irresistible day outdoors.

We kept on pedaling except when called to a halt by western grebes, canvasbacks, scoters, coots, and great blue herons that became a common sight. By the time we reached Seaside, it was gray, cold, foggy-damp, and three-thirty. We were starving. We had bicycled forty miles.

Moving slowly, I spied a sign announcing a motel room with two beds for $15.95 off season. We found we not only had two beds but two rooms. They were small, but we got the bikes in and still had space to walk. We shopped for groceries and ate in our rooms, munching happily as rain pounded the roof and we watched local television.

Seaside, Thursday, October 16

At The Coffee Mug, I liked the family atmosphere and sourdough toast for breakfast. The kids came by for orange juice, a kiss, a whisper to Mom, and their school bus. After eating, I phoned my mother and discovered that she planned to drive to the mountains in North Carolina for a week. A few friends would visit her there for a day or, perhaps, my cousin would stay overnight. I felt sad that, at eighty, she would have to drive five hundred miles each way alone. She found driving relaxing and looked forward to being in the mountains. I wished her a good week.

We had journeyed many short days without a day off, so I declared a rest day. Bea announced she needed exercise and departed for a walk. I just wanted to sit quietly, alone. I needed to vegetate. I washed my cycling shorts, wrung them out in a towel, turned the heat down to low, hung them on the hot air vent to dry, and then stretched out to read *Travels With Charlie*.

Bea soon exploded through the door and exclaimed, "I'm freezing!" She rushed over to the heater, flipped it to high, and rubbed her hands together, blowing on them and talking non-stop. "Let's go eat as soon as I get warm. It's really cold out there, but this is a great place for bird-watching, lots of ducks." I was hungry, too, and put down my book. "What's that smell?" Bea asked.

"I don't know," I said, putting on one shoe. "It's my shorts!" I hopped to the heater, still carrying the other shoe, and grabbed the shorts. We looked at the smoking blob. The polypro saddle insert had melted. It hardened before our eyes as it cooled. Looking at each other, we burst out laughing. Bea offered me her spare shorts, which were too small.

Actually, I had a serious problem; my other pair of cycling shorts was thinly padded and uncomfortable. The ride to lunch was cold and raw, for it was damp and the temperature was in the low fifties. After eating, we biked along the boardwalk and walked, pushing our vehicles, into the mall portion of town. At the Jubilee Gift Shop, Lou Ann Baty asked where we were from. We told her about the perimeter trip.

"I'm fifty-seven. How old are you?" she asked.

"We're fifty-six and sixty-one."

"Really? Would you mind if I call the local newspaper?" We looked at each other. "No problem," I said. "We only give one interview per state."

She suggested we would enjoy the town better without pushing our bikes, and put them in her storage room. Fred Bassett, the reporter, would meet us here in a half an hour. We found something to eat and returned just as Fred arrived. He had forgotten his camera, so we reclaimed our bikes and rode to the newspaper office.

Inside, we enjoyed Bassett's skilled interview. He put us on the front page of *The Seaside Signal's Senior Magazine* and wound up his report saying: "The personal recollections and energy made this reporter want to hop on his old three-speed and join them, but they said he'd have to stand in line. They said they'd had hundreds of similar offers from people all along their route."

Back in the motel, I relaxed and read about Seaside's first residents, the Clatsop Indians, who made cloaks from strips of bark bound together and coated them with fish oil to repel rain. Lewis and Clark came in 1805 and made their camp at what is now Fort Clatsop. On one short expedition to study the area, they found the Clatsops on the beach boiling seawater to obtain salt. They adopted the same practice since they needed salt to preserve meat and fish for the winter and for their trip home. In 1955, the salt cairn was dedicated as a national monument.

In spite of my melted pants, we had enjoyed a fine day. I wondered if the world needed adversity to strengthen cooperation.

Seaside, Friday, October 17

While we were packing, we realized it was too wet and too cold to travel, much less camp. We rode through a light mist in the dark to a farewell breakfast at The Coffee Mug. This time the owner's wife waited on us.

Regulars sat at the counter listening to Charlie, who reminisced non-stop: "Used to get a pound of coffee and a stick of candy for two bits. Now you have a hell of a time finding a good banana. My grandad bought a brand-new Model T in 1919. The second day he had it, he tied a chain around the rear axle and started pulling up stumps. Well, sir, he jerked the rear axle right out from under the car, and my grandmother nearly beat him to death with a baseball bat." Charlie waited for laughs, sipped his coffee, wiped his mouth on his arm, and continued, "Andy caught an eighty-pound salmon by the tail. He wrestled with it all day. Late in the afternoon a fellow came by with a gun and shot the salmon." Charlie took a deep breath and announced that he hadn't bought coffee for thirty days, due to the generosity of his friends. He remarked, "If the government finds out, they'll cut my Social Security."

When Mrs. Coffee Mug, Beth Weaver, brought our check, she told us the restaurant had been open only two weeks and it seemed to be going well. We certainly liked the breakfasts and lunches we ate there. Beth heard me mention I was from Washington and she asked me to call her sister who lived in Woodbridge, Virginia, only thirty miles from my house.

"Sure, but I won't be home until December when we break the trip for the holidays."

"That's O.K. Here's the phone number. I think she'd like to talk to someone who has seen our place."

It was January before I got around to calling. I remembered The Coffee Mug as a home on the road, and it was good to hear the owners continued to do well.

In the rain, we reluctantly left Seaside. We never saw the sun while we were there, but the place and the people were so

radiantly charming we hardly noticed. Our route was beginning to get hilly, and, in view of the rain, we bypassed Cannon
Beach and Hug Point State Park. After stopping to photograph
an "Elk Crossing" sign near a bridge, I looked over into the
gully. Two black-tailed deer were watching me!

At Arch Cape, we mailed our letters, and I phoned my
cousin Jack Floyd, also my stockbroker and business advisor. I
decided to make an investment we discussed. Breathless, I
walked out of the phone booth. I had just spent a lot of money!

While I was on the phone, Bea talked to a woman who
said she got disgusted with local politics, quit teaching, and
became a "handyman." She invited us to extend our stay in
Oregon by visiting her for a few days. I was tempted.

Bea closed the conversation, "Thank you, but we really
have to get south. We're too late already." Near Manzanita the
rain stopped and the world looked brighter. Along the route,
we had a good look at several harlequin ducks. Since we were
high on a bank, we didn't worry them. We watched with our
binoculars for a long time and nibbled on wild blackberries
when the ducks submerged.

The cheese factory in Tillamook took up more time. As
we walked inside, Bea said she certainly hoped we could get
some curds, a form of milk from which cheese is made. We did,
and as I sampled them for the first time, I wondered how I could
have lived in Switzerland without eating curds. The cheese
factory reminded me of that year in Switzerland when I was
seventeen. My Swiss student friends taught me to appreciate
long walks, skiing, and the outdoors. From that year, outdoor
activity was no longer a diversion; it became a necessity.

It was almost dark, and we entered a nearby motel. We
had not been the only birds flying south along U.S. 101. South-
bound "snowbird" traffic had included every type of live-in
vehicle and van, as well as tightly packed cars and station
wagons. Coming toward us were local cars and pickups with
gun racks or fishing poles. Many vehicles towed boats.

Tillamook, Saturday, October 18

While I was walking around outside the motel to test the
morning air, a man inspecting his boat on its trailer asked, "Are
you bicycling?"

"Yes, are you fishing?"

"The Chinook salmon are running."

"Is that what those small fishing boats in Tillamook Bay were doing yesterday when I rode past?"

"Probably. You can catch two salmon a day or seven a week. Each fish weighs about forty to eighty pounds. I drove here yesterday from Portland to get my share."

"Do you hunt, too, or just fish?"

"I used to like hunting bear, but, after I got one and skinned it, it looked so human that I didn't want to hunt anymore."

"Are those wool overalls that you are wearing? I've never seen them before."

Taking his hands out of the pockets and pulling on one strap, he replied, "Yes. I really like them in this weather. They're warm and flexible." The only pants of similar material I had seen were heavy underwear worn by the winter team trying to climb Mt. Everest in 1972 when I had hiked almost to base camp.

He advised, "Don't go over to the beach today. Stay inland on 101 south where the traffic will be lighter. You might also get away from the fog for most of the day. It's quite hilly on the coast and you couldn't see anything."

Taking his suggestion, we covered twenty-two miles in pale intermittent sunlight before stopping at the southern end of seven-mile-long Lincoln City for lunch. The pastures along the way smelled like cattle, silage, grass, and wet hay, and I was reminded of spring days in a Swiss valley farm village. We saw cows of every hue: some light tan, others heavier brown with white faces and chests, and Holsteins in black and white.

I'd been out on the highway so much that I'd grown unaccustomed to city traffic. A car making a right turn almost got me, but I managed a quick stop which wobbled me off the bike. The driver came to a halt, turned off the engine, and put her head into her hands. The rear fender slightly brushed my rear pannier. No harm was done, and there was no need for discussion. I rode on until lunchtime.

By the time we stopped in Lincoln City, my bottom hurt from lack of padding. Today, I had layered, but that wasn't like having padded bicycle shorts. It was cold enough that I was wearing underwear, short pants, long pants, a wool short-sleeved shirt, a T-shirt, and my lined Gore-tex raincoat. My shoes had not been dry for weeks. I was chilly when motionless or coasting, but just right when spinning along about fifteen miles an hour.

We rolled on to Boiler Bay where we briefly abandoned our bikes to look for whales. We saw one whale, but didn't know what kind it was. Signs along the bay warned of coastal hazards: high waves, deep water and strong currents, logs that roll in the surf, and high, steep cliffs. Nothing I had read exaggerated the rugged beauty of the Oregon Coast. To be closer to the sea, we got off 101 for a time on the Otter Crest Loop.

We continued on to Newport Motel, where we were pleased to have a kitchen in our room. We shopped for food and prepared dinner of pork chops, rice, and sauerkraut. Although Newport, on Yaquina Bay, is proclaimed the Dungeness Crab Capital of the World and is noted for shrimp and oysters, too, we passed them up. I don't like to pick crab, was too lazy to peel shrimp, and failed to think of oyster stew. Cooking, even in a kitchen, was limited by our pot and pan supply and our energy.

Newport, Sunday, October 19

For the first time since we could remember, the sun dazzlingly bright in a cloudless dawn. The day's riding was hard because of the hills, but no finer views were anywhere. Old Yaquina Bay Lighthouse, established in 1871, dominated the coastline.

We continued along the coast to Sea Lion Caves, where we went to see the sea lions. Days later, the joy, amusement, and excitement of watching them was a clear memory.

Florence, Monday, October 20

It was raining when we awoke, and I was hungry and tired. On the way to breakfast, we saw a library, a good refuge on a rainy day. Bea returned to the room to sleep, and I drafted our joint letter and my trip notes at the library. By noon, I went back to get Bea. I enjoyed being alone and she had slept well, so we shared a companionable lunch. We talked about taking time to rent a dune buggy for a ride tomorrow on our way south.

Florence, Tuesday, October 21

The next morning only the weather was gray, and we

pedaled down the road. After waiting a half hour until the dune buggy place opened, we found no one would come to drive the buggy for another two hours. We left disappointed, and went to one of the dune overlook parks where we admired the birds and small, red-bellied, dark brown squirrels.

Our next stop was a big sawmill at Gardiner. From outside the fence near the water, we watched several large logging trucks being unloaded by cranes on tracks. In the water nearby were ibis, and a wonderful humped-over great blue heron that faded into the background so perfectly it was visible only as a reflection in the still water.

Further down the road, we heard crashing noises in the trees overhead. Someone was throwing rocks at me, but their aim was sloppy. I saw the boys in a parking lot near a pickup and kept pedaling. My thought on one level was, "If he owes me a near-miss rock pounding from some past life, it is paid, and I am glad he didn't owe me anything worse." On another level, "If the guy thinks so poorly of himself that he has to feed his ego by throwing rocks at a woman, I should feel pity rather than anger." On a third level, "Assuming he couldn't tell how old I am but realizes I am a woman, disguised in these cycling clothes and helmet, perhaps I should be flattered by the 'flirtation.'" Then I watched Bea turn her bike and ride directly toward the group.

She pulled out her recorder, read the pickup's tag number, and said, "You should be ashamed. Stop it." When she returned to the highway, the rock thrower and I were both speechless. I thought she would be knocked flat.

On the Coos Bay Bridge there were so many cormorants out sunning their wings or fishing that we stopped at the bridge summit and watched the show through our binoculars. One harbor seal seemed to be observing us as it floated on its back. Feeling chilly, we rolled off the bridge toward a motel for the night. Daily, we hoped for sun; we were ready for relief from the penetrating damp and cold. Nevertheless, we adored Oregon.

Coos Bay, Wednesday, October 22

We pedaled into the thundering morning truck traffic on 101. As we rode into Brandon on the bike path, we found it lined with ripe blackberries. In town, we supplied ourselves with cheese curds at the factory and lunch at Eat'n Station before proceeding down Myrtlewood Lane, that portion of 101 resplendent with myrtlewood factories, shops, and trees.

Inside a shop, we learned that myrtlewood grows exceptionally slowly and is among the hardest woods known. The proprietor told us the small tree we'd leaned our bikes against was over a hundred years old. Southwestern Oregon is the only place this symmetrical, broadleaf evergreen is found in America. (It also grows in Israel.) Artisans craft its spectacularly grained wood into beautiful objects; neither of us could resist buying something and having it sent home. The wood's colorings vary from satiny gray to multi-colored grains of red, yellow, and brown, revealing many burls and patterns. The wood is so heavy that green, unseasoned logs will not float.

After pedaling fifty miles by two-thirty, we arrived at Port Orford, an attractive, historic coastal town and the westernmost incorporated city in the contiguous states. The town's natural deep-water harbor makes it a busy fishing center.

By the time we selected a motel, it was darker and quite cold. I seemed to be getting more tired, with no ability to snap back. I had been having a fatigue-type diarrhea for the past three days. I huddled in bed while Bea shopped for food. She brought back yogurt and orange juice, but I ate only the yogurt.

Port Orford, October 23, 24

I could barely pedal the twenty-eight miles to Gold Beach and insisted on a halt about noon. We decided to take a break from bicycling and registered for the all-day Rogue River jet-boat trip the next morning. I did sleep an hour in the afternoon, but then couldn't sleep again until after midnight. It was rare for me to have trouble sleeping.

I knew I was ill, but was certain the only problem was stress. I needed about four days alone with a fat interesting book to read. Nevertheless, I went a hundred-and-four miles round trip on the Rogue River jet boat. Although I felt like a sack of flour lumped on a seat, only eyes moving, I thoroughly enjoyed the trip and my body's inactivity. By the time we returned, however, I was cold, exhausted, pale, and had diarrhea again. I slept twelve hours, and awoke weak, headachy, and dog-tired.

Bea went to the hospital emergency room and told the

nurse she had a sick friend at the motel. The nurse said she would come and get me in her car. Too weak to argue, I was hauled off to the emergency room. They took blood for tests and gave me some pills and brought me back to the motel. All I wanted was rest.

Muttering about getting south to the famous California sun, Bea arranged for the nurse's husband to drive us in his pickup to Crescent City, sixty miles south, where he deposited us in a motel.

Crescent City, California, October 25, 26

The best help came from on high. It rained so hard there was no question of us going anywhere, and I recovered, slogging over to Denny's for food a couple of times. When the rain slackened, Bea went off on her bike, and I returned to the room, bed, and a book.

During lunch at Denny's we met Sally, who seemed to be a vagrant when she came inside to dry off from the rain. We had almost finished eating when we noticed her loaded bicycle outside. She was cold, wet, and alone. Bea invited the girl to join us for coffee. We offered her apple pie, and she took it heated, a la mode, please. She was riding down the coast, too, but hadn't decided where to stay for the night. We left her at the restaurant.

I returned to bed, watched TV, read, and slept away the afternoon. Eating dinner didn't appeal to me, but we returned to Denny's where we saw Sally again. She told us she was returning south from Alaska on her bicycle, but she carried no stove and only an open tube tent. We didn't think her equipment suitable for Alaska. She told us of crossing the Gulf Coast from Florida to Louisiana in four months. Apparently we both looked incredulous, for she continued, "Well, I stopped to work." I thought her eyes and mouth sent different messages. "How big is your motel room?" she asked Bea. She left when we did, but we were walking, and she pedaled off.

Basically, we agreed we didn't trust Sally. We had listened to her, fed her, shared stories, and chattered about bicycle touring. At first, we had talked openly; then we had withdrawn. Although we felt guilty, we were relieved that our impressions were similar. Meeting her reminded us that all bicycle tourists aren't the same. Bicyclists, on the whole, are worthy of trust. I get angry when I meet a bicyclist who doesn't live up to or enhance that reputation.

In the rain at Crescent City, we made the mental transition from Oregon to California. I resented having been hauled into California in a pickup, but acknowledged that although it's impossible to go back, one can go again.

CHAPTER ELEVEN

Getting South to California Sun

Crescent City, California, Monday, October 27

California felt looser, more relaxed, like muscles after exercise. Economically, it appeared less depressed: fewer closed or boarded-up store fronts, fewer "for sale" signs. Gone were the high-heeled boots of the west and the fishermen's boots and wide suspenders of the Oregon coast. As we proceeded south, people looked more assured, cosmopolitan, and confident.

Anticipating the sight of our first redwoods, I felt especially privileged. I remembered a passage from a friend's letter: "I think everyone has a dream to do what you have accomplished. It's a shame we can't always fulfill that dream; when you have other commitments, you just can't take off and do as you please. We just go on dreaming — some day...."

In Del Norte Coast Redwood State Park, my bike wobbled as I tried to see the tops of the redwoods, over three hundred feet high. Where the sun shone through the trees, steam billowed from the thick bark. Our two-lane road snaked through the forest, redwood trees crowding so closely we could touch them as we rode. I read the markers of dedication from individuals and garden clubs as I pedaled the quiet avenue among peaceful, natural skyscrapers. The thick forest allowed little sunlight to penetrate. Fog clung to the branches and slid over the road often enough for the few cars to need lights. I particularly liked peeping into the forest when a ray of sun spotlit a bit of moss, a leaf, or a limb. Emerging into brilliant sunlight, we paused to watch a herd of elk placidly grazing in a meadow. Had we stepped back a hundred years?

After four and a half days off the bike, all symptoms of illness were gone, but I was weak. We halted at a motel in Orick forty-two miles south of Crescent City.

I read the National Park Service handouts, learning that the name "redwood" derives from the first description in Spanish, "*palo colorado*," meaning red trees. The coast redwood, *sequoia sempervirens*, lives to be about two thousand years old unless the wind blows it over. (The trees lack a taproot, and their broad, shallow root systems are sometimes inadequate.) A living tree has no known killing diseases, and insects cause no significant damage. Fire is its worst natural foe, but usually only to the young trees. On mature redwoods, the bark grows as much as a foot thick, protecting the tree from flames. From southern Oregon to Monterey, redwoods are found within thirty miles of the coast. Eons ago, in a warm and humid prehistoric climate, the redwood dominated much of the Northern Hemisphere, including what is now the Arctic. Now the coastal fog belt protects the remaining forests. Fog decreases the trees' loss of water through evaporation and transpiration and adds moisture to the soil.

In this area there is fog every morning which lasts until afternoon. When it burns off, another fog bank may move in before sunset. We had three to five hours of midday sun, when it wasn't raining.

Orick, Tuesday, October 28

We continued through the redwoods for 23 miles before stopping for lunch in a cafe among the trees. I was exhausted, and we agreed to make this a short day when we found a motel tucked among the redwoods at the edge of Trinidad. Our room had a kitchen. We could "camp" in a warm, dry tent!

That afternoon in Trinidad, we met Axel Lindgren, a Swedish-Irish-Indian. His grandmother was the last medicine woman of the Yurok tribe in a village near the Kalamath River. Axel was carving an eighteen-foot redwood canoe using only an ax and plane. Later, to hollow out the canoe, he would use an adz. He explained, "All chips are saved to burn the outside of the canoe, making it smooth to cut down resistance as it moves through the water." He told us about the community spirit of Indian villages. Whatever food was caught was shared by all. He felt one of the worst of the white man's inventions was the deep freeze.

"Why is that?" I inquired.

"Now, rather than sharing food, it is hoarded."

Trinidad, Wednesday, October 29

We had gone to sleep so early, before nine, so we were both wide awake at five-thirty. I began writing a letter while Bea fixed cream of wheat and orange juice. It was still pitch dark at five minutes to seven, so I continued writing.

Bea went out to inspect the weather. At seven ten it began to rain, hard. I saw no reason to depart, but Bea was ready to go. In preparing to leave, I couldn't find my rain pants, then I dropped my bike off the porch where it fell upside down in the mud.

As I headed out to Route 101, I realized I had never ridden a bike in such heavy rain. Even cars were pulling off the road. I was crying as hard as it was raining, and my stomach was doing flips. I rode for two hours non-stop to Eureka in the downpour. There I stopped at Debbies Donut, peeled off some of my wettest outer layers, and went inside for hot chocolate. Bea followed for coffee. As we drank, puddles collected under our feet. The rain stopped, and small patches of blue sky appeared here and there.

We were on the road again, stopping every now and then to admire the view. At the Hungry Hutch in Fortuna we ate lunch, and the ride to Scotia was increasingly pleasant. We passed a log heap that was over a mile long.

Dominating downtown Scotia were two buildings constructed entirely of redwood with columns made from trees across the front. Fancy wooden trim and ornamented doors decorated the buildings, which appeared old and had never been painted. The town of Scotia, owned by the Pacific Lumber Company, was obviously a company town. Its wooden look-alike houses were generally gray, and all grass was trimmed and edged to the same standard of excellence. After arranging to tour the sawmill early the next morning, we crossed the river to Del Rio and found a motel. Where was that California sun?

We decided to eat dinner in our motel room, and I went out to the phone booth. Mom told details of her mild heart attack, alone in the North Carolina mountains. I called the doctor, who counseled there was no cause for alarm and that I should continue the trip.

Del Rio, Thursday, October 30

I was up and out early. A lovely crescent moon hovered above the parking lot where I waited for Bea. It was pleasant, quiet, and uplifting.

We rode through the dark main street of Del Rio and across the river into Scotia, ate breakfast in a cafe, and were standing at the gate of the mill at seven-thirty when a loud whistle blast sounded and the mill came alive with activity. We stepped through the gate and began a self-guided tour, following yellow arrows painted on the floor and reading descriptive plaques on the walls and handrails. At the Bellingham Barker powerful jets of water removed the bark, sometimes six inches thick, from redwood and fir logs. This bark was carried by conveyor belt to another building where it was ground up and used as fuel to power the mill, to heat and light the town, and to make high-quality insulation.

The debarked logs slid out of a chute on a conveyor to a saw that cut them into twenty-foot lengths, which were snatched by metal fingers, rotated, and flung to the headrig where lengthwise cuts were made with a large bandsaw. Data on each log's dimensions and type were collected by the scaler. Using laser scanning devices and hydraulic lifts and jacks, the sawyer inspected and judged each log before each lengthwise cut. The sixty-foot headrig bandsaw was my favorite machine. I watched as slabs were cut from log after log and sent to the edgerman. From a glassed-in booth, the edgerman set circular saw blades to produce marketable grades and widths of lumber with the least amount of waste. These boards, up to twenty feet long, still needed to be trimmed to market lengths.

We walked on a catwalk overlooking twirling rollers that transferred the wood from place to place. As lumber emerged, men snatched it and wordlessly sorted it into high stacks of newborn planks. Elsewhere, boards slid down a conveyor to a sawyer perched on a cushioned stool before fifteen levers controlling fifteen circular saws. With fingers flying among the levers and his feet pushing and releasing pedals, he conducted a concerto for saws. We spent two hours on the self-guided tour. I easily could have started again and spent another two hours there. Instead, we looked at the fish-rearing pond built to rehabilitate the salmon and steelhead population in the Eel River that flows past the mills. The young steelhead spend almost a year in the pond before release into the Eel River for migration to the ocean. Most return in the third or fourth year to spawn. Steelhead, unlike salmon, do not die after spawning but return two or three times to lay eggs.

The pond fish are fed a special diet of "Oregon Moist Pellets" that comes in graduated sizes for each size fish. The pellets contain fish grain, kelp, and vitamin supplements for a nutritious, well-controlled diet. The pond (it looked like a tank to me) can accommodate one hundred thousand fish annually. Most of the land in the Humboldt Redwood State Park was formerly owned by The Pacific Lumber Company. It was held in trust for decades until funds were available for formal acquisition by the Save-the-Redwoods League for the State Park System. The Pacific Lumber Company is proud of its preservation of these mighty trees, and of its policies of balanced harvest and planting.

We turned off Highway 101 into Avenue of the Giants near Pepperwood, entering a thirty-three mile portion of road which winds along the Eel River through redwood groves. Through over a hundred miles redwood forest, we continued to see the sign "Live Burls." At Gwen's Shop, where live burls were grown, we stopped. Gwen explained, "Redwoods characteristically develop growths called burls, wart-like protrusions made up of dormant buds. For some reason, a bud will divide and redivide instead of growing into a branch. Occasionally this is caused by injury to the tree, but it is usually a natural occurrence. Many people purchase live burls that contain the living buds, ready to sprout and grow when placed in water. These can be kept in a dish as a house plant for several years. The burl can then be planted in soil where it will root and continue to grow."

We continued along the banks of the Eel River and entered Garberville. I noticed a greenhouse in a parking lot across the street. "I'd really like to look at that greenhouse. How about investigating the motels and pick one for us tonight?"

"O.K." Bea pedaled off.

Paul Johnson, who was marketing the Solar Prism Greenhouse, gave me a tour. Molded all in one piece and looking like a fiber-glass quonset hut, the structure absorbs light and heat on rainy, foggy, or overcast days. In summer, Paul assured me, it reflects excess light, and on very hot days, it helps keep things cool. Not being a gardener, I thought it would make a grand all-weather tent. It got dark as I followed Bea to the motel.

Garberville, Friday, October 31

At six a.m. Bea opened the door and stuck her head out for a weather report. Fog. We dressed hurriedly and walked to the Eel River Cafe, whose flashing neon sign showed a chef flipping pancakes. We were greeted by a witch-waitress with a pointed black hat, green face, silver eyelids, and jolly smile. The other waitress, in a pink negligee, nightgown, and hair curlers to match, inspired my laughing comment, "It didn't take you long to dress for work, did it?"

"It took an hour longer than usual," she giggled. "Normally I get up at five, today I had to begin at four to be dressed this way!"

Quite a novelty! I had never seen grown people costume themselves for Halloween. We didn't go to work at the CIA in costume. The cook, dressed as a gypsy, was writing "Happy Halloween" in orange and black on the white menu board. Other customers were joking and talking. They were the regulars, the morning news exchange service. After a jovial breakfast, we returned to the motel and pedaled out of Garberville at sunup.

We sailed down the Highway 101 freeway shoulder into a valley where a few remaining wisps of fog hung, then up the evenly graded hill on the other side. Going up the hill, my legs felt like old rubber bands. I was dizzy. Bea suggested a dose of sugar might help, and we stopped for Coke and coffee.

Everyone talks all the time to everyone else in California. During our brief time in the restaurant, we became acquainted with the owner, two people at the bar, and a couple from Malibu. Gene Abrams was selling NutriWheat and Apollo BioDrink, which is imported from Japan and is supposed to replace coffee, tea, cola, and alcohol. His wife was learning to be a psychological therapist. They took our photograph and gave us their address along with an invitation to call when we came through Malibu.

We rode on for some time before coming around a bend in the Eel River, shortly before Leggett, where there was a cafe with five logging trucks outside.

"This must be a good place," I shouted to Bea.

"Let's go," she flung over her shoulder.

Several drivers came out as I was taking off my helmet and gloves.

"What's your load?" asked T-shirt.

"I'm moving fast — carrying sailboat fuel," chuckled Sweat shirt.

One of the parked trucks carried wood chips. It looked like a normal eighteen-wheeler, except the trailer almost touched the ground between the wheels. Their soft tops and wire mesh rear doors ensure a lovely aroma, along with the biggest air blast of any truck I know. I usually could identify an approaching chip truck by its sound.

In the cafe, one young man sat on a counter stool. "Are you the chip truck driver?" I asked.

Smiling, he whirled around on his stool, and replied, "Yes. I'm Jim Smith."

I commented, "We've been passed by a lot of chip trucks and I'd like to compliment you drivers on your courtesy to bicyclists. I know it is work to haul a big truck like that around, but the drivers seem to give us as much space on the road as they can. That wind blast is horrid for us. Where do the chips go and what are they used for?"

"Wood chips are made from clean barkless scrap wood after lumber is manufactured at a sawmill. Clean chips are delivered to a paper mill. I'm carrying bark mixed with trash chips — knots, bark, and scrap wood run through the chip machine. This also goes to the paper mill where it is burned for fuel to run the mill. Any excess electricity is sold to Pacific Gas and Electric. Sometimes we carry shavings that are used to make pressboard or to make Prestologs by adding paraffin and sawdust under pressure. Now they are making pressboard logs."

Jim had a master's degree and had taught school but couldn't support his family as a teacher. He still coaches sports. He and the waitress were in the same high school class, and she runs an auto repair school for dropouts.

When Jim departed, we ordered and ate lunch. Other truckers at the next table talked in loud voices about how they hate bicyclists. They would have liked to eliminate them. Many bicyclists feel the same way about trucks.

We rode ups and downs before turning on Route 1, also known as Hollow Tree Road. Civilization was quickly left behind as we climbed into the mountains and headed for the coast. With this turn, we completed the two-hundred-mile northern section of the 1,019-mile bicycle route along the California coast. The five-hundred-mile midsection is characterized by secluded stretches of two-lane highway cut into the coastal cliffs. The road is steep and strenuous and the views are outstanding. This portion was highly recommended for bicyclists who have touring experience and are in shape. First, we had to climb Leggett Hill, over a thousand feet in four miles of switchbacks, our guidebook advised. I puffed and turned pedals for over an hour, admiring the views, delighted by the absence of traffic and the presence of warm sunlight. We drank most of our water and ate all of our fruit.

Then came a three-mile descent, a level mile or so, and an additional five-mile descent along Cottoneva Creek through three relatively flat miles, including the abandoned community of Rockport and its closed-for-the-season demonstration forest. We climbed again for two miles and were rewarded by a two-mile descent that ended on a bluff about fifty feet above the surf.

I reached the bluff first, and stopped. Bea pulled alongside. Exhilarated, we rummaged in our bags, looking for something to eat. Westport, where we hoped to find a motel, was five more miles. I expected the campgrounds to be closed like so many we had recently passed.

"Did we eat all of that fruitcake your mom sent?" asked Bea.

"Brilliant!" I shouted. I had forgotten it. In the bottom of my pannier were two pieces. I lay on my back, my head propped on my helmet, and watched a roughlegged hawk soar on the thermals as I nibbled fruitcake. The sun was shining brightly. What could be finer! It had been a perfect day: crystalline air, sun, trees, and car-less.

On the coast road, we passed rock formations in the surf, arch rocks, and grassy, treeless hillsides. The seascape scrolled by at ten to fifteen miles an hour until we entered Westport, a weathered coastal village on steep bluffs. We rolled to a stop before an inn. Three signs announced, "Closed," but a gray-haired woman stood in the open door. Bea yelled, "Can we get a motel room in this town?"

"Right here," came the welcome response. We entered and were shown such a lovely room we asked, "Can we afford to stay here?" The owner, Thelma, laughed and quoted an off-season price less than we expected. She had been away on vacation until two days ago and added, "The restaurant isn't open, but I'm making soup if you want some for supper and I'll do breakfast for the lodgers. Split pea soup will be ready in about an hour."

Walking toward our room, Bea observed, "Two hours — let's go to the grocery." She was accurate almost to the minute. I acquired a lesson in how the laid-back California attitude readjusts all clocks. As a stop-gap, I drank a quart of orange juice and Bea a quart of chocolate milk to wash down Irish oatmeal cookies and Fritos.

Thelma had severe arthritis and needed my help in replacing a light bulb before we sat down to soup, hot bread, and fresh carrot salad with her and Alex, another guest. Throughout dinner, Thelma greeted by name each Halloween ghost and goblin child who came to the door as she dropped candies in their bags. We admired them silently. Among visits by trick-or-treaters, we learned that Westport, a town of a hundred people, recently installed a million-dollar water system and sent a local boy to school to learn how to operate it. Thelma, a sixteen-year resident, and two other women run the Westport Inn and Bakery. The seven people she hires make her the largest industry in town, she told us, a smile on her face and a "Sweet Grandma" necklace showing through her open-necked shirt.

Fed and sleepy, each with a handful of trick-or-treat candy, we went off to bed.

Westport, Saturday, November 1

Just after sunup, which wasn't early by our standards, we cleaned our bikes and put our clothes in the motel washer and dryer.

At breakfast, I learned that Alex, newly graduated from college, was touring the country by car. He was interested in our bike trip and suggested we stop and camp at his parents' home in Sunshine, Maine. He gave me elaborate directions, drew a map, and quite seriously said if we didn't go to Sunshine, we hadn't seen Maine. He would arrive in San Francisco tonight. Since the nights were too cold and damp for us to camp between here and San Francisco, I asked Alex to take our tent, kitchen panniers, and sleeping bags in his car and leave them with our friends to await our arrival. He readily agreed. Each of our loads would be about fifteen pounds lighter for the hilly trip to San Francisco. We still would carry about twenty pounds each (the bike shop, the cameras, and a few clothes). We previously lightened our load by mailing a fourteen-pound box to San

Francisco. Arthur and Cynthia Leeper, our hosts there, were receiving us as houseguests one piece at a time.

By midmorning, we put the chains back on our bikes, hung our reduced loads on the racks, and rolled out of Westport. I wistfully thought of sitting on the terrace drinking coffee and talking as long as I liked, were I alone. Instead, I drank in sun and sights while our wheels rolled.

There was hardly a cloud in the brilliant blue sky except along the horizon where a few flat ribbons hung above the blue of the sea that merged into emerald along the beach. A large chevron formation of ducks flying south skimmed above the breaking waves. I could hardly watch where I was going for looking seaward, yet the smell of eucalyptus trees roped me to the land as I rode past. I felt both relaxed and energized.

Soon we were rolling down Main Street in Fort Bragg, named for Confederate General Braxton Bragg. We passed its sawmill, stopped to look at trees in the Georgia-Pacific nursery, and found splendid turkey sandwiches at Egghead Omelettes. When Bea went to find the restroom, she followed directions through the kitchen, across a courtyard, along a brick walkway to an outhouse. It was padlocked! She returned to the table laughing and suggested I not drink any more water.

Our ride continued among yellow California poppies and Scotch broom until we passed the turn off to Mendocino and stopped to see it from an overlook across the water. Mendocino began with a rough cabin built by a shipwrecked traveler in 1851. Now it is a well-known artists colony with restored New-England-style architecture, seen on the TV series "Murder, She Wrote." At the overlook, I noticed a car from Georgia, my native state. Although I hadn't lived there since I was eleven, I consider myself a Georgian, so I spoke with Lee and Virginia Howard from Smyrna.

We thoroughly enjoyed the ride along the cliffs but by three o'clock, it was getting cold and we decided to stop. We passed the Albion River Inn which looked expensive. There was no other accommodation, so we returned and got the last "garden" room, happily accepting apologies that there was no view, for the room was bright and the price was lower. On a high bluff, the view from the inn overlooked the sea and the river. We made reservations for dinner and drank complimentary wine delivered to our room. "Some bicycle tour," we laughed! After our showers we strolled around the bluff and garden admiring the sunset beyond the sea. There were several Anna's humming birds and blooming flowers in the garden.

We donned formal dress for dinner — long black pants and black, long-sleeved jersey for me and long black tights with a brilliant red jersey for Bea. I didn't feel particularly out of place. In California, anything goes. As we were seated by the head waiter, both of us giggled about the luxurious tablecloth, big cloth napkins, goblets, a wine steward, all the trimmings of an elegant dinner. We were starving. Dinner was a three hour event — much too long for us. We began to nod and almost fell asleep before the food arrived. I enjoyed the wood fire, candlelight, and piano music, but neither of us would have eaten such rich food had we been less hungry or had an alternative. During the night, our digestive systems were stressed by the rich food and the wine, and by eating so much so late in the day.

Albion, Sunday, November 2

For the second day in a row, the sun rose gloriously without fog or mist. In spite of heavy fatigue I was pulled outside by the fresh, salt-tinged air.

We laughed at a "llama crossing" sign and were soon moving slowly across the intricate wooden bridge over the Albion River. The Inn chef didn't cook breakfast on Sunday morning, and I was hungry. Ten miles of riding beside fields where sheep grazed placidly brought us to the thriving hamlet of Elk where a grocery provided us with coffee and sweet rolls. People came for Sunday newspapers while we rested near the storefront. Everyone greeted us.

Wheeling southward, we saw dairy herds roaming farmlands. Our road cut through these pastures bounded by oceanside cliffs and inland forests of redwood and fir. When we rolled from the bluff-top pastures down into Point Arena, a tiny, friendly city, I was exhausted.

After lunch at a health food restaurant, we registered at a motel, where our neighbors were abalone fishermen. They hung their wet suits in the sun and charcoal-broiled chicken in the parking lot. We inspected a ten-inch abalone shell and learned the fishermen pry them loose with an abalone bar used like a crowbar.

I took to bed.

Point Arena, Monday, November 3

The next morning, I stayed in bed and ate leftovers, while Bea went out for coffee. By nine o'clock, Bea, incredulous that I wasn't up, decided to go for a ride to see the lighthouse and museum. I wanted to go to the beach and see the lighthouse, too, but I knew I needed rest. When Bea came back, we went to lunch at the cafe and then I returned to nap and plan our trip south of San Francisco. She brought turkey sandwiches back to the room for supper.

Point Arena, Tuesday, November 4

When we got up, Bea decided we should leave before breakfast, so we ate the remains of a sandwich, split an apple, and rolled along. Ten miles of riding would bring us to Gualala for breakfast, I hoped. We rode far apart and I reveled in the solitude.

Along the way, we were studied by a black-tailed deer before it bounded out of sight. Loons fished in the Gualala River and hawks and vultures soared. I watched the long roll of fog draped over the sea, coloring it gray. Off to the left, the sun climbed higher. By the time we reached Gualala (like Point Arena, a town of about five hundred), a long, gray-blue cloud had expanded high over the sea.

At breakfast, someone said, "You must be the last of the bicyclists." We were certainly at the end of the season. We were told that people refer to Point Arena as "funky," Gualala as "artsy-crafty," and Sea Ranch as "resorty." Refueled, we continued. I watched the fog rolling, boiling, drifting, twisting, and turning like smoke as we pedaled through patches with droplets I could actually see.

Shortly after midday, we turned into Fort Ross State Historic Park under brilliant sun. In spring, 1812, ninety-five Russians and forty-nine native Alaskans came ashore here and built houses and a sturdy wooden fort—the village and fortress of Ross. They came to hunt for sea otter, soon depleted, and stayed to grow wheat and other crops for the Russian settlements in Alaska and to trade with Spanish California. Trade between the Californios and the Russians technically was illegal, but the Californios were as eager to sell grain as the Russians were to buy it.

When the Russians decided to leave California they tried, but failed, to sell Ross to the Mexican government. In 1841, John Sutter of Sutter's Fort in the Sacramento Valley removed the abandoned arms and ammunition, as well as herds of cattle and sheep, to his Sacramento domain. On land Sutter acquired from the Russians, gold was found that began the Gold Rush to California.

As we rode away from Fort Ross, Highway 1 followed the coastline. At times, the road was just inches from a precipitous, plunging ravine, with angry surf gnawing furiously at the base. Many hills were steep, and I marshaled my strength, coaxing my loaded bike over the crests. Straining up demanding hills, then careening down around hairpin curves, I pedaled furiously to gain momentum to attack the next hill. Up and down we went, constantly challenged and then rewarded — swooping down, shouting with exhilaration, the surf roaring like a freight train. Cobwebs glistened in the early morning sunlight, and we were draped with long gossamers. Clad in a brilliant orange shirt and black pants, I reminded Bea of a kite sailing down the road with a tail of cobwebs streaming behind. Often, a lone cypress tree overlooked the ocean, gnarled, distorted by the constant wind, indomitable as the early settlers. To our left were brown, lumpy hills speckled with sheep; to our right was the Pacific, as blue as the sky. A dream-like veil of mist wandered from surf to land and, as we rode through it, I felt magically charged. Gone was my fervor to reach the next city and the next. We paused. Siren-like, the mist whispered, "Stay." Like Ulysses, Bea felt smitten.

Hunger brought us back to the mundane world — we found a snack in our bags and moved on. The fog closed in as we pedaled quietly through Jenner, a town of seventy people, and continued through gradual darkness to Bodega Bay. The fog thickened to mist, then rain. Cold, wet, and hungry, we tumbled into a motel room.

Bodega, Wednesday, November 5

The morning light was gray. I went along at a comfortable pace. Bea was out of sight ahead. At the turn off to Inverness I met two men on bicycles. They knew the area well and advised me to stay on Route 1 because, without a fog bank, it would be prettier than the alternate route inland and traffic would be about the same. I enjoyed the contact with bicyclists and their interest in our tour.

An hour or so later, I came upon Bea sitting on a log watching ducks, eating crackers and cheese. I joined her and began to munch. We were looking across a smaller bay just south of Drake's Bay. I calculated we had seventeen miles to reach the Golden Gate Bridge. It was clear now and should be a spectacular ride. We began to climb, and I didn't overtake Bea until the outskirts of Sausalito.

The grading and repair of the highway was poor. Rock slides had wiped out the road so often its surface was a patchwork of textures between tight hairpin curves. The lack of shoulder was complemented by a lack of traffic. Occasionally I glimpsed Bea, over a mile ahead and high above me as I inched up the cliffs, improving my view of the Pacific with each crank of the pedals. At the top, at the pass on Mt. Tamalpais, I looked one last time seaward, knowing there would be bay rather than ocean vistas for the next few days. I scanned the sky, which was graying with incoming fog, and then swirled joyously down five miles of hairpin turns into Sausalito, taking deep breaths when I went under the eucalyptus trees and admiring the homes.

Bea stopped to put on another shirt. It was getting darker, damper, and cold. We continued together. I had to find the bike path and guide us through the city. Finally, we saw the tall orange towers of the Golden Gate Bridge rising ahead. Bea was hungry, but there was no time to stop, for we were already racing the sunset. Darkness would come in about an hour and a half. We would probably take two or more hours to reach the Leepers' home if we kept moving steadily and I didn't get lost. Bea was frightened at the prospect of riding over the bridge during rush hour. My concern was whether or not I could find the bridge! I did. Crossing, we rode side by side.

"Isn't this wonderful? We are two feet above that horrendous traffic," Bea sang out. Then she read the sign, "Caution cyclists: Gale Force Winds May Occur."

"Jane, we'll be blown off the bridge!"

"Not if you stay on your bike. It's heavier than you are." A hundred yards further the wind strengthened and became so cold that we stopped and put on our rain jackets. The brilliant yellow was probably a good idea in the fading light, anyway. We rode slowly, dodging the pedestrians. It was hard to balance and travel slowly enough to savor the quiet inner joy and exhilaration of accomplishment that I felt.

At the end of the bridge, I studied the direction of the bike path. As long as it went downhill and generally to the left I would follow it. All the cars had their headlights on, but it wasn't completely dark yet. Bea followed, quite slowly. Sometimes she dropped out of sight, and I'd wait. When she appeared, I set off again immediately, allowing no opportunity for talk. Food was at the end of the ride.

I went ahead, and stopped and asked a woman where Bay Street was. It was one block away — fine. We rode along Bay Street, and after finding the house I leaned my bike against the door and began walking back to help Bea. Apparently dizzy and sick, she was pedaling toward me. We rang the bell shortly after five.

Arthur Leeper ran down the stairs and gave me a bear hug. I was delighted to see him. He stowed the bikes in the garage hallway and we carried our clothes panniers upstairs. Our sleeping bags were already here. Slumped in a chair in the kitchen, Bea ate crackers, cheese, water, milk, and coffee while Arthur cooked chicken for dinner and we chatted. As soon as his wife, Cynthia, came he served dinner and we continued talking. Bea, revived by food and liquid and stimulated by people, concurred that I had not exaggerated when I told her how nice Arthur and Cynthia were.

I felt very much at home spreading my mattress and sleeping bag on a beautiful old Tibetan Rug. Bea lay down and fell asleep immediately. Perhaps it was the seventy-three miles, or the glory of the scenery, or the cold weather, or the warm reception, or cumulative fatigue that delayed my falling asleep. I was thrilled and incredulous that I had ridden from Detroit to San Francisco on my bicycle.

San Francisco, Thursday, November 6

Bea marveled at the houses perched precariously on steep hillsides. "Modern cliff dwellers inhabit this city," she announced as we climbed aboard a cable car. She was fascinated by Chinatown, so we got off. "It must be as large as Dayton, just Chinatown."

My fun was in wandering a step behind to see what caught her eye. Having lived in Singapore and traveled to Southeast Asia, I felt at home in Chinatown. Bea wandered into a shop with window displays of plucked, flattened ducks and whole chickens dripping fat off their tails, legs, and wings. We devoured huge bowls of hot rice soup with pork meatballs. Much of the day, we rode the cable cars.

We wandered into the Wells Fargo exhibits in the bank headquarters. My favorite was a simulator for driving six horses. I sat on a box, placed my feet in braces, and pulled on the weighted leather reins while Bea exclaimed about simulated stagecoach motions. Gold dust, nuggets, and various types of rock embedded with gold were displayed. We walked around a Concord stagecoach which carried eighteen passengers, nine inside and nine on the roof, on the Great Overland Mail Routes from Montana to Mexico and from the Mississippi River to the Pacific Coast. As I looked at the stage, I thought about riding across Nepal from Pokahara to Kathmandu on the roof of a bus with dozens of passengers. My, how comfortable that was compared to riding on the roof of a stagecoach!

In midafternoon, cumulative fatigue hit. I suddenly lost interest in everything except lying down. We returned to the Leepers' exhausted. We invited them out to dinner, but were overjoyed when they suggested that we pay, they cook, and we eat at home. The salmon was perfect, but starved as we were for vegetables, their salads were life-giving tonic.

I had decisions to make about the rest of the trip, mail to answer, a joint letter to write, and, most importantly, I still hungered for "down" time. Cynthia would be away at work on Friday, and Arthur had things to do away from the house most of the day, though his office was at home. They would be attending an all-day function on Saturday. We decided to leave early Sunday morning, to give them the day at home together and bicycle through the metropolitan area on Sunday morning in the least congested traffic of the week.

San Francisco, November 7, 8

I climbed up to the roof where I spent some time looking over the city and harbor, writing. Bea talked with her daughter, Beth, and yielded to pressure to get home for Thanksgiving, so we discarded thoughts of taking the train across the country. I made reservations for us to fly out of San Diego on November 25 and to return to San Diego on January 31. Bea's first grandchild was due to arrive the first week in January. My mother was not doing well, and I wanted to spend time with her. With the whole of January, I could also complete my income taxes, have everything ready to mail, and forget about the IRS for the rest of the year.

As we cleaned our bicycles and I cooked my chain, we talked and agreed to stay in motels the rest of the month, for few campgrounds were still open. A few friends on the route south had invited us to stop over and, theoretically, we could travel faster with lighter loads. We sent the tent and most of the kitchen equipment in a box to my friends Homer and Dorothy Shaw in San Diego. For many years I had treasured the friendship of John and Homer Shaw and their wives, Janet and Dorothy. John and Janet lived near my home in Washington, D.C., while Homer visited when business travel brought him to the East Coast. Sometimes Dorothy came, also. Dorothy and Homer often invited me to San Diego, but none of us envisaged me arriving on a bicycle. They agreed to store our bikes in their garage for December and January and help us get launched on the second part of our journey.

Satisfaction soared as decisions were made, tickets and reservations settled, and letters containing our plans were mailed to our families. We completed our preparations and washed our clothes. Three days hardly had been time to re-group and revive, and we hadn't seen as much of the city as we would have liked.

We recalled earlier parts of our journey for the Leepers and talked about how we felt like Alice, opening doors to new lands with unique languages. In North Dakota and Montana, we were entranced with grain and farming. We enjoyed a private concert and became acquainted with the logging indus-try. We watched fish harvested in rivers, lakes, and the ocean by people, seals, and sea otters, and saw whales blow and swim. Scraps of local history had stimulated us. We'd learned much in four thousand miles of bicycle travel, and agreed that what we'd noticed and understood represented one grain in a fifty-pound bag of rice.

San Francisco, Sunday, November 9

Cynthia and Arthur fixed breakfast for us, then sat on the steps while we hung the panniers on our bikes and checked our gloves, helmets, and maps. Lovingly sent off, we made our way slowly, enjoying the city while most motorists were home in bed. We proceeded to Golden Gate Park where we rode like other Sunday bicyclists, side by side, talking of our delightful and comfortable visit with our San Francisco hosts.

Two hours of leisurely bicycling took us to Daly City where we climbed a hill high enough to provide a fine overview of San Francisco, including the tops of the Golden Gate Bridge towers. Beside us, the houses were an asymmetrical pile of children's blocks stacked up the hillside, with a plate glass window where the alphabet letter should be. The coast road with a good shoulder stretched before us. A tail wind reached out, our legs warmed up, and we whirred along.

After stopping at Montara for toast and orange juice, we pedaled along Half Moon Bay, watching a couple ride horses in the surf. We passed large greenhouses and a field of pumpkins. Hills rolled by on our left, and the shining sea spread endlessly on our right. Turning inland, we rode through cultivated land. First, I noticed miles of fields with the largest ferny plants I had ever seen. Eventually, I recognized artichokes at the ends of stalks atop the plants, like flowers. A plant with cabbage-like leaves growing off a three foot stalk turned out to be Brussels sprouts. A crew harvesting them cut the ripe stalks, shearing off the leaves in one operation and the sprouts in another. Leaves and stalks were strewn about the field while a conveyor belt hoisted the sprouts into the air and dropped them into a truck. In stores near the fields, three-foot stalks without leaves but with all the Brussels sprouts still attached were for sale.

Shortly after noon, we stopped on an overlook to watch surfers, pelicans, and a hang glider take off as we ate sandwiches and apples. Directly overhead was a multicolored hang glider twisting and turning like a huge kite. The pilot, his legs encased in a cover like a sleeping bag, resembled a soaring wasp. We could hear the wind blowing his jacket sleeves. A flock of determined sea gulls flew beside him, turning as the glider turned. He came in for a landing, just missing the utility wires over our heads, swooped up, and then turned around for another try. Finally, he tilted the brilliantly colored wing to rest. The show over, our sandwiches gone, we mounted our bikes.

Homer Shaw had told me I should call and meet his sister, Joan McIntosh, and her husband, Mac, who live in Santa Cruz. I have a mild phobia about telephoning, so I put off calling Joan and Mac on the pretext that I didn't know when we would reach Santa Cruz. About one o'clock I spotted a phone booth. We had already cycled fifty-five miles and were pleasantly tired, but the day was too fine to halt. Santa Cruz was about thirty miles ahead. Joan answered the phone and invited us for dinner. I looked at my watch, expressed some uncertainty, and then agreed. When she asked where we would stay, I replied, "In a motel."

"We live in a mobile home park, but we have a small motor home. You could sleep in that if you want." Delighted by the prospect, I accepted.

We hurried over pleasantly rolling terrain to reach the McIntosh home before dark. I just couldn't keep up with Bea. She wasn't going any faster than usual. My bike just wouldn't go. Twice I got off and looked it over. I carried one pannier and two sleeping bags; Bea carried two panniers; nothing was rubbing. I couldn't figure it out. Finally Bea rode beside me, then behind, then alongside, inspecting my bike. Then laughed, "You're riding with your brakes on! No wonder you're tired and can't keep up." We adjusted my rear brakes — one brake pad had gotten stuck against the wheel rim. I must have gone ten miles that way, too tired to figure out the problem. When I got on the bike again, it was like riding downhill with a new pair of legs.

We found the McIntosh home just as darkness was thickening. As we leaned our bikes against the motor home, a neighbor approached.

"Are you looking for someone?" he asked.

"Yes, the McIntoshes said they would be home from church soon. They're expecting us."

"Right, just checking. We look out for each other here, you know."

Our hosts returned and scooped us inside for dinner as though we were long-lost daughters. It was Joan who coined the phrase, "gentle California weather," which typified the day and the kindness that enfolded us.

Santa Cruz, Monday, November 10

We had kept our sleeping bags, planning to sleep over-night at a hostel in a lighthouse. Mac warned us that during fall and winter, homeless people usually fill the hostels. Low night-time temperatures, closed campgrounds, and decreasing day-light confined us to motels. We now had five or six fewer hours of daylight per day than at the beginning of our trip.

During a convivial breakfast, we planned to meet in

February south of San Diego where Mac and Joan would be spending some time in their camper. We talked about traveling together from there to New Mexico, Arizona, and, perhaps, as far as Big Bend National Park.

By eight, we were on the road, overlooking Monterey Bay. Our route to Capitola was rolling, pleasant, without steep hills. Now the traffic was farm trucks carrying vegetables and fruits instead of eighteen-wheelers with logs or lumber or chips. Vehicles were expensive German imports instead of American sedans. Two-seater sports cars replaced two-seater pickups. Sun finally had displaced rain and fog.

We went on to Aptos where Cats Incredible Cafe caught our eye. Bea was suddenly thirsty for coffee. She was uncharacteristically tired and found reasons to stop about every fifteen minutes. In spite of the recent social care and feeding, we were short on reserve energy and stamina. The forty-three miles from Santa Cruz to Seaside exhausted Bea, so we ducked into a motel for long naps before supper.

Seaside, Tuesday, November 11

I realized it was Veterans Day when we discovered all the eateries were closed. Finally, we found a snack at Red's Donut Shop near the limits of Monterey, a city curled around the bay. We followed a smooth bike path as wide as a small highway along the bay, spurred on by the sea lions' barking.

We watched the sea otters wrap themselves in kelp as they sunned and fed themselves. On the wharf, we indulged in omelets at The Cove Restaurant where we watched the gulls and pelicans through a wall of plate glass while a fire crackled nearby.

On we went past John Steinbeck's Cannery Row, the former sardine cannery now a shopping mall. In a park full of flowers and hummingbirds I watched a ground squirrel with a spotted coat near a statue of the monarch butterfly. It was an ideal place from which to look upon Monterey Bay. I would have preferred to spend ten days on those ten miles around Monterey Bay, instead of three hours.

A tailwind propelled us through even more spectacular scenery. We passed a golf course where one deer stood observing the players and another slept in a sand trap. At Sea Lions' Rock, we stopped to watch sea lions and pelicans fishing, and the people who watched the animals. A ground squirrel took its head out of a clear plastic cup it was licking to watch me. Through my binoculars, the sea lions looked black or silver gray when wet and shining tan as they dried in the sun.

A sign on 17-Mile Drive warned that bicycles must detour, so we missed Pebble Beach and got sweaty hauling ourselves over Spy Glass Hill, Ronda Road, and Sunridge Road to Highway 1. I adored the homes and views. Our feet cranked us to the top of the hill and we flew down the other side straight into Carmel. As we opened a restaurant door, Bea said, "Sorry, I'm just no ball of fire today." Sleeping all afternoon yesterday and twelve hours last night hadn't revived her.

I was fit, the weather grand, and I had to keep a rein on myself not to be impatient. I reminded myself how I felt when I was tired and wanted to rest. "We have the whole afternoon to spend at Point Lobos State Reserve, only a few miles from here. Joan and Mac insisted it's the number-one must-see place on the whole California coast. We'll take our time." After a relaxed and restful lunch and few miles of pedaling, we arrived at Point Lobos named after the Spanish *lobo marino*, sea wolf or seal.

We got off our bikes at an information station and walked along the Sea Lion Point Trail. Bea admitted, "The sore throat is worse, and all I can think of is that I want to lie down." She did lie down on a rock in the sun, for a while. Singing sparrows perched in the bushes, and the ground squirrels scurried everywhere. After a few minutes, Bea sat up and began to look through her binoculars for sea otters among the kelp. Harbor seals basking among the rocks were easy to see. The crashing of the waves was drowned out by the sound of the sea lions' barking. We joined a walking tour along the Cypress Grove Trail. On the guano-covered rocks were pelagic and Brandt's cormorants, brown pelicans, gulls, and murres. Beechy ground squirrels, like prairie dogs with fluffy tails, popped up here and there, while Sister Anna Voss explained that "having taught science for fifty years, a little bit of it stuck." She pointed out a two-foot-high mound of twigs — the nest of a dusty wood rat. This rat collects shiny objects, and Sister Anna found a hoard of smashed aluminum cans in one nest.

Overhead was one of two naturally-growing stands of Monterey cypress trees remaining on earth. (The other stand is across Carmel Bay on Cypress Point.) It was to save the cypress that this park was originally reserved. Around on the north-facing slopes, a reddish velvety alga was especially noticeable on trees and rocks. There was a delicate lace lichen bearding dead understory limbs. The alga and lichen do not harm the trees.

During part of the tour we were accompanied by a phoebe flycatcher. Sister Anna completed our tour by pointing out two contrasting rock types that dominate the reserve: Santa Lucia granite, a coarse-grained igneous rock that solidified one hundred ten million years ago, and the Carmelo formation, a sedimentary rock at least sixty million years old.

Bea was feeling worse than ever. We went back three miles to a motel on the Carmel River, where she went to sleep at once. Since our room had a small kitchen, I went to the Safeway. After dinner, Bea went back to sleep at seven, and I was asleep by eight. We had crammed a lot of sights into twenty-eight miles of bicycling.

Carmel, Wednesday, November 12

Pedaling south across the Carmel River, I knew we had a longer day than we could handle to reach San Simeon, almost a hundred miles away on a road that included steep, long hills. They would be our last on the coast.

Point Sur, a miniature Gibraltar connected by a sliver of land to the precipitous coastline, was our favorite view in a day of spectacular scenery. Dulled somewhat to the beauty by our hard day and Bea's continuing sore throat, we wheeled into the forest to the town of Big Sur. We had expected a surf-side town. Big Sur is located along scenic Highway 1 approximately one hundred fifty miles south of San Francisco and three hundred miles north of Los Angeles. Historically, the name Big Sur described the unexplored and unmapped wilderness along the coast south of Monterey — *El Sur Grande,* the Big South. Today, Big Sur is the ninety-mile stretch of rugged coastline between Carmel and San Simeon. Highway 1 is flanked on one side by the majestic Santa Lucia Mountains and on the other by the rocky Pacific Coast.

Coffee, cherry tarts, and information from the Big Sur River Inn store fueled our continued pedaling uphill. With hardly a breath for speaking, we pedaled on as fast as we could, covering the thirty miles to Lucia in about two hours. There we lunched on sandwiches and learned the Sea View Motel had a vacant room, but it was too early to stop. We already had done fifty hard miles.

Off we went uphill. The afternoon sun, a headwind, and more hills drained our remaining energy. Finally, too exhausted to ride the flat country we reached, we agreed to catch a ride and got off our bikes. Two young people from Colorado took us aboard their pickup for the fifteen miles to the San Simeon motel complex. Sitting in the truck bed with our backs to the wind, we exclaimed over the mountains turning purple. It was dark on the road, and the last flecks of rose disappeared into the Pacific as we hopped out at a motel.

San Simeon, Thursday, November 13

In the morning, we lay in bed listing our aches: wrists, fingers, palms, toes, feet, seats, legs, arms, and knees. Soon we became convulsed with laughter that we were "all stove up."

Cycling three miles to the castle entrance, we saw hawks and the Hearst estate zebra in a pasture with cattle. We learned about family history, the gardens, and the architecture on the tour. I noted the blue and white Chinese bathroom carpets and the words "San Simeon" incorporated in a copper gutter design. After two morning tours, we cycled "home" for lunch.

I read, washed gloves and socks, and adjusted my bike. The fog bank rolled in, resting gently on the other side of Highway 1 until sunset. Bea, who felt "ratty" and "no ball of fire," slept all afternoon.

San Simeon, Friday, November 14

Bea wasn't fully recovered when we left San Simeon and rode into San Luis Obispo where we ate brunch. Afterwards Bea felt sick and attributed her condition to the chili we ate. Turning inland on country roads provided a welcome change from the seascapes. We went through Corbit Canyon and the Nipomo Valley, spinning along with few stops, past Victorian homes and miles of Arabian and Apaloosa horse ranches. The names Bee Canyon, Deer Canyon, and Badger Canyon Roads appealed to me. We came to rest at the Motel 6 in Santa Maria about four o'clock. Bea went immediately to bed.

Santa Maria, Saturday, November 15

The next morning, our road sliced in straight cuts and right angle turns through fields of red peppers, beans, and other vegetables, and past the city dump. We rode about twenty miles through Foxen Canyon, a dry, narrow valley, with sparse vegetation and a few oak trees. For several days, we had smelled licorice from a six foot high weed, perhaps wild anise. Whenever we rode through eucalyptus groves, I came out refreshed by the aroma. We passed grape arbors and red Brangus, white Brahma, and long and short horn cattle which looked like they had bicycle handlebars on their heads. The animals looked blankly at us. I stopped to observe an acorn woodpecker in some oak trees. As I looked around me, I just couldn't imagine anything on earth that I would rather be doing than this bicycle trip.

As I rode along, a couple of dogs dashed out a farm gateway and chased me. One dog's teeth caught my heavy wool sock and broke the skin on my leg. We rode a half mile or so, until I got close enough to yell at Bea to stop. We looked at the bite; the skin was barely broken and the scrape was cleaning itself by bleeding. We went back to be sure the dogs were inoculated. No one was home, so I copied the car tag numbers and noted the mile post nearest the house. There was no name on the mailbox and nothing inside the box to tell me who lived there. The dogs had flea collars and were obviously pets. We rode a mile or so and stopped to clean the wound. I washed it with Joy (our bathing, clothes, and hair soap) rinsed it from my water bottle, then doused it with merthiolate.

Charmed by the town of Los Olives, we stopped for lunch, but Bea didn't eat much. We proceeded past Lake Cachuma along the San Marcos Pass Road. In an hour, the four-mile climb to the top sapped all our strength. Soaring from the pass to Santa Barbara, I was pleased to pilot us to the home of my friend Jean Tanyhill at Samarkand, a retirement community, without mistake or detour. Delighted to see us, Jean had reserved a guest suite for us for two nights.

In spite of Bea's feeling sick, we had completed one hundred forty miles in the two days since San Simeon. Throughout the Pacific Coast one or the other of us had suffered symptoms of extreme fatigue: diarrhea, headaches, stomach upset, aching muscles, and inability to sleep. Jean and I chatted while I soaked in the hot tub before dinner. We hadn't seen each other for years, so there was a lot of catching up to do. Bea and I were both tired and went to bed not long after dinner and a splendid sunset punctuated by Santa Barbara's twinkling lights.

Santa Barbara, Sunday, November 13

Bea felt worse, so Jean and I went to breakfast. Although I took her a meal, Bea only sipped the orange juice. We were certain she had a high fever. She insisted on sleeping most of the morning and didn't want medical help.

Jean and I toured the delightful gardens, dining area, pool, and living quarters at Samarkand. The people we met at every turn were hospitable and seemed cheered that two women not much younger than themselves were doing a bicycle trip.

Jean wanted to drive us around Santa Barbara. Bea got up to go with us, though she said she felt faint. We drove along the shore and had a splendid, relaxed lunch at the Moby Dick Restaurant on the wharf. Later, we also toured the Santa Barbara County Courthouse, which has been called America's most beautiful public building. I was too tired and Bea too sick to excel as tourists, but Jean's guiding was sensitive, and I absorbed a great deal.

When we returned, Bea called her sister, and asked her to come the next morning to take us to her home in Northridge, near Los Angeles. Bea felt too ill to ride a bicycle. She went back to bed.

I quizzed Jean about earthquakes. I had never been in one. Jean is a fire warden and worries more about fire, which can sweep through a canyon in an unbelievably short time, than about earthquakes. She is supposed to have an earthquake kit ready for evacuation, but she doesn't. She does keep four gallons of water in plastic jugs, a flashlight, and boxes of food ready. She also has an oil lamp filled and ready to light. "Here, no one talks or bothers about an earthquake. It will come. We can't worry about it," she told me.

Santa Barbara, Monday, November 17

Bea was up and down a lot during the night and feverish. Bea's sister Elsie arrived just before lunch with her friend Mildred. I disassembled the bikes and put them in the rear of the station wagon, piled the panniers around the frames, and tucked the wheels on top. We said our goodbyes to Jean.

It seemed hard for Bea to sit up on the drive, and she lay down on the sofa as soon as we reached Elsie's home. We had planned three to seven days to stop over with Elsie and explore the Los Angeles area. We expected Bea to recover with rest and being with her family. After napping during the afternoon, she rallied during dinner, telling her family and their friends stories of our adventure. Everyone suggested something we must see and offered to take us. People dropped by or checked in by phone, delighted that Bea came to visit. The welcome gave Bea quite a boost.

Northridge, Tuesday, November 18

When I awoke at five-thirty, Bea was doubled over in a knot. She said, "I was up a lot during the night. Maybe I have appendicitis." By nine, Elsie had not been able to reach the doctor.

"Is there a hospital near here?" I asked Elsie.

"Yes, quite a good one, not far."

"Then, come on! If it's appendicitis we can't wait." Bea agreed immediately, and we piled into the car and headed for the hospital. Bea was admitted, examined within an hour, and operated on a couple of hours later. Her appendix had ruptured. She would have to stay in the hospital until Sunday so the incision could drain. Our tickets home for Thanksgiving were for Monday evening.

I had not expected to see much of Los Angeles through the smog. I expected to find a busy, crowded city stuffed with cars. Instead, it seemed spacious. Buildings were not so tall and traffic wasn't all that bad. It seemed everyone in California came from somewhere else. I wondered if that was why people were so friendly. "Where did you live in Georgia?" I asked Elsie.

"Fitzgerald. It's a mill town in the southern part of the state. I lived there sixteen years. My husband was killed in a motorcycle accident."

"I lived in Columbus until I was eleven. What did you do in the mill?"

"We both worked there. I had different jobs and raised my kids." Elsie also talked about her parents and about Bea."I'm the oldest, then came our three brothers. I'm ten years older than Bea. After three brothers, you can imagine how delighted I was to have a little sister. She was premature. Everyone thought she wouldn't live. She was so small her first diapers were Father's handkerchiefs. She was always Mother's favorite, but she was my favorite too. Bea was a live doll for me. I adored her, still do."

At Elsie's house we called Bea's daughter, Beth, to tell her about the operation and that we had sent flowers to Bea with all her children's names on the card.

I liked Elsie; her traces of Georgia accent made me feel at home. She reminded me of my Aunt Katie in her compassion, patience, and humor. As we sat down to supper, Elsie told a story of her childhood. She didn't understand why she wasn't permitted to play with a neighbor child who was half-Indian. She was lonely. "Perhaps that, too, contributed to my joy at receiving a little sister." As I bit into turnip greens, cooked the Georgia way, I complimented the cook. Who would have thought I'd feel so at home with Elsie?

I had trouble staying awake long enough to phone my mother to tell her I would arrive the Tuesday before Thanksgiving, a week earlier than expected. Mother was thrilled and comforted by having a phone number where she could call me back.

Northridge, November 19-22

I wrote our joint letter, then went to the hospital to visit Bea, who was sleepy and dopey. Too tired to do anything fast or demanding, I went home and cleaned both the bicycles, thoroughly. Elsie didn't really like to drive, so I used her car for errands and filled it with gas.

Late in the afternoon, I drove us to the hospital where we had a short visit. Bea said, "My eyes won't focus, but there's no pain." She smiled. With Elsie directing and me driving, we reached Mildred's for dinner.

The next morning Bea was up, walking around and ready for company. She said, "I thought I was going to die. But it was all right. I didn't mind."

The days sped by, eaten up by hospital visits, enjoying Bea's family, and trips to the bike shop. My bike needed new front shift levers, a new front derailleur, and brake adjustments. Bea's brakes needed adjusting and my bottom bracket was loose again.

On Saturday I was still tired. Elsie and I had a quiet breakfast, and I set off by bike to visit the San Fernando Mission. I pedaled quietly, pleasantly surprised to find this portion of L.A. wasn't the concrete jungle I expected. I spent a long time at the mission, reading about the mission's place in Californian and American history.

I was the only visitor in some of the mission rooms, quietly reading my way from exhibit to exhibit. Then like hitting the jackpot, the whole collection of historical coins from my perimeter trip began to fall into place. Traveling slowly around the edges of America's coasts and borders was giving me the geographic structure of the country, the sense of the earth, weather, seasons, and outdoor life, and the tangible feeling of personal discovery, whiffs of how today rests upon two hundred years of yesterdays.

Here in the Fernando Mission, I paused over fine examples of "Willow Ware" from the early 1800s, the world-famous blue and white china with the bridge, tree, and house. As a child, I ate off a plate of similar design. It inspired tales and stories as I uncovered the image by eating the food. I was amused that the contents of the rooms, except for the rugs, were itemized. As in Tibet, I presumed, rugs were common, necessary household articles. They were not considered works of art. Knowing little of California history, I was astonished by the display of fourteen flags flown in California from 1542 to 1849.

A glance at my watch showed it was time to pedal toward the hospital where I arrived to find Bea in splendid spirits. She took me to the glass corridor to see the sunset. "I come here every day now, but there is no one to share it with. Thank you for coming."

Northridge, Sunday, November 23

Sunday morning Bea called from the hospital saying she could leave. She sat in the sun while I finished separating our gear. I had Bea's prescription filled and Elsie stirred up lunch before her son and daughter-in-law drove us to San Diego. They took an inland freeway route so that we could see different sights than those we would see on our coastal bike trip, planned for February. During the drive, we stopped frequently for Bea to walk around the car so blood clots would not develop.

We found the Shaws' home easily, and Bea's relatives returned home. Homer and Dorothy, a retired nurse, fed us and Bea went to bed. I thanked them for insisting we call Joan and Mac. Sometimes I feel like I have a lot of foster families. In the morning, I met the mail carrier to give him outgoing letters. "How is your trip going?" he asked.

"Fine. But how did you know about it?"

"I've been delivering mail for you," he smiled. "I'm glad you arrived O.K. I've always liked bikes. Once, when I was younger, I rode to Santa Barbara." He still looked young to me. From the kitchen window, Dorothy watched the humming-birds on the deck. Homer showed us the sparrow hawk that lived in the eucalyptus tree in the back yard and called my attention to three types of eucalyptus. Then we hung the bikes upside down in the garage. I put all the panniers in a box so they wouldn't fall all over the place, and took the usable food into the kitchen. The Shaws said we were having Santa Anna weather — clear and sunny with five percent humidity, seventy-eight degrees during the day and fifty at night. I felt so good, so rested and fit. I would have liked to jump on my bike and roll on.

During that rest day at the Shaws' I weighed everything on their bathroom scales. My panniers, including contents, were 34 pounds; Bea's were 21 pounds. My weight was 165 and Bea's 128. I had to add the front bag with camera, helmet, and sleeping bag and full water bottle, for 12 more pounds. The bike weighed 30. So my total weight without any food was 240 pounds. Bea's including stove fuel and bird book totaled 190. We carried about 30 pounds each in addition to ourselves and our bikes when we had no camping gear, and about 50 pounds each with full camping equipment, and minimum food. People often asked us how much everything weighed.

The Shaws drove us to the airport where I got a wheel-chair and pushed Bea to the boarding gate. We sat in silence. We had reached a watershed in our trip, and although we'd agreed to a rendezvous in January, there were no guarantees.

We boarded the plane and traveled to Atlanta, where we changed planes. I had a short wait, she a long one. The stewardess suggested I deplane early, for we were late and I had to run for my connection. Bea had to wait until all other passengers had deplaned. As I stood in the aisle, she looked at me and waved, saying nothing. I copied her, turned, and was pushed down the aisle and out of the plane by the rest of the passengers.

I took three deep breaths and ran for my plane.

Looking out the window at the clouds, I realized I was committed to finishing this trip. Perhaps I would look for a new partner. Perhaps it would work out for the Shaws to sag us across the desert — that might be fun. I would like knowing Joan and Mac better, too. A glimpse into the RV subculture would be interesting.

Soon, I was looking down on the Potomac River. A page had been turned, and I was beginning a new chapter. Among the clouds, Route 301 and the old Potomac River Bridge fifty miles south of Washington slid under the wing. There was my friend's farmhouse shining white upon its hill as it had for over one-hundred years. I recalled the story of the elderly woman who once owned the house sitting on her sofa informing the young, spit-and-polish Yankee lieutenant, "No, young man. This is my home. This has been my home for seventy-four years, and if your captain must blow it up, then you do so with *me in* it. I will not leave. Leave is what *you* must do — now." It was the only home the Yankee Navy left standing along either side of the Potomac.

Washington, D.C., November 25 - January 30

During the two-month holiday, I focused on personal business, reading, writing, and planning for the next stages of the trip, as well as family and friends.

The day after arriving in Washington, I called Bea to be sure she had gotten home safely. Two weeks later, I mailed her a copy of the joint letter I wrote in Los Angeles. A friend in New York had thanked me for these letters and nicknamed them "Pedalgrams." I decided to use that title during the rest of the trip.

My mother's health had improved, though she hadn't her usual energy, mostly because of medication that kept her quiet and decreased her blood pressure. She maintained the best medicine was having me home for the holidays and encouraged me to return to the trip so that she could finish it vicariously.

I wrote a letter to Joan and Mac McIntosh, proposing we travel together from San Diego to Big Bend. They responded favorably, saying they might enjoy a different type of RV travel, and they were already planning to go to New Mexico in

February. Perhaps we could coordinate our trips. I worked out a schedule and sent them a draft. Mac proposed some camping spots. He had always wanted to do a raft trip on the Rio Grande and, if the timing worked out, they would consider going that far with us.

By mid January, Bea returned books and clothes that had been sent to her home during the trip with a note saying, "A lot has changed in my life." I wondered if she meant she was not going to resume the trip. My plans were to rent a car at the airport in San Diego and drive to the Shaws, reclaim our bikes, drive to Santa Barbara, and turn in the car. We would then bike back to San Diego and visit the Shaws and tour the area, if that suited their schedule. I intended to visit the Viegs in Claremont while Bea visited her family.

I made tentative plans for Newport Beach, Tucson, and El Paso. Because of the desolate terrain, I worried about cycling the Arizona and west Texas parts of the trip alone. After Texas, I could complete the journey by myself and enjoy it more. I was becoming more comfortable with the prospect of continuing alone.

While I was home, friends and family told me I had become more considerate and a better listener than before. No one had called me "intense" for a very long time. Perhaps retirement and life on the road had taught me something.

I kept in shape for bicycling by shoveling snow during two snowstorms, each of which dropped ten to fifteen inches. It was grand to be outside in really cold crisp weather. Linda Bell, who planned to travel with me on the East Coast for a week, led me on a few miles of cross-country skiing. The car doors froze. Gutters, heavy with ice, fell off my house, and most other houses on the block. I had gained fifteen pounds, and counted the days till flight time for southern California.

WINTER ON THE MEXICAN BORDER

CHAPTER TWELVE

Changes in Southern California

Washington, D.C., Saturday, January 31

My neighbor, Susan Harper, bravely drove me to the airport. Earth movers were scooping snow off Memorial Bridge and dumping it over the railings into the frozen Potomac River. My flight was an hour late, but I would arrive in plenty of time to make the connection in Atlanta where Bea and I would board the same flight to San Diego. We hadn't talked for two weeks, and the three or four conversations we'd had were strained.

When the plane landed in Atlanta, I claimed the phone nearest my next boarding gate and called my aunt and uncle. When I hung up, a woman sitting next to me excused herself for overhearing. She said she was going to Tucson by plane and our bicycle trip sounded interesting. Then I saw Bea sitting nearby, reading a book.

"Glad to see you. How do you feel?"

"Great. I'm ready to go," she responded quickly, but nervously.

"How is the baby?" I asked, meaning her first granddaughter.

"Baby is fine."

"I guess it was hard for you to leave."

"Yes, very. I've got to go back soon." I wondered what that meant.

The woman from Tucson began asking questions about our tour. Bea got up and wandered; I responded, then asked questions about the Tucson area. Then I was on the phone again until time to board. Bea and I were assigned seats one row apart, across the aisle from each other. As the plane rolled away I asked if her friend Kate was coming to sag us through the rest of Texas after the McIntoshes returned to California, a plan Bea promoted.

"How's Kate? What are her plans?"

"She's ready to come. She wants to drive her van and accompany us, but she's still caring for a friend who has cancer."

I told her my plans. "I've tickets to go home from El Paso between the fifth and eighth of March. The McIntoshes said they would travel with you while I'm gone." I showed her the article about maxi-saver tickets, and suggested, "You could go home at the same time if you prefer." She didn't answer. I stretched out my legs and began to read.

Waiting to change planes in Houston, the woman going to Tucson remarked, "I should think you would be very thin from bicycling all that way."

Laughing, I replied, "I would be if I didn't eat so much." Actually, I was disappointed not to have lost any weight. I *had* lost two dress sizes — a splendid compensation — and I felt wonderfully healthy. Now, I vowed to eat less junk and more vegetables in hope of losing pounds.

From the San Diego airport, we drove to the Shaws' to spend the night. After breakfast, they departed for church, and we put our bikes and panniers in the car and drove to Santa Barbara, to arrive before dinner as Jean requested. At first, it was a quiet trip. I had nothing to say and was busy driving. Then Bea began to talk.

"I've been in therapy all of December and January. When I got home, all I could do was sit and cry. My children were concerned. They made the arrangements and insisted."

"What were you crying about?"

"When I got home, I didn't know. I just cried all the time."

I looked straight ahead. I was driving through L.A. on the freeway with "Hollywood" on the hillside in front of me. It was Sunday morning and traffic was light. After a long silence, I asked, "Are you still in therapy?"

"No, I completed the course and won the prize for the most progress. Have you ever been in therapy?" she asked me.

"No, but I taught group process."

"It's the best thing that ever happened to me," she said. "Getting on that plane was the hardest thing I ever did."

"Would you like me to take you to your sister's?" Maybe Bea didn't want to be here. After all, it had been an exhausting trip and she'd just gotten over having surgery.

"Of course not. I'm going to do this bike trip. I'm doing the perimeter whether you do it or not!" That was my line! I returned the car in Santa Barbara, and we rode our bikes less than three miles to a reunion with Jean at Samarkand. She had reserved the same room for us and, after dumping our stuff there, we went in to dinner. Jean's friends greeted us by name. Later, when Bea went to bed, I went to Jean's apartment to talk about her holiday trip and mutual friends.

On the way back to my room, I sat in the garden for a time to organize my thoughts. I wondered how I could make it easy for Bea to leave this trip and also save face.

Santa Barbara, California, Monday, February 2

At five, Bea got up to take a shower. After I took my shower and came back into the room, Bea was looking at television. She walked outside, saying, "I'll meet you at breakfast."

On morning news I heard that the director of the CIA had resigned. My work for the CIA seemed a long time ago, as though it were someone else's life, not my own. For thirty years, when I walked through the building exit, the data base in my head disappeared. When I went back inside, it was restored. Living that way became so normal that I couldn't remember any personal business when I was at work. I had to write reminders and stuff the notes in my wallet so that I couldn't buy my lunch without seeing them. Routinely, I separated my thoughts governing work and the rest of my life. Perhaps I had an exaggerated singlemindedness, but I was not the only CIA employee who lived that way. In retirement, I had become one person and had shed the fear and stress that, without intent, I would mistakenly reveal some shred of information to the wrong person at the wrong time.

After breakfast with Jean, we walked back to our room to hang our panniers on our bicycles and pedal off. I was grateful to Jean and ready to get going. I waved as my bike rolled down the hill, headed south. Bea followed.

Looking ahead, I saw the smog line just above Ventura. We descended to the bike path past the wharf where Jean and I had enjoyed lunch when Bea was so ill. That seemed more like yesterday than two-and-a-half months ago. Today, I was wearing shorts and a T-shirt. Some change from bundling up to shovel snow!

The Pacific Ocean was absolutely flat — still, like a lake. From a distance, I watched two surfers talking with their bodies, arms and hands describing relationships of boards and waves. Two brown pelicans skimmed along without flapping their wings, close enough to the water to break its surface. They raised their heads a bit, flapped, and skimmed on, leaving not a ripple on the gray water.

We continued riding around the great arc of the bay until we reached Ventura County Park, a wide place in the road several feet above the sandless shoreline where waves slammed against a rock wall. Beside Highway 1, we stood on a hillside to watch the sea. I couldn't believe I was riding in shorts in February and observing porpoises frolicking and ducks feeding. Bea told me she was homesick.

We soon entered Ventura where we stopped. Bea's computer wasn't working. I thought the battery might be the problem. I suggested, "There's a camera store. Perhaps you can find a battery that will fit your computer." Without a word, she handed me her bike to hold.

Bea returned triumphant, and put the Cat Eye into its holder on her handlebars. We continued along Main Street until we stopped for a light and she moaned, "It still doesn't work properly." Later, we spotted a bicycle shop. Bea went in to have her Cat Eye checked. The camera store had sold her the wrong battery, and the bike shop replaced it. I sat on the curb while she rode back to town to return the first battery.

I waited, thinking about Bea's remark about being homesick. I really do not know what homesickness is. Certainly, I have never felt it. I couldn't believe I was sitting on a curbstone in Ventura, California, looking at the mountains, houses, palm trees, gulls, and enjoying the intoxicating air. In the sun it was too warm, in the shade it was too cool — conditions reminiscent of Nepal or Kashmir. Here, however, I could drink the water.

When Bea returned, we continued south along Telegraph Road, passing groves of lemon and orange trees. Bea had the map, and had been navigating. She rode either just in front of or just behind me, never more than twenty-five yards away. It was a nice change to have company, even when she didn't talk. Air blew through the thin fabric of my shoes, pleasantly cooling my feet. There was a bluish haze all around, and as we headed inland, the air became drier and drier. We continued through strawberry fields with the pickers at work, under a stand of eucalyptus trees, past a lemon company, a citrus company, and a large turf farm before Bea stopped.

"I'm ready to call it a day," she volunteered. "How far is the motel?"

I said, "Six or seven miles. Let's slow the pace."

She set a pace about three miles an hour slower, and we stopped several times to rest. Heavy traffic kicked up dust on the road, and the shoulder wasn't wide. I, too, was ready to stop. Today we could be flexible because the ride from Santa Barbara was too far for one day and not far enough for two full days. We didn't know how Bea's operation would affect her riding or how inactivity would affect mine.

The day's sixty-three miles ended at Motel 6 at Simi. As we rolled our bikes into our room, Bea said she wanted to eat as soon as she cleaned up, and asked if I wanted to join her.

It was only about four-thirty, and I wasn't hungry. Maybe establishing a routine with more space between us would be a good idea. "It's a little early for me to eat. Perhaps, if you take long enough with your shower, I'll be ready."

"I'm going now. Do you want to go?"

"No. It's a bit early for me."

After forty-five minutes, Bea returned, smiling.

Simi, Tuesday, February 3

The next morning I resolved to make the day fun. Although more convinced I could do the trip alone, I still didn't want to. Neither of us had an alternate partner ready to jump on a bike.

Bea phoned her sister and told me, "Elsie said that her daughter-in-law is very ill. It's her back again, and she's confined to bed. Elsie's caring for her and won't be able to take me sightseeing. I don't know what to do."

"I'm sorry to hear that, but perhaps the visit will turn out better than you expect." We ate in silence, and meandered back to the room. It wasn't light enough to ride. I cleaned my teeth and readied my bike. We rolled our bikes out and headed down the highway toward Elsie's house, twenty miles away.

We came into the Los Angeles area over the Santa Susanna Pass, and reached Elsie's house by nine o'clock. Elsie had gone out and was to return about noon. I phoned the Viegs.

They said they would come for me by midday.

As we sat in the beautifully sunny garden, we both knew it was time to talk. We could not postpone it any longer. Conversation was difficult and stilted. We agreed the trip was a great privilege and that we both wanted to continue together. We also agreed that getting along with each other wasn't enough. We had to get along and have fun, too. We also agreed on three options: continuing to Texas and seeing how things went; Bea stopping here and now with her family; and Bea's returning home out of homesickness. It was Bea's choice.

Not long after Elsie returned, the Viegs came for me. While everyone was talking, I began to roll my bike toward the car. "You leave your bike here!" Bea ordered.

"No. I'll take it so that, wherever I am, I'll have it when a decision is made."

As I opened the car door to get in Bea commanded, "You call me!"

"No. You call *me* when you know what your plans are." I closed the door, and we drove away. I thought I was free. I would ride from Claremont to San Diego and see how I liked the experience before making my next decision. I suspected Bea couldn't quite believe that I could or would go without her. Neither could I.

For the next two days I enjoyed the company of the Viegs. Although I had known Elizabeth forty years, I was only now becoming acquainted with her husband, John. During the thirty-mile drive to Claremont, I developed an appreciation for John's sense of humor. "There are six colleges in Claremont," he told me. "It's the only town in the country where if there were a sign saying 'Heaven' and 'Lecture on Heaven' everyone would head for the lecture."

"So we would like you to attend a lecture tonight," smiled Elizabeth. "John and I are among the organizers of Claremont Association for Mutual American/Soviet Understanding, a cooperative series of eight lectures. We'd like your company, and we thought that the subject would interest you: Russian and Soviet Views of the U.S.A. Hans Rogger, Professor of Russian History at UCLA, is to speak. He's also a member of the Academic Council of the Kennan Institute for Russian Studies in Washington."

I was interested. "My only reservation is my limited wardrobe. I wouldn't wish to embarrass you."

They laughed. "This is California. You can wear *anything* here. Anyway, for these lectures, people dress casually."

Hans Rogger traced the origin and development of envy, competition, and fear within cultural and political contexts. He related fear to the classic dilemma of leaders: How far can one loosen control without losing control? It was an interesting hour.

Claremont, Wednesday, February 4

John retired from Pomona College, where he was department head for many years. Each college at Claremont sets its own requirements yet shares libraries, research, laboratories, and sometimes faculty — the Oxford system.

The Viegs' home was an example of the Cliff May house, one that let the light in through large panels of glass but kept the sun out with an overhanging roof, and was partially prefabricated.

Elizabeth and I hardly could stop talking. She read me a summary of her experience advising German and American leaders on women's activities from 1946 to 1949. We shared stories of life in Berlin that first hard winter after the war. She had been asked to organize educational affairs for German students, and I had attended the first American Dependents High School in Berlin. She was interested in my first cross-cultural experience when some German students, formerly active in the Hitler youth, heard that students had written a constitution for student government. They came to learn what we had done. We became exasperated because the German visitors couldn't understand that it was not a peace treaty between the students and the teachers. They refused to accept that we, not the teachers, had written it, using the Constitution of the United States as a guide. We realized our philosophy of government was subtly ingrained in us, and we were ill-equipped to explain, interpret, or defend what we had written.

During the afternoon, Elizabeth and I drove to visit The Huntington Library, Art Collections, and Botanical Gardens. In the library, I gazed at Chaucer's Canterbury Tales, reavowing to read it someday. In the gallery, originally the Huntington residence, I saw Lawrence's *Pinkie* and Gainsborough's *Blue Boy*, two oh-so-common pictures that many people assume were painted by the same person. It was interesting to contrast the styles, brush work, and colors.

Outside in the Huntington Desert Garden, I learned

about xerophytes, plants that have adapted to a lack of water. The garden introduced me to plants common across Arizona, New Mexico, and Texas. I saw my first jojoba, a bushy, evergreen desert shrub. Female jojoba plants produce large, edible seeds that contain almost fifty percent oil, which is used as a machine lubricant, in cosmetics, and in food. I saw century plants, with and without flowers. Their sweet sap is used to make tequila and pulque. Other century plant species produce a leaf fiber called sisal, used for making rope. The variety and beauty of the cacti held me spellbound.

Later, when we finished dinner and the dishes, we consumed most of the coconut macaroons John baked with a little instant "guidance," he grinned, from Betty Crocker.

Bea had not phoned, and I needed to tell the Viegs when I would be leaving. If I did not hear from her, I intended to get on my bicycle in two days and ride to Newport Beach to visit a college friend's brother, then continue on to San Diego. Perhaps Bea and I should not split up now, in this way. I picked up the phone and dialed.

We decided to meet on Friday in a place convenient for my hosts. After John, Elizabeth, and I consulted, we called back with the idea that we meet at the Disneyland Hotel on Friday at noon. Elsie could drive Bea there. It was settled. We would continue pedaling to San Diego.

I phoned the McIntoshes, explaining, "I'm not certain Bea will continue beyond San Diego. I wanted to tell you that this discussion is going on and ask if you'd be willing to keep our plans if I am the only bicyclist?" They replied that were I alone, they would worry. I gave an inaudible, internal sigh. What I said with a laugh was, "With only me, there would be fifty percent less to worry about. All I need is good company to meet and camp with in the evenings." Their responsibility would be to call the State Police if I failed to show up at night. They decided to talk about it; they were coming south anyway. "Well, I don't want you to feel any obligation. We're doing this for fun. If it isn't fun for you, forget it." I was satisfied that I had done my best to get them off the hook should they want to change their minds. I went to sleep looking forward to another day with Elizabeth and John.

Claremont, Thursday, February 5

Driving on Thursday to the Los Angeles County Museum of Art and the Tar Pits, Elizabeth and I talked about my continuing the trip. "Everyone agrees that we're better off together and neither of us should undertake this trip alone," I told her. "I don't think it's unsafe, but I'm not sure I'd want to travel alone. In large metropolitan areas, for example, we can't leave the bikes, even for a few moments, even locked, because the valuables are in the panniers. I think we'll go our separate ways soon, but I don't know exactly when."

At the museum, we turned our attention to Monet and Pissaro paintings and a wonderful display of netsuke, miniature Japanese carvings. We rested during lunch on the terrace before walking over to the Tar Pits. I had never heard of them, but Bea said they were the most important thing to see in L.A. Elizabeth and I saw the remains of pools of bubbling tar. Inside, a display showed how animals stuck in the seeping tar were sucked into the pools. Other animals came to feed on the dead and were in turn trapped. Birds were attracted by the water that covered the tar. Eventually, a bone pit containing horses, wolves, vultures, and small birds built up. The bones settled into a mass of deeper sediment as they became saturated with tar. From 1913 to 1915, bones of more than eight thousand mammals and birds were excavated here. Nearly all the skeletons assembled and displayed are of animal and bird species now extinct.

Next, we visited Bullock's Wilshire where Elizabeth shopped for a dress and a suit in the elegant Art Deco style department store. The wooden elevator creaked as the operator took us up and down. Many shoppers, wearing hats, white gloves, and fur coats, were of the same period as the building. I walked around proudly in my black cycling tights topped by a brilliant yellow and orange Italian racing jersey.

Thoroughly pleased with our day, we drove past the Coconut Grove, along Wilshire, to Sunset, past Vine. The long-heard names became real for me. Although I didn't take the glitzy movie or television industry tours, I did get a good feel for the burgeoning presence of New York City artists swelling the population.

Claremont, Friday, February 6

I had never seen a lemon tree except at a distance, and Elizabeth's was heavy with fruit. She planned to donate lemons from their tree to a bazaar, and I picked them for her. Next to the lemon tree was a kumquat tree. Elizabeth spared enough from future jelly for me to fill my pockets. While bicycling that day and the next, whenever I, like Pooh, was hungry for "a little something," I'd pop a tree-ripened kumquat in my mouth and crunch slowly.

John and Elizabeth wanted to participate in our departure, and I believe they, too, would have liked to join us. Bea, with bicycle, met us in front of the Disneyland Hotel. We hauled my bike out of the car while making introductions. Bea explained the gears while I hung on my panniers. We waved, pedaled out into West Street, and waved again as the Viegs drove past us on their way home. It was hard to leave them.

We turned left on Harbor Road. When we crossed the Santa Ana River, I opted for the bicycle path, exchanging stoplights for birds. There were cinnamon teal, western grebes, northern pintails, blue legs, yellow legs, a white crane, great blue heron, American egret, marsh hawk, black neck gulls, stilts, the ever present mallards, and my favorites that day, the widgeons which were so close we could see their green eye stripes glittering in the sun. Along this river, I watched the bird of my Avocet computer was named for in winter plumage.

The bike path led us to the sea where we followed Balboa Drive's beachfront homes, and Isle Avenue, where the bike path continued south between the shore and the houses. After passing yacht basins, boat docks, and the Ulmer Sail Company, we stopped to walk to the end of a rock jetty to watch the surfers.

I explained to Bea that a college friend's brother, Harry Boon, and his son were expecting us to spend the night at his home in Newport Beach tonight. The next day, I intended to ride around and visit the area before attending the international men's volleyball game between China and the United States in the evening. Arranging the game and publicizing it had been a project of Harry's, and I thought seeing an international-level game would be fun. The Shaws were not expecting us until late Sunday afternoon or Monday. We would ride out to the campground to meet the McIntoshes on Thursday. Bea didn't like the schedule. She didn't want to see the volleyball game or to wait until Thursday to get going on our trip.

At the appointed time, we reached Harry Boon's home and his son, Hunter, let us in. The side of the house away from the street faced the water, a narrow channel full of sailboats and motor boats bordered by a small beach. Bea went out and sat on the beach; I was glad to sit quietly indoors. When Harry came home, he invited us to join him, his girlfriend, and Hunter at a dinner theatre to see *Camelot*. When Harry insisted, Bea agreed to come. I had never seen the musical and enjoyed Elizabeth Howard's production.

Newport Beach, Saturday, February 7

Arising at dawn, I ate an orange and packed my bike. Harry came downstairs to see us off, and we had a short visit while Bea got ready. I was disappointed at having to miss the game, but Bea was firm about moving on.

We rode forty miles into the wind along the coast. Pedaling through Camp Pendleton, I thought about the Vietnamese refugees who had lived here and about the dear Pham family, who lived in my apartment briefly in 1975 until they found a place of their own. Now, talking to myself as I pedaled, I made a speech to the Pham family: "I take my birthplace for granted, but your family and people like you from all over the world came here with nothing. Because of you, America will be a better place. I know it's hard to leave your country, but I am glad you came here." Camp Pendleton, in my mind, was Camp Vietnam.

Since it was Saturday and we were on a major bicycle route, there were many bicyclists and I was delighted by their company. I stopped at a phone booth to call Homer and confirm that we would arrive on schedule the next afternoon. We registered at a motel; Bea went at once into the shower. I was neither hungry nor tired, so I shouted to her, "I'll be back after a while," and went to a nearby bicycle shop. Preparing to ride without such heavy loads during the next month, I installed new chain rings. Later, I would change the tires from one-and-a-fourth inch to one-and-an-eighth inch, the smallest my rims could handle. I planned to carry tire tools, patch kit, one tube, a couple of tools for adjustments, camera, film, food, water, microcassette recorder, pump, extra shirt or raincoat, and map. Everything else would go in the RV.

Leucadia, Sunday, February 8

We watched the surfers at Elijo Beach as we rode along, and read signs advertising Shear Madness Hair Cutting, Clone Duplication, Inc., and Fleet Feet Triathlete Shop. Two balloons appeared suspended in the quiet, early Sunday morning air. People were jogging, taking surfboards out of their cars, putting on wet suits, and sitting on their tailgates drinking coffee and enjoying the beginning of a lovely day. Had I been alone, I would have stopped to talk with some of them.

I remembered a conversation with a bicyclist I met yesterday, who theorized the numbness in bicyclists' hands results from poor posture. If you ride with a straight back and do arm and back exercises and stretches before and after bicycling, the numbness and pain diminish. I tried sitting with a straighter back and exercising my hands and arms while riding. It seemed to work.

I turned into the road to Torrey Pines State Park and pedaled up to the top of the hill to the museum. Bea followed. As we walked among the Torrey pines themselves, we were accompanied by Steller's jays. I took a lot of photographs to try out my new close-up filters. I saw lemonade berry whose sour seed coating can be made into lemonade, and spice bush, yerbasanta, and California buckwheat, whose leaves and blossoms were used by Indians for teas and poultices.

We were about to mount our bikes after a couple of peaceful, interesting hours in the park when a ranger stopped his truck, and asked, "Do you have a chain tool? Some people down the road broke their chain."

"I have one," I volunteered.

"Would you have time to help them? I don't think they would know how to use the tool."

Bea had been complaining of hunger. I glanced at her and asked, "Are you too hungry to stop?"

"No, but I'll wait here."

"Where are they?" I asked the ranger.

"Just at the curve as you come up the hill."

I hadn't been on a hill in a long time, and I coasted before halting on the curve. It took no time at all to remove the broken link and recouple the chain. I hated the grease. Delighted to be able to continue their Sunday ride, the couple thanked me and invited me to come see them in Del Mar. The park ranger returned and offered me a ride up the hill in his pickup. I thanked him but said I'd rather pedal the quarter mile than lift the bike into the truck. He laughed. Bea joined me at the top and we continued into La Jolla where we ate soup and salad for lunch.

The area has the best bike path system I had seen anywhere, and, along the San Diego River, we watched American widgeons and coots. Shortly before three, I called Homer and said, "You don't need to pick us up. We're coming along the bike path to El Cajon and should be there in about an hour and a half." We had a fine ride uphill from the coast, and we arrived within ten minutes of my estimate.

It was a friendly reunion, and they were solicitous of Bea's health. I invited them out to dinner, and we settled on Monday night, when the McIntoshes could join us. I had bought an art book in Los Angeles for us to give Homer and Dorothy. Bea gave me a check for her half of both the dinner and the book.

Dorothy served dinner: chicken, rice, green beans, fruit salad, and carrot cake. We didn't hold back on the cheese and cracker appetizers, and I ate all the hot sourdough bread. I telephoned Mac and Joan, and we agreed to go sightseeing together tomorrow.

El Cajon, Monday, February 9

I awoke early and lay still, thinking of pedaling east following a zigzag route along the Mexican border. The third portion of our perimeter trip would present differences in weather, terrain, direction, and group composition. We were about to embark on a different mode of travel, sagged camping. We would set off early and arrive late; our RV "parents" would leave late and arrive early for day's end sharing. They would buy the food, plan and cook the meals, and carry all our gear except our day packs. We would ride our bicycles and enjoy the evening camaraderie. Our distances should increase from fifty or sixty miles a day to seventy or ninety, using the same energy because we'd be carrying less. (Far apart towns in the southwest necessitate higher daily mileages.)

The McIntoshes would experiment with traveling slowly and moving their recreational vehicle daily rather than weekly. I expected to ride long and hard through barren areas and pause to savor parks and wildlife refuges. Overnight stops would be planned two or three days in advance since the McIntoshes said reservations were necessary. No more joint letters would be sent to our friends. Bea had decided to write hers separately, and I would write *Pedalgrams*.

My list for the day included buying a one-person tent, batteries for my new belt beacon and camera, arranging tickets home from El Paso, sending home a box of unneeded extras, finding AAA maps for the states ahead, and putting my bicycle in order.

I drove my bike to the shop in Homer's truck. The gears had not changed properly since the new chain rings were installed. I needed a new chain, a tire, and riding shorts. Although it was not badly worn, my old chain was clogged with dirt I couldn't remove. It had been six or seven thousand miles, as had the freewheel. The shop, Wheels 'n Things, had a Centurion Pro Tour 15 like mine in stock. The mechanics were knowledgeable, and I felt comfortable with their advice.

Bea and I spent the rest of the morning talking, packing my box of extras, and sorting the contents of our panniers. I called several shops, trying unsuccessfully to find the Eureka Crescent tent I wanted. I would use one of Bea's two tents. She had brought a pup tent from home when she came back.

After the McIntoshes arrived, Homer drove us all to Point Loma where we stood between the lighthouse and the ocean and looked west at the sun upon the shining Pacific. Whales were blowing and waving their flukes. Beyond them, to the south, were Mummy Island, the mountains of Mexico, the salt cliffs. To the east spread San Diego harbor. Homer pointed out the yacht club, which currently exhibited the America's Cup, the Navy ships, a hospital ship, and highrise modern buildings of downtown. One of them, reflecting light, reminded me of a giant champagne glass. I adored Point Loma and San Diego, including the bushtit we saw near the lighthouse. Homer told wonderful stories.

When we returned home, Homer and Mac installed a new aerial on the RV and the new bicycle rack they had bought for us but would also use for their grandchildren. Bea set up and checked both tents, and I put my new belt beacon together for use in fog. During an evening at a Japanese restaurant, the Yakitori II, we completed our plans for the journey.

El Cajon, Tuesday, February 10

We spent the day shopping with Dorothy, visiting with Homer, reading, resting, and packing. I spent hours on the phone and writing notes. I arranged to see Charlotte Mesick in Tucson and to meet the Hulls near Douglas, Arizona, and I contacted the local bike club in El Paso. My bike sported new one-and-an-eighth-inch Specialized Turbo/S tires to cut down road resistance during the month it carried less.

El Cajon, Wednesday, February 11

Shortly after eight, we began a long free ride from the Shaws' neighborhood down through El Cajon. At a bridge, we went up a short hill. At the top, Bea waited. "You go first until we're in the country," she said.

Off I went, making a couple of turns that brought us into Route 54, where Bea passed me. It was good to be in the country again. At Jamul, Bea was far ahead, and I turned into the post office for stamps. I returned to my bike and continued. Bea had gone back to look for me. Fortunately, she saw me when I re-entered the highway.

A lovely ride on Campo Road led southeast and continued until we reached Telegraph Canyon Road, where we turned into the Jamul Valley. Heading toward Otay Lakes, we entered the Thousand Trails Campground, Pio Pico. Following the gatekeeper's directions and recognizing the Scottish flag on the RV, we found Joan and Mac. The place was alive with birds — Audubon's yellow-rumped warblers, scrub jays, acorn woodpeckers, house finches, and brown towhees. We saw several western bluebirds on the roof of the bath house in excellent view without binoculars.

Our site was under an old, well-pruned live oak in a flat canyon that I would have called a valley, surrounded by gentle hills covered with scruffy bushes. The clean air held moist fog that admitted sun intermittently.

Homer and Dorothy drove up to join us and wish us well on our trip. We shared a jolly meal and marked the occasion with photographs. The Shaws departed as the day waned. We put up Bea's tents, and I covered my bike with the new plastic tablecloth I brought to protect it from the dew. When Joan called us, we assembled in the RV for supper. I was grateful for warmth inside, for it got cold as soon as the sun sank behind the hills.

Mac assured me Joan really liked to cook, and that four required no more work than two — it just eliminated leftovers. During dinner, we discussed finances and agreed that Bea and I would pay half the camping fees, food, and gas for the car and stove as well as contribute to cover the supplies already on board.

Thousand Trails, Thursday, February 12

Pio Pico was so pleasant that we all agreed to a rest day before beginning our journey. Morning entertainment was provided by the scrub jay and brown towhees looking for a drink in small mud holes by the water hookups. I watched an acorn woodpecker who sat patiently on a water spigot, waiting for a drop to form and then taking it into its beak before it fell. Wearing wool pants and three shirts, I was chilly. I couldn't find my socks.

I cleaned and sorted stuff during the morning. After lunch, we went for a swim. The heated pool was really warm, and I luxuriated in the hot tub. Joan and Mac joined me there.

Back at the campsite, Mac and I decided to hike among the hills. Bea was out walking, and Joan was cooking supper. Bea's trail intersected ours, and she joined us for a last view of the Pacific and a look at Lower Otay Lake with the hills of Mexico in the distance.

Thousand Trails, Friday, February 13

Clouds of mist over the hills above us had not yet descended into our canyon. Along the Otay Lakes Road, my attention was distracted from Audubon warblers by a hawk on a nest, and three others standing by in the trees. They appeared to be all brown with yellow on the top back of the tail, but the flat light obscured the colors. Then, among Brewer's blackbirds, I continued to spin along the road through quiet, pleasant farmland.

After six miles, we climbed into the mist. I stopped to turn on my new belt beacon which flashed orange every second. Weighing only a few ounces, it replaced my bike's red generator-driven tail light, which had not burned very brightly going uphill. In the fog, I couldn't see more than a hundred yards, but the pulsing flash ensured I could be seen.

I continued climbing and emerged gradually from the fog shortly before passing a sign that pointed to Mexico, two miles away, and another that confirmed I was on Route 94 East. Ahead, the hills receded, their canyons full of billowy mist. The third leg of this journey was really underway!

As I rolled by Pass Cafe and Wydell, I shifted down one gear and pedaled faster. I wasn't accustomed to hills and wanted to protect my knees. If they began to hurt, it was already too late. Every bicycling magazine and professional riders advocate stretching before and after riding. I never did anything except occasional back exercises.

At Potrero, when we had ridden about eighteen miles and reached twenty-three hundred feet, there was another ridge before any descent. It was mainly horse ranch country. There were old oak and fruit trees, and the rocky hillsides were covered with scrub. I soon crested a hill and had begun to coast down when I found myself speeding through Dogpatch U.S.A. It wasn't on my map!

Less than an hour after eating apples and bowls of soup at Campo, we stopped at Outdoor World Campground. It was about noon, and we had covered forty miles. Our Scottish flagship had not appeared. Before long, the McIntoshes arrived and we selected a campsite among old oak trees which harbored a white-breasted nuthatch.

I talked with Joan and called Lajitas to make reservations for our Big Bend raft trip. It was warm and cozy in the RV, and Joan suggested an after-dinner game of Scrabble. Bea responded with zest. I chose to watch. "I can't spell at all, and it will spoil the game if I participate."

Bea concurred, "She really can't spell."

Outdoor World, Saturday, February 14

After a night of mist and rain, I crawled out of the tent on almost dry ground. The clothes I left pinned to tree branches were still dripping. Birds announced the clear, crisp, cloudless dawn.

While taking down the tent, I found my binoculars on the picnic table, where they had been all night in the rain. I dried them as best I could and attached them to my bike in the sun later that day. Eventually, the moisture inside disappeared. We took off. As I pedaled over a rise, I heard a wheeze and a metallic groan, alerting me to windmills atop the hill. Then down we pedaled until we reached Jacumba, a town with a derelict hotel and a wide main street, showing economic suffering. After a ten-minute rest, we continued past the airport, still in San Diego County on Old Highway 80. We rolled down a six percent grade for nine miles and entered Imperial County. It was a beautiful ride, but when the macadam changed from smooth to rough, I dropped three miles an hour, though I made no changes in pedaling. I knew the surface was important to a bicyclist, but I didn't realize it could make such a difference.

Next we encountered Highway 98, an old concrete road where tar-filled cracks had shriveled into humps. A crosswind out of Mexico buffeted us until, at West Side Canal, we turned north and headed into our campground on the outskirts of El Centro. "That was the worst road surface of the whole trip," pronounced Bea, and I agreed. We found our flagship waiting after a fifty-seven mile ride.

The air was very dry, and I went to take a shower. The hot water felt so good I didn't want to come out. When I did, I put on my bathing suit and slid into the hot tub. Bea packed her things and waited for a friend who was visiting relatives nearby. The two of them had planned to camp for a few days, and she took both tents. I spread out my bivy sack on the sand and secured my mattress and sleeping bag inside, hoping all the RVs, dogs, and cats discouraged snakes. At least, there were no bugs. The worst problem for me was the lights that stayed on. I decided to sleep wearing my hat.

Mac and I watched a crop-dusting plane that flew below the valley level into a canyon, spraying its dust against the backdrop of Mexican hills. When Joan called we turned to face a row of palm trees silhouetted against the pink and orange, fuschia and magenta sunset.

I walked around the campground after supper. The walk was an RV-life education. Some people set out potted plants to form a garden. Most people had a step block of some sort and a rug-sized doormat. Animals were restrained. The moon rose behind the palms, and there was a faint fragrance of kerosene in the air. Last night, we had slept at three thousand feet; tonight, at only one thousand, would be warmer.

I put on all my clothes and went to bed under the stars and campground street lights. Looking up, I saw only the stars and imagined myself a cowboy. A saddle for a headrest would have been nice. I wasn't tired, and the night was splendid. I took a long time to go to sleep.

El Centro, Sunday, February 15

I awoke early as usual but lay happily in bed until the RV door opened. We had breakfast before my first day of riding alone. Nervously, I turned toward flat, direct Interstate 8 where bicycles were banned. It was early on Sunday morning, and I didn't think there would be a problem. Hanging over the valley between the highway and the Mexican border was a white, wispy layer of ground fog around the base of Mount Signal. On the other side of the road grew miles of carrots, sugar beets, and asparagus. The flagship, headed for church, passed me. I rode fourteen miles the first hour. This was living! Spinning along effortlessly, I felt like there must be an outboard motor on my bicycle.

I hoped traveling alone would help me determine the direction for the rest of my life. I had maybe twenty years ahead — what should I do with them? This year was my rest, my vacation, a transition from hard work, tunnel vision, and commitment. What should I do with the person I had become?

I began to peel off layers of clothing and stuff them into my almost-empty pannier. I tried listening to my tiny radio for an hour. The Spanish stations were best because the music was good, and I couldn't understand the advertisements, but I soon tired of extraneous sounds. I just didn't like being distracted from the sights, sounds, smells, and perceptions of the country around me. I preferred the rhythms of bicycling, the sounds of the bike wheels, watching the traffic, and listening to the birds.

The wind picked up a bit, but I had a wide, smooth shoulder. There was scenery at the edge of the road too: S hooks, pieces of tire, lugs from wheels, weights, beer cans, and bottles. Within two feet of the road surface, the shoulder was blown clean by passing vehicles.

I turned the radio to an American station, and paused ten minutes to rest while I ate a peanut butter sandwich and a granola bar. Then I spun on without frequent stops and starts. I had forgotten how pleasant setting my own pace, listening to my own body could be. "Up a Lazy River" played on the radio — it suited my mood.

I stopped in the shade of an overpass to eat fruit. I

passed the All American Canal and came into a area of sand dunes, where I turned off to see the remains of the Old Plank Road. What I found first was another American subculture in full Sunday-afternoon blossom. There were scooters, and two-, three-, and four-wheel all-terrain vehicles running around in the sand. Campers, cars, trailers, pickups, and tents were scattered everywhere among the dunes. An NBC Sports van was set up, antenna extended.

"What's happening here today?" I asked someone.

"They're having races. People come from Los Angeles and all over. This is one of the best places in the country for this sport." Behind him, I saw whole families, following each other in long lines of ATVs up and down the dunes, much like groups of skiers swooping down a mountain.

I asked where the Plank Road was. He pointed, "Right down there." In use from 1914 to 1927, the seven-mile-long Plank Road was the only means early motorists had for crossing the treacherous Imperial Sand Dunes. The eight-by-twelve-foot sections were moved by a team of horses whenever the shifting sands covered them. Double sections placed at intervals permitted vehicles to pass.

Glad I didn't have to ride on *that*, I rolled along rather slowly, watching the dune buggies. Then, as suddenly as they had begun, the dunes were gone. The terrain flattened to a gentle roll.

Over the American Canal, I sped again, a little uphill, a little down. I pedaled at twenty-four miles an hour down, and it was lovely. Yuma would appear soon. A grand finale beat in my head, like the drum roll for a final curtain, as I crossed the border into Arizona. "What a day this has been!" I sang at the top of my voice. "I'm gonna like traveling by myself! I think I'm gonna like it!"

Along the Canadian border, my left thigh and calf had sunburned; now it was the right leg's turn. No one took much notice of me. I was masquerading as a day cyclist with a small front bag and a limp rear pannier.

Being an old lady on a bicycle is complicated. Stopping to get out my glasses to read the map meant taking off the sunglasses, finding the reading glasses and putting them on to look at the map, taking them off, looking through the binoculars to read the road signs, and then donning reading glasses again to check the map before knowing which way to turn.

I crossed the Colorado River separating California,

Arizona, and Mexico, not realizing that it was also the Pacific-Mountain Time Zone line, and pedaled through Yuma. Safely on the road leading to the campground, I stood outside a fast food store drinking a chocolate milk. A horse, with saddle askew, galloped down the street kicking up dust from the shoulder. "It usually heads for home," a girl sitting on a moped said.

I bought a thirty-five dollar tent at a camping store. It would do while I was sagged, but was too heavy to carry on the bicycle. I would have to buy a lighter weight tent in Tucson, the next large city. The McIntoshes went to the grocery and then we stopped for dinner at the Imperial China Restaurant.

I had ridden seventy-three miles, absorbed too much sun, eaten too much, and I wasn't back at camp to pitch my tent until almost ten o'clock. I hadn't slept long enough the night before; no wonder I had a headache. I put up the tent in a driving wind, wishing Bea had told me she was taking her two tents. I did not miss Bea. I'd had a fine day, and was ready to continue the trip alone.

Flat on my back in the tent, I thought of my wonderful day of bicycling. I'd had enough of companions. I was tired of people, not of bicycling.

Jane pedaling at Lewes Ferry, Delaware.

Jane fixing a flat
tire in Brooklyn,
New York.

LINDA BELL

The Centurion
loaded for
traveling.

Sunflower reaching for the sky in North Dakota.

Suzanne Toomey

Linda Bell at Verrazano Narrows Bridge in New York.

Georgena Terry holds a Terry bicycle.

Wee'l Turtle in
Dunseith, North
Dakota.

Floyd Hartman

Rafting on the Rio Grande River.

Courtney Gaines

Janes setting up
her Crescent tent
in Barnegat,
New Jersey.

Jane poses with a pancake near Jacksonville, Florida.

Centurion bicycle protected in its plastic "garage."

Photo finish: Jane completes her trip in Detroit, Michigan on August 30, 1987.

CHAPTER THIRTEEN

Rolling Free in Arizona and New Mexico

Yuma, Arizona, Monday, February 16

Although I would have a fine tailwind and a good flat road ahead, the McIntoshes deflated my dreams of biking my longest day, about one hundred twenty-five miles to Gila Bend, by wanting to stop overnight at Dateland. I felt control of the bicycle trip had shifted to other hands. Decisions were based on factors that had nothing to do with bicycling. From reading bicycle stories, I formed the impression that the driver of a sag wagon should follow the whims of the cyclist. People who never read bicycle articles were much more democratic.

At eight-thirty, I rode out of the camp, heading east with a five-to-fifteen mile tailwind, anticipating a predicted high temperature over seventy. Lettuce pickers were busy in the fields as I wheeled by at about eighteen miles an hour making no special effort. Rough pavement soon slowed me under a cloudless sky.

I was anxious not to miss Hank and Dottie Hull, who were to phone me at Gila Bend and might be there in person. Shortly before eleven, the flagship passed me. We waved, shouted that all was well, and then continued. I had ridden thirty miles when a car towing an outboard motor boat passed. A sign hanging on the boat read, "Just Add Water."

There was a gradual fifteen-mile climb up to the pass into the Mohawk Valley. Savoring speed, I swooped to the rest stop near the bottom of the pass. I filled my water bottles, drank one of them dry, refilled it. I rested at a sun-shielded picnic table and watched a loggerhead shrike atop a utility pole.

When I was on the road again, the wind changed directions enough to be annoying, and my body was drying out from too much sun. By the time I reached Dateland, at two, eagerness to continue had wilted, and I knew stopping was a good decision. The flagship waited for me as I came down the exit ramp. They drove over to the campsite, and I went to buy some dates and eat a bowl of soup and a fresh date milkshake. Although I felt tired after eating, I biked over to the camping area, set up the tent, and put my stuff inside.

Noting how far away the bath house was, I rode my bike there over the grass. When I came out of the shower, both tires were completely flat! Only then did I notice little white balls, about the size of English peas, with whiskery thorns. Hundreds of these thorns, goatsheads, were stuck in each tire. I had to push the bike back to the flagship. All my plans — for lying in the tent, reading a book, and resting quietly—dissipated while the goatsheads let the air out of my tires. It was my first flat tire in over 5,000 miles.

I spent the afternoon working on my tires. Foolishly, I tried to patch the tubes before realizing I should just throw them away. I pulled the thorns out of the tires with tweezers. Then, carefully testing with my fingers, now bloody, I smashed the thorns I couldn't remove. My angry mood lightened by sharing a big platter of Joan's spaghetti with empathetic companions. The delicious dates wouldn't be the only thing I remembered about Dateland! The next day's ride would be short, but I needed at least a whole day off the bike. I was beginning to exhaust my reserves.

I sprayed my right leg and arm with what I thought was Solarcaine. Wondering why the hot burning failed to diminish, I turned the can in my hand. Athlete's foot spray!

I unfolded the new ground tarps I bought in Yuma and placed both over the top of my tent to shield it from the streetlight directly overhead. RV parks had so much light that I wished I had brought a black sleep mask. Instead, since it was cold at night, I slept with a hat pulled down over my eyes. It was wonderful for my hairdo! By day, I had sweaty helmet hair; each morning my hair was squashed from sleeping with the hat.

Dateland, Tuesday, February 17

Although I had told the McIntoshes I would eat break-fast at the cafe, they were up early and invited me to join them. While we shared bacon and eggs, Joan and Mac related stories about their children. It was hard to leave.

To avoid goatsheads, I carried the bike on my shoulder to the highway, then rode carefully, avoiding anything on the road, as though I had expensive silk tubular tires. I could hardly see the cafe for the eighteen-wheelers parked around it and longed to go in for another breakfast with the truckers. Instead, I left temptation with the date palms and followed my route through rocks, sand, and scrub brush.

In less than an hour, I needed to peel off a layer of clothes. Before ten o'clock, I changed from the photo-gray glasses I normally wore as a protection from dust and bugs into new, dark glacier glasses with leather side pieces to cut the glare. I had brought them for this terrain. The day before, my eyes had felt unusually tired and strained from glare. The flagship caught me and passed by slowly, headed for Gila Bend. I waved and signaled no problem.

I was riding parallel to the 1859 Butterfield Stage Route and parallel to the railroad that first came along here from west to east in 1879. I wondered how many people had taken this one-hundred-and-eighty-two-day route on foot from Inde-pendence, Missouri to San Diego. Along the way, they would have seen, as I did, fine stands of saguaro, the giant cactus that takes one hundred fifty years to mature. I also passed cholla with its silver fuzz of spines and ocotillo, a plant which looks like whips and exists on about six inches of rain a year.

As I pedaled over the relatively flat valley floor, moun-tains and outcroppings rimmed the distance. Ahead of my front wheel, drainage ridges appeared after every five pedal rotations. Spectacular mountains were too far away for photo-graphing with a wide-angle or even a standard 50mm lens. Using a telephoto to show the mountains would make a picture without the feeling of space the scene itself presented. Over-head were dispersed vapor trails and wisps of cotton-candy clouds. The Blue Angels practice in this area, but I saw only the contrail of a commercial jet — high and straight and smooth.

I'd heard that the desert was flat, even boring. Explor-ing the desert on a bicycle, you soon realize its flatness is an optical illusion. I found the desert fascinating, awesomely handsome. The scale was almost too large to comprehend. There were many plants strange to my eyes. The irrigated gardening that I passed reminded me of a trip I had taken north of Hue in South Vietnam. There, I had watched wooden, human-powered, bicycle-like pumps lifting water.

The only disadvantage of bicycle travel with an RV sag was that I was so well sustained, even catered to, that I hadn't met anybody. In tent campgrounds, people talk a little; RV people don't talk as much. Perhaps RV camp acquaintance develops more slowly because the people usually don't move every day. The McIntoshes had never traveled every day and wondered how they would like it. I would have preferred to ride longer days and then stop for two or three consecutive nights.

My body was tired and screaming for rest. The days were not hard, just repetitive. This was my fifth day. My leg was becoming more sunburned even though I wore full-length tights. With a few minutes off the bike, I'd be ready for the last ten miles to Gila Bend. I found a ditch with a few bushes to act as privy. After stretching a moment, I ate a carrot.

I watched a small plane spraying cultivated fields, making pass after pass across the highway ahead of me. On the ground were two men with large orange flags, showing the pilot where to spray next. The plane came right at me, pulling up just high enough to clear the wires along the highway. How can people say it is boring here? As I descended the exit ramp to Gila Bend, I felt like sounding trumpets.

I found the mobile home park and my flagship shortly before one o'clock. After a short visit with Joan and Mac, I set up my tent, pitching it on a little patch of grass under a palm tree. A car rolled in and, as the dust settled, Bea and a young woman hauled camping gear from the trunk. Bea was exuberant, and we all talked at once. They went back to San Diego for sightseeing and camped in the mountains. Bea introduced us to Betty, who had to get to Phoenix to turn in her car and catch a plane. She drove away as suddenly as she arrived. I went back to my afternoon of puttering and chores before showering and lying down in my tent to read. Joan came to see me there. I told her I thought I'd ride into town to check out my bike and see the place. "Do you need anything?"

"Yes, we need milk."

I set off and found motels, laundries, fast food restaurants, and RV parks clustered in a dusty tourist strip along the highway before I returned with the milk.

When we went in to dinner, Bea told Mac and Joan about her trip. We discussed the next day's schedule. Joan had made reservations at Crazy Horse Campground and RV Resort in Tucson; tomorrow we would stay at Coyote Howls in Why, and we would spend one night at Organ Pipe. The McIntoshes favored staying overnight only in campgrounds, and my suggestions of a long day's ride followed by an extended rest were overruled. This wasn't my bike trip anymore. Our travel together reminded me of a pair of panty hose — one size fits nobody. I escaped to my tent and continued brooding.

Gila Bend, Wednesday, February 18

In this part of the rugged Sonora Desert, winter is warm and sunshine constant. There were many flowers, and the rock forms and colors were lovely. As we passed through a military gunnery area, planes circled overhead. Signs warned: "Danger: Do not leave right-of-way on main-traveled roads. Use roads open to public only. Observe all warning signs."

After only an hour on the road, I felt quite tired. Bea was ahead of me again, not so far that I couldn't notice she often rode with her hand on her right side. I wondered whether she still hurt from the operation. Bea seemed fresh and rode fast. Riding my sixth successive day, I was feeling sluggish.

There had been no vehicles for a quarter hour. I looked down at the white line sliding past the right side of my bike. That was it! When I finished riding the white line all the way around America, I would have closed the door completely on my past life, seen and learned something about my country, and decided what to do with the years ahead. I resolved to focus upon the present and not try to open a door until I reached a house. If I let everything shake down in my head, if I relaxed and loosened my compulsions, a new goal and the path to it would unroll as I walked upon it. First, I would write about how I had followed the wiggles and squiggles of the white line, a small segment of a long journey.

Ahead, Bea was waiting. I watched a tumbleweed, like a giant silver spider, as it hopped and somersaulted in front of me. We entered Ajo, "where the summer spends the winter." While sitting on a bench and eating an orange, I observed the Spanish-style architecture, the glaring whitewashed buildings, and the green plaza shaded by several kinds of palm trees.

I pulled out *Discovering Yuma* and began to read about date palms, which have a life span of up to two hundred years and can grow over one hundred feet high. Although I only tasted a few varieties, my favorite was the medjool date, originally from Morocco.

I asked Bea if she would like to explore the museum. It turned out to be closed, but we had a good view of the open-pit copper mine before returning to Highway 85 and heading south toward Why.

One story claims that town's name derives from days when motorists referred to "The Y." Another states that a post office name must contain at least three letters and the pronunciation of "Why" and "Y" are similar. The roads there lead to Tucson, to Ajo, or to Mexico. On the border, about twenty miles south of Why, is Organ Pipe Cactus National Monument. As we bumped over the railroad tracks leaving Ajo, Bea stopped and said, "We only have ten miles to Why. I'd like to ride it like a time trial and see how fast I can cover that distance with this tailwind." I had been dragging all morning, but the rest and food had revived me. I decided to keep up as long as I felt comfortable. Bea started off. Several bike lengths behind her, so did I.

A slight downgrade helped us as we whirred along as fast as we could go, about twenty miles per hour. Traffic was fairly brisk. Bea pedaled steadily. I rode with intent. When an oncoming car was about to blow me backward, I curled down, reducing the effect of the rush of air. When a car or a big truck came from behind, I sat straight, squared my shoulders to the wind, and tilted my head to catch as much blast inside my helmet as possible; then I hard pedaled three strokes to maximize thrust as the blast hit me. It was fun and not particularly hard to keep up. Although I was not close enough to draft, being paced provided a challenge. Bea was a smooth rider; I was more erratic. When I got too close, I soft pedaled, keeping up the same rotations. I didn't want to pass her. We kept about two bike lengths apart. I gained a little extra momentum by pedaling normally up the rises and hard pedaling down the other sides when it appeared I might be falling back. I was comfortable in my highest gear, but I was getting tired. I knew I shouldn't go on much further at this pace, but we were very near Why. I slowed as we entered the campground. "That was fun!" I exclaimed.

Why, Thursday, February 19

Just after first light, I awoke and lay in the tent reading and listening to the coyotes howl. I discovered that, by the mid-nineteenth century, Fort Yuma had already been linked to San Diego, more or less by the route I pedaled. A stagecoach line, the San Antonio to San Diego Mail, also used the road. This service was superseded in 1858, when John Butterfield established his semi-weekly mail and passenger run from Missouri to San Francisco by way of El Paso, Tucson, and Yuma Crossing on the Colorado River, and continuing on to Los Angeles and San Francisco.

While taking down the tent, I interrupted myself to watch a cactus wren which seemed to observe me in return. A jackrabbit dashed across the road as doves waddled about. When everyone was almost ready to go, I phoned the Hulls, left a message, and found a place to lock our bikes until we returned from Organ Pipe. Mac didn't like looking through spokes or handlebars as he drove.

The last rain here occurred over a month ago, so nothing was in bloom. The landscape wasn't very interesting from inside the RV. When we arrived at the camping area, a gila woodpecker and a cactus wren welcomed us, and a red-tailed hawk circled overhead. At the visitor center, I learned about some of the plants I had been calling scrub and in the shop, I bought myself a Golden *Birds of North America*, the same book Bea carried. For the rest of the day, Mac drove us on the twenty-one-mile Ajo Mountain Drive, a undulating, graded, dirt road. I would have loved to follow the route on my bike. It was especially nice, however, to have the whole RV water tank at the ready. Mac stopped at almost every turnout as we wound along the desert foothills through impressive stands of organ pipe cactus.

Driving up the side of the basin five miles from the Mexican border, we noticed that many saguaros had holes which had been excavated and used as nests by the gila woodpecker or gilded flicker. I learned to recognize the palo-verde (green-stick), a common pale-green tree. The green trunk, branches, and twigs color the desert all year.

We reached rock outcrops of the Ajo Mountains, a colorful range formed from layers of volcanic materials. The darker striations in the cliff walls are lava and basalt, and ribbons of light yellow or tan are compressed volcanic ash. We stopped for lunch and walked around a bit, careful not to touch anything. All the plants were sticky, and some thorns and spines were sharp indeed. Mesquite and ironwood were common, too. I tried to learn to recognize these plants, knowing my daily rides for the next month or more would be enhanced by knowledge of the desert environment.

I had passed jojoba plantations several days ago, and now it was interesting to see the plant up close. Years ago, on a visit to explore caves and canyons near Monterrey, Mexico, I had seen cacti in bloom. I remembered finding the desert colorful and interesting, but now there was a feeling of softness, and I felt a quiet joy to be in the desert.

Organ Pipe, Friday, February 20

We drove back to Why and retrieved our bicycles at the campground. The last few nights had been increasingly cold. By mid-morning winds were blustery and, Mac thought, dangerous. On the drive north, they blew across the road, causing the flagship to flutter and buffet in the wind. Turning toward Tucson, we would have the best tailwind of the whole trip. I thought we could bike all the way through the Indian reservation and into Tucson, provided we stopped dillydallying.

It was still cold, but only because we were standing still. Mac told me that Bea felt it was too cold to ride, and would travel in the RV. He proposed we all ride in the RV to within twenty or thirty miles of Tucson. By then, it would be warmer, and we could bicycle the rest of the way. While talking, he looked at me apprehensively.

I wondered what had happened to Bea's proclamation, "This is a bike trip — no vehicle rides for me!" I looked down the road at the clouds and felt the wind on my cheek. I was exhausted and defeated, not by bicycling, but by the tug and haul of our pulling at each other. Aloud I agreed, "O.K., that's a good idea. Let's go." Mac visibly relaxed at my compliance, and a smile broke across his face. We were soon heading down the highway with the bikes hanging on the flagship's front rack.

After we registered at the Crazy Horse Campground, I called Charlotte Mesick. She suggested I spend the night at her home and meet her friends. On her way to a luncheon the next day, she would bring our mail to the campground. Then, I would bicycle to her house, seeing something of Tucson, and stay overnight.

During an afternoon tour of the Rincon Mountain area of the Saguaro National Monument, I told Joan about my plans to visit Charlotte. She commented, "You'll be back before Bea leaves on Tuesday. We agreed to stay here that long and take her to the airport. She wants to see the Desert Museum on Monday, so we'll drive her there."

"That will be perfect," I said. Apparently, Joan didn't know this was news to me. Thinking quickly, I added, "I'll just meet you on Monday at the Desert Museum since I want to go there, too." I could get around on my bike.

"We don't feel comfortable hanging around El Paso for four days during your trip home," Joan continued, "So we think we won't go to Big Bend, and will head north or back home from El Paso."

"That's fine," I said with real enthusiasm. "I'll call this weekend and cancel the float trip reservations." That ought to tie things down. The stretch I was really worried about cycling alone was from El Paso to Van Horn and if I didn't have help there, I'd rather get on with this trip alone — the sooner, the better. With more of the puzzle pieces in place, I felt all smiles inside.

We decided to eat at a restaurant near the park entrance. Beyond a wall of glass spread the desert. Close up were bird feeders. We could hardly order or eat for looking at the Gambel's quails with teardrop topknots bobbing as they fed calmly on the other side of the glass. Pyrrhuloxia and northern cardinal males and females abounded. So did phainopepla. Our food, when we remembered to eat, was as good as the show. The staff disturbed a vedin by walking through the feeding area to drop bread on the ground. Our waitress told us the bread was for the peccary (javelina) that would come about eight-thirty. We decided to come back later another evening to see the animal. Fed and in good humor, we returned to camp.

Tucson, Saturday, February 21

Even though I borrowed a blanket from the RV and wore wool socks, long cycling pants, several shirts, and a hat inside my sleeping bag, I felt chilly and awoke earlier than usual. With the street lights overhead, I read until I heard Mac suggesting that Bea get breakfast for herself. I already planned to eat at the nearby truck stop.

On the walk to the restaurant, I noticed that many of the trucks were coated by snow. One of the drivers told me there had been snow in the pass to the east but it had been raining at Las Cruces, New Mexico. As I returned, the campground was alive with finches. Bea was waiting at the picnic table to talk with me. She said, "I've made the decision to leave on Tuesday."

I went into the RV to say good morning to Mac and Joan. They told me Bea was going home because she needed to establish an apartment. She sold her house in December, and she wanted to be with her grandchild and find a home for herself. Joan said I shouldn't take Bea's decision personally. What was I supposed to say or do? I went back outside to tidy up. Finally Charlotte arrived, met everyone, took my clothes, gave me directions and a key to her house, and left for her luncheon.

After I checked plans one last time with Joan and Mac, I rode my bike to the Pima Air Museum, went inside to look at several displays, then rode across the valley to Charlotte's home on a northern elevation above Tucson. Pedaling calmed me. The day was beautiful, and the decisions were firm. How fortunate I felt to spend the next two days with Charlotte and her friends.

I stopped at Bob's Bargain Barn where I bought a one-person Crescent tent, attached it to my bike, and pedaled toward Charlotte's home, ready for solo travel. Charlotte's dog and I were getting acquainted when she arrived. Although we met only once or twice before, Charlotte and I had lived in or visited many of the same places and kept discovering more people we both knew. We talked about where and when we had worked, traveled, and gone to school, and recounted stories of our mutual friends and families. It was just the sort of evening I needed.

Tucson, Sunday, February 22

The last day of the Tucson Balloon Fiesta got us up early and out to a field to watch the mass launching of over eighty balloons. The area was alive with hawkers, observers, and dust. After my experience with the goatshead thorns, I wondered how and where balloons could land without tangling with thorny plants. While watching, I told Charlotte of taking my mother for a balloon ride on her seventy-fifth birthday. She adored the trip, and my photographs had turned out so well I put them on exhibit in my office building.

Charlotte drove me to Mission San Xavier del Bac, the Dove of the Desert, for a quick look, then through downtown Tucson to show me the University of Arizona's campus. Back at her home, we dressed to go to lunch at Tanque Verde Ranch with friends. Tanque Verde Ranch is an old-time cattle and guest ranch with an authentic history of pioneering, cattle rustling, and Indian battles. Looking out the ranch house windows, I had no trouble imagining billowing dust clouds kicked up by Don Estervan Ochoa's mule train or the swaying Butterfield Stagecoach on its way to Tucson in the 1880s.

Tanque Verde is Spanish for "green pool," a name given to a sizeable area east of Tucson, where deeply colored pools of artesian water are common along the creek beds. Near Cottonwood Grove are grinding stones once used by Indians who settled along the creek. We enjoyed the Sunday buffet. I was feeling normal and civilized again.

On our way home, Charlotte took me to Gallery in the Sun, Ted DeGrazia's studio. The buildings, which the artist and a group of Indians constructed from local materials, were as interesting as the paintings. Looking at the art and trying to learn something about the artist dissipated my fatigue and sent me forth refreshed.

On our way to dinner, we stopped by to see Bitsy Reaves, who had gone to Randolph-Macon Woman's College as I had. Bitsy is incapacitated by rheumatoid arthritis. After training her dog to help her, she began teaching other handicapped owners to train their dogs to help them. This became her business, Handi-Dogs, Inc. Charlotte is a volunteer.

We reached the Saguaro Corners Restaurant on Old Spanish Trail at the same time as Bea and the McIntoshes. No sooner had we sat down than the javelinas appeared for dinner, too, darting among the bushes and rocks. They looked like giant pig-shaped sunfish flitting about.

After dinner, I put my extra things in the flagship. I would ride my bike from Charlotte's home to the Arizona-Sonora Desert Museum to meet Bea and the McIntoshes the next day. We parted for the evening. It had been a long day, and I fell asleep in my room soon after reaching Charlotte's home.

Tucson, Monday, February 23

Monday morning was dark and cold, and the forecast called for high temperatures in the forties. Charlotte had to run a golf match, and I set off to ride thirty miles to the Desert Museum. She sent me on my way photographed, armed with clear directions, rested, and encouraged.

A tailwind breeze sped me along the first ten miles, and gravity pulled me downhill along Silverbell Road where Charlotte played golf. I wondered momentarily which century I was riding in as I passed a covered-wagon camp, complete with horses, tents, and numerous wagons emblazoned "Vision Quest."

Then came a long climb over the Gates Pass on a narrow road with little traffic. Coasting down from the pass, I arrived ready to explore the museum with the McIntoshes and Bea. We went in together but set a time and meeting point and wandered in different directions. At last I saw an American eagle! Later, I was lying on my side in the aviary taking a picture when two elegant women stepped around me.

"Now that's getting the most out of your visit!" one of them remarked, as I looked up from my camera. They wanted to know where I was from and what I did. When they heard I'd retired from the CIA, one of them chided, "Oh, you're one of the bad guys!"

"That's a matter of opinion," I grinned.

Then she asked seriously, "Do you think the bad reputation is created by the politicians?"

I responded, "Every time the CIA's reputation takes a nose-dive in the press, our number and quality of job applicants skyrockets; we get more money from Congress and more private letters commending us. Assume I've stated facts, and make your own decision." I liked the style of these women and delivered my reply with a smile. The outpouring of good will toward me from strangers continually lifted my spirits. After lunch, we hung my bike on flagship's rack and climbed inside to motor back to Crazy Horse Campground.

I packed away my temporary tent, now part of flagship's equipment, and set up the newly purchased Crescent. At four pounds, it was a little heavy, but it was more comfortable and half the weight of the temporary one. While Bea packed her bike and panniers into a box for travel, I sorted, organized, and reviewed my stuff. Joan prepared dinner, and

Mac brought the accounts up to date so we could settle. Each person made an effort to ensure that our dinner was pleasant. Accounts settled, I went to bed with renewed assurances that the flagship would accompany me as far as El Paso, a few more days. I felt sure the McIntoshes would gently encourage me to cancel the trip and stay home when I visited my mother. They still considered bicycling alone too dangerous.

Crazy Horse Campground, Tuesday, February 24

Since there was no hurry to get up, I lay in my sleeping bag, covered with two extra flagship blankets, and read a book until Mac came to talk with me. As we walked around the campground, he said that he and Joan slept poorly and talked during the night. A severe storm, including snow, was expected during the next two days. They thought it would be foolish to go to higher elevations and get caught in a snowstorm. Since the weather was changing, they would prefer to return to the warmer climes of the coast and not continue to El Paso. They just could not accompany me any further, but hated to have to tell me.

I couldn't hurt their feelings by telling them how thrilled I was to be on my own. "I'll continue with my plans," I said with all the firmness I could muster.

I had time to think while riding my bike to a store to retrieve a box out of a dumpster. My heaviest equipment, stuff that I planned to carry home on the plane from El Paso, went into the box along with everything else I couldn't stuff into the panniers. There was no time to change back to heavy duty tires. I tied one of them on top of my load and put the other in the box. I took down the tent, pumped my tires, zipped the panniers, and hung everything on the bike. Mac stuck his head out the RV door to invite us to breakfast. Finally ready to roll, I went in, sat down, and quietly ate. They agreed to mail my box at the post office, and I left twenty dollars to cover the postage.

All the loose ends appeared to be cared for, and I thought I'd better get on that bike and ride out of there before I lost momentum. It would be so easy to give up and sit down. If I did, my U.S.A. perimeter trip would be history. I told Bea, Joan, and Mac goodbye, put one leg over my heavy bike, stepped on one pedal and began to turn the crank. I wobbled the overloaded bicycle into the road.

I passed the truck stop, thinking I should buy food for the day, but I was afraid to stop turning the pedals. Speeding down Interstate 10 with a tailwind, I left Tucson under a black storm cloud visible in my rear view mirror. The decision was made. The action was taken. The stress of indecision slid from my body like fat off a roasting chicken. I was glad to be on the road again, self-reliant, on my own. From the top of a rise, I turned and looked at the black clouds where Tucson had been. It was probably raining there, but I was in the sun! In my rear view mirror, I saw lightning split the blackness.

I turned due south on Route 83 and into a headwind as I headed for Sonoita, over two thousand feet above Tucson. Climbing began in earnest and continued, connecting ever-shorter straight stretches of road between hairpins. The wind blew in my face, increasing my effort and cutting my speed. As I continued uphill, sun often splashed the road. The sky ahead was blue but in my rear view mirror, it looked like night.

After two-and-a-half hours, my shoulders ached. Balancing the bike with such a heavy load, the heaviest I ever carried, was hard. I had not ridden a fully loaded bike since Washington State. It was chilly when I paused briefly to rest and eat an apple. The road became steeper. After riding another ten miles, I felt much more tired. I stopped at a shelter and lay down on the picnic table to flatten my back. Somewhat rested, I walked around in circles to keep warm and as I replaced a lost bike rack screw, I noticed hunger. I had nothing else to eat. The chill wind urged me back on the bicycle. It was six miles to Sonoita. Although I was riding in the sun, occasional hail fell like fine, prickly rain. After one hairpin turn, the wind buffeted me off the pavement into the sand, but I didn't fall. I walked a few hundred yards.

On the bike again, over the pass, I soon rolled into the intersection that was Sonoita. In a tiny grocery, I drank hot coffee, ate junk food, and heard good news about the road ahead. It was rolling or downhill all the way to the next town, Huachuca City, twenty-five miles away. When I started off, the sun was still ahead of me and black clouds were at my back. A tailwind pushed me along.

The afternoon was glorious, and my fatigue disappeared. Rain pelted down for about five minutes as one of the clouds overtook me; then one end of a rainbow hovered over the highway center line just ahead. The rainbow moved down the road for a time, drawing me forward before skipping out over the cacti and the mountain.

By five o'clock, I was sixty miles from Tucson. Hungry, wet, and extremely tired, I stopped at a gas station and was told the nearest motel was ten miles away in Sierra Vista. There was nowhere to camp and I doubted I could pedal another ten miles into the wind. Certainly, I could not do it before dark. I asked several station wagon or pickup drivers for a ride, but no one was going my way. I really did not want a ride. I just wanted to be safe, dry, and warm for the night.

I mounted the bike again and began to turn the pedals, not efficiently, but they kept turning. It got dark and rained hard before I arrived at the main street of Sierra Vista. As my Avocet turned seventy miles, I leaned my bike outside the Western Motel office. Since it was still raining, I didn't feel foolish walking into the office dripping wet. They gave me a cup of coffee and a room. Showered, dry, and warm, I ate and fell into a self-satisfied sleep.

Sierra Vista, Wednesday, February 25

When I awoke, my body ached, and I didn't feel like moving one inch. I heard light but steady rain. I would take a day off to rest and prepare my bike and myself for the adventures ahead. The weather prediction was for rain the rest of the week. In Tucson, the airport was closed. Flash flood warnings had been announced, and people without heat in their homes were suffering. I got out of bed and looked out the door to bring the weather report from general to specific: fog, a dusting of snow and slush, and intermittent light rain.

Mid-morning, I walked through light snow flurries that melted on impact and misty rain, never getting my raincoat or shoes more than damp. For warmth, I layered four shirts under my coat. Being home in "real" winter for two months had acclimated me to the cold. I found the Gourmet Bakery and ate what was to become a favorite meal for any time of day, huevos rancheros: two eggs, over easy, atop two soft corn tortillas, the whole covered with hot tomato sauce and served with hash browns. The Gourmet Bakery was the classic town cafe and communications center. One large table and several smaller ones were occupied by men and women wearing cowboy hats, plaid shirts, jeans, and boots.

The clouds were lifting and here and there, a ray of sun

penetrated sporadically. Cars were decorated with snow but the streets were dry. It looked and smelled like early spring.

I went back to my room, wrote a *Pedalgram* to my friends, made the copies and stapled them at the Paper Clip shop, and carried them to the post office. My commitment to completing the trip alone was underscored in writing, fifty copies worth. There was no turning back.

The Paper Clip employees told me about the route ahead to Douglas. It was straight, almost flat, and with little traffic. Only one person in the shop had been to Douglas. The extent to which people remained at home surprised me. I had grown up in motion, and my home was wherever I slept. I found it hard to identify with people who had never traveled from their birthplace to the next town.

After learning the next day was expected to be clear and sunny, I ate General Tzo's Chicken at a Chinese restaurant. There, I talked with a couple who had served in Fulda, West Germany, for several years and now "homesteaded" here in Sierra Vista. Ambling back to my room completed my day on foot.

Sierra Vista, Thursday, February 26

Bright sun glittered off the snowcapped Huachuca Mountains as I walked to the Gourmet Bakery for breakfast. I had relaxed enough to realize I was quite tired.

There was a police officer in the bakery. I asked him about the road to Douglas. He said that it should be clear, dry, and uncongested. His optimistic report gave me confidence. After selecting two oatmeal cookies for later in the day, I paid my bill and strode out to my bike, hoping I'd be seeing Hank and Dottie Hull at the Double Adobe Campground between Bisbee and Douglas, where we had agreed to meet.

I chose Route 92, flatter than the other possible road which wound through higher elevations in the Mule Mountains. The map indicated that I would climb less than a thousand feet, proceed due south almost to the Mexican border, and then parallel it before turning north to Bisbee and then southeast to Douglas. I had approximately sixty miles, a half-day ride, ahead. The thermometer at the bank showed thirty-nine degrees, and the post office flag indicated a tailwind as I pedaled out of town.

Twelve miles of gentle uphill took me closer to the Huachuca Mountains. There was a little snow on the ground beyond the road shoulder. Although the wind behind me had picked up, I stopped to remove one shirt. Water dripped from everything in sight. Birds chattered and leapt about on the cacti, utility wires, and trees.

My road descended and was shaded by a few black clouds. As I sped along at twenty-eight miles an hour, my fingers got cold. Unwilling to slow down, I warmed them in my mouth, one hand at a time. I would slow soon enough on the flat valley ahead.

I passed the Coronado National Memorial where, in 1540, Francisco Vasquez de Coronado entered what is now the United States. A snow devil whirred up by the wind danced across a field as I continued through Miracle Valley, and a black cloud briefly loosed snow upon me. In the crisp, clear air, I almost felt that I was skiing.

Soon, I came to Bisbee's city limits sign. Naco, Mexico, was about three miles south across the border. The town of Bisbee was a mile-high refuge for retirees and artists and a favorite movie set for nineteenth-century stories. I rode through a few blocks of the old town on the edge of an open mine pit before returning to the road to Douglas.

After traveling thirty-five miles, I was getting tired. Although I knew the rest of the ride would be easy, I wanted to allow plenty of time to visit the Hulls. I began to roll downhill at thirty miles an hour. Along the way, I flushed several road-runners. The birds would run awhile, then fly up and glide into the bushes. I hoped they had cleared any lizards and snakes from my path. I passed a small airfield and a large copper smelter and arrived at the Motel 6 in Douglas shortly after two o'clock.

I phoned the campground. Hank and Dottie came right away to pick me up in their car. The rest of the afternoon and evening, I reveled in non-stop talk with Hank and Dottie. They drove me back to Bisbee, and up and down the gullies and ravines. Squeezed into odd lots were turn-of-the-century houses, some on streets so steep that the postal service would not deliver the mail. In the heart of town was the renovated Victorian Copper Queen Hotel, where Theodore Roosevelt had been a guest, as had General John J. Pershing when his forces invaded Mexico in pursuit of Pancho Villa.

When we returned to the campground, there were balloons festooning the front of the mobile home and posters proclaiming, "Welcome Bea and Jane, U.S.A. Perimeter Tour" covered the windshield. People came out to shake hands and welcome me. I was sorry Bea missed the celebration.

Lou Sirois, owner of the quiet Double Adobe Campground, asked my permission to call the newspaper in Bisbee. Although rather nervous about being interviewed alone, I agreed. Lou arranged for the editor to come to the campground the next morning.

The rest of the evening was spent enjoying Dottie's home-made chili and listening as Hank and Dottie shared their thorough knowledge of the area. For the next three days, I traveled on their advice, well guided and assisted.

Douglas, Friday, February 27

When I looked out of the window at five-fifteen, snow was falling. I was glad to be in a motel snugly protected from the desert winter. Lou Sirois picked me up after breakfast for the interview.

Larry Ketchum's article in *The Bisbee Observer* was headed "Seeing America — Retired Cyclist Halfway in Journey Around USA." After the interview, I waved goodbye to Hank and Dottie as they headed west. I spent the early afternoon exploring Douglas before going over to Mexico to buy some Nescafe, a stronger blend than ours. For many years, I had hauled coffee back from England, Switzerland, and Mexico or asked friends to bring me the foreign blends I favor. In Mexico, I bought two large jars of coffee and mailed them home.

In Douglas, a couple from an RV recognized my clothes and bicycle and said, "We passed you yesterday and I thought you were a man. It never occurred to us a woman would be out here alone on a bicycle."

Laughing, I replied, "It never occurred to me either, but here I am."

After seeing the Phelps Dodge Mercantile store, built in 1902, I visited the Cochise County Historical Museum. The most interesting exhibit was the caretaker, who told me "I'll be ninety if I live to St. Pat's Day." He had come to Douglas from St. Louis for his health.

In the next block, I parked my steel horse and entered The Gadsden Hotel, built in 1907. Everyone, it seemed, wore cowboy boots. Many men wore big-brimmed hats and had long, dangling mustaches. The hotel lobby, built in 1929, has a high ceiling decorated with Tiffany stained glass murals. Its focal point is an Italian marble staircase. Several movies have been filmed here, including *The Life and Times of Judge Roy Bean*. Thorton Wilder wrote a book while living at Gadsden Hotel.

Douglas, Saturday, February 28

Up early, I read, had breakfast, and then rode out of Douglas at first light.

In Apache, a "town" of three houses, a stone marker stated that in nearby Skeleton Canyon, Geronimo, the last Apache chieftain, and his followers surrendered in 1866, bringing Indian warfare in America to a close. For about ten miles ahead, there were mountain walls on either side, where the road's bluish line zipped the valley together. My eyes wandered the expanses of earth tones and stared here at a rock, there at a variance of color, now at a pair of hawks soaring. The road was mine except for a few roadrunners. Row upon row of mountains rippled into a gray-blue haze.

When I came to Rodeo, a few feet across the New Mexico state line, I was thirsty. I drank some orange juice and then rode off, hoping to pedal the ten uphill miles to Portal in less than an hour to allow time for lunch and sightseeing.

At the Portal Cafe and Motel, I ate soup, unloaded my bike in my room, and met a local resident who volunteered to guide me through Cave Creek Canyon. He was pleasant and friendly, but I was a little put off by his curly hair and beard that fluttered in the breeze as we cranked up the canyon road talking about bicycles. He also pointed out the best campsites where bird watchers stay and said he picked up enough odd jobs to keep his bank account solvent. He had lived hand-to-mouth for ten years, camping out with no job. He parked his truck and camper off the road high up to catch the sun. Why had I thought this guy a bum because he had no steady job? I didn't have a job either! I had to keep correcting my mental illusion that I was on vacation.

We climbed rather steadily for over three miles, and I felt a little tired. I decided to forego the nearby frozen waterfall in favor of a hot shower. Thanks and goodbyes were almost as brief as the thirty-mile-an-hour exhilaration of the downhill run to Portal.

At supper, three generations of the two families who own and operate the cafe and motel crowded into the cozy eight-table room that opened into the grocery store. The other overnight guest was a truck driver whose rig was stuck on a mountain road where he had driven illegally. Usually, one truck driver a week gets stuck trying to avoid the scales. After supper, he watched TV and I watched the birds until it got too chilly. At night, temperatures dropped rapidly from the sixties to the teens.

Back in my room, I nervously considered the next few days along Interstate 10 in New Mexico where bicycles were illegal. No other road could take me from Lordsburg to Deming and Las Cruces. Originally, I planned to stay along the border on Route 9, but I had learned water and food would be difficult to find. I couldn't carry enough for that distance through isolated terrain.

I planned to travel Interstate 10 for sixty miles on each of the next three days, stopping at Lordsburg, Deming, and Las Cruces. I would then ride straight to the El Paso airport to catch my afternoon plane home. When I returned, I could switch to lighter clothes and carry less cooking gear.

Portal, Sunday, March 1

The twittering of birds woke me, and I went out to watch them. Grinkos, cardinals, titmice, woodpeckers, black and white sparrows, and gray and yellow warblers sang merrily as I walked to breakfast and back to my room.

Every morning, I climbed upon my bike and turned its wheels into the unknown. I pulled on my warmest gloves, for the seven-and-a-half-mile descent would be chilly, invigorating. In the valley, I reentered New Mexico and passed irrigated land where wisps of cotton were caught in the cacti along the road. Meadowlarks sang on the fences and sprang aflutter out of the brush as I passed. It was a day to soar with the hawks and watch over the fields like the kestrel on a utility wire. I watched the hunting birds as I pedaled, wishing I could identify them, but not wanting to stop. I climbed a long slope that took me out of the valley on to a plateau and looked back to where Cochise and Geronimo led their tribes. I headed north to pickup Interstate 10 at Road Forks.

At the truck stop, I ate from the salad bar and spent an hour sitting in a comfortable, warm room full of bantering people. Refreshed, I rode past the "no bicycles" sign down the ramp and along the interstate shoulder. Traffic was light, and I pedaled happily beside long distance trucks and RVs.

In Lordsburg, I found a motel on the east side of town. Its office was the parlor of a house resplendent in oriental rugs, paintings, and ornate furniture. During the night, when rumbling trains awoke me momentarily, I felt concerned about reaching my plane at El Paso. I knew I was becoming overtired when I began to awaken, even for short moments, every two or three hours.

Lordsburg, Monday, March 2

I entered the Border Cowboy Truck Stop Restaurant before daylight and was on the road shortly after eight. I stopped to watch ducks and again to buy orange juice and refill my lower water bottle. Soon, at 4,585 feet, I passed the Continental Divide. Traveling east with the flow of water, I was making good time on the high prairie plateau. On the long gradual downhill to Deming a policeman passing in a cruiser ignored me, a lone, trespassing bicyclist. I ate some crackers and carrots from my pocket, looked across the yucca and brush, and kept going. When I descended a small hill into Deming, a sign announced three state parks, pure water, and "fast ducks." Duck racing, I found, is a local sport.

I continued through town to Motel 6, rejecting a campground for a larger, more comfortable "tent." Campgrounds were fun but Motel 6 was private, and familiar. Every room had the same floor plan. I knew where the light switches were, and the windows would open to fresh air. I checked in, showered, read for two hours, and watched TV, but still wasn't rested enough to feel like eating. The next Motel 6 was in El Paso, far out on the west side of town. Perhaps I could get that far the next day. It would be a long trip but from the El Paso motel, the airport would be a short ride across the city.

East Deming, Tuesday, March 3

On the highway again, I cycled into a lovely morning, amusing myself by catching the wind blast from trucks and riding it like waves of surf. The shoulder surface was rough, and wind blew across my path. Two roadrunners stepped lively across a field, flew a little, ran again. On I went, past a trading post, blacksmith, laundry, and lots of evenly spaced pecan trees. A police helicopter flew over but gave me no signal. No police cruiser came to get me.

After pedaling forty-nine miles, I could see the rim of the alluvial plain sloping into Las Cruces. I turned off the interstate to Route 28 and stopped at a bakery in Mesilla for a half-hour rest and food. Refreshed, I continued. I would try to reach Motel 6 in El Paso. I could afford to push myself, because my trip home would be a five-day rest from biking.

I crossed the Rio Grande! It wasn't very wide but the current was swift. Years ago, near Los Alamos, I had been surprised by its narrowness. My idea of a famous, great river had been conditioned by the Potomac, the Chattahoochee, and the Rhine at Bonn. Perhaps, in the desert, a great river is one with water! By two-thirty, under clouds floating in from the east, I observed plowed fields full of huge blackbirds, some holding their tails up like roadrunners. A car full of people slowed, stared at me, and then continued. A few miles further in Vado was a campground, but I felt good and decided to head for El Paso.

At a grocery in Berino, a woman said thirty people on bicycles came through about a week ago. They had started from Florida to cycle the perimeter of the U.S.A. She didn't think they would make it to the west coast. She told me it was five miles to the motel in Anthony or fifteen miles to the outskirts of El Paso and Motel 6.

It was only four and, if I pedaled fast, I could reach the motel before dark. A truck carrying vegetables passed me, dribbling red peppers down the road. Rolling well, slightly downhill, downstream, I entered El Paso's city limits. Whee! I checked in as the sun disappeared. The desk clerk said it was a hundred miles to Motel 6 in Deming. My Avocet recorded ninety-three. I felt well satisfied with myself.

I called Mary Lou Parker, a member of the El Paso Bicycle Club, with whom I had corresponded. She would meet me the next afternoon and take my panniers to her house. Dr.

Bill Reynolds would lead me on a cross-city ride to the airport. There, Mary Lou's father would pick up my bike and store it. When I returned, Mary Lou would meet my plane. It was wonderful to talk with a bicyclist.

I had entered Texas that day, on a bicycle! I felt like a fellow hiker who kept asking on my first trip to the Kashmir Himalayas, "Do you believe this?" My fatigue dissipated in exhilaration.

El Paso, Texas, Wednesday, March 4

As usual, I was up early, eating fruit while I packed and cleaned the chain superficially with a paper towel. I was tired, and this was a lay-about day. I read for an hour and then pedaled over to the university where, after lunch, I lay on the grass, basking in the sun and waiting for Bill Reynolds.

I saw a man walking toward me, pushing his bicycle. His name was Mack Shreve, a truck driver and psych major who was on his way to class. Later he wrote me a letter describing his feelings:

"When I saw your loaded-up bicycle, I knew a friend was nearby. I guess nothing is more moving for me than a person longriding. Recently a friend and I pedaled about twenty-five miles east where we'd gone a dozen times in the past by car. There was a profound difference in being there with our bicycles. I looked at the long road disappearing into the horizon and was proud as heck that I'd motivated myself out there with my own juices, so to speak. Being there seemed to have so much more significance! As you can see I'm hooked! I make U-turns whenever I see a full-dressed bicycle!"

Bill Reynolds arrived, and we rode to Mary Lou's office where we put my panniers in her car, leaving out what I would need on the plane. Bill, a retired dentist, adores bicycling. He rides around the city daily and seemed pleased to escort me to the airport. Unfortunately, we went down a street covered with fresh tar which adhered to our tires and collected sand, gravel, and debris. We stopped at a filling station and cleaned the tires and splattered frames as best we could with paper towels. Jim Parker met us at the airport and hung my bike on his car rack. I waved goodbye and put myself in Delta's hands until I would reach the East Coast and home.

Another passenger asked if the long days of riding in

the desert had been dull. Had it been dull in early morning to stand stock still, hesitating to bring the binoculars to my eyes because a pair of bridled titmice were hardly fifteen feet away?

Had it been dull to ride past a prairie dog village, watching them scamper from hole to hole calling warnings, leaping, putting heads up to see what the fuss was about. They sat on hind legs like squirrels, furiously shaking their tails. Too soon, they were behind me.

Had it been dull watching hunting birds flying low over bushes and grasses, hovering, dipping, skimming, disappearing to the ground — perhaps without touching — then sliding into another hover or glide?

It was interesting, beautiful, stimulating, exciting, but *never* boring. From a car, it's difficult to perceive the subtle variations of the land, see the animals, or smell the air, snow, or rain. I didn't remember the towns where I cycled through a commercial strip of fast food places and gas stations, but I remember old buildings and historical markers I would never have stopped a car to read.

Getting away from responsibilities at home was difficult, and staying away had been hard. I knew a phone call could terminate my trip. I realized how great a privilege it had been to live in a society of trust. At the CIA, every person was thoroughly investigated and tested. We knew we were an elite group, and we took pride in it. Some entrusted their lives to another's discretion. Since leaving that company, the best people I have encountered are bicyclists.

CHAPTER FOURTEEN

The Rio Grande Valley
of Decisions

Baltimore, Maryland, Sunday, March 8

My mother took me to the airport in Baltimore. "I'd like to go with you," she laughed, "but, I'm eighty, after all. I'll have to be content to bicycle by phone." I promised Mother another visit when I reached the other side of Texas, and I promised to stay twice as long. The rest had been fine and her encouragement sustaining. I was ready to continue my trip.

Mary Lou Parker greeted me warmly when I walked out of the airport gate at El Paso with one pannier, my luggage. That evening at the Parker home, the family offered advice about the route and what to expect on the way. The next day's ride to Van Horn was long, over a hundred miles.

I told myself I was not afraid. After all, I had traveled alone all over Southeast Asia, and on short trips in Mexico and longer trips in Nepal and Kashmir. At home in America, when I wanted company, I could telephone a friend. Alone on the road, I had learned, I could take the initiative to talk.

Over the years, I developed the notion that every person is shy or reserved to some degree with strangers. I was confident I, a lone woman, threatened no one.

El Paso, Texas, Monday, March 9

I slept comfortably under a handmade quilt. In the morning, the Parkers helped me finish packing the bike and pumping the tires. I was surprised that the front tire had become completely flat during my four-day absence. I would watch it. After we took pictures, Jim, Mary Lou's dad, escorted me in his car. Under Interstate 10 at the frontage road, we waved, and I was on my way again.

Scraps of sentences flashed through my head: "Aren't you afraid? You're so brave. We're so glad to meet a real adventurer. Thank you so much for sharing your trip with us." Could anyone have been more kind or hospitable than the Parkers? At the junction of Routes 375 and 20, I found a Safeway and bought three oranges and two rolls for snacking. The checker asked, "Where do you come from?"

"San Diego."

"Where are you going?"

"Florida."

"Wow!" She called the bagger over. He commented on my rear view mirror.

"It's a helmet mirror," I told him. "It doesn't create wind resistance, like one on the handlebars, and it's steadier, so I can see better. Best of all, I adjust it by moving my head."

After five days, it felt good to get some exercise and be back home on the bike. There was little wind, and the cloudless morning smelled fresh as I left the city limits of El Paso. I decided not to hurry, but to keep going as fast as possible for as many miles as I could. I followed Route 20, rolling between Interstate 10 and the Rio Grande, pedaling in the same direction as the water flow, slightly downhill. Near the Renklin Canal, rows of pecan trees lined up in full battle array. On a tailwind, I entered the town of Tornillo, the largest town before Sierra Blanca, and passed the border control office, closed in the daytime. The Mexican border was seven miles south. The canal continued on my right, along the flat, loamy valley. Beyond were fields of young pecan trees about half the height of the utility poles. A sign warned: "Anyone picking pecans from the trees or off the ground will be prosecuted according to law." I saw large and small blackbirds and a family picking pecans off the ground. Another sign indicated Sierra Blanca to be fifty-three miles away. I had traveled thirty-one miles.

The Parkers were concerned about where I would camp if I got tired and couldn't make it to Van Horn. I had thought the culverts under the road would be good, but they had vetoed that, saying they are used at night by "illegals." Everyone advised me not to be out at night along this border.

Rolling along the Texas Mountain Trail, I passed about thirty bee hives. On the Alamo Bridge, I paused because I liked the name and leaned my bike on the bridge rails. When I resumed pedaling, wind was dead behind me, and it was cool in the shade, hot in the sun. At McNary, a ghost town, I took the bicycles-prohibited interstate since there was no other road. There was little traffic, so I rode the white line to avoid the rough shoulder until, at a farm road, I exited toward a truck stop and food.

At lunch, I was told I was approaching a ten-mile hill. Out here, ten miles just means "a piece" or "a space" — it shouldn't be taken too literally. The hill proved to be about ten miles up, ten down, and then ten rolling. On a downhill grade through Sierra Blanca, I noticed I had traveled seventy-six miles and had only forty miles more to reach Van Horn. It was two-thirty, and I felt good.

A train slid by silently. Because I could see so far, the train looked close, but I could hear nothing. The movement caught my eye, as did the antics of prairie dogs, hopping in and out of their holes, alerting each other, shaking their tails. I crested a ridge and swooped down at thirty miles an hour into Van Horn, Culbertson County, and the Central Time Zone. I had lost an hour and gained one-hundred-seventeen miles worth of confidence.

The *Texas Travel Handbook* told me that Van Horn, with three thousand people at four thousand feet, grew at the junction of Bankhead Highway and Old Spanish Trail in the mid-1800s. Van Horn rests in a wide basin devoted to irrigated farming and is surrounded by mountains. Tourists flock to Van Horn for its climate and camping; hunters come for white-tailed and mule deer, pronghorn antelope, and upland game birds.

I found a motel room, food, and sleep in quick succession, satisfied to have concluded the day's journey I dreaded. My last thought before sleep was that people are never presented with trouble they cannot handle if they are willing to accept the opportunity and exert sufficient effort.

Van Horn, Tuesday, March 10

Under cloudy skies, I left Van Horn, "Where the Sunshine Spends the Winter." Well, it forgot where it was supposed to be that morning! I assured myself that kinks of unwillingness in my body would dissipate faster through movement than rest. I had a slight headache and my jaw was sore to the touch. Was a dead tooth acting up or was the pain from a surface gum irritation? I did not want to get sick.

West Texas seemed empty. I passed a historical marker noting the arid terrain's only dependable water supply and I saw old windmills whose blades or whole tops were missing. None was spinning. Their era had been blown aside by technology, and larger fields now contained irrigating machines.

I began to watch a pair of hawks. Then, just below the birds, I noticed two pronghorn antelope pressed head to head, horn-locked, not fifty yards away. I stopped, but could hardly take my eyes off them to reach the binoculars as they pushed and shoved each other. When I began describing the scene into my recorder, the animals pulled their heads apart, never moving their feet, and twisted their necks to look at me. We silently observed each other, frozen in time. They began to wander away, and seeking my longest lens, I unzipped the saddle bags. One buck stopped. I continued to assemble my camera, and one antelope, head alert, cautiously walked toward me, putting his feet delicately into the grass, upon the earth. Through the camera and the binoculars, I got clear views from several angles of the magnificent animal with its white necklaces and rump, wonderfully curled horns, and markings. Although I was too far away for the 135 mm lens to fill the frame, I shot some photos anyway before the pronghorns quietly walked out of sight. What a thrill the animals had been!

As I resumed pedaling, I saw another bicyclist with panniers coming toward me. As he got closer, I crossed over, dismounted, and waited until he stopped. Removing his radio headset, Bill Horne introduced himself. He was riding to speak against drug abuse. He was taking the perimeter too, and had covered over eight-thousand miles since he started from Chicago. "Be careful at the border," he laughed, "They had a shootout in Lajitas while I was there." Chuckling, he continued, "Everyone scared me to death about these roads, but there's really no problem. Just don't be out at night. There's a good cafe in Valentine, and there are motels in Marfa and Presidio." He took a Rio Grande float trip, and advised, "It was cold in the canyon. Take a sweater." We both had long rides ahead and moved on long before I had talked enough. I was disappointed that I forgot to take Bill's picture.

An hour later, I saw a group of fifteen pronghorn antelope, females and young lying among the grass in a low place. When I stopped to look, three stood up. We watched each other.

In Valentine, I stopped at the cafe for lunch, and rain sprinkled my bike for a few minutes while I ate. In restaurants, I was trying Mexican dishes to learn what I liked best. Soup and salad or tacos for lunch weren't too heavy when I had an afternoon of pedaling ahead. I went on until I reached Marfa and found a snug motel room. After shopping for groceries, I consumed milk and cookies before showering. I flopped on the bed and rested until dinner time.

After dinner, I washed clothes, checked the bird book, and ate more milk and cookies. My head ached and my jaw hurt, even though, except to eat, I had not worn my lower denture for two days. I took aspirin and hoped the headache would disappear.

Marfa, a former water stop on the Texas and New Orleans Railroad, is a trade hub and a center for soaring in gliders. Marfa's Chamber of Commerce folder described local cattle, sheep, and goat ranches. Water supplied by city-owned wells is plentiful and so pure that chlorination is unnecessary. Majestic mountain country reached eight thousand feet into clear sky. Being here felt good.

Marfa, Thursday, March 11

In the motel parking lot, I met John B. Ashford, a young geologist who worked for the Water Board. After answering a few questions about my trip, I asked him about the area's geology. He said I would ride across a basin, out over its edge, and down a slope several thousand feet to the Rio Grande River Valley. John recommended the lodging and food at the Balia Inn in Presidio. Located across the street from the Border Patrol offices, it would be safe.

In my room at the Thunderbird Motel, I checked the map mileage for yesterday's trip against my Avocet and found them within a mile of each other. Satisfied that my Avocet was accurate, I decided I could leave town as late as mid-morning and arrive with ease in Presidio by four.

After breakfast, I had noticed a dental office next door to the restaurant. Perhaps the dentist could at least tell me whether the pain in my jaw was serious. It wasn't. Dr. Roy F. Slaton repaired my denture and medicated an ulcerated gum.

I rode around the County Courthouse on my bike, admiring the native stone and bricks used for its construction in

1886. When I was almost out of town, a young man on a mountain bicycle hailed me in the street. "I'm the only biker living in Marfa. Maybe you've seen some of my cartoons published in bike magazines." He was so talkative that I forgot to ask his name or take his picture as we babbled about bicycles and components. Most of what I had heard about bicycling and camping in Big Bend he corroborated.

I pedaled south across the basin, stopping at the Border Patrol station. The officers concurred that the motel opposite their headquarters was where I should stay, that I should not camp, and that the road to the park was safe.

"Are you permitted to comment on whether or not I should go to Mexico?" I asked.

"My wife, mother, and sister don't go anymore," he replied.

"That's good enough for me. Thank you."

The afternoon proved unique and special. The sky, which had been heavily overcast, was now light blue and sprinkled with popcorn clouds. Pushed by the gentle hand of a warm tailwind, I passed an unusual number of deer-crossing signs. On each sign, the deer's nose had been squirted with international orange paint. I watched scissor-tailed flycatchers and the killdeer who flew beside me from time to time. I talked to myself, sang, spoke into my recorder, and read billboards describing the Lajitas Museum.

Sometimes the road appeared to lead straight to the sky, but it didn't look or feel uphill. I took off my helmet, hung it on the back of the bike, and pushed the wet hair back from my forehead to get a little sun on my face and dry my hair. I breathed deeply, realizing I had not been in a place I liked so well since my last hike in the Himalayas. I saw one vehicle every quarter hour.

At about forty-four miles, having climbed from Shafter, I reached the basin rim and began to roll downhill. There was tar over a layer of gravel on the road. Some tar was soft in the hot sun, and the road felt as slick as ice. I rode carefully, making no sudden movement, until the patches disappeared.

Ahead lay the Rio Grande Valley. A living map spread before me, every detail visible. The small town on my side of the river was Presidio, and the dust and haze beyond hovered over the Mexican city of Ojinaga.

By five o'clock, I had covered sixty miles during the laid-back, five-hour day. I was off the plateau and feeling warm, good. On to the Gulf of Mexico!

Presidio, Friday, March 12

My day's route would cover fifty difficult miles, up and down hills. Bill Horne said his heart almost popped out of his chest when he walked up the fifteen percent grade which lay ahead of me. I had walked eight-percent grades but wondered if I could push my heavily loaded bike up a fifteen percent incline. *El Camino del Rio,* Spanish for The River Road, is the popular name here for Farm Road 170. It took me from Presidio to Fort Leaton and I would follow it toward Big Bend National Park. Texans hail it as a spectacular drive, a road in a land of primitive magnificence, a road that careens over mountains and snakes through canyons.

I watched a congregation of ducks before threading my way through a little gorge with only a sliver of pasture between me and the muddy, winding river. The bluebonnets were two feet high, a blaze of blue, nodding in the breeze. I felt wafted along by their soft, sweet fragrance.

A couple of bends in the road took me over a small rise and down a little slope through the town of Redford, consisting of a shed, adobe ruins, and a store that wasn't open. A van with "Outward Bound" on the door panel and Minnesota tags stopped at the store. The men in the van told me they were running two programs in the area, one for the trustees and another for the public. Their activities included rapid running, rock climbing, and canoeing along the river. They were busy, and I went on. They waved as they passed me later.

Coming up a short, steep hill, I turned into an overlook to rest. As I watched the swirling river below, I drank water and ate a few peanuts. The heat felt good, but this was only March. A big RV pulled in, and a couple got out and introduced themselves as Dot and John McDonald from Langhorne, Pennsylvania. They were stopping for lunch and asked me to join them. I told them I really was not hungry but would enjoy talking. They invited me in and we sat around the table. The McDonalds said they wander in the RV until they get cabin fever — about six weeks — and go home. They advised me to spend my day along the road which they thought more beautiful than the park itself. I enjoyed their company and emerged rested, but I still had not done The Hill.

The sweet smell of bluebonnets propelled me along, and encouraged me as I came to The Hill. Steep it was, but short. I walked the top half, pushing my bike. The crest view was worth every drop of sweat. A car full of boys pulled up, and they all tumbled out, admired the view, and told me they spent one night of their spring break in the basin at Big Bend Park. This was about the tenth time I'd been told not to miss the basin. "Hell on the bike," Bill Horne had said, "but worth it." The boys jumped into the car and sped down the hill. Quiet returned, and I watched the river current. Its muddy color was between the gray of the Indus and the red of the Chattahoochee.

When I started down, the hill was short and steep like the beginning of a good ski run. I had to use brakes at first; then I could let the bike run, as I would my skis, as the grade became more gentle and I had space ahead.

The center of Lajitas consisted of wooden shop buildings along a boardwalk. I headed for the campground and old store nestled below the ridge along the river. A few feet from the Rio Grande, a narrow island cut off my view of the river and created a chute of water in front of my campsite. I put my tent under the only tree. Over a nearby picnic table was a thatched sunshade.

At the River Bend Tour Office, my bicycle clothes were my introduction. Beth Garcia greeted me by name and told me I could take a day trip through the Santa Elena Canyon tomorrow. The bus would bring my bicycle and panniers when it came to pick us up. Instead of returning to Lajitas, I would enter Big Bend National Park by water and camp on the riverbank at Cottonwood.

Satisfied with this plan, I showered, talked with Paul, the manager of the campground, and set up my tent. The front tire I had been watching since El Paso was flat. The sun had exhausted me during the last hour of riding, probably because I had run out of water about two or three miles short of town and had been drinking conservatively for some time before that. I had just completed the shortest but hardest mileage of the past four days, for a total of three-hundred-five miles.

At the other end of the campground, a local restaurant was catering a picnic for a bus tour. I asked to buy a dinner, then piled my plate with brisket, potato salad, slaw, chicken, and bread. I saved the chicken and potato salad for the next day's lunch and ate the rest.

It felt good to lie flat, with a straight spine, to stretch, to do nothing. Bats made little noises. The stars were brilliant. Best of all, I liked the idea that I didn't have to go anywhere the following day.

Lajitas, Friday, March 13

I slept well the first night in my new Eureka Crescent tent. It was long and narrow, and the net side could be left open for ventilation or zipped up for privacy and protection from the weather.

I walked up to the bathhouse and tried to phone my mom again. I had tried several times the day before and again there was no answer. On my way back to my campsite, I planned my day. I needed to clean the stove and the bike, repair my flat front tire, and investigate a slow leak in the rear one. With the river handy, I could inspect the tubes and patch them. I would switch to the heavier tires.

The family at the next campsite asked me to join them for breakfast. Ed Levesque, a marathoner, was just returning from a run. We would eat after he showered. Ilona Levesque came to get me for breakfast, and introduced me to Chad, Andy, and Christie. Since I'd be around the campground all day, I volunteered to keep an eye on their gear while they went off to explore. After they left, I washed the pots and pans from breakfast and began work on my bike, thrilled to have a whole day with nowhere to go!

Submerging the tubes in the river revealed tiny leaks, pinholes made by goatshead thorns at Dateland. Apparently, I had failed to remove all the stickers from the tire casings. Each time I went to the water's edge to test my repairs, I was carefully observed by a great blue heron hunched sleepily on a tree limb. For four hours, he stood there. I tried some photos and watched him with the binoculars between tire-mending and bike-cleaning chores. Great-tailed grackles wandered about squawking, but all work stopped when a vermilion flycatcher sat in the sun, turning this way and that on the live-cactus fence, and a black phoebe visited the willow tree near my picnic table.

Later I walked uphill to the office and beyond to the town. A woman standing in a doorway asked in a strong, quiet voice like a musical instrument, "You're walking up and down. What's happening?" She was Angie Price, owner of Crazy Angie's store.

"I'm trying to find someone to cash my traveler's check."

"How much?"

"I only have one twenty left and I'd like to keep it. Fifty or a hundred?"

"I could do fifty."

There were lovely clothes and many interesting items in her store. "I'm sorry I can't buy anything; my bike is too heavy already."

Angie said that before she married, she had come here as a tourist, adored Lajitas, and became a river float trip guide. "This place is gonna grow. Real estate's the biggest thing in town. In a few years, this will be a going place. They say snowbirds don't spend, but winter's still best for business. People don't come in the summer. They think it's too hot, but it isn't."

I liked Lajitas. I could probably live there and be happy, too. It was midafternoon when I carried my bike over the grass, up the stairs to the gravel parking area, and rode to the old store that was a step back in time. It reminded me of many country stores in isolated places being discovered by hungry and thirsty bicyclists. A mile down the road, I knew my legs needed rest. Leaving Tucson had stressed me mentally and physically. I stood over my bike and considered visiting the museum. I'd already seen many, many small museums, but everyone had said not to miss this one. Reluctantly, I rolled downhill.

A bus tour pulled up as I was locking my bike, and I hurried inside to buy my ticket. A one-hour lecture and walk-through would be given for the group, and I could tag along. I recorded tapes of Eunice Chenoweth's wonderful tour.

At the three-dimensional diorama of wildlife, she said, "The pig-like peccary, or javelina, has poor eyesight, and can see only about ten feet, but the nose is good for about three-quarters of a mile. It eats prickly pear cactus, spines and all." Eunice talked fast; I really had to concentrate. "The American eagle's talons hit its prey at fifty-five to seventy-five miles per hour. Its claws act like a latch lock. The bird can fly carrying three times its own weight. An average American eagle weighs between seven and eight pounds, and prey under twenty-five pounds is fair game. The bird has three-stage vision: panoramic vision like ours; telescopic vision, which enables it to see a bird in flight at five miles; and micro-vision, which can lock in on a running mouse." She continued, "A turkey buzzard feeding on the road needs plenty of time to get off the ground. A driver who doesn't slow down for him may find the buzzard has dumped its food on the car's hood." Eunice went on to describe an early 1900s mining district adobe home. "They took old crankcase oil and turpentine, mixed it together, and poured it on the floor to make a linoleum-like finish. The oil held the dust down, and the turpentine killed the vermin. Window panes were made of brown paper bags. Oiled, the paper became translucent, letting in the light and keeping out dust and vermin. A well-maintained adobe will last a hundred years.

"Everything used to build the adobe structure was free off the land. From talechi, a local clay, you make a thick, green mud pie, and to that you add stone and straw. The stone acts like a furnace, and the straw gives tensile strength. Simply press a thick, gooey mud pie into a wooden frame, lift the frame off, and press some more mud in till you run out of mud. Let it lay three or four days, and it will be hard enough to handle. Let it air dry. At 110 to 120 degrees out here, we bake some pretty good bricks."

She moved on to a display of tools. "These are fence cutters. If you had them in your pocket, no discussion, no contest — one year in jail. This tool is for dehorning cattle, and these are for shoeing horses. Here's hand-made barbed wire, it was cheaper to make your own. When you're a month's round trip, a hundred miles, away from supplies, you protect your food at all costs." One wire had pieces that twirled and made noise in the wind. "When a storm tended to stampede the cattle, the noise made by the fences would cause the herds to bunch up in the middle of the fields, instead of stampeding through the fences."

After an afternoon jammed with information, I pedaled quietly to the campground and fixed and ate supper. I finally was able to talk with my mother. Mom assured me she was fine and that I shouldn't worry.

Lajitas, Saturday, March 14

The day of my raft trip arrived at last. Looking forward to it pulled me through desolate areas when I doubted my ability to bicycle alone. I rolled up and packed my tent sadly, for I liked the campsite. I debated about staying another day, returning after the raft trip, and then bicycling out but vetoed backtracking. I walked my loaded bike to the office where I said goodbye to cheery Beth Garcia and boarded the bus which would carry me to the river.

At the shore, I met David Linebough, our guide, and Iowa farmers John and Ellen Shaw. Guides in training to lead river trips came in a second raft. People from a church in El Paso were launching a dozen canoes. They didn't look experienced.

David explained that the water was fast, four feet above normal for this time of year. We had nine miles to go before reaching the canyon, nine miles in the canyon, and another mile before takeout. There was one Class IV rapid in the canyon, but the river was easy and safe.

A black-capped phoebe catching flies swooped in front of our boat as we swirled quietly along the river past banks sparsely covered with scrub or cactus. Rapidly traversing the river, we pulled over to a flat sandbar. When the second raft arrived, the staff quickly set up a picnic. As we ate, we watched the canoeists. Some came first on foot to look at a "hole" David warned them about. One by one, the boats floated through a slot on the other side of the river. One canoe overturned, and several went well past the bend where they were supposed to stop, but there was no real trouble. The canoeists intended to portage the Class IV rapid. We would ride through it if it seemed safe. Otherwise, we would walk, and David would take the raft.

As we floated through the canyon, layers of slanted rock created the optical illusion of water flowing uphill. Cliff swallows and canyon wrens accompanied us. The river, twisting and turning, muddy and fast, was not warm enough for swimming. We three tourists got out of our raft above the Class IV rapid while the trainees and David studied the water. One or two canoes had come, halted, and begun their portage. An empty canoe went down. The Shaws and I reboarded our raft. David was taking us through the rapid. We paddled according to his directions and shouted over the noise of the water. We twisted this way and that, bounced through the splash, swirled, laughed, and then pulled over to the shore between rocks.

About that time, several canoes sped down the river, too fast. A man and a boy were thrown into the water but scrambled to a nearby rock. Another man climbed to a rock across the river where the current was so strong we dared not go, and their canoe disappeared downstream. Yelling for us to hold on, David pushed our raft into the rushing current. The man and boy climbed in with us for the ride to shore. The other man sat marooned in the sunshine. Behind him rose a steep cliff. Downstream from his perch was a rapid and a drop that was too dangerous for our boats. The navigable rapid was on our side of the river, not his. The roar of the water prevented communication.

For the next hour or so, other canoeists portaged over the rocks while we waited. David said there were two rafts we passed that perhaps could reach the man, and he waited upstream for them. When one came, it missed the man's rock and was swept down the river. David walked back over the rocks to us. The passengers on another raft that came along were old people and couldn't risk a rescue attempt. (We, of course, were only in our fifties, not old!) The sun was sinking.

Just then, a tiny two-man raft slid across the current, between rocks we couldn't get through, and clung to the man's rock. They got him in. We watched them slide down the waterfall, out of sight in the churning spray. Up they bobbed as the boat sprung free. They made it through the hydraulic! Cheers went up, even above the noise of the rapids, all along the river.

We floated quietly on the current, picking up two lost canoes. We also picked up paddles, life jackets, bottles, and gear. When we landed, we left the canoes and gear on the shore, took everything out of our raft and carried life jackets and paddles to the bus. The trainees carried the rafts.

The bus delivered me to a long double row of cottonwood trees where I pitched camp before supper. I rode up to the store to phone my mom about her cardiological exam. She told me she was all right but needed a lot of rest. I promised to call more often. She knew how hard it was to find a phone in good working order. When I awoke in the night, I heard coyotes howl.

Cottonwood, Big Bend, Sunday, March 15

While I heated water for oatmeal, I noticed Steve and Mark, two high school boys from Alpine, Texas whom I met the day before, huddled at their picnic table. They looked cold.

"You guys want some coffee?" They came over with cups, and I served them the rest of my coffee. Mark planned to enter the Air Force after graduation, and Steve wanted to learn more about computers. We were joined by fellow campers, Armando and Cindy, graduate students from Austin. The park ranger told us we were in a group space reserved for the night and would have to camp elsewhere if we were staying. Mark and Steve packed up and departed for home, but Armando and Cindy claimed a vacated site and asked me to join them. I did.

Still tired, I was indecisive about my day's plans. Armando invited me to drive with them up to the basin. With their little car partially unloaded, there was room for me in the back seat. I had read there was a horseback tour, just the thing. Too tired to walk, I could sit on a horse!

It was unexpectedly curious to whiz through terrain similar to landscapes I had seen during the past four days. From the car there seemed to be no animals or fragrances, and the sense of moving among the land, rocks, and wildflowers was missing. I wondered what cycling the same road the next day would be like. I was prepared for the thousand-foot climb and the few steep hills.

We reached the basin, parked the car, and set a time for reunion. I called the stable and discovered there was space for me on the next two-and-a-half-hour horseback-walk to the Window. I called my mother and found she was improving but discouraged. I worried about how to manage if I had to get home in a hurry. Since there was no time for a proper meal, I grabbed a cherry pie and a large V8 on my way to the stables.

At noon, walking down the hot narrow trail, I imagined the time when Indians used the place as a fortress. Our road had come through a narrow, steep gap in the rim. A thousand feet below, a desert meadow was protected on all sides by a natural stone wall. Emory Peak, the highest point in Big Bend National Park, towered nearby. I didn't have to be a geologist to sense the time and forces that shaped this land — it *felt* old.

Walking the narrow, rocky trail, I realized my shoes were wearing out. I was glad to mount my horse, relieved not to move my feet or body in any direction. The horse provided an elevated view as well as a gentle back massage.

It had not occurred to me to carry my water bottle, for it was always attached to my steel horse. When I returned, I was parched and drank a lot of water, some juice, and milk while waiting for the Armando and Cindy. They had hiked part of the basin rim and were tired, too. At Cottonwood Campground, we cooked and ate supper together.

Cottonwood, Monday, March 16

When Armando and Cindy packed to leave, they found room for my panniers, sleeping bag, and tent. They would leave them for me at park headquarters. I kept only binoculars and cameras for the ride to Panther Junction. I pedaled the thirty-eight miles up from the river slowly, anticipating a downhill slope toward Marathon.

Beyond Castolon, during the tiring and tough ride up grades that felt steeper than they looked, I realized I was more tired mentally and emotionally than physically. I felt the desert sapping my will. I was worried about my mother.

The bluebonnets were encouraging, and recognizing the candelilla pleased me. The plant looks like huge bunches of straw with small leaves and white blossoms. The powdery coating on its branches is a source of wax used in lipstick and floor polish.

When I reached Persimmon Gap, the first steep uphill was behind me, and ahead the road looked relatively flat. I might even have a tailwind. Soon, with honking horn and waving hands, the students passed me. They were certainly kind to adopt me during their spring-break weekend.

On the next hill, I couldn't stay in a low gear because a gear-shift lever was loose. The Allen wrench required was in the panniers, not in my front bag. Mistake. I rigged a shock cord to hold the gear lever down. Part of the last twenty-four miles had been on a hard-packed dirt road under construction. My heavy tires, halfway between those of a racing bike and an off-road bike, were just right.

I switched directions at the main road leading to Panther Junction and park headquarters and, chased by a threatening cloud, I reveled in the push of the tailwind. At headquarters, a woman in the restroom suggested her thirteen-year-old daughter could watch my bike while I went to the office to retrieve my panniers and a camping permit. She said there had been tornado warnings. No wonder the clouds looked strange!

While standing in line to speak with a ranger, I talked to several students on spring break and learned winter visitors to the Rio Grande Valley are called "Winter Texans." When my turn came, I was welcomed with, "Oh, you're the bicyclist! All your things are here."

I had realized I left my bifocals on the ground at the water pipe in Cottonwood. A call was made to the ranger there to ask if they'd been turned in. They had not. My glasses were comfortable, even though the lenses were scratched and needed replacing. I hated to lose them. I felt discouraged.

It cheered me up when the thirteen-year-old girl, Durinda, asked if she could interview me for a school report assignment. As she and her mother, Linda, stood with me in the camping-permit line, I talked about my trip and Durinda took notes in full sentences on the back of an envelope. Her mother, who had left the line several times, returned. The campsites available were primitive ones in the desert without water. Amid lighting and thunder, the rain had begun. Linda announced, "We're going to Marathon. The weather's getting worse, and you shouldn't be trying to ride in this wind. There's room in our van for you, your bike, and all your stuff. Please, come with us." My feeling that I had been officially adopted by the State of Texas was reinforced.

I glanced in two directions; one view showed falling snow, the other brilliant sunshine. Behind both was the blackest daytime cloud I had ever seen. Its bottom was collapsing in a terrible squall. I knew Linda's proposal was wise and, though I accepted the ride, I hated not being on the bike in that tailwind! We bolted through the pelting rain to their van. There, Linda introduced her husband, Noland Young, and his mother, Delores Young. Rain, snow, sleet, and sun bounced off the van during the seventy miles to Marathon. Noland slowed the vehicle when we saw deer or wild javelina. They recounted hunting experiences to match my biking tales.

Tornados were predicted during the night. They decided we should all stay at the same motel in Marathon. I was glad I'd be indoors instead of at a campsite. The temperature had plummeted, and the wind almost blew us off our feet as we raced for our rooms. Linda told me, "The owner gave us permission to cook in our room, and our ice chest is full of meat. Please come and eat with us. We'll let you know when dinner's ready."

As I rested in my room, I removed my contacts but found I couldn't watch TV — I couldn't see that far. I couldn't rest my eyes long, for I had promised to call my mother. Mom's words said I should continue my trip while, against her will, her spirit pled with me to return home. Her doctor had urged me to continue the trip. Getting to Corpus Christi by the date I promised Mom meant less time touring in Texas. I felt pressured by schedules. I might be retired, but I had not yet abandoned deadlines. Durinda came to get me for dinner before the telephoning was done. I made a last, quick call to learn my bifocals still had not been found.

My friends had set out a feast. Sliced venison, elk patties, and beef steaks made choosing difficult. I just ate some of each. My hosts reminisced about hunting trips on horseback in Colorado. They knew the route Bea and I had biked over the Yaak because they had hunted there. They had special Columbian horses whose natural gait was like Tennessee walkers. I told of Rajistan saddles and the handsome nomad who galloped up to offer me a ride on his horse.

My hunting story was about killing a young buck with my new car even though I was braking hard and trying not to hit the animal. It was the last day of hunting season and according to Maryland law, the buck was mine. When I requested a deer tag, the orange-coated hunters were angry, for my new car bagged the only deer in the area. One angry man complained, "It's just not fair! I bought a new gun, took two weeks leave to come out and hunt. Now, I have to go home and tell my wife I spent that money and got no deer. It's just not fair." Although the venison hadn't lasted long, I hung the skin on my wall, and the story had amused my guests for years.

Marathon, Tuesday, March 17

"Texas has adopted me," I sputtered through toothpaste. I was to join the Youngs for breakfast, and they had invited me to visit their part of northern Texas as soon as I finished bicycling the perimeter.

At midmorning, they drove west, and I slowly pedaled east. The wind was still blowing my way. Before leaving Marathon, I stopped to explore the Gage Hotel, a restored West Texas establishment of the 1920s. It had original pine floors and woodwork, and each room was furnished with antiques. Pedaling out of the River Valley on to the desert plateau the day before seemed far away, in another lifetime.

I checked the water bottles again — full. I hoped I was carrying enough water to last until Sanderson, fifty-four miles away. The map indicated no other towns. Before leaving Marathon, I mailed home a package of non-essentials, ridding myself of almost four pounds. Wheeling effortlessly through town, I was blown by a strong tailwind, the residue of last night's storm that had crashed tornadoes to earth north, west, and south of us. There was almost no traffic and the road was more downhill than up, and I had all I needed for a good bicycling day.

At Housetop Mountain Campground, I stopped to drink and use the restroom. When I took off my rain jacket, the wind that had been so helpful felt chilly. Although I stopped several times, I covered twenty miles during the first hour.

From the hilltop, I flew down the slope at thirty-five miles an hour without pedaling. A motorcycling couple slowed down and rode beside me. They clocked my coasting at thirty-eight m.p.h., although my Avocet read thirty-four. Their Kawasaki was so quiet we could talk without difficulty. It was fun rolling down the road at that speed, talking as casually as though we were sitting around a swimming pool. When they went on, I sat on my bike experiencing the full effect of the west wind, which inspires many bicyclists to fly west to pedal east.

It was getting hot and I took off my gloves. The highway turned, giving me a half-mile of crosswind. It felt good to pedal though I did not seem to slow down much. With another turn, I recaptured the tailwind and my free ride continued. On the ground were creosote bushes and a few weeds — no more yucca, not much grass, and no bluebonnets.

At Sanderson, I ate breakfast at the Oasis Restaurant. A border control officer in the cafe said, "We catch many fellas trying to jump on the train that runs beside the highway." To find a motel or campground, I would have to continue to Langtry, another sixty miles.

By one o'clock, I was rolling again. The downs swooped me into the ups. I climbed out of the canyon and moved easily at twenty and thirty m.p.h. on a plateau. Watching the scenery scroll by, I savored the illusion of seeing forever. My world was the highway, the railroad, utility poles with wires that sang, flat earth where sparse vegetation grew in miniature, and an azure sky. After I passed through Dryden, a goat ran along with me for about fifty yards before giving up the chase. The clouds acquired a pinkish tint, and the wind pressure was beginning to soften. Normally, in the afternoon, it freshens. Perhaps the storm winds had blown out, and normal winds were resuming.

I stopped for something to eat and drink at the Exxon station at the turn-off to Langtry. The store had a few motel rooms, reasonably priced, and it looked as if the windows would open. I had to choose, after a hundred fifteen miles, between staying and visiting Langtry, or proceeding another twenty miles to Seminole Canyon State Park to camp. I would have to buy food and carry it to the park, and it was after four o'clock. I'd completed a good day, and decided to stay put.

After dumping all my stuff in the motel room, I rode my bare bike downhill into Langtry and entered the Judge Roy Bean Visitor's Center. There, I stepped into the original 1920 Jersey Lily saloon, billiard hall, and courtroom. Alone, I mentally filled the space with beer smells, redneck jokes, and the clack of billiard balls. Closing time shortened my visit to the dioramas and garden. I followed the dictates of my stomach to the local cafe.

For dessert and an after dinner stroll, I pedaled up to my

motel room, smiling at myself. I had not wanted to stop. I wanted to ride my wave of elation to Seminole, or Lake Amistad, or Del Rio. I had to eat, however, and I knew I couldn't ride too far on any day if I expected to ride again the next day.

This caution was a spillover from the tutelage of Swiss friends. In years of ski vacations in Switzerland, I never had a serious injury because my friends saw my fatigue before I felt it. Near the end of every day they would tell me on the lift, "This is your last run." Usually, I wanted to squeeze one more run into the afternoon, but they were right. The snow would have iced and the temperature would have dropped just when my fatigue was high. My friends ensured I never took that last run. I felt their training had safely halted me once more.

The motel owner said, "You may need extra heat tonight. I'll come and light the heater for you." The antique gas stove had a lever on the side and a hole for a match. It threw out a gentle, steady heat.

Langtry, Wednesday, March 18

I lay reading about Judge Roy Bean, the West's most colorful justice of the peace, who presided over America's frontier in the last decades of the nineteenth century. Railroad historians claim Langtry was named for a construction foremen. No one, however, told Lilly Langtry that. She was a famous British actress, whom the judge idolized but never met. She visited "her" town in 1904, months after the judge died.

I packed, glided downhill to the cafe, and leaned my fully-loaded bike against the wooden rails intended for tying horses, an appropriate place for my steed. While Betty, the owner, prepared breakfast, I studied the map and estimated sixty miles to Del Rio.

"Yesterday," Betty told me, "there was a hail storm in Del Rio." She said my next thirty miles would be hilly. I now know people use a word like "hilly" in relation to where they live. She meant the route would continue to flatten as I proceeded east.

As I pedaled out of Langtry with slightly tired knees, I watched two great blue herons take off, one a few minutes after the other. When I reached the Pecos River, I stood and looked over its expanse for some time. Deep in its escarpment, the water ran wide and sparkling, an anomaly in this arid land. I could understand how the Pecos was important in the history of the border area and Texas. A few more miles took me to Seminole Canyon State Historical Park. Some of North America's oldest pictographs, believed to have been painted eight thousand years ago, are visible there.

Seminole Park appealed to me, and I thought about staying to camp, but I had no food and there was none to be bought. My shoe soles were not tough enough for me to enjoy walking the trails. A more serious deterrent was that the camp area was on a hillock, thoroughly windswept. It would be cold in the wind and the tent fabric would rattle, keeping me awake. I would have to come back someday. Perhaps I would spend my next twenty years going back to visit places from this trip!

Halfway to Comstock, I met two young men with backpacks and panniers, but no bicycling gloves. Cycling west into the wind was debilitating them, but they hoped to hold out for the next few miles. At Seminole Park, they planned to sleep all afternoon and try riding at night when the wind would, perhaps, be gentler. I empathized, telling them how I had thought I would never get across Montana. One bicyclist, on spring break, soon would return to school; the other was riding cross-country to San Diego. Since I was never awake after ten, I wondered what biking in the nighttime winds would be like. Good lights would be needed. I wondered, also, how much nocturnal desert wild life they would see. After talking about life on the road, we parted.

In Comstock, I leaned my bike against the cafe wall and unzipped my front bag to get out my wallet. It wasn't there! I searched the pockets, three times. I checked my rear jersey pockets, and then began rifling through the panniers. Could the wallet have fallen out? Where did I last use it? I didn't remember using it since I paid a fee at the state park. I would call the park. As I turned to look for a phone booth, a small pickup truck with a park logo was coming up the hill. I watched, hoping, as it stopped. The driver motioned for me over and handed me my wallet.

Nick Chavez found it when he was cleaning the restrooms, and he took it to Lois McRantalr, the entrance fee official. When they had looked inside, they had found a bicyclist fee receipt for fifty cents. She remembered me because she had never collected a bicycle fee before and had to look up the charge. Lois remembered that I was traveling east because she had told me about the road and the Comstock cafe. Since it was time for Nick to make his run to the post office, they decided he would take the wallet and try to find me.

"What would you have done if I had gone past the post office?" I asked.

"Oh, you wouldn't have gotten so far I couldn't have found you!" he smiled, refusing my offer of a reward.

"What *could* I do for you? Perhaps the park rules don't allow you to accept a reward." His eyes concurred. "Could I write a letter of thanks to your boss?" Again, only his eyes responded. I asked for the name and address, and wrote and mailed the letter later that day.

As I rode out of town after lunch, I realized I had not taken a picture of Nick. I had taken no photographs of the Youngs, of the grad students from Austin, or of the boys on the road. Why was I carrying two cameras and two extra lenses if I wasn't using them? I had been too busy socializing.

During the afternoon, the terrain continued to flatten. I looked forward to the flat land but I knew once I came to the Gulf Coast, I would not see a real hill again until I reached New England.

The hot air began to smell fresh. I hadn't noticed the smell of the air for a long time. Over a rise, looking somewhat out of place, Amistad Lake appeared. Birds, green grass, bushes, and trees nestled in the hollows. The blue-green lake water was surrounded by desert banks.

I entered the outskirts of Del Rio, at an elevation of under a thousand feet. I passed lakeside campgrounds but there were no stores or restaurants. I kept pedaling until I saw a sign for my favorite campsite when I am hot, tired, dirty, and wish to stop early in the day — Motel 6. By four-thirty I had checked in.

When I called my mom, she said she needed me to come home and sign some real estate papers. Without realizing it, she made a transparent excuse to get me home. She moaned about taking so many pills. They made her too draggy to do anything — and she had a lot to do.

Now that her house was for sale, she was probably having second thoughts. I knew she didn't want to move, but the place was large and remote. I was glad she made the decision herself, because I knew it would be hard to sell the house she and my father had designed and built. She'd lived in it alone longer than they lived there together.

Del Rio, Thursday, March 19

My idea of luxury was reading my way into and out of the world each morning and evening. For thirty years, I had sprung from sleep to feet and run all day at top speed just to stay in the same place and, like Alice, run even faster to get anywhere. All day long, I wobbled into the wind that sapped my energy and blew my will power to smithereens. Before I had completed twenty miles, I was cold and hungry, and the road seemed hard and hilly, the terrain lackluster. Three times I stopped to watch a scissor-tailed flycatcher's antics. I could see every detail as he posed on a fence and then flew, displaying his distinctive tail. His dance through the air made the day worthwhile. Only a dozen more miles would take me to Eagle Pass, my short-day goal. Reaching my long-day goal, Carrizo Springs, seemed improbable. I had no idea what I would find at either place. The wind was hard. The day was hard. But bluebonnets had returned to the roadsides, and yellow poppies bobbed their blossoms. The wind changed, and I sped up to nine miles an hour. Balance took more effort at slower speeds. By two-thirty, I was still pushing my bike into the warm wind down a straight highway, achieving thirty-eight miles in five hours. If I stopped immediately, it would be the shortest and hardest of the past four days.

Ahead, through a tunnel of pecan trees, a yellow light winked. At Mary's Cafe, just beyond the light, I dismounted and leaned the bike against the cafe window. Off with the gloves, wet and sticky, and the helmet. I could hardly walk. Only one customer was inside. I walked past the mismatched tables and folding chairs. A woman looked into her coffee cup and sucked on a cigarette. As I went to the counter, I noticed the owner's table covered with letters and newspapers.

"What would you like?"

"One order of everything — I'm starving." I smiled weakly.

"Coffee?"

"No, a large milk, please." I paced around and nodded to the seated woman. The waitress brought the milk and menu. Since I didn't feel like talking, I sat back-to-back with the other customer. I ordered tacos — salad, meat, and bread all at once.

The seated woman wanted to know where I came from. I twisted around in my chair. "Today, from Del Rio," I said. "It was hard pedaling into the wind." I had developed a pattern of naming the closest place when I didn't feel like telling my story and a more distant place if I felt more like talking. Often, whatever people asked, I supplied a short polite answer and asked them a similar question.

This trip had taught me to listen, to learn more about other people than they learned about me. I had grown tired of repeating my story, and what they had done was new and more interesting. For the first time, I wanted to listen more than I wanted to talk.

Feeling stuffed, I waddled out to my bike and wondered how I could pedal it another eighteen miles. Five miles beyond Mary's Cafe, I reached a campground and RV park. It contained no campers. The wind had become worse, and a few drops of rain threatened to become a downpour.

The owners of the campground, Bev and Ben Bowman, suggested I camp under the palm trees close to their house. "The Rio Grande is only half a mile behind us and 'wets' come through occasionally. We'd feel better if you were nearby."

While pitching my tent, I noticed a pair of ducks circling. Heads bent low and feet stuck out, they landed in a pecan tree near my tent. Ducks in a tree? I dropped the tent pole and picked up the binoculars. With the help of the Golden bird book, I identified them as black-bellied whistling ducks. When my tent was up and I had showered, I continued to watch the ducks in spite of occasional raindrops and a lot of wind.

I locked my bike in the restroom to keep it dry and stowed the panniers there. Glad to camp, I spent most of the afternoon and evening lying in my tent reading and resting my back.

The Bowmans brought me a plate of food for supper. I was pleased because I had worried about lighting my stove in the wind and I did not want to cook in the laundromat on top of a washer. There was more wind than rain, and Ben told me the forecast was for clearing weather.

Bowman Village, March 20, 21

In the gray dawn, raindrops fell sporadically. The Bowmans told me I could stay another day and camp in the trailer they used in the summer as a carry-out restaurant kitchen. Not liking the headwind and still feeling tired, I accepted their offer. During the morning, I swept the rat droppings (but not all of the smell) out of the trailer, moved my kitchen equipment to the stove grill, struck the tent, and made a comfortable sleeping-bag-and-mattress-bed on the trailer floor. Obviously, I hadn't escaped housework!

I rode to the store with Ben when he went to fill his car with gas. He had taken the day off from his job as maintenance man for the irrigation system in Eagle Pass and spent the morning preparing for a family fishing trip with his brothers and sons. They would fish the Rio Grande for catfish.

As we returned from the grocery, Ben showed me a road where an array of grackles, blackbirds, and black-bellied whistling ducks reside. Later that morning, I rode there on my bike with binoculars and bird book. I saw a brown-headed cowbird, bronzed cowbirds, great-tailed grackles, Brewer's and red-winged blackbirds, and a black-necked stilt. There were perhaps fifty whistling ducks as well as many mourning doves and killdeer. In the afternoon, I walked through the cow pasture to the Rio Grande. From the bluff where I stood I had a good view of the sandy, low bank on the other side. Crossing the Rio Grande would be a physically undemanding, ankle-cooling process. Since first sighting the Rio Grande near Las Cruces, New Mexico, I had followed it as closely as possible. I had floated upon its surface for twenty miles and had ridden along more than half of the international border it carved between Mexico and Texas. I planned to continue along its north bank to Brownsville.

After scanning the river water once more, I turned and walked a half-mile back through the field, slid through the barbed wire fence, trod the cow pasture, and looked up to see whether there were any interesting birds visible in the palm trees. The row of eighteen sixty-year-old palms, the outstanding feature of Bowman Village, were alive with hooded orioles whose orange feathers flitted in the sun. Were it mine, I would have named the campground Oriole Palms and advertised to attract birders.

The whole valley appeared to be for sale. Even the Bowmans were thinking about selling, after fourteen years here. For two years, the drought was so severe that irrigation was prohibited, and the oil crisis brought two years of severe economic troubles. The Bowmans were located off the beaten track for tourists, and Mexicans who formerly crossed the border to shop no longer came. Everything except the peso was coming back, slowly. The wets were still arriving; many people kept beans and rice to feed them. The area, although far from prosperous, must have looked like paradise to Mexicans. It was unsettling to see, at home, the same conditions I observed in developing, economically struggling countries.

After lunch, I went into the A & M Grocery run by Orange County, California native Hispanics who were interested that I had biked from their home. A couple from Colorado who just arrived invited me for peppermint tea in their RV. They asked my age. When I told them, they said they thought I was in my thirties. He showed me a three-inch thick book that listed where they had traveled. This year they had wintered in Harlingen to be south of the frost line. South Padre Island, they said, had been jammed with over seventy thousand vacationing students. The spring-break crowd would continue until the end of the month, but I'd have no trouble camping because the kids stayed in motels, condos, and hotels and filled up the best restaurants. We joked about a course in Yuppie 101 at South Padre Island.

I lay on the sleeping bag for about two hours, letting my mind wander through the day's scraps of conversation. People whip up so much discussion about my being alone that I wondered if they were kind because they felt sorry for me. I hoped not. I didn't want to affect people that way. For the first time in over a year, I had done nothing at all for two days; I had been without the pressure of a schedule or someone else to consider. I really enjoyed it. I wrote thank-you letters to all the people I'd recently met and answered some of my mail. It would be dark by seven.

Bowman Village, Quemado, Monday, March 22

Two full days of relaxation had made me ready to get moving. Staying here and collecting myself had been imperative, and the Bowmans had certainly helped me. I felt good, and my body was rested. If I had a headwind, I had a headwind.

As I pedaled out of the drive a little after seven, it was overcast and looked like rain, as it had every other morning. I spotted another scissor-tailed flycatcher, admiring its fighter-pilot maneuvers. White and yellow poppies grew along the shoulder of the road. There were more leaves and some beginning blossoms on the bushes. The terrain rolled, and the headwind was slight. Someone wearing an extra-large cowboy hat passed me in a small car. I passed through Seco Mines, which had a Hispanic flavor. After entering Eagle Pass, a dusty town of twenty thousand, I bought two Egg McMuffins, ate one, and put the other in a pannier for later.

Out on the road again, I rode through gentle mist which gradually disappeared. The creosote was beginning to bloom, and on the shoulder were red and yellow black-eyed Susans and rusty, mauve, yellow, green, and pale yellow wildflowers. Tiny green leaves were unfurling. There seemed to be a dozen shades of yellow and twice as many shades of green. The fragrance was intoxicating, delicate, a real perfume. I would continue on the straight road as far as my eyes could see.

After traveling thirty-five miles by midday, I stopped at a roadside picnic area. People from Minnesota arrived and asked to share my table. They gave me a tiny, delicious tangerine-orange and several other snacks.

Soon after leaving the area, I saw a wild turkey run and then fly a little before disappearing into the bushes. Above was the clearest sky I'd seen for almost a week. The headwind picked up. The harder I turned my pedals, the sooner I could stop! After fifty-four miles, completely beat, I arrived at Carrizo Springs. The old houses with front porches upstairs and down reminded me of New Orleans. In a grocery, I supplied myself with fruit, canned tuna, and juice.

Carrizo Springs, Monday, March 23

I hesitated to look at the treetops, for fear they would indicate a headwind. The bike was ready; I was ready; I was hungry. I rolled downhill to a restaurant at the route junction, where I filled up on soggy pancakes. When there was enough daylight for good visibility, I drank one more glass of water and left. Outside, a strong tailwind greeted me.

Morning weather reports mentioned a west wind, my tailwind, and tornado warnings for San Antonio. My route, far from the banks of the Rio Grande, ran southeast and converged with the river again at Laredo, eighty miles ahead.

In Asherton, the first and largest town on my route, only the dogs were awake. For protection I now carry a small spray can of Halt. Only once or twice during the entire trip did I have to squirt a dog. Back in the open again, I observed desert plants and bushes with tiny yellow blossoms in many shades from pale yellow to almost orange. Wildflowers wagged their colorful heads in the breeze as I rode by. The Texas State Department of Highways and Public Transportation plants and preserves wildflowers in a program of beautification that has spanned more than forty years. The department is the nation's largest landscape gardener.

The route so far was a succession of gradual up-and-down grades. The presence of eastern meadowlarks indicated I was truly headed east! I startled crows in the road eating small packets of salt. McDonald's feeds everyone. I observed gates with cattle guards. Some were elaborate security systems, others only fence posts. There were stone gates, iron gates; many had crossbeams with names or logos.

With fifty-two miles behind me, I stopped at another roadside picnic shelter. After stretching, I ate tortilla chips and salsa and lay flat on my back in the sun. Just as I was mounting my bike, a car came along dragging a boat on a trailer supported by one tire and one wheel rim, sparks a-flying. Two miles later, I passed the driver, kicking the tireless trailer wheel.

At two, I reached the Texas Tourist Bureau in Laredo. There, allowing ten days at home, I bought a round trip ticket from Corpus Christi to Washington, hoping I could bicycle to the airport on time. I resolved to do the best I could and, if necessary, take a bus at the end. I would not place myself under any more pressure.

I checked into a motel about three. After an early supper and a trip to the grocery, I applied Tiger Balm liniment to my knees and Solarcaine to my arms, legs, and face before falling asleep.

Laredo, Tuesday, March 24

Laredo's streets set me singing as, a little stiff in the joints but rested, I walked in the morning air. It was still dark during breakfast at Juleps Restaurant. I pedaled south through modern Laredo to find the old quarter. This city of ninety thousand is the major international crossing along the Rio Grande border between the United States and Mexico. Since the Spanish established it by land grant in 1755, seven flags have flown over the city, more than anywhere else in Texas. I crossed streets running at right angles and stopped abruptly at a bluff high above the river. Then, I continued south toward San Ygnacio, planning a fifty-mile day that would end in Zapata.

Out on the road, warning signs about trespassing reminded me of Bill Horne's caution not to leave the right of way.
He had said these signs meant that a Texan would shoot before
asking questions, so that "trespass" and "suicide" have become
interchangeable words. It is important for bicyclists to understand the sacrosanct nature of Texas land ownership.

As I continued toward Zapata, I noticed Chevron signs
on gates, no doubt indicating oil wells somewhere beyond my
view. Much of America was invisible from the highway. A
border patrol inspection station was my next stop. I felt more
sociable after an officer permitted me to use their privy. Since
the day was getting hot, I removed my long pants and rain
jacket and stowed them in a pannier.

Once people, especially women and youngsters, realized I am female they seemed to relax, to discard fear. How safe
I felt traveling was directly related to how women were considered and treated in that locale. In Texas, I was quite comfortable.

I pedaled into Zapata County. The road shoulder was
rough and, once again, I cycled on the white line. I identified a
white-tailed hawk and great egret. Bea taught me that looking
over bridge railings for birds, ducks, and snakes can be reward-
ing. Halfway across Arroyo Dolores, I saw water below, and I
decided to stop on the bridge, lean my bike against the rail, and
look. My eyes almost popped out!

I flung off my helmet and sunglasses, grabbed my
binoculars, and stared at a big, spotted cat ambling along well-
trodden grass beside the stream. About the size of a large dog,
with white spots behind its alert ears and a short tail with a
black fuzzy ending, it was a bobcat. I watched as the cat turned
uphill and began to stalk, moving ever-so-carefully into an all-
fours *plie* into the grass. It continued to move forward, creeping,
occasionally flicking its tail. Then it stood, intently, like a bird
dog on point. As some of the tension drained, the cat moved
two steps, then sat. Cars and RVs were rumbling over the
bridge; I didn't need to be quiet. I ran the few steps to my bike,
seized my camera and telephoto lens, and assembled them
quickly. When I looked again, the cat was gone.

I ran to the other side of the bridge, and there it was,
quietly walking the same path, looking this way and that. I took
a couple of pictures, but I was behind the cat now, and it was too
far away for my 135mm lens. I resumed binocular watch. The
cat came to a log and walked across it to an island in the stream.
It tested its haunches like a dancer flexing in the wings, waiting

to go on. Then it leapt to the next island, then leapt again, holding a log with its front claws and quickly pulling its hind legs out of the water. Vigorous shakes sent water flying. A few more steps, and the bobcat disappeared into a bushy thicket.

I had been holding my breath and had to gasp before picking up the camera and crossing the road to my bike. What disarray — panniers unzipped and stuff hanging out, helmet and sunglasses along the edge of the road, and a lens on the pavement. I laughed and reassembled my belongings. A king-fisher flew under the bridge. I rode on, hardly noticing the oil pumps or the distant tick of natural-gas-line machinery.

I ate an apple as I pedaled, smiling at how the process changed when I had gotten false teeth. I'd always held the apple horizontally, with thumb and forefinger on the top and bottom, taking the first bite out of the side of the apple. Many people with false teeth believe they can't eat apples — not true! Now I hold the apple upside down with the top, or stem, in the palm of my hand. I bite into the base of the apple, using my teeth and my hand to leverage the first bite. After the skin is penetrated, the bites are easier.

Bluebonnets, not so tall as in Big Bend but just as sweet-smelling, bloomed along the road. I turned off the highway and pedaled sedately down a one-way street in San Ygnacio, my only town for the day. It was interesting, old, and authentic. I rode slowly, squaring my shoulders and sitting with dignity, responding to the formal Spanish architecture.

At the next corner was a charming town square with trees, grass, and a bandstand. Deciding to eat lunch on a park bench, I sat down in the sun. It felt good to take off my helmet. I drank a can of V8 and ate my last roll. My second bottle of water was almost gone, but I had a third bottle, and Zapata wasn't far. Today there was no need to hurry.

Two couples wandered over from RVs parked nearby, and we introduced ourselves. Alan and Jean Sheridan lived in International Falls, and Olaf and Marion Grumdahl in Duluth, Minnesota. I told them how much I enjoyed the museum in International Falls. The Sheridans asked if I remembered the antique Chevrolet in the museum. I did.

"It's mine! I loaned the Chevrolet," Alan smiled, "I go to visit it when I'm home."

They wanted to take my picture, and I took theirs. I asked about their travels. Having spent the cold months further south, they stopped here on their way north to visit the camp-ground where they had often wintered. Like many Winter

Texans, they took the same routes home and saw the same people traveling in each direction. With two rigs, they communicated on the road by CB, and they met other friends during overnight stops. They told me most of the birds, human and feathered, had already migrated. I had been dreading the day, a long route with only this one town.

At a flea market, Jean bought a book about a woman who, in her sixties, rode a horse across America. She thought I might like to read it. When I got home, there was a package containing the picture they took and the book, which I thoroughly enjoyed. Before saying goodbye, we visited a tiny museum together. I had not expected men to be so interested in my trip and was quite overcome by their encouragment.

Back on the highway, I heard the wires humming. Each time I passed a utility pole, the tone of the hum changed. Ahead was a straight strip of highway, then a big sign, "Welcome Back Winter Texans."

I was in Zapata, named for Antonio Zapata, a hardy pioneer and fierce Indian fighter. It was built on top of a hill instead of sheltered in a dip, meadow, bowl, or valley. It was new, very recently built; I expected an old town, more like San Ygnacio.

A woman getting out of a Honda Accord waved to me. I stopped, and we talked. She told me her name, that she had recently married a rancher, and had lived there less than a year. She wanted to talk with me because she had hitched around the States and Europe, bicycled on tours alone and with a group, and really liked the vagabond life. She said there were javelina and deer on their ranch and that coyotes run along the fences by their car. Since she had to do her shopping and I was getting hungry, we parted. After eating at the Dairy Freeze, I rode downhill and across a long bridge that led to camp.

I registered for a tent site at Bass Lake RV Park. Many RV parks don't allow tents, but Dave Delorme, the owner-manager, welcomed me and led me to a grassy spot at the water's edge. Before I could get the tent out of its storage sack, two women arrived to help me, and two others came to watch. I was tired and appreciated help. We put the tent up behind an oleander bush to shield it from the wind. My RV neighbor reparked his car to provide an additional windbreak. I sat on a veranda to talk briefly, and then slipped away to take a shower. When I returned, people invited me to join their bingo game. I ate a quick sandwich and hurried to the recreation building. When I walked in the door, I heard my name called. The women saved me a place at their table.

Sonia Delorme, park owner and caller, asked me to tell a little about myself before the first game. I did briefly. She then asked for a particularly exciting incident from the trip. I liked to answer such questions by describing something nearby, so I told them about the bobcat.

Sonia asked, "Where did you see it?"

"I was on the bridge over Arroyo Dolores between here and Laredo," I said.

"We saw you there, looking over the bridge!" Sonia exclaimed. "I wondered who you were, where you were going, and where you'd be staying tonight. I can't believe it — here you are!" Several other people in the room also saw me. My story satisfied their curiosity.

I won the first bingo game. They all cheered. My previous games were played in Army clubs as a teenager. Later, I won another game. My winnings paid for my cards and my four-dollar tent site. The woman who brought gum drops for our table teased me about trying to steal her husband, the man who moved his car to shield my tent from the wind. Several people offered me a bed inside their mobile homes, but I needed solitude.

Zapata, Wednesday, March 25

When I awoke, the wind was still blowing hard and the light rain that pattered on my tent during the night had become an unsteady drizzle. The air was chilly. I reached for my binoculars to see snowy egrets and another bird which looked black in the half light. It was the size of an egret, with black legs and a very long beak curved down like a curlew's. Looking forward to a quiet day, I got dressed and walked the quarter-mile to the restaurant for breakfast, ate, and returned to my tent. Several campground residents heard weather reports that confirmed my suspicion more rain was on the way. I decided to stay another night.

Sonia told me she and David had searched America for just the right place to buy before selling their motel in Niagara Falls. Running this camp made them feel like they were on vacation, too. "No matter what you need in this park, there's someone to provide it or to help," Sonia explained. "Many brothers, sisters, cousins, and friends come here from the same small towns in Ohio or Iowa."

"You can't walk across this park with a hammer, spade, or any tool in your hand," Dave pointed out, "without ten people following you to help. Whatever needs doing, someone who lives here knows how to do it. We set aside an area for gardens so residents can grow food or flowers. Many of these people are retired farmers, and they like to grow a little something. The garden produce is for the whole park. Although there are many large RV parks nearby, this park, with its seventy-six spaces, is our town. It's our way of life, our livelihood. There's nothing else around here, no shopping malls, no square dancing —we don't appeal to the night-life crowd. We offer people an all-water view, fishing, and small-town atmosphere."

As I walked toward my tent, Annamarie and Ray Fox invited me in for a visit. Annamarie grew up in Germany and lived in Kaiserslautern, where the couple met and married. Annamarie and I shared an understanding of those terrible years in Germany during the late forties. Even though our experiences were quite different, we had known similar social and cultural conditions. During those years, Americans and Germans were forbidden by law to associate and were further separated by language and economic divergences.

When the Foxes asked me to stay for lunch, they didn't have to insist. I was hungry for conversation. Annamarie served German creamed cabbage, mashed potatoes, bratwurst made by a *wurstmeister* in Toronto, pepper steak, spinach salad, wine, and fresh fruit. She told me about her father's surviving the Battle of Stalingrad and coming home on foot. He was captured at the Battle of Moscow and imprisoned in the Soviet Union for over two years. He and a friend escaped by digging out under a fence and walking across Poland to Germany. On the way home, he lived for a time with a family on the Volga. They helped him across the river and got him a bicycle which he rode the rest of the way. Annamarie was fourteen when her father returned to their village.

While she was talking, images of Berlin in 1946 scrolled through my head: the bulletin boards where people patiently stood in the cold and snow reading every message, looking for lost friends and relatives. I remembered displaced persons in the camps and on the streets, old bent women digging in the forest with soup spoons for roots to burn for heat and cooking, people carrying impossibly heavy loads of wood and goods on their backs or their bicycles. I even saw a bathtub transported by bicycle! The afternoon slid by.

Many camp residents asked me about my travels, so I asked Sonia if they had a program scheduled that evening. They didn't. I suggested that I bring my bicycle, meet with anyone who wanted to ask about my trip, and try to answer questions. She put up a notice on the board. After errands in town, I got the bike and panniers ready, to use as "exhibit A" in the evening's talk.

About twenty people came to hear me. I spent twenty minutes outlining my bicycling retirement trip before trying to answer questions. When I began, the audience was composed mainly of women. Several men played pool in the next room. Toward the end of my talk, there were more people, including some holding cue sticks.

They asked me unexpectedly detailed questions about the bike. Nearly everyone in my audience had bicycle-riding grandchildren, and my listeners wanted to go home with new knowledge. What did I do in the rain? "I get wet!" Then I pulled my raincoat out of a pannier and showed it, modeling the slit-zip underarm holes and the long tail cover. I showed them my towel — about a foot wide and a foot and a half long. "This is my beach, bath, kitchen, and hand towel. It takes a shower after I finish." I showed them my cameras, lenses, and film, told them about my system for getting mail, described the joys of sleeping outdoors, talked about my food and explained how my diet changed with the weather. I drink more and eat more fruits and vegetables when it is hotter.

One man asked what film I used and I replied, "Fuji, slides." He wanted to know why. (Everyone else in the room knew he retired from Kodak.) I explained that I had used Kodak film for years, but my personal preference was for Fuji slide color saturation. I always had slides made at Kodak because I preferred their quality control and processing.

One man said, "If you don't want to answer this question, that's all right. We will understand. Do you carry a gun or a weapon?"

"No," I laughed. "I carry no gun. It would be too heavy, and require a license. The main reason I don't carry a gun is that it could be used *against* me as well as *by* me. In addition, if people knew I had a gun, I might be bothered by someone wanting to steal it. I do, however, have a weapon, but it doesn't look like one. I carry Halt, like the postal carriers, for use against dogs. It's a tear-gas type product that could, in an emergency, be used to give me time to get away from an attacker. I paused and looked all around. They waited. "I have two secret weapons in my head. The first is prayer; the second is the conviction that, unless I have made it necessary or possible to be attacked by my own actions or provoked something by my behavior, I will not be troubled.

"Thank you very much for coming and asking questions that made me think and were interesting to answer. Thank you again for welcoming me to your RV town — I'd love to live here too. But I have set a goal for myself and I must leave tomorrow," I concluded.

Many residents asked me to stay another day. I almost yielded when Ray said he wanted to take me fishing. If I had not already planned the flight from Corpus Christi home to visit my mother, I might have stayed. I would have liked to take wildflower and roadrunner pictures. I also wanted to sit and do nothing.

For the next morning, the radio predicted a nor'wester, a good tailwind for me. The excitement and thrill of talking to an enthusiastic audience made it hard to sleep.

Zapata, Thursday, March 26

Quietly and slowly in the early morning, I showered, packed everything, and was about to creep out of the park. Ray and several others were already up and about. Each wished me well, asked me to stay, and thanked me for coming. Ray said he admired my commitment more than anything. "You set a goal, and you are committed to accomplishing it."

"Thank you, for that and for everything," I said as I waved goodbye. Wearing my ultra-bright yellow rain jacket, with a caution light blinking sixty times a minute on the back of my bike, I felt confident traveling through the mist. By afternoon, the mist thickened, but the tailwind never faltered. I took off the sunglasses that protected my contact lenses because I couldn't see well enough through them. I had to remember to duck my head or close my eyes whenever a vehicle splashed by. By noon, I had pedaled over fifty miles. I was thoroughly wet, and the thought of camping grew increasingly unattractive. I decided to go for distance and relieve my apprehension about reaching Corpus Christi in time. I continued through Dreamland and Mission and passed a turn-off to the state park that had been my goal.

Traffic increased, and damp gray mud clung to the whole bicycle and to my body from the waist down. Wondering if the desk clerk would register someone covered with ninety-three miles of mud, I entered Motel 6 at the edge of McAllen. I was grateful to be given a room.

When I stepped out of the shower and was about half dry, I removed the remaining bags and the Avocet from the bike, pulled it up on its rear wheel, and rolled it right into the shower stall. Fitting me and the bike through the door was a tight squeeze. I turned on the water and twirled the front wheel, splattering me with mud and water. It was easier to move the shower head than the bike. Eventually, most of the mud was transferred from the bike to me and the shower stall. I certainly couldn't dry the bicycle with motel towels. I bounced it up and down on its rear wheel, then wiped it down with my hand-towel, and semi-carried it back into the bedroom. If you want to give a bicycle a shower, that's how it's done! (A hose works better.) I showered again, and washed my hair and my towel.

Clean again, I ate a whole avocado and the second fish sandwich Annamarie and Ray prepared for me. The weather prediction was for clouds and occasional showers in the Rio Grande Valley for the next three to five days.

I decided that from Brownsville I would proceed to Laguna Atascosa National Wildlife Refuge on Road 1847 and then turn west, taking Highway 77 to Raymondville. This route would allow time to visit the King Ranch, but it would omit a sixty-mile ride to South Padre Island and back. I had eaten many Texas grapefruit and given them to friends, so I regretted the route would bypass Harlingen and the citrus orchards.

How many times, I wondered, had I eaten my weight in oranges on this trip alone? My juice consumption could fill a swimming pool! The next time someone asked what sort of fuel the "engine" on my bicycle used, I said, "orange juice."

McAllen, Friday, March 27

Mud dried on my panniers overnight. I took them outside and beat them together like a pair of small rugs, and went in search of breakfast. I followed Route 336 out of McAllen due south toward Hidalgo in mild, partly clearing weather. My arms and legs ached, and my knees were sore, but they had been worse. Since movement seemed to oil the joints, I kept going, gradually becoming more flexible. My arthritic feet had never felt better than during the trip when they received a daily massage from pedaling. I had two hundred miles to cover in four-and-a-half days to reach my flight from Corpus Christi.

I went around the edge of Hidalgo and, leaning my bike against the best non-littering sign I'd seen anywhere, "Don't Mess With Texas," I bought some juice in a grocery. At the Santa Ana National Wildlife Refuge, I bought a ticket for an hour-and-a-half lecture and train tour. I sat on the edge of my seat the whole time. I saw the sora, Inca dove, ladder-backed wood-pecker, tri-color (Louisiana) heron, broad-winged and Harris hawks, plain chachalaca, blue-winged teal, northern shoveler, least grebe, and green jay. I watched a nutria on land and in the water. Many species living at the Santa Ana refuge are threat-ened or endangered. We were told that Spanish moss doesn't draw its sustenance from the host tree, but receives nutrients from humidity, rain, and air.

After drinking all the water I could swallow, I refilled all three bottles, pedaled back to the highway, and turned south-east. The next day, I would head north and continue north and east until a big left turn in Maine took me back to Detroit.

The wind along the Military Highway was light, com-ing from behind. I had bought a pair of fish grippers, which I attached to my handlebars to extend my reach. Using them, I could sit up straight on the saddle, stretching and resting my spine. They were helpful on flat, smooth roads if there was a slight tailwind. The straighter I sat, the broader my back. The broader my back, the more there was for the wind to push.

Squashed carrots littered the road. A few were so large they didn't look edible — perhaps this crop was intended for making juice. Although I was quick to laugh at jokes about milk growing in paper boxes, I realized that I'd accepted uniformly-sized carrots in plastic bags without question. Beside the vege-table fields stood a historical marker about the Spanish explo-rations of east Texas in the 1600s. I looked from the historical marker to onions in the field.

I was pedaling furiously to meet an airplane schedule, and the grueling pace was no fun. I always said I would cancel the trip when it was no longer fun. Talking to myself, I thought, "You should be glad for what you've been able to do and can do. Jane, don't let it get you down! You're doing the best you can, and you have the privilege of doing it. A month for this part of the trip would not be enough. Don't worry."

Vegetables turned to city as I followed Route 802 around the outskirts of Brownsville. I arrived at Motel 6 minutes before the sunset winked its last bloodshot eye.

SPRING ALONG THE GULF COAST

CHAPTER FIFTEEN

Texas Turning Points

Brownsville, Texas, Saturday, March 28

At breakfast, I met three cyclists gathering for a day's ride. When we talked about routes, they recommended a motel off the main highway in Raymondville. My body's tiredness had melted during the mile-and-a-half round trip for breakfast. I was O.K. again! Earlier, heavy clouds pulled over the sky like some giant down comforter, but slivers of lighter, almost blue spots were now opening. Although the skies promised to clear, I couldn't yet predict the wind.

Heading north among fields of peas, onions, cane, and parsley, meadowlarks cheered me on. After stopping in Los Fresnos for milk and crackers, I pedaled through the humid air among ponds and lakes full of wildlife, over a straight, occasionally rolling road. Scissor-tailed flycatchers came along, too.

Miles of hard pumping eastward into the wind taxed my resolve. I kept going until I got to the Laguna Atacosta National Wildlife Refuge, spurred by the knowledge I would have a strong tailwind on the return trip. I arrived with empty water bottles and a weakened inclination for sightseeing. In the Visitors Center I traced the long history of the coastal area from prehistoric times to the era of Spanish settlement, to ranching and farming, to World War II training bases, to its present economy and culture.

I took the Bayside Tour which winds through dense brush and past coastal prairie. At Osprey Overlook, I met music teachers Cynthia Gonzales and Elizabeth Gomez. "Are you on spring break now?" I inquired brightly.

They looked at each other, suppressed giggles, and one of them said, "Yes, but we call it a weekend. Today's Saturday."

When our laughter subsided, I couldn't resist saying, "Now, that's retired!"

"But you're not professionally retired. You're doing something. You aren't making a profession out of retirement."

"At the schools where you teach, is everyone bilingual?" I wanted to know.

"Yes, but they seldom speak English."

"What could I learn about the Spanish-Mexican culture that I might not notice?"

"You came into Texas at El Paso. What you've seen will change. You'll learn, observe the changes. When you get to Corpus Christi, it'll be quite different from the Valley."

Cynthia and Elizabeth, third generation Americans, were charming. So often, I didn't realize how lonely I was until I met someone and talked awhile.

The wind blew me away from the coast, through Rio Hondo, past the Confederate Air Force Museum into Combes where, on Route 77, I headed north to Raymondville. Following the breakfast bikers' directions, I found the Raymondville Motor Inn, a big, old place getting a facelift. With ten thousand people, Raymondville was a larger town than I needed. I wasn't looking forward to the ride to King Ranch. It would take a whole day on a straight, hot, desolate road. The idea of sitting still and letting a plane carry me appealed greatly. I was ready for my spring break!

Raymondville, March 29, 30

When I awoke, the wind was blowing hard from the north. A headwind. I ruled out going to King Ranch and declared a rest day in Raymondville. I welcomed being stranded on Sunday. Fishing for one of the three hundred local varieties could have made a tempting lunch, but today I gorged on newspapers and sports television.

Since weather conditions were the same the following morning, I caught a bus to Corpus Christi. The driver let me stow the bike in the baggage compartment. I hooked bungees around the front panniers to secure them and rolled the bike in at an angle on the sides of the tires, letting it rest on the panniers. Bus companies usually require bicycles to be in a box. As we sped along the seventy-three miles to Kingsville, I still felt tired. I watched wildflowers whiz by the window. There was a wonderful, rosy red flower I remember seeing before. I wondered how it smelled.

The bus began to slow and then stopped. I looked all around. We were nowhere. The driver directed a nod to his rear view mirror, and a man got up and walked off the bus. We continued. A mile or so down the road, we stopped at an inspection station. An inspector boarded, asking, "Is everyone an American citizen?" We nodded in reply. The bus rolled on at top speed to Kingsville, where we disembarked for a twenty-minute break.

When we were back on the road, I unfolded my map and watched the signs. We would go right past the airport on the expressway. Although the driver probably wasn't allowed to stop, I asked anyway.

"I will if I can, when we get there. I'm allowed to stop, but not to open the baggage box." He paused. "How fast can you get your bike out?"

"*Very* fast," I said.

He stopped. I grabbed my bike. The bus was gone in seconds. Only two miles ahead into the wind lay the airport. I was glad to get off the bike and wheel it into the terminal.

Although my ticket was for the next day, I could take the same flight today and leave in less than an hour. I called Mom to meet me. Where to leave the bike was the problem. The attendants at pay storage and two car rental desks would not accept it.

Finally, I went to Budget Rent-a-Car. In Port Angeles, my bike had been stored in their repair garage for a dollar a day. The Corpus Christi garage was an open-air, fenced area. I told the Budget manager, "I'll sign a release of liability. I can't go unless I can store my bike. My mother has a heart problem, and I have to go home."

Two men drove to the fenced area while I pedaled behind them. I locked the bike to itself and covered it with both ground cloths to protect it from rain. The men drove me back to the terminal. I thanked the manager, Edward T. Vawser, and vowed never to rent a car from anyone but Budget. Dripping with sweat, I entered the plane.

During my days at home, I was happy to observe my mother was getting better.

Airborne, Wednesday, April 8

It was chilly on the plane back to Corpus Christi and I thought about putting on my rain jacket, but I was too lazy to get it out from under the seat. It was late at night when I stumbled sleepily off the plane. I was dreading the trip out to claim my bicycle.

At the Budget car rental counter, the clerk smiled and greeted me, "You must be the bicyclist I'm looking for. We have your bike right here in the office." My offer to pay was cheerfully rejected. I hung the panniers on the bike and trundled it out of the terminal building.

Outdoors, I was really cold, not just chilly. Frantically, I searched for the rain jacket. It was gone. It must have rolled out of the over-filled plastic bag under my seat and flown away in the plane. I went to the counter and filled out a lost item form. In my heart, I knew the jacket was gone. I had my chance when I was so cold during the flight.

I put on my *Washington Post* emergency jacket made of paper, and found a driver to take me and my bike to Motel 6. Almost asleep on my feet, I was excited to be traveling again. At the motel, I was thrilled to be "home." I never turned on the light and was asleep before I lay down.

Corpus Christi, Texas, Thursday, April 9

There would be no more flights home from this trip! At Charleston, South Carolina, I would take a week off in May and drive with cousins to meet my mother in the North Carolina mountains. After biking to Lewes Ferry, Delaware, I would spend the month of June helping Mom move. In July, I would ride with my friend Linda Bell from the Cape May, New Jersey ferry to Long Island, New York to attend GEAR. Continuing alone through New England, along the St. Lawrence River, around the Great Lakes and back to Detroit, I intended to complete my journey before Labor Day.

The most difficult aspect of this tour had been to disentangle myself from "normal" life long enough to complete it. I almost envied the pioneers who had no telephone contact with their former homes. They said their goodbyes, departed, and lived in the present. The age-old struggle between freedom and responsibility remained with me.

I put on all my clothes: short pants, long pants, sleeveless T-shirt, T-shirt with short sleeves, T-shirt with long sleeves, the paper jacket, and covered the whole assortment with a windbreaker vest. I didn't look stylish, but who could with a white mixing bowl strapped on her head? I wore new shoes that were the same brand, model, and size as my old ones. I knew they would feel foreign until they molded to my feet and toe clips.

While at home, I had read *Fit for Life*, a book which outlines an eating program for weight loss and health. During the trip, I firmed up my muscles but lost only five pounds. The appeal of the *Fit for Life* program lay in the possibility of avoiding a sick feeling while riding the bike after eating. Its concept of using less energy for digestion and more for activity sounded practical. Blood couldn't work hard in my stomach and legs at the same time.

I decided to eat only fruit, which requires the least amount of digestive energy, before noon, vegetables and carbohydrates at midday, and vegetables and protein for the evening meal. I planned to adhere to this program as closely as possible until I reached Jacksonville, but I was dubious about avoiding milk and milk products.

Having eaten only fruit for breakfast, I headed east on the North Padre Freeway. I soon realized a policeman was following me. When he turned on his red light and hit a short wheeze on his siren, I pulled over.

"You are on a freeway. Bicycles are not allowed on the freeway. Please go over to the frontage road."

"Yes, sir. Could you tell me how far the frontage road goes?"

"It doesn't matter. You can't be out here."

"Sir, did I misread the signs? It seems that every half a mile or so the road changes from freeway to highway and back again."

"If you don't get off of here I'll have to give you a ticket. You get your bike over that bank right now."

"Yes, sir." I hoisted the bike over the curb, making it look tougher than it was, rolled it down a cement embankment on to the frontage road, proceeded a few miles until I came to the next End Freeway sign, then got back on the lane-wide shoulder. The frontage road had stop lights, more traffic, and no shoulder. Away from city, fingers of marsh stretched among the developments up to the road. Pelicans, terns, sea gulls with black heads, and traffic noise kept me company. I hadn't learned to identify many shore birds. The saline marshy smell filled my nose and lungs. I spun along easily over the Kennedy Causeway to Padre Island National Seashore which stretches over a hundred miles along the Texas Gulf Coast. Among the three hundred fifty species of birds sighted at Padre, I saw great blue herons, sanderlings, gulls, terns, meadowlarks, marsh hawks, great horned owls, sandhill cranes, and many varieties of ducks and geese.

I turned north to Mustang Island. The area reminded me of the Georgia coastal islands where I vacationed as a child. I was content to glance at the information center and walk out on the beach to the water's edge. I stuck my fingers into the Gulf of Mexico. It was tepid, not quite warm enough for a swim. I didn't remember touching the water of the Pacific. At midday, it was warm, and I wore only shorts and my cycling jersey. On I went to Port Aransas, a nice town of about two thousand, where refinery and oil smells reminded me of New Jersey. I boarded the little ferry across Aransas Pass as brown pelicans watched.

After lunching on a large salad and rolls, I headed for a campground near Rockport, eleven miles north. A lone scissor-tailed flycatcher welcomed me back to Texas!

It was taking time to shift mental and physical gears and build up my vagabond momentum. All the glitter had fallen out of the afternoon — I was going through the motions, just pedaling. Although I was flushing scores of ducks and cranes, I hardly noticed.

Now that I had overcome the fear of traveling alone, had learned to camp, to tour with another person and alone, why was I here? Was the effort worth it? Maybe I should have been spending my time some other way. Was a year too long for a vacation?

In Rockport, I pedaled over the Copano State Fishing Pier past the Sea Gun Sports Inn which advertised eight a.m. boat excursions to see the whooping cranes. I'd be there the next day, I thought, as I rolled on a few more miles to the Goose Island State Recreation Area. I picked a site shielded from the wind and phoned my mother.

Setting up camp took longer than usual. I had lost the habit. All my panniers had to be dumped, sorted, and repacked so that I would have at least a vague idea where things were. I tried to keep things in the same places, but no system worked for long. My back and arms hurt, and I still hadn't gotten the bike seat, which was moved while my bike was in storage, properly adjusted. Traveling seventy-three miles after being off the bicycle over a week was too ambitious.

After pitching the tent, I explored the swimming area on Aransas Bay and admired a famous thousand-year-old oak tree known as the Lamar Oak, Bishop's Oak, or the Goose Island Oak. Best of all, I liked the comfortable live oak trees near my camping spot, stopovers for migrating fall and spring warblers. A thin cat with only one good eye ventured near, sat, and watched me. My slightest movement or glance made it shy away. I wondered if it had been mistreated.

It felt good to be alone outdoors. As I puttered around the campsite, I began to unwind. During the night, I was awakened briefly by a visiting raccoon. I noted the brilliant stars and went back to sleep.

Goose Island, Friday, April 10

The cough which had bothered me since I returned to Texas was worse. A slight headache and extreme thirst seemed to indicate fatigue. When I peeped out of the tent, there sat the little cat. Had it been there under the oak trees all night? Patience like that needed a reward. I mixed the last of my powdered milk with water and put it out for the cat. It drank very deliberately, lapping slowly, its single eye constantly alert. I could learn a lot from that cat.

The thicket shielded my tent from wind but not from dew. I should have pitched it under a tree. I shook the tent vigorously to get rid of as much dew as possible and then upended it on the picnic table to dry. It would be packed last.

I climbed on the bike and left the campground by seven-thirty. On the highway with a tailwind, twenty-one miles an hour was a nice, easy pace on a flat road.

At Reyno's Food Store, the owner commented, "Congratulations, you're the first." I looked puzzled as I presented two bananas to be weighed. "You must be the first, because none of the others have come in here yet." We both laughed. Like so may storekeepers in small American towns, he was accustomed to an occasional visit by bicyclists in groups of two, three, or five. When I told him what I was doing, he asked, "Who's financing this?"

"I am. It's my first retirement project — a vacation to figure out what I'm going to do with the rest of my life."

Back on the road, I passed through Hog Bayou, the first place I'd noticed the word "bayou." Everything was green. I saw and heard red-winged blackbirds in the shrubs and observed white pelicans flying and a couple of whooping cranes near Chocolate Bayou. There was not a cloud in the sky, not one, not anywhere. Grasses waved in the light breeze. What a day!

At Port Lavaca, home of over ten thousand people and The Fighting Sand Crab Team, I added the Magic Scissor and Hair Port to my collection of offbeat beauty shop names. I crossed the bridge to Point Comfort, a small community consisting of a shopping center housing the police station, library, Alcoa offices, and the City Cafe. I didn't see anything else. Everyone in the cafe talked to me. The food was good, all homemade, but it was the people who made the difference. I felt so much at home that I forgot the tip until I was miles down the road. During the afternoon, the headwind picked up and held on to me. At times, I could only crank along at seven miles an hour. A sign in a Texaco station cheered me: The Key to Success Is the Urge to Move On.

In Palacios, a town of under five thousand, shrimp boats lined one side of the main street and buildings lined the other. I found a motel, splashed in the shower, coughed a lot, decided I liked my *Fit for Life* diet, and joined the rest of America watching "Wheel of Fortune" on TV.

Palacios, Saturday, April 11

Although my cough persisted and the chilly, gray morning was not encouraging, I was ready to travel by nine o'clock.

On the outskirts of Palacios, I passed a mobile home park that looked like a permanent Vietnamese suburb. The community, old enough to have accommodated the first Vietnamese refugees in 1975, contained a car for each home, an outdoor market, and a community center. Several signs were written in Vietnamese.

I recalled flights over the Mekong Delta and my visits to Vietnam during the late 1950s, but most of all I thought of the Phams, refugees who shared my one-bedroom apartment in Washington for two weeks.

The marsh and the sea with a touch of salt in the air

would be familiar to many Vietnamese. They would feel comfortable and thrive, as I did, in ninety-five percent humidity. The Cajuns, coming here as refugees, had started the shrimp industry. Now, Vietnamese refugees had revitalized it.

The road was smooth and free of traffic. Fourteen miles slid by effortlessly until a turn changed the tailwind to a crosswind. Near Wadsworth, I came upon the South Texas Nuclear Project and took a while to ride around it. The Visitors Center of the Electric Generating Station of the Nuclear Project was open.

Inside, the staff was preparing an Easter egg hunt for employees' children. No tourist buses were expected. One of the workers told me the day was the coldest they had experienced all winter. It seemed pleasant, like spring to me. I asked, "Have you had a lot of protesters at this plant?"

"No, we don't have protesters in Texas." Eyes glittered and laughter danced from face to face.

On the north side of Wadsworth, further away from the power plant, smooth pavement was replaced by a rougher farm-road grade of pavement. For a while, the countryside looked like the eastern shore of Maryland and Virginia. Away from the coast, amid rolling hills, a metal gate across a farm road provided a place to lean my bike. I sat on the ground and leaned against the gate, too. A cow pawed the earth while I ate an avocado and saltless potato chips for lunch. Meadowlarks provided music, and a black and white bird appeared and disappeared from time to time. People in passing cars waved.

The area felt comfortable, like home, like Georgia, like south coastal Georgia. It was Saturday, and people were out cutting grass. I thought of my little yard, and how much I enjoyed puttering there and feeding the birds.

Riding through Brazoria, I added The Hair Rustlers to my list. Fifteen miles ahead was a campground and motel at Surfside. Although I was traveling on a busy road with no shoulder, I felt better than I had all day. As I continued through Lake Jackson, I noticed the temperature was up to seventy-five. When I entered Clute, a Dow chemical city of ten thousand, my Avocet registered sixty-eight miles. A Motel 6 sign appeared down the road.

I've never liked to bicycle late on Saturday afternoon. After three or four o'clock, the beer that's driving around behind steering wheels has begun to affect highway behavior. Besides, good sports programs are available on television. I turned in at Motel 6, and the desk clerk recommended eating at Rolland's, a few doors away.

As I ate a delicious bowl of gumbo, an electric player piano kept the place hopping. Mr. Rolland cautioned me that bicycles are not permitted on the bridge leading to Surfside, and recommended a very early start.

Clute, Sunday, April 12

Eating nothing but fresh fruit for breakfast shortened my morning routine and since I was planning to ride only thirty miles to Port Bolivar, I would have hours of leisure time.

On the road, I met Don Rainey from Longview, Texas. He urged me to spend as much time as possible in Galveston and especially recommended seeing the Bishop's Palace. Thinking a big seaport town would have little of interest, I hadn't planned any sightseeing.

Riding along just behind the sand dunes, I was astonished that vehicles could drive on the beach. Little roads and tracks were everywhere. The water was the color of wet sand. Beyond the causeway over San Luis Pass, a sign informed me I was entering the city limits of Galveston. City water hydrants protruded from otherwise-barren sand. Development along here seemed to have come to a halt.

I blended right in with the Sunday afternoon runners, walkers, and bicyclists along the Galveston seawall. Built as protection from hurricanes, the seawall runs parallel to Galveston Beach and the Gulf of Mexico and rises seventeen feet above mean low tide for about ten miles. I'd been riding with only sand between me and the flat, shimmering surface of the gulf so long I took the calm seascape on my right for granted. Since my bike was fat with panniers, I had to ride cautiously among the people, but I still made good time on the seawall without the delay of stoplights.

I turned off Seawall Boulevard to take a few photographs of white houses with unusual shutters and to find the Samuel May Williams home. Prefabricated in Maine, the house was brought to Galveston by schooner and erected in 1839. One of the earliest Greek Revival houses, it had survived the 1900 hurricane that devastated Galveston. I realized Galveston reminded me of New Orleans, Charleston, Savannah, and Annapolis, yet retained its own special charm.

Aston Villa, built in 1859, withstood the Civil War, the 1900 hurricane, and a recent threat of demolition. The restored grand Italian mansion was being readied for a wedding and reception.

After a ferry ride to Point Bolivar, I could absorb no more, travel no further. I collapsed in front of the TV.

Port Bolivar, Monday, April 13

I was beginning to suspect my cough resulted from the cleansing effect of my new diet. So far, I hadn't felt hungry although I was eating less. I'd see how the regimen went for a few more weeks. Except for coughing and being tired and a bit despondent, I felt good.

On the road, I found a phone booth and called Gay Baker, who suggested I visit her mother on my way through Port Arthur. I wondered if her mother would like to house a dirty, tired, lonely bicyclist. Before I finished eating an orange, Gay called back to confirm arrangements. Her mother, Opal Wallace, invited me to arrive at her home in Port Arthur between one and five the next afternoon.

I'd do a short day, rest at Sea Rim State Park from afternoon to late the next morning, and cover the twenty-five miles to Port Arthur by early afternoon. When I reached Port Arthur, I would have completed my ride through Texas. If company and a sense of accomplishment didn't revive my enthusiasm, I'd go home from New Orleans.

The morning surfside journey loosened my joints. Relaxed and with a better outlook, I came to a small bridge over a canal. Nearby, fishermen were throwing nets into the water. I leaned my bike against the historical marker which identified the strait as Rollover Fish Pass. Years ago, ship captains avoided the customs station at Galveston by rolling over their barrels of merchandise from the gulf side of the peninsula to the bay and then taking them to the mainland.

I walked toward a man who was casting a net into the water and bringing up an occasional shrimp or small fish. I took some pictures, hefted the lead-weighted net, five feet in diameter, and went on my way.

In their beachside meadow, four cows ran along beside a fence, accompanying me until another fence blocked their route. Red-winged blackbirds were out in force. When one flew straight toward me at eye level, I could see its red shoulder pads glittering in the sunlight as the black wings pumped the bird forward.

I reached Sea Rim State Park about two-thirty, and the ranger suggested I pitch my tent right on the beach next to the picnic table. "It's better than being with the mosquitoes behind the dunes. It'll be all right tonight. It's off-season, and you'll enjoy it more there." Imagine being told to pitch my tent on the beach!

I staked the tent and stowed the panniers under the picnic table to protect them from dew. I wrapped my bike tightly in an extra plastic ground cloth to protect it from sea spray and salt air. After finishing my chores, I walked around the Interpretation Boardwalk, two feet above the marsh surface, which provides the visitor a sense of the watery landscape. People at the other end of the trail seemed to disappear into the marsh grass. Although I concentrated on the grasses, I also saw common moorhens, gallinules, and American coots in a pond. I would, no doubt, see thousands of miles of marsh grass during the next two months.

The gentle wind, without barriers on the beach, blew out the flame of my stove. Under a shelter, I made a stew of leftover vegetable soup mix, macaroni, and red cabbage. While it cooked, I ate an avocado that finally had ripened. This would be the ninth night I had spent in my new tent. In warmer weather, I could camp more often. I anticipated a good night's sleep and lolling about on the beach until mid-morning. Although the ranger had told me that there was a tornado watch until seven p.m., the thick clouds were already clearing.

Sea Rim State Park, Tuesday, April 14

The unfamiliar sound of waves roused me briefly during the night. At dawn, I watched the sun rise from the sea into a clear sky. It was chilly as I snuggled in my sleeping bag. Finally, with toothbrush, soap, and towel in hand I set off for the restroom. On the stairs I met a ranger who was looking for me.

"There was a phone call for you. I was just coming to find you."

"Who called?"

"Opal Wallace. She wants you to call her back right away. It's something about your appointment with the mayor."

"My what?"

"You can use the phone in my office."

I called and listened to the plans. "Yes. I can be there in good time — not to worry. No, I do not need a police escort! I won't get lost, and will be on time." I hung up. "Thanks for coming to get me. It seems I have an appointment this afternoon at two to receive a key to the city of Port Arthur in the mayor's office." I had to leave right away.

I showered and packed my gear, elated enough to move efficiently, but not enough to rush. It took me a half a mile to get up to speed, and I saw the brown station wagon Opal told me to look for. It slowed to a stop, and I got off my bike and leaned it against the front of the car. "Howdy, Mr. Bean."

"How did you know my name? Opal must have found you." Mr. Bean was the backup, ready to give me the message in case Opal failed to reach me.

I sped along at twenty miles an hour with a fine tailwind. The day was warm; I felt tired. It was my sixth day without a rest day. Looking over the watery landscape and drawing in deep breaths of salt marsh air, I was happy.

At Sabine Pass, after buying an orange and a banana, I turned into a headwind, and kept going. If the attention of television and newspaper coverage failed to encourage my flagging enterprise, it deserved to die in New Orleans, I told myself. I was getting lonely and losing steam. I ate the banana and pushed my legs to crank Centurion into the wind at less than half my former speed. Getting up the nice little hill to the bridge over the Intracoastal Waterway almost put me afoot, but I raced down the other side, swooping along into Port Arthur.

Even with three sets of detailed directions, I managed to get lost. Three officers at the Police Headquarters Motor Pool cautioned me to be careful, and the one named Clancy gave me more directions. I set off again and, a few blocks later, one of the policemen nodded and pointed as he passed me in his squad car. Ten minutes after I found Opal's home, newspaper people arrived. First, David Cruz took photos of me in the street, riding and standing over the bike looking at a map. Opal and I agreed to stop by the newspaper office for the interview with Jackie Wickliffe after the ceremony at the mayor's office. The TV people called and asked me to bring the bike along so that they could videotape me riding around the city streets.

Opal drove her car, and I rode the bike back downtown with the panniers stuffed with newspapers! After my arrival was recorded on tape, we wondered where to leave the bike. I rode over to the police station, half a block away, and Clancy kept it with all the stolen and abandoned bikes in the police garage.

The mayor's secretary, Muriel Blanton, put us in a conference room to wait. The TV crew began interviewing me. As the cameras whirred, Mayor Malcolm L. Clark made a kind speech and gave me a key to Port Arthur, the Energy City, and a certificate proclaiming me an honorary citizen. Outside, the camera people wanted footage of me riding my bike, so I rode around downtown Port Arthur. It was like a ghost town, definitely a depressed area. The buildings that had not been torn down were boarded up — blocks and blocks of them. Opal followed in her car while the footage ticked off.

At long last, my day as a public figure was over, and I rode back to Opal's for a shower and a visit. I sneezed a lot, and the insides of my head seemed to be running out my nose. Opal thought my malady was more an allergy than a cold. Ellen Gay, Opal's daughter, called and we had a good chat and laugh about Port Arthur having so little news that they needed me. Opal told wonderful stories about Ellen, herself, Port Arthur, and a friend in her nineties who said she didn't mind being fat because balloons don't wrinkle!

I could hardly stay awake to see myself on the ten o'clock news. My piece included a sequence of feet flying around the pedals, gears changing, wheels turning, and me riding through town, "salad bowl" on my head and a smile on my face. I even adjusted my rear view mirror — what a ham! The commentary was my own voice, taken from the interview. I was glad they left out my face — it looked rather haggard. The piece convinced me that what I had done was remarkable. I fell into bed exhausted, and hoped I would never have to move again.

Port Arthur, Wednesday, April 15

I awoke on "tax day," pleased that my forms were filed well in advance. I then remembered the newspaper interview, hopped up, and opened the front door to get the paper. There was my picture in color — front page center! Being the focus of such publicity meant real retirement from the Central Intelligence Agency. I once worried about speaking to my neighbor,

Carl Bernstein, a then-unknown reporter for *The Washington Post*. For thirty years, I had trained myself to assume reporters could read my mind and to avoid even thinking about anything classified when a reporter was nearby.

What a way to spend my last day in Texas! I was proud of riding around the edge of Texas from El Paso to Port Arthur. El Paso is closer to Los Angeles than to Port Arthur, and Port Arthur is closer to Tampa than to El Paso. Texas is BIG.

The article began: "Jane Schnell's sun-baked cheeks and sparkling eyes reflect the outdoor adventures she enjoys." I was quoted as saying, "I'm doing what a lot of women are doing these days once the children are grown and out of the house. A woman can do anything she wants to do, and if she doesn't, it is something in her own mind holding her back."

Opal drove me on a sightseeing trip after breakfast. We took my bike along and stopped at Spokes and Sprockets where I met the owners, Gene and Liz Tomlinson, who read about me in the morning paper. Gene tightened the bottom bracket on my bike and checked the wheels and everything else for adjustment. While he worked, we talked at length about the trip. He wouldn't let me pay him.

We crossed into Louisiana to find tourist folders about my upcoming route, returning by way of Beaumont in order not to miss any portion of the Golden Triangle, then tarnished by depressed oil prices. Along the way, Opal told me stories, anecdotes, and bits of local lore. We ended our day with dinner at Sartin's Seafood Restaurant, devouring barbecued crabs, fried shrimp, and fish. I was happy when Opal insisted I stay an extra day. What a gloriously interesting, amusing hostess she was!

I went to bed hoping Port Arthur would soon be as rejuvenated as I felt. The city's people gave me a new key to commitment, a new joy in my journey, and renewed courage to complete the perimeter route. They had found me interesting, and I loved them for it.

CHAPTER SIXTEEN

Deltas, Bayous, and
Sugar Sand

Port Arthur, Texas, Thursday, April 16

I had cleaned the bike and cooked the chain the night before, so I was ready for a prompt departure. After breakfast, I waved goodbye to Opal and pedaled her now-familiar street. On my way to the police station to thank Clancy for his help, I observed some Vietnamese people converting a Methodist church into a Buddhist temple. The sun was shining, and I was taking to the open road again.

I pedaled up the high-arched Gulfway Bridge across the Intracoastal Waterway and sped on whirring wheels down the flat marshland roadway among the blue grosbeaks, indigo buntings, eastern kingbirds, and summer tanagers of Pleasure Island. Egrets, herons, and blackbirds were plentiful in the marsh grasses on both sides of the road. A tailwind carried me happily over another bridge near Sabine Pass and into Louisiana.

Just before reaching Johnson's Bayou, a car honked, stopped, and the people waved. I stopped to talk with them. Debra Debault and her father, M. G. Wells, had seen me on television and read the newspaper article. From experience in international political science, I thought that public memory of press coverage was only one day deep. I was surprised and pleased at recognition a day later and in another state. We talked about Michigan, their former home, and my travels there. They told me so many times to be careful that I asked what I should be careful about. "There are a lot of KKK and

Cajun people who keep to themselves in this area. They don't
like outsiders." I interpreted their fears for me as results of
legend and misunderstanding. Clancy had told me to be careful, too, but police always feel the need to watch out.

Mr. Wells pulled a twenty dollar bill out of his wallet
and handed it to me. "That's not necessary," I stammered. He
insisted, "I want to contribute to your effort. My daughter finds
it very meaningful."

"Thank you, thank you very much." Abashed, I ear-
marked the money for splendid dinners. Later, when I stopped
to buy a sweet roll and banana at Johnson's Bayou Store,
another woman recognized me and identified me to other
customers. While I ate, we talked, and they also told me to be
careful.

After riding another ten miles, I paused to look at the
beach. It was warm enough for gnats. My riding shorts and
sleeveless shirt provided little insect protection. After resting
and enjoying the gulf view, I rode fifteen miles through marshlands, and pushing my bike, I walked to the Cameron Ferry.
When we docked, after all the cars had gone, I pedaled off. At
the hardware store, Jackie gave me directions to a motel in Oak
Grove, near Creole.

"Does it look decent from the outside? Would it be all
right to stay there?"

"Yes, but I've never been inside, and I don't know
anything about it." If the motel had a bad reputation, she would
know. I thanked her and pedaled through town.

At a doughnut shop, I asked the clerk, "Do you know
anything about the motel in Oak Grove?"

"No."

"Could I look in your phone book?" She handed it to
me. I tried calling but got only static and buzzing.

"The phone never works to that town," she said flatly.

If I could stay at Oak Grove, I could divide the mileage
through the heart of Cajun country between two days. Satisfied
that I had been careful, I walked out of the doughnut shop. I'd
go to Oak Grove and hope the motel was open. My alternative
was camping.

The motel, just where it was supposed to be, was open
and clean. The young man in charge told me there was a
restaurant about a mile away along the bayou toward Creole.
I sat down at the desk in my room and wrote seven thank you
letters. I continued to write in the restaurant while I ate salad

and a large bowl of gumbo, the new staple of my diet.

The combination filling station, grocery, and restaurant was run by Betty and Oberley Theriot. Their good-tasting drinking water came from a deep well. Crawfish was their specialty. Betty boiled them, filling the room with the scent of cajun spices. As they cooked, the dark green crawfish turned deep red. I desperately wanted to try them but had no idea how to go about it.

An affable young man ordered two portions of crawfish and, while he waited, he came over to my table and asked about my trip. I pushed aside my letter and invited him to sit down. In a voice booming with charm and self-confidence, Teddy Boussard told me about his home and business in Grand Chenier. He said he had written and sold several hundred country music lyrics and traveled frequently to Nashville. His other business was selling fish wholesale.

Teddy invited me to stay at his place over the weekend so that I wouldn't be on the road during Easter. I thanked him but refused. "Hang around and I'll take you out on a crab boat," he winked. His offers, I felt, were indicators of hospitality and friendliness, not to be taken literally.

"Teddy, your crawfish are ready," called Betty.

"Have you ever eaten crawfish?" Teddy asked me.

"No," I admitted.

"Come on, then, have some of mine. I can't eat them all, and I'll show you how. Betty makes the best boiled Cajun crawfish in the whole world."

We walked over to the counter where a bundle of crawfish steamed in a bowl. Betty cut the plastic net holding them together. Teddy went to work on them. After eating three or four crawfish, he twisted off the head of a large one, twisted and pulled the tail with his other hand, and offered me the whole tail lump. I tried it — delicious! Caught up in his excitement and thrilled to feel so comfortable, I picked up a crawfish and turned it over in my fingers. He showed me several times how to twist off the head, hold the tail and, using my thumb, squish out the lump of meat. Inept, I certainly wasn't going to get fat on crawfish or deprive him of his meal by eating too fast. Teddy explained that I was in *real* Cajun country and traveling toward *tourist* Cajun country.

As we left the restaurant, Oberley, wearing a big cowboy hat, was bagging fresh crawfish. I watched him dump them out of a large croaker sack into an empty laundry hamper. From there, he scooped some up in a gallon bucket. He then stretched a plastic mesh bag over the top, upended the crawfish into the net and knotted it. Since he picked up the wiggling crawfish with his hands, they obviously didn't pinch like crabs.

"Do crawfish live in fresh water?"

"Yes. We seed them in the rice fields where we've planted a special tender grass they like to eat. That's why they grow so large."

Louisiana was proving to be as friendly as Texas. Traveling here was much like being in backwoods Burma. Everyone knew me as a foreigner, just as they knew each other.

Oak Grove, Good Friday, April 17

It was fun to pedal through the thin film of ground fog and watch and smell the marsh awakening. When the sun was up, I stopped to photograph a family's catch of crawfish. "What do you use for bait?"

"Melt."

"What's that?"

"Cow insides," one person ventured tentatively. They weren't sure what it was, just that it caught crawfish. The ride beyond Grand Chenier was flat and pleasant despite the bugs that came out as it grew warm. A summer tanager let me catch a glimpse. There were a variety of blackbirds, cranes, egrets, a blue-winged teal, coots, gulls, terns, and a multitude of unfamiliar wading and shore birds. I spotted a few baby gators and enjoyed multitudes of wild lilies and iris. A rat scurried across the road. At the western edge of the Rockefeller Wildlife Refuge, a pair of Canada geese with babies waddled nonchalantly. Located at the southern end of the Mississippi River migratory flyway, the refuge is the winter home of hundreds of thousands of waterfowl which nest much farther north. Birds that winter in Central or South America use it as a resting spot. The marshy waters provide a nursery for fish as well as a haven for birds.

Since there were no guided tours, I headed back to my bike. I was just in time to meet Clark Hoffpauer, Sr., former director of the refuge. He told me one of his favorite sights occurs early in the morning near Pecan Island when thousands of swallows fly up like smoke, catching flies. He recommended that I visit the restaurant his family runs on Bourbon Street, the

Cajun Crawfish House, when I got to New Orleans.

I pedaled past the end of the refuge along a straight road through the marsh grasses. Not far along, I was rewarded with a wonderful view of male and female orchard orioles and a multitude of swallows. Along the route, people were fishing or crawfishing. All I could see in any direction was grass and marsh. After I crossed the Intracoastal Waterway, I descended from the bridge at over thirty miles an hour! Marsh gave way to inland farms with cattle and rice fields, some of them flooded for crawfish farming.

About four, I arrived in Abbeville, closed tight for Good Friday. I asked at several small shops about a campground, but I settled for a motel near a shopping center.

The grocery store couldn't cash my hundred-dollar traveler's check, and I had no smaller denominations. The motel required cash, and I would need money for the long weekend. The drug store cashed my check when I bought some nail clippers. As I returned to the grocery, I heard gunshots of duck and Canadian geese hunters on the outskirts of town.

After dinner, I washed my hair and read tourist folders. The next day I planned to tour Abbeville, visit Avery Island and historic Franklin, and try to reach Morgan City where I could camp. There was also a campground near Avery Island in case I wanted to stay there longer.

Abbeville, Saturday, April 18

As I ate an early breakfast of oranges, I read about Abbeville, founded by a Roman Catholic missionary who named it after his hometown in France. When it was light, I pedaled around the charming town and Magdalen Square, surrounded by a brick wall with a fountain in the center. I saw the C. S. Steen Syrup Mill, the Rivina Rice Mills, and the St. Mary Magdalen Church, reputedly the most beautiful church in Acadia. The bridge over the Vermilion River and the small shops made an attractive town. I stopped at the motel to pick up my panniers and, once again, headed east.

It wasn't long before I entered Iberia Parish. The first settlers had come before 1765 when a few families arrived from Acadia, now Nova Scotia. *The Cajuns*, a historical novel by Lee Davis Willoughby, provided me background information on both Louisiana and Maine.

Before turning down the road to Avery Island, I entered the tourist information office in New Iberia. I learned bicycles are not permitted on the island and that it is too large to explore afoot. Disappointed, I rode toward Franklin and visited Oaklawn Manor, a fine antebellum mansion built in 1837. Although twice burned, it has been restored. The house faces the bayou across a lawn shaded by centuries-old oak trees. I particularly enjoyed seeing the owner's collections of Louisiana waterfowl carvings and antique bird prints.

Bicycling through Franklin provided a journey back into the steamboat era. Many fine old homes and aged trees remained between the highway and Bayou Teche, where steamboats had anchored. I continued following Route 182 to Garden City where a boy in a pickup stopped to greet me. Several hours earlier on Highway 90, he and his brother had yelled out of the truck, "Where are you going?"

"New Orleans," I had shouted back over the traffic noise.

"Where are you from?"

"San Diego."

Here he was again. "I'm just going home—do you want a cold drink?"

"I do need to fill my water bottles."

"Follow me. It's less than a block." He turned down a street, and I followed.

At the house, I drank water and filled my bottles before meeting the other brother and their parents. I settled an argument between the boys over how far I could go in a day. One had insisted on twenty-five to thirty miles and the other on fifty to eighty. Barry and Danny Luke were driving to Houma in the truck and asked if I'd like to go along. Although tempted, I declined. I drank another glass of water and chatted with Barbara and Ray who told me the boys were competing in a calf roping contest that night. Reluctantly, I left for Morgan City.

I wondered if the heat had addled my brain! Taking a ride to Houma would have given me a straight-shot, one-day ride to New Orleans. The distance from Morgan City to New Orleans was too far for one day's biking. Several people warned me about Houma. "It's a rough, bad city—dangerous. Don't go there," I had been told.

Rolling through glass and other litter, I huffed and puffed up the bridge leading into Morgan City, then whizzed down the other side and headed out of town toward Lake End

Park and Campground on Lake Palourde.

I wasn't prepared for what I found — a fantastic, lakeside thirty-acre lawn overhung by moss-draped cypress trees and sprawling live oaks. There were shower and restroom buildings, picnic pavilions, and a beach along the lake. All sorts of vehicles, from elegant whales to tiny pickups, were parked at spacious sites. I situated the tent under a tree to prevent dew, and in the shadow of a trunk to block light. Finally settled, I sat down and began to unzip my kitchen pannier.

The campground was bathed in the aroma of char-grilled food. I pulled out my stove, some noodles, a can of chicken, and a few carrots. The food wasn't very appetizing, and I was too tired to feel hungry. Two eighty-mile days in a row had been exhausting, and New Orleans was still a hundred miles away.

As I began to unfold the legs of the stove, a woman walked across the road and called out, "Don't open that!" When she reached my picnic table, her face shining with smiles, she added, "Please don't cook. We are three couples, all friends, over there, parked together. We have plenty of food, and we want to fix you a plate."

My lack of hesitation in accepting wasn't even polite. "I'd be delighted, but I'd like to visit with you as well."

"Fine, it'll be ready in about fifteen minutes. My name is Theresa Thibodeaux."

Quickly, I showered and dressed in a clean but rumpled long-sleeved cotton shirt and my long, black, velvety slacks. They need not know I was wearing my pajamas! Theresa introduced me to her husband, Phil, and to John and Yola Rogers, and Harold and Joyce Hebert. They served crawfish etouffe, fried catfish, potato salad, green salad, cantaloupe, bread, and sodas. I told them I almost turned into a bowl of gumbo and adored all the Cajun food I'd tried. They were afraid the seasoning was too hot for me, but I thought it delicious.

They asked about my trip and laughed at my stories which, I hoped, were interesting enough to be my contribution to the meal. They told me stories too, about a man in Lafayette, Black Callier, who remembered the old ways and sold vegetables from a wagon to send all his kids to college, and a ninety-six-year-old man who plays the French accordion in Martinsville. They laughed about French people being unable to understand Cajun French. The Cajun language is now taught in schools, and people are bilingual.

They said I should have come through Lake Charles and that the Cameron area, where I had traveled, was rough and dangerous. Everyone considers home safe. I decided safety is a state of mind, an attitude of the familiar, which one could choose to carry around or leave behind.

They called themselves Cajun Roadrunners, part of a group of ten families who toured together in RVs. By the time we finished eating, it was dark and I was sleepy. I excused myself and was soon zipped into my tent.

Morgan City, Easter Sunday, April 19

The chatter of blackbirds and grackles at dawn precluded further sleep. About seven, I crawled out of my tent to start the day. An Easter sunrise service was in progress in the pavilion, and many townspeople had come.

While I was upending the tent in the sun to dry, a young boy on a bicycle stopped beside me. My rear tire was flat, and I began to take it off as the boy watched. One of his tires was deflated, too. I found a glass slash, probably from debris on the bridge. I put tape on the inside of the tire, patched the tube, and remounted them on the wheel. I pumped up the tires and went to wash up. When I returned, I noticed the boy's father helping repair his son's tire.

Theresa hailed me, "Happy Easter!" They had set out two big baskets of eggs and candies. "We wanted to fix you a basket and leave it at your tent last night but thought it might frighten you if we made a noise." She handed me a plastic bag. "We'd like you to take some things for your trip today. Please choose anything you like." I filled the bag with wheat fig bars, an egg or two, and some candies that might not melt. They showed me their RV, a thirty-one foot Encounter.

I wanted to know more about Cajuns. A little nervously, I asked Theresa, "Do you feel you fit in, do other people treat Cajuns well?"

She smiled, took a deep breath, and replied. "If you had asked me that twenty-five years ago, I would have been embarrassed, and I would have said I felt second-rate. The government of Louisiana discovered the Cajun culture is a commercial asset. They recognize and promote Cajun culture as important to Louisiana. We're proud to say we are Cajun."

"Just what is a Creole?" I asked.

"Originally, it was a mix of Spanish, Mexican, or French with Anglo-Europeans. The term is often used to mean a person of mixed European and African heritage. Most Creoles live in New Orleans."

Phil asked me to stay for an early lunch. I asked him how crawfish and rice were raised in the same field. He explained that rice is grown only every third year and, in intervening years, the milo grass which crawfish eat is planted, and baled alfalfa is put out for nesting.

After lunch and goodbyes, Phil and Theresa walked with me to the bike. She said, "Thank you for being with us. You're the most interesting person I've ever met in my whole life." Undone, I rode away as quickly as my full stomach and my wobbly legs, melted by emotion, would allow.

Morgan City, where the first Tarzan movie was filmed, slid behind me, and I reached Tribodaux on Bayou Lafourche. Cajuns call it Main Street. I continued along the banks of the Bayou Lafourche to the motel at Raceland.

It was a beautiful, traffic-free ride until the tire I had just repaired breathed a sigh. I should have known better than to ride on a cut tire. Without removing the panniers, I removed the wheel, threw the tire away, and replaced it with a slightly used, fold-up spare. While I was making repairs, a woman peeped out her front door and then slammed it shut. Later, she looked again, "What are you doing? How long will you be?" she cried.

Perhaps watching me was making her nervous. I chuckled, "Fixing a flat tire. I'm just leaving."

Across the road, a young family was out in the yard. Two youngsters ran over, handed me a cold Coke, and asked if I needed help.

"No, thanks a lot." I was tempted to ask if I could camp there, but hadn't the courage.

At Raceland, after fifty-two hot miles, I collapsed on the motel bed. Riding the same distance the next day would bring me to New Orleans and the Mississippi River, a milestone.

Raceland, Monday, April 20

When I returned the motel key, the desk clerk, who looked like Frenchy in *Casablanca*, told me that going through town would shorten my route by three miles. As I left, a couple out walking agreed it really was shorter. Thirty years of cross-checking every piece of data at least three times, preferably using separate sources, obviously influenced my route-finding.

Through town I pedaled, over the bayou and past the sugar mill. Beyond town, I entered fields of clover waving green and purple in the morning breeze. I smelled honeysuckle. I had *some* dinner the night before — fig bars, jelly beans, and a lollipop for dessert! At midnight, I ate a pear. An apple and orange had constituted breakfast. Now, on Route 90, rolling along a wide smooth shoulder, I ate an orange. By nine-thirty, I reached Boutte thinking only of food. Two pancakes and grits solved the problem, and I rolled on.

There were wild Louisiana lilies and iris in the swamp by the road's edge. Birds could be heard but were seldom seen among the spring leaves, although herons and egrets became visible when they flew. Occasionally, a spotlight of sun through the trees reached feathers of a creature in the water.

At Westwego, I turned on Route 18 and continued east until another flat tire halted me in a derelict shopping center. I sat on the curb and pulled out the limp tube, replaced it with a new one, pumped it up, and went bumping over litter-strewn streets, carrying no spare tires and only one extra tube. Flats on three consecutive days underscored failure to follow my own rule: fix it right the first time.

From Gretna, a ferry took me across the Mississippi River, and I bounced off at Jackson Avenue and kept rolling. New Orleans felt good, comfortable. I wondered if everyone responded positively to the city. When I spotted The Bikesmith, I stopped to buy a new tire and tube, a new Third Eye rearview mirror to replace the one I'd broken and temporarily repaired, and a tire patch kit. I also exchanged my erratic Avocet for a new one. Employees Steve and Frank were interested in my trip and talked with me when they weren't busy with other customers. Frank suggested a longer but more interesting departure route along the shore of Lake Champlain.

I soon passed Tulane University and Newcomb College and arrived at Ann Rhea's daughter Wendy's house about two-thirty. Lil Holt, a next-door neighbor, was sitting in the porch swing, as expected. I introduced myself, left my bike, and walked across the street into a delicatessen. I was starving, but a big salad satisfied me. Lil let me into the house and I took a nap and read some of Wendy's magazines until she came home from work. What a privilege it was to sit quietly in a home!

Wendy is a developmental geologist. "What exactly do you do?" I asked her.

"I take the data from oil field surveys and measurements and figure out what it means," she said.

New Orleans, Tuesday, April 21

As usual, I was awake early, trying to plan my route and a rough schedule from New Orleans to Jacksonville. My mom called to say she sent the things I had requested to the post office at Grand Bay — maps, a campground guide, a tire, and personal mail. She wanted my itinerary, which I promised to mail at once. During the morning I completed route planning and wrote a *Pedalgram* that told friends I'd reached New Orleans.

About ten, I rode the streetcar to town. The hedges and larkspur were in spring bloom and smelled wonderful. Larkspur grew wild in our yard when I was small and was my favorite because I thought the flowers looked like small rabbit heads. I called it "the rabbit flower." Now, a woman on the street identified it for me.

The streetcar line began operation in 1835. Cars pulled by horses were replaced by steam-driven cars, and the lines were electrified just before the turn of the century. The New Orleans system claims to be the oldest continuously-operating one in the world. The windows were open and the breeze floated through. Sometimes crape myrtle bushes brushed a protruding elbow. We rounded Lee Circle and continued to Canal Street, where I got off and took to my feet.

I bought film before wandering down Royal and Bourbon Streets and through Lafayette Park, where a high school orchestra from New York played Mozart. Occasionally, I heard an extra-loud trumpet or saxophone from the other side of the square. From the river boat *Natchez*, a whistle summoned tourists to the Mississippi River. This was obviously not a daytime portion of the city; groceries were being delivered to the restaurants, and the shops were taking down their outside shutters at noon. In the park, artists were at work. I wandered about, comfortable and happy. When I was a child, the old slave block was a major attraction; now, it wasn't mentioned on my maps, and I didn't know where it had been. I sat in the sun on a bench on the levee and looked across the water. The *Natchez* whistle blew again. Its load of tourists drifted on, and so did I.

At an antique gun, sword, and coin shop I inquired about the sword designed by George S. Patton and issued in 1913 as the last U.S. Cavalry sword. I had never seen one, and they had one I could examine. I had always wanted one. It had a straightened blade designed for attack, in contrast to more defensive curved blades.

Footsore, I boarded the streetcar for my trip back along St. Charles Street. Since I couldn't bring myself to break my nostalgic mood, I rode to the end of the line, walked around to another car, and then rattled back to my stop.

When I got home, I sat in the swing on the front porch. Lil Holt joined me, and we talked until I got hungry. Once again, I went to the deli for a big salad and sat outside in the shade eating it. Then I pedaled to the Tulane campus post office to mail home packages of non-essentials and returned through Audubon Park. This was my last "friend stop" until Jacksonville.

New Orleans, Wednesday, April 22

New Orleans doesn't wake up early, there was no significant traffic along Broadway and Jeff Davis Drive. I saw Lakeshore Drive with its waterfront houses — modern, huge, of various styles. On the outskirts headed east, I took the old road past fishing cottages.

Near the Intracoastal Waterway, I met two bicyclists, Joyce Rochette and David Ruoff, who had begun their trip a month before in Baltimore. Cycling for cystic fibrosis, they planned to continue to Alaska and return to Baltimore in November. Their fundraising would take them through the larger cities and involve them in television, radio, and print media publicity. There would be no quiet slipping in and out of New Orleans for them. For their work, they got funding and were outfitted with the latest sleeping bags, tents, bicycles, and panniers. I was glad to be on my own.

After a rest and snack at Fort Pike Park, I crossed the Pearl River into Mississippi. There was no more marsh. A tailwind sped me among the pine trees. At Waveland Hospitality House, I consulted with the volunteer and selected a nearby camp. But at the gate, I was informed that the grounds were private. Angry, tired, hot, and hungry, I was relieved when the gatekeeper decided to let me stay one night. He said, "The nearest store is five minutes away."

"By car," I interjected.

"But," he continued, "food is available at the Pavilion. All you can eat for a dollar-fifty." The meal consisted of cheeseburgers, lettuce, tomato, onion, and cookies, and it was good. I specialized in lettuce, tomato, onion, and cookies. The retirees were not any more interested in me than I in them. I rested in my tent, feeling dull and full. I fit right in!

Later, I phoned my mother. Mom assured me that she was feeling fine, more energetic because she had run out of pills. She suggested I try to reach the home of her college roommate Dot Rowlett near Jacksonville before Dot left for England. I could stay one night with her and as long as I liked during the week that she was away. Once again, a deadline pressured me to move fast.

Gulfport, Mississippi, Thursday, April 23

After encountering an entertaining frog in the restroom at four-thirty, I didn't go back to sleep. Daylight was slow appearing but, because my tent was right under a campground light, I could read. When I pulled the black mask back over my eyes and lay flat again, whippoorwill calls and the sizzles of an electronic bug-zapper kept me awake.

When there was enough light, I pedaled to a Winn-Dixie for breakfast. After eating a cantaloupe and a banana, I stored two bananas, mushrooms, and an avocado in my panniers. The fruit stoked my legs through Gulfport at sixteen miles an hour until I stopped at the historic last home of Jefferson Davis, which faces the ocean between Gulfport and Biloxi. I stood on the lawn and looked out over the Gulf of Mexico, and I hoped some day war would be allowed to rest in peace.

I watched a pair of cardinals, not nearly so brilliant or large as the western species. Easterners dress with less flash and flair than their western cousins! Mounting my iron horse, I galloped down the coast into Biloxi, reigned in at a historical marker, and read about the sights. After enjoying exhibits at the Seafood Industry Museum, I visited the outdoor fruit and vegetable market to replenish my supplies. It was fun to wander an open market full of Vietnamese shoppers and vendors!

I hated to bypass inviting state parks and commercial campgrounds, but my mail awaited just beyond the Alabama border in Grand Bay. By mid afternoon, I had picked it up and settled in a campground. Mockingbirds and jays chattered as I rested in the shade.

Grand Bay, Alabama, Friday, April 24

While I was packing, a woman from a pickup truck-camper greeted me and asked, "Are you going on a long trip?"

"Yes, I'm riding around the perimeter of the United States."

"That's great. My husband and I just retired, and we're going to visit our daughter. This is the first time in our lives that we've been able to take a trip without hurrying. We saw all your gear and thought you might be a writer, off by yourself. Do you take back roads?"

"Yes."

"That's an interesting way to travel. You must see a lot that way." Her eyes focused on my bicycle as I slowly walked toward the campground exit. She accompanied me until I passed her camper, then watched me out of sight.

Relaxed, I pedaled into a slight wind. Pines and oaks lined both sides of the road. Among them, Carolina wrens, red-headed woodpeckers, eastern kingbirds, an indigo bunting, and an oriole kept me company. My flashiest companion was the scarlet tanager. I sighted an osprey nest with young in a dead tree along the road and anhingas hanging their wings out to dry.

At Bayou La Batre, I restocked my fruit and vegetable supplies and bought a twelve-foot extension cord and a four-watt night light. Many campgrounds had electrical outlets and when I wasn't sleepy at dark, the light would be useful. As I finished paying, the cashier said, "Hurry back." I hadn't heard those words for years. They reminded me of Georgia. Another local expression I caught once in a while was a favorite of my father's, "Much obliged."

When I was rushing and stressed all day, I was more tired. If I just ambled along, I accomplished just as much but felt better at the end of the day. Fatigue seemed related to attitude. Now, I was riding at a more relaxed pace. Oyster shells were everywhere when I reached Alabama Port and turned south for the long trip out Cedar Point and over the causeway to Dauphin Island. I rode through marsh again along the west side of Mobile Bay to the ferry. It was a small ferry and a long ride across the entrance to Mobile Bay. I'd selected this route not only to remain along the perimeter but to avoid city congestion.

After the ferry crossing, I stopped to watch two scarlet tanagers in the topmost shoots of neighboring small trees. Through my binoculars, I saw them sitting quietly. Their feathers glittered in the sun much more brilliantly than the feathers of the summer tanager of Sabine Pass, Texas. Fleetingly, I glimpsed an oriole, something that was probably a warbler, and a female blue grosbeak.

After a hot, twenty-mile ride along sandy Mobile Point that separates Mobile Bay from the Gulf of Mexico, I paused at Gulf Shores. When I had finished a lunch of fish, squash, cole slaw, and okra, I pedaled a few miles into Gulf State Park for the afternoon and night.

Public campgrounds in the East have a minimum charge, and the attendants usually thought it odd when I requested a discount because I had nothing to hook up — nothing electrical, no water hose, and no gray water to dump. This time, I came prepared with my four-watt night light. My light worked wonderfully well, providing brighter and safer illumination than a candle or flashlight.

CHAPTER SEVENTEEN

Beached on the Spanish
Main Panhandle

Gulf Shores State Park, Alabama, Saturday, April 25

After a chilly night, I wandered along admiring the seascapes. Since I was going fewer than thirty miles, much of the day would be for rest.

At nine-thirty, I crossed the state line into Florida. "I'm on the East Coast!" I yelled to the sand dunes. "Well, almost." Blue gulf water appeared beyond sand white as sugar. I'd left the Mississippi mud behind.

Now that I had a light, I needed something to read. I stopped at Coquina Village, and wandered into Page and Palette, Inc. I couldn't help complimenting the owner, Betty Jo Wolff, on the quality of her book selection. It had been a long time since I'd found a book or magazine display without junk. I bought three paperbacks and chatted until other customers arrived.

I continued pedaling along the rather barren, wind-swept coastline to Big Lagoon State Park. Although I had only traveled twenty-seven miles, I was very tired. I put up the tent and intended to spend the rest of the afternoon in it reading. With only two rest days in the past seventeen, I traveled nine hundred-twenty-seven miles and averaged sixty-two miles a day. Just being in Florida raised my spirits in spite of fatigue.

A couple walking by introduced themselves as the Jimmy and Vivian Vaughn from Destin. We talked. Vivian, recovering from heart surgery, took short walks frequently during the day. Since I was near the Vaughns' 310 Airstream motor home, they stopped by my tent to chat. They told me they use their motor home for hurricane evacuation. They just transfer their food into the motor home refrigerator and go. Most of my route for the past week or more had been through hurricane country.

I was concerned about the bridges at Pensacola and asked their opinion. They suggested I travel with them in their motor home. They planned to return to Destin the next afternoon. The Vaughns convinced me it was an opportunity to cross sixty-two very similar, congested miles and have a rest day at the same time. We would leave in the early afternoon. That would solve the bridge problems, and I needed the rest.

I walked over to say hello to a woman with children camping across from me. Peggy Bailey was as happy as I was for someone to talk with. She'd been divorced three years and was working as secretary, bookkeeper, and interior designer for a builder, selecting rugs, fixtures, and colors for his houses. She adores her job, and I would like it too, I thought. She said she would love my sort of trip, that she wouldn't be afraid, but that she doesn't ride a bicycle. The kids were on spring break, and she had taken the week off for a camping expedition. She invited me to supper, but I said I needed to eat up what I'd been carrying. I didn't have enough energy to be more social.

Big Lagoon State Park, Florida, Sunday, April 26

I awoke too early, so I switched on my light and read. Eating fruit in bed had become a luxurious habit while camping. At midmorning, I washed my hair and my long black pants and began to write thank you notes and a *Pedalgram*.

Peggy showed me raccoon paw prints on their picnic table. The critters ate crabs the kids caught and left in a dishpan under her trailer. After devouring two paper envelopes of Kool-Aid, the raccoons left a sticky, pink trail.

Vivian, Jimmy, and I shared a pleasant afternoon driving in the Airstream. Shortly before we reached their home in Destin, Vivian told me they would be delighted to have me stay overnight with them. Southerners are so generous and kind that I can't always tell if they're just being polite. Though I consider myself a Georgian, Southern subtleties escape me. I enjoyed the Vaughns' company and was amused that their home was on Mountain Road, where the altitude was ten feet.

We went out to eat red snapper, and they showed me

the town and the beach. He owns and operates his own fishing tackle business and she works there, too. They make their own fishnets. I learned to recognize their nets and continued to see them in shops during the rest of my trip across Florida.

Destin, Monday, April 27

I rode an eighty-three-mile day along the shore, through Panama City and Tyndall Air Force Base, to Mexico Beach where I found a campground. Morning doves were everywhere, and there were little ponds full of blooming lilies and cypress knees in the water near the road. Hour after hour, the view was sand, water, and pine trees. Singing eastern kingbirds failed to raise my spirits. I felt sick, tired, and ready to quit. Perhaps being in a home overnight had stirred in me a trace of homesickness.

During the past few weeks, I had, for the first time in my life, been unable to sleep well. My spirits were as blue as the gulf. There was no silver rim to my wheels or glitter to my spokes as I rode. Although I kept both feet on the pedals, I seemed to have no best wheel to put forward. Fatigue, like a leaky tire valve, was deflating my will power.

Mexico Beach, Tuesday, April 28

The first vehicle to pass me in the morning was a logging truck. Its long skinny timbers and overall size were smaller than what I'd seen in the Northwest. At Port St. Joe, after passing a wood-processing plant, I rested at a monument commemorating Florida's first constitution.

Wheeling along, I watched yellow and purple wild asters nod among a multitude of curiously-shaped grasses and blooming weeds. The dandelions were lemony yellow, and a few blackberries were ripe. The smell of pine sap, sometimes like turpentine, pervaded the air. Further west in Florida, motorists seemed almost hostile, but here they beeped, honked, and waved.

When I entered the cafe in Apalachicola, I had ridden thirty-five miles. Waiting for my vegetable plate, I noticed the clock on the wall was an hour faster than my watch. I had crossed into the Eastern time zone. "I'm really on the East

Coast," I tried to encourage myself.

After lunch, I pedaled through streets with old houses and along the river bank to the Apalachicola dock. By 1930, this was the third largest cotton port in the country. I could still see some of the forty-three cotton warehouses and brokerages made of brick and faced with granite. I stood on the pier and looked over the rambling river delta.

Then I rode northeast. Chip trucks and pickups full of oyster sacks sped by. There were frequent patches of new road, bracketed by broken, twisted, or burned trees. Florida has no shoulders on its roads and this part of the state had relatively little traffic. Heavy traffic on north-south routes prompted me to omit the southern Florida coast from my journey.

At Carrabelle Beach, I stopped for a while and walked through the surf in water quiet as a lake. I wondered whether I liked Apalachicola so well for itself or because, in my family, it was praised as a special place for vacations and fishing expeditions. My cousin, Frank Schnell, told me several of our ancestors lived at Apalachicola. Another famous-in-the-family relative was a steamboat captain on the Chattahoochee River. In his day, the boats traveled upriver as far as Columbus, Georgia.

I headed on toward the Holiday Campground in Panacea. From the bridge across Ochlockonee Bay, I saw the campground on the water. The setting was glorious.

Nearby at The Oaks Restaurant, I ate broiled grouper, grits, and salad. The placemats depicted the family of Alton and Ora Oaks, who founded the restaurant. In family tree style with an oak leaf motif, the chart named each "acorn," including the "grandacorns," "great-grandacorns," and the "nuts" they married.

Panacea, Wednesday, April 29

At the grocery in Panacea, I bought kiwis, the only ripe fruit. I asked the girl in the grocery, "Is there anything down this way in town I should see?"

"No, you 'bout slap through town," she replied.

Heading into a slight wind, I had to exert myself. I was depressed; after all the time spent on the trip, I still had no idea what I wanted to do with the rest of my life. What would I do all day if I didn't ride my bike? When the road turned, the headwind disappeared, and though I didn't pedal as hard, my speed jumped from eight to twelve miles an hour. My mood, too, leaped forward.

At the last possible junction, I decided to ride the extra mileage to Wakulla Springs and Lodge. As I turned into a quiet road, a gray fox crossed in front of me. On fast feet and with a long, bushy tail, it looked about three times as big as a squirrel.

The Indian word "wakulla" means "mysteries of strange water." The origin of Wakulla Springs is unknown. The water, perhaps arising from an underground river, forms a basin one hundred eighty-five feet deep and eventually flows to the gulf sixteen miles away. Ponce de Leon and his companions are said to have wintered here. Now, a forest of live oak, magnolia, pine, and cyprus trees encircle the springs and create a four-thousand-acre wildlife sanctuary.

As I walked beside the basin pushing my bike, some young men in the swimming area yelled, "How many miles have you been?"

"About eight thousand."

"Wow! Welcome to Wakulla County!"

Soon after I left the springs, the rail under my seat broke. To avoid sitting crooked, I jammed the sleeping bag as far beneath the seat as it would go. I'd have to buy a new seat in Jacksonville.

When I came to a small state forest campground at Newport Springs, I decided to stay overnight. A young man beginning to climb the fire tower invited me to climb up and enjoy the view after I got settled at my campsite.

I had no idea how high the tower was until I began to climb the steps. It was a long huff and puff. My legs, accustomed to going around, not up and down, protested long before I reached the top. I was shocked at how out of breath I became.

When I reached the top of the tower, the young man told me that watching for fires across the highway along St. Mark's River was his responsibility. He added, "Last year was pretty good for us, but it's very dry this year."

"What do you have to do to be a fire fighter?"

"You have to have a high school diploma and take an exam. I made more money at my previous job," he said, "but I like fighting fires. If you aren't happy doing what you're doing, I think you should find something else."

"What do you like best about it?"

"I don't know. I just like it. I like scraper work, making

firebreaks."

"Do you wear special suits for that?"

"We didn't, but now they've just come out with jump-suits and earmuffs containing radios." After a final look at the expanse of pine tree tops, I told the young firefighter goodbye and descended the tower steps.

For the first time, I was spending the night in an empty campground, good practice for when and if I had to camp alone somewhere. I pitched my tent back in the woods behind a picnic table in a spot that would minimize my being seen if anyone drove through during the night. If people didn't know I was there, they couldn't bother me.

When camp was all set up, I went to try the solar heated shower. Drastic changes in water temperatures gave me a few spots that looked and felt like sunburn and put me out of sorts. The "on" button controlled both hot and cold water. I tried every stall, running from one to the other dressed in soap bubbles, trying to rinse without becoming an icicle or scalding my skin. The water was fit for instant coffee or iced tea, but not me!

Newport Springs, Thursday, April 30

After a quiet sleep on a soft bed of leaves in the woods, I was still tired. As I headed toward Perry, the vehicles passing me were trucks: logging trucks, eighteen-wheelers, or trucks carrying loads of pipe or woodchips. No cars or RVs passed. Startled by my approach, a large white egret with her young one took off out of the grass. They climbed steeply, pulled their necks in close, and tucked up their feet — they looked like planes with wheels retracted. The birds flew away through a windless sky. I just pedaled, not thinking, just enjoying pedaling.

Coming upon a wayside picnic area, I stopped to see if there was any water. A man walking toward me called out, "Hello. I'm glad you turned in. We passed you and wanted to find out what you're doing." After answering briefly, I asked about him. He and his wife make sand pictures. Not knowing what he was talking about, I asked to see one. It consisted of colored sand pressed between two pieces of plastic held together by a frame. Turning the picture upside down made the sand create a different design.

He explained, "I trained as an electronics engineer but quit my job. I wanted to get out from behind the desk, away from the crazy stuff that goes on, the petty tricks. I enjoyed the work, I didn't like the politics and the crazy bureaucratic palaver. This is a new project for us, and our business is really taking off. You could sell photographs at the arts and crafts shows. They would really go well."

"Maybe someday," I replied, "but now I have to get down the road." I certainly understood petty tricks and bureaucratic palaver. I recalled a colleague who years ago asked me why I was wasting myself working at the CIA. She thought I was unappreciated, under-utilized, and wasting my talents. She didn't understand why I did it. Neither did I, then.

At work I had lacked the confidence to confront the unknown. In recent years, I have learned other people perceive me as more intelligent and capable than I perceived myself. I knew I could do things, but I held myself back, dependent on someone else's confidence in me rather than my confidence in myself. My self-confidence was so low during work years that I had to wait for a boss or colleague to expect action before I could proceed. Underestimating myself was a closet illness I didn't know I had, and I was too stubborn to ask anyone anything.

It took the office of training to teach me confidence. Even there, I had a boss who told me I took too much of his time seeking approval. He made me so angry I switched to a different position where I resolved not to seek approval. Fortunately, that boss was swamped in work and was happy for me to present him with finished products that I prepared without much input from him. The saving grace for me was his inability to say anything negative even when he should. I worked hard and devotedly. When I learned enough, the repetition stopped and I retired.

At Perry, I bought food for lunch and supper before heading toward the Suwannee River. Perhaps I'd stay at a campground or motel in Bradford. Along the road, I came upon an all-black work crew cleaning litter out of the ditches. The white overseer asked, "Do you have a match? The boys are about to have a nicotine fit." I stopped and dug a pack of matches out of the kitchen pannier. The overseer had a big "Department of Corrections" patch on his shirt sleeve. As I remounted my bike, he offered me some Kool-Aid. Since I had plenty of water, I thanked him and went on my way.

After cycling through farmland for a while, I entered

Mayo where I saw a motel back from the road under large old oak trees. I decided to stay. Ultra-clean, the large room had screened windows on both sides. I lay down almost an hour before mustering enough energy to take a shower. As the motel owner filled my plate with barbecue and cole slaw from the family grill, he told me Mayo is the county seat of Lafayette County. I was too tired to sleep. I rummaged in the panniers and ate the remaining mushrooms, read a while, then ate an avocado. I slept a couple of hours, ate three slices of bread, then went back to sleep. I kept waking about every two hours, much more frequently than usual, and finished the night by eating a banana and a bunch of grapes. By the time I got up in the morning, I had eaten breakfast! I was still tired, but felt a lot better. "If I can just pedal another hundred and twenty miles, I can rest a whole week," I told myself.

Mayo, Friday, May 1

I felt revived and ready to go. My water bottles were filled, and one included the juice of a fresh lime. The tires were pumped and the camera was loaded with film. On the outskirts of town, I entered a feed store and weighed myself, and the bike — one hundred sixty pounds for me and eighty-nine for the fully loaded bike. My weight included shoes, clothes, gloves, helmet, and my last glass of water.

As I wheeled past scores of chicken farms, I saw lavender, fuchsia, pink, purple, and white impatiens growing along the road and recognized chinaberry trees and wild plum bushes from my youth. Impatience grew within me, strengthening my desire to *be there*. Through wispy ground fog, I heard larks singing and saw chickens, cattle, and irrigation machines that made patterns flinging water around the pasture grass. I never changed gears but changed the rhythm of pedaling for my own amusement. Riding along the white-painted line was like riding a long balance beam.

Beyond the bridge in Bradford, I stopped at the Steamboat Restaurant. I'd been twenty-two miles and was ready to quit. I was too late for breakfast and too early for lunch, but I was able to order a bowl of grits followed by fresh strawberry and lemon meringue pie.

As I proceeded through Fort White, the terrain began to roll a little, and it was a pleasure to glide downhill even if I had to climb again in the heat. I headed for O'Leno State Park, located very near the Sante Fe river sink where the water flows underground for about three miles. After forty-three miles, I tumbled into a campsite, certain I couldn't go any further. The next day would be a long one. I was exhausted before two o'clock. Lying flat on my back for two hours and reading brought me back to life.

When I moved to the picnic bench to continue reading, four little gray squirrels with white bellies appeared. One had a nick in his ear. He sat on the table and watched me turn the pages. Although feeding wildlife was not allowed, I gave him half a peanut. A mother raccoon wandered over to my table and sniffed around. She sat down, had her portrait taken, and scratched an ear before wandering along.

Although I was too tired for conversation, I phoned my mother. Her house was still on the market; she thought she might not move in June. Changing her plans upset me, too. I had just completed my highest mileage ever in three weeks, over thirteen hundred miles, double the pace I had anticipated, to get home to help her move. I decided that my scheduling would no longer be keyed to Mother's plans. I was tired, and I was tired of the trip. I wanted to get it over with—immediately. I, however, had said I was going to do it. I wanted to do it. I would do it. Iwillfinish. It was all one word!

O'Leno State Park, Saturday, May 2

Forty minutes took me from sleeping bag to bicycle. Ground fog was thick, and no one else was stirring. As I left the park I saw white tailed deer and tanagers and heard unidentifiable bird voices. On Route 18, where the fog was thicker, I hung my safety blinker on the rear of the bike and turned it on to flash orange every second. Spotting an eastern cottontail, I said aloud, "Hello, rabbit." It was so small, half the size of a western jack rabbit. Its ears were smaller, not extra-long like those of his western cousins.

After the fog dissipated, I turned off my blinker. Trailers transporting ponies and horses passed me. At Lake Butler, people were preparing for a horse show. I would have loved to stay and watch, but my schedule forced me on. Three women bicyclists approached, and I prepared to stop. They kept going but answered shouted questions. They were traveling from North Carolina to Gainesville. I hadn't seen many bicyclists, and I was sorry they wouldn't stop. Gainesville wasn't far, and perhaps they also were tired and rolling on automatic pilot. I'd reach Dot's "landing strip" by evening, but it was too early in the day to start pushing. I was still warming up.

Just before noon, I arrived at Starke, where three women told me, "The Shriners' parade for burned and crippled children is about to begin. We'll be serving lunch after the parade. Have lunch with us and make a contribution." I stood on the corner and watched the parade. The number of vehicles, the patterns they drove in, and the costumes set me laughing. It almost seemed that the band was playing to celebrate my arrival on the East Coast! The musical umpahs blended with my thoughts, and "Iwillfinish" began to thump in my head.

After the parade, I was at the front of the line for the chicken dinner, and the ladies really piled up my plate. Before the crowd around the lunch counter became too thick, I made my donation and was already on the road out of town. The rhythm of my pedaling feet kept repeating "Iwillfinish."

As I was passing a fire tower, the watcher aloft yelled, "Come on up, there's a nice breeze."

"I'm too tired to climb the steps, and have to get to Jacksonville this afternoon." I stopped on the roadside, and we shouted at each other. The firefighter said, "The haze is bad. I can't see more than ten miles, and usually I can see twenty. It's dangerous today. Everything's so dry, I might not be able to see a fire."

"Not on your watch, I hope."

Penny Farms, the only town on my map before the river, consisted of a gas station and a retirement home for ministers. Its golf course stretched along my way, and I stopped to lie down on a bench under a tree at the sixth tee, par three. In the middle of a hot day, there were no players in sight. I poured water down my throat and refilled my bottles at the faucet. After twenty minutes, I was ready to go. I never stopped being amazed at how tired I could be and how quickly I became rested.

I estimated twenty or thirty miles to go. I reached the St. Johns River and began to pedal across the bridge as a sailing regatta passed under its span. The river looked like swamp water; the color was created by tannic acid from cypress trees. Spectators leaned over the railing on the hump to watch the regatta. I joined them, admiring the catamarans sailing underneath. It was the annual Palatka to Hibernia Race. I sometimes really miss sailboat racing.

Cooled by the breeze of coasting down to the end of the

bridge, I turned upstream toward Orangedale and Mandarin. Although the last miles to Wesley Manor seemed the longest, Dot's request, "Try to get here in time for dinner," tugged my unwilling feet around in circles for eighty-five hot, sunny miles. I had done it! I had reached Jacksonville's outskirts.

Wesley Manor retirement village, a group of one-story buildings in an old turpentine forest, is bounded by Julington Creek on one side and a small lake on another. Azaleas bloomed everywhere. I wanted a shower first thing.

Dot laughed, "If you can still shower in six minutes, you'll have time before dinner."

On the way to the dining hall, we walked down Main Street, a twelve-foot-wide sidewalk protected from sun and rain by an overhanging roof. It connects the apartments with the library, post office, dining room, and other buildings. Dot explained, "The builders were given the 'Test of Time Award' by the Florida Association of the American Institute of Architects." She chuckled, "Here we've *all* met the test of time!" Dot was supervisor of art education for the Jacksonville Public Schools until her retirement in 1970.

In the spacious dining room, Marion Colson joined us for supper. Marion had taught enameling. Her mentor was Kenneth Bates. Having read Bates' book, I was impressed. After dinner, we visited Marion's apartment to look at her enamel work. "I haven't taught enamelling for years," Marion laughed, "but I'd love to teach you to shoot pool!"

Dot told me I could stay in her "cell," as she called it, as long as I liked. Although I would not have access to the dining room, I would be able to use Dot's car. A quiet room of my own, a car, and time to do nothing—it sounded like heaven! I looked forward to spending the next few days among the books, tapes, and art supplies in Dot's room.

Wesley Manor, May 3

Riding her large, stable tricycle, Dot accompanied me to breakfast. I rode my bare bike, and we wheeled quietly toward the dining hall. On Main Street, we passed a tractor-towed cart with benches on the sides and a "Rapid Transit" sign on the rear.

Although only half the residents were present at breakfast, table-hopping and extended conversations were common.

I was pleasantly reminded of my visits with Jean Taneyhill at Samarkand in Santa Barbara. Wesley and Samarkand were the only continued-care retirement homes I'd ever visited, and I wouldn't have minded living at either one. I found myself looking forward to such a way of life — when the time came. My mother, on the other hand, would be moving to an Atlanta apartment which offered housekeeping and one daily meal. She had chosen modified, independent, apartment life. Except for the minimum age requirement and in-house activities, it was much like any apartment.

Dot spoke enthusiastically about her ten-day tour. "Jerry Holcomb, whom I call Gung Ho because she's always ready to do something interesting, got me into the trip," Dot said with a twinkle. "Not everyone could persuade me to fling away half a year's pension in ten days. As you get older, do-it-now presses you harder."

The group planned to fly to New York, cross the Atlantic on the QE2, rush around London's museums and historic buildings, explore Stonehenge, Salisbury, and Bath, ride the Orient Express, and visit the Hard Rock Cafe before flying home on the Concorde. Just hearing about it made me feel exhausted. I was glad I didn't have to do it.

After pedaling around the sixty-acre village, we drove around the neighborhood to a few places I would never have found on my own. Unready to inflict a museum upon my feet or a city upon my senses, I vetoed a trip to Jacksonville. My body, mind, and emotions were overloaded.

In my life of fortunate travel opportunities, I had seen enough European cathedrals and Asian temples for several lifetimes. My once-keen interest in architectural history had dulled, and interest in world art was superseded by concentration on world politics. Recently, the outdoors and birds had replaced indoor things, and world affairs had been set aside in favor of an interest in colonial and current America.

Spotting a historical marker interrupted my thoughts. "Harriet Beecher Stowe House," I read aloud, "Stop, please. Let's see what she was doing here." It was much tougher to read markers from a car than a bicycle. Dot backed up and we read that Calvin and Harriet Beecher Stowe bought thirty acres in Mandarin for their winter home, which later became a year-round residence. Our next stop was at The Church of Our Saviour, organized in 1880 by an Episcopal missionary. The first congregation had attended Bible readings led by Calvin and Harriet Beecher Stowe.

As we drove back to the Manor, I composed an immediate agenda: buying a new bicycle seat, cleaning the chain and the whole bike, buying film, writing a *Pedalgram*, reading the pile of mail, answering it, and telephoning everyone. I wondered if three days would be enough!

"Mandarin has quite a good paper. Would you mind being interviewed?" Dot interrupted my thoughts.

"An interview would be fun. Mom likes the pictures. I made a rule — one interview per state — but there hasn't been one since Port Arthur."

"Since I won't be here, I'll have it arranged through the activities director. You won't have to do anything unless the paper calls you."

My quiet day off the bike sped by. I'd been alone so long that company seemed more important than rest, an out-of-character feeling for me.

Wesley Manor, Monday, May 4

I was sorry to say goodbye to Dot and her sense of humor. She could get a laugh out of anything. Only recently I learned she founded *The Old Maid*, the first woman's college humor magazine in the United States. It was still published when I attended the same school. My mom was business manager.

After waving the travelers goodbye, I drove Dot's car to Jax Beach, found Sue Shine's house, and felt comfortable with the reserved, almost shy, person I met. When I had been in Tucson, Charlotte Mesick had given me Sue's name and insisted I should meet her. Sue, a retired Foreign Service traveler who returned to her hometown, now volunteered at the local historical society. Sue guided me to the Beaches Area Historical Society to begin a day of touring. I focused on lighthouses and ships.

At Pablo Historical Park, our attention shifted from ships to railroads while we looked at locomotive seven, a twenty-eight-ton steam engine built in 1911 and used to haul cars loaded with cypress logs. From there, we drove to St. Augustine to visit the Gonzales-Alvarez House, the oldest house in America. Originally a one-story, coquina stone dwelling, it was built in 1702. Later, a porch and a wooden second story were added. Since 1918, the house has been preserved by the St. Augustine Historical Society.

We walked down Charlotte Street, through the Castillo San Marcos, another coquina structure. The fortress was the only historic building I remembered visiting with my aunt and uncle before I was old enough to attend school. At that young age, spending my first night in a hotel and brushing my teeth in water that smelled of sulphur made a greater impression than the rest of the city.

I really wanted to bicycle into St. Augustine, and arranged to meet Sue there on Friday morning. She was wonderful fun to tour with. We had not visited the Fountain of Youth, which Sue's mother remembered being relocated three times during her lifetime!

When I returned, there were notes for me under Dot's door. In the morning, Katherine Terwilliger would take me to meet the activities director who was to introduce the program for the residents about my trip. Marion arranged the newspaper interview, they would phone for an appointment. My schedule was filling up, and I decided to stay a week instead of a few days. There still wasn't enough time for everything.

Wesley Manor, Tuesday, May 5

After Marion brought me bananas for breakfast, and Katharine Terwilliger introduced me to Suenell Spiro, I presented a talk similar to the one I made at Bass Lake Campground.

The most interesting question came from a man who said, "In your talk, you mentioned having a 'one-man-tent.' Shouldn't you call that a 'one-woman-tent'?"

I could have kissed him for asking! A big smile spread over my face. "I believe the people who change words like chairman to chairperson reveal their ignorance of the English language. In my view, the 'man' in 'chairman' is used in the sense of mankind and has no reference to gender. Therefore, my use of 'one-man-tent' is correct English." There was massive applause. I was still smiling.

While I was packing away biking equipment I showed the audience, many people came with further questions. One woman thanked me saying, "We like to have speakers who don't feel they have to tailor their talks to our interests. We like to hear about what other people are doing. It doesn't have to be something we can do." I shook her hand.

Katherine Terwilliger, an author and historian, took me to the dining room for lunch, and I truly enjoyed her company. A Wellesley graduate, she is doing research for a book on the design and history of Wesley Manor. I wished I felt more sociable. The village was a gold mine of experience, but the people seemed tired of talking to each other. After lunch I retreated, intending to nap.

After reading about native plants, I looked out the window at the pines, palmettos, and a few scattered hardwoods. I had just learned that the white, fragrant flowers of the palmetto attract bees and, therefore, make the plant important in honey production. Before air-conditioning, churches were supplied with light, stiff fans made of palmetto leaves.

In midafternoon, I cleaned the drive train and cooked my chain. My Centurion was ready to march again. As I talked to friends along my East Coast route, plans and a schedule for the next two months gradually solidified.

Because I know the East Coast, because it is home to me, because the novelty of my bike trip had worn off, would the ride north be dull? Had I bitten off a bigger chunk of America than I could pedal? Was I ready to quit and unwilling to admit it? My curiosity wasn't yet satisfied.

Wesley Manor, May 6-7

Marion brought a couple of sweet rolls and we nibbled as we talked. At noon, I met Peggy Saunders at the bus and joined the group of village residents going to Cedar River Seafood and Oyster Bar. I got home just in time for an interview with Deborah Squires of the *Mandarin News.*

I described the grueling pace I maintained to reach the Manor, thirteen hundred miles in three weeks from Port Arthur to Jacksonville, with only two days off the bike. I attributed my fatigue to higher temperatures, humidity, and more sun during longer days.

"After you've gone around the country, what next?" Deborah asked.

"I'll probably do a series of cross-state rides as breaks from learning to use a computer to write about this trip." I wanted to let everything soak in, but hoped, someday, to write a book.

For the first time, I had no doubt I *could* finish the trip, but I had lingering doubts whether I *wanted* to finish. Well, I had to get to GEAR on Long Island to deliver my scheduled talk, and Linda Bell was planning to accompany me through New Jersey, Manhattan, and Long Island. I'd only been to New England by car for two weeks thirty years before. Maine in August on a bicycle should be perfect. I'd also enjoy another trip through New York State and pedaling along the St. Lawrence River. Visiting GEAR friends in Buffalo would be great, but grinding back to Detroit probably wouldn't be fun. With the goal so close, I might as well go for it. I'd bicycled well over eight-thousand miles and estimated fewer than four-thousand miles ahead.

The next day I'd write the *Pedalgram* about the journey from New Orleans to Jacksonville, and answer my mail.

Wesley Manor, Friday, May 8

Leaving only overnight things in the room, I stowed my bike, panniers, tent, and sleeping bag in the back of Dot's car. After driving to Orangedale, I parked the car and bicycled to St. Augustine. Sue Shine would meet me, bring me back to the car, and take my baggage with her. The next morning, I would bicycle from the Manor to Sue's house, stop for a last visit, and continue up the coast.

My legs felt unwilling, but I pedaled twenty-five miles through heat and traffic, through flat farmland and marsh to St. Augustine. My first sightseeing stop was Nombre de Dios Mission, founded in 1565 and reputed to be the first mission to the country's Indians. I stopped again at a large sphere made of coquina, and went to read its plaque. It was the zero milestone for the Old Spanish Trail that had led to San Diego, California. What a surprise! Although I had traveled the trail backwards, I had arrived! I took photos to mark the occasion.

After lunch, Sue followed me in her car as I approached the Bridge of Lions. Waiting for the drawbridge to be lowered, I talked with Sheila Fowler and Roy Harvey, the only other people afoot. I interrupted their questions about me, preferring hearing about their trip.

"We're taking the *Aeolus*, our boat, up the inland waterway," they replied. "It's a twenty-eight-foot sailboat, the one out there with the light blue hull."

"I used to sail a lot, just a little sixteen-foot racing boat, but I sometimes miss it. Where are you coming from?"

"We spent the winter in the Keys and are headed for Chesapeake Bay at about fifty to eighty miles a day."

"That's just my speed. I'm going there, too, on roads and ferries. Do you think I might get a boat ride across from Fernandina Beach to St. Marys? Would anyone consider taking a bicyclist?" This was a new, on-the-spot, idea. The East Coast is so marshy, it's hard to stay near it on a road.

"*We* would certainly like to take you! Try asking the harbormaster at Fernandina."

Sue was waiting for me on the other side. Sue's company and the enthusiasm of the sailboat people fired my eagerness to get back on the road. I was ready to head north.

Wesley Manor, Saturday, May 9

Pushing my bike, I left Dot's apartment, rode out of the Manor, and turned north on Highway 13. I stopped at an International House of Pancakes where two "live pancakes" waved from the driveway. I laughed, "Since I've eaten so many pancakes on this trip, I should have my picture taken with a pancake!" The pancakes were willing. Then I proceeded to Southside and Butler Boulevards. Five days ago, I read an article in the *Times-Union* by Robert Blade that said although three roads run between Jacksonville and the beach, the only road suitable for bicyclists was off limits to them, but all the bicyclists use it anyway. It was timely advice.

On the highway, I stopped to pick up a fifty-cent piece. Curious. I seldom found coins outside cities. When I leaned over to pick it up, I saw another, another, and still more — four dollars in fifty-cent and dollar coins. They were all within two feet of each other between the road edge and the grass. Big scars cut through the mashed grass, and metal bits and plastic debris indicated an accident. It was the most money I'd ever found.

Sue's house was the last one before the marsh began. After walking through the marsh, we watched the birds coming to her feeder. For the first time, I sighted a red bellied woodpecker and male and female painted buntings. A black-throated blue warbler ate worms nearby. When the squirrels came, undeterred by attacking jays, we ducked into the house for a comfortable conversation and lunch.

As I rolled my wheels north up the road just behind houses facing the beach, I decided that I wouldn't like to live in Florida, although I consider it ideal for visiting. I like all four seasons. Then I realized I had pedaled too far. A fence blocked the road. I loathe backtracking.

I was glad to see a man on a bicycle approaching. He said I'd have to return a few miles to Atlantic Beach and turn.

"Is that really the only way?" I pleaded.

"Well, there is a way, but I'll have to help you with your bike." We pushed our bicycles through sand, across pine needles, toward a twenty-five-foot wide creek with two large, black pipes spanning its green scum. He explained, "They grease the pipes to keep the school kids off them. I brought a shovel yesterday and sprinkled sand for traction. Let's use the pipe on the right."

I backed across holding the handlebars, and he steadied the rear wheel as we gently rolled my bike, heavily laden, to the other side. Since I didn't want to ride the rest of the afternoon covered with green creek scum, I was very cautious. Nimbly, he retrieved his bike, picking it up and carrying it across. While we pushed our bikes through patches of sand, he told me, "That's the Ferry Road over there. Just go to the end of it, and you'll find the boat." He pedaled away.

In Mayport, as I watched the approaching ferry, a man got out of his pickup and came toward me saying, "I hope you won't take offense, but I think you are the oldest person I've ever seen riding a bike on a tour. I just wanted to tell you I think you're great, just great. Good luck!" He turned on his heel before I could recover from surprise or say thank you. Then, after several strides, he turned again, stuck his thumb up, and yelled, "Go for it!"

It was a short, pleasant ride across the St. Johns River to Ft. George Island where I disembarked, paid my dime fare, and continued. The road to Little Talbot and Amelia Islands cut through wooded areas, crossed bridges, and traversed miles and miles of marsh grass. At Fernandina Beach, I saw a woman working in her garden. "You look tired," she said. I stopped, and she introduced herself as Ruby Crankshaw. She told me the park wasn't far away.

I continued, feeling out of sorts, ill-tempered from fatigue as I approached the left turn to Ft. Clinch State Park. A guy in a truck came up behind me, turned on his loudspeaker, and barked, "Move over. Get off the road!" Calling his bluff, I moved from the edge into the middle of the lane. "Get out of my way!" blasted the voice. I pedaled on, pretending to hear nothing. Then his voice became terribly nice, "Please, get out of the way so that I can get by." It was only fifty yards to the intersection where there was an additional lane. Without further comment, he pulled up beside me and turned right. I turned left.

I rode past the entrance to Ft. Clinch Park to the town and the harbor. At the harbormaster's office, workers and boat owners convinced me that crossing the St. Marys River by boat would take three times as long as riding my bicycle around the shore and over the bridges.

I pedaled toward to the park and was about to turn in when another bicyclist caught up with me. Sam Ankney had spent the day riding up the coast from Daytona Beach. He was returning from supper and already had chosen a tent site. "The park's full," he informed me, "but you could share my site if you wish."

"Fine, I'll pay my half. How much was it?"

"Eleven dollars. We still have a long way, four miles to the site." There was no traffic, so we rode side by side, swapping stories as the sun began to set. I had not eaten, and I had no lights for my bike.

When we reached the site, I flung up my tent, zipped everything inside, and hopped on my bike to return to town for supper. The sun was sinking, and I was starving. Service in the Bamboo Restaurant was ultra-slow. After I refueled, the five-mile ride back to my tent was not so tough as the miles to find food had been.

Sam and I sat at the picnic table talking about tents until it was quite dark and I was extremely sleepy. He had a Sierra Designs Divine Light tent which weighed just under three pounds. Sam also showed me a piece of plastic plumbing pipe he had used to make a tent-pole carrier with a screw top. It was heavy but convenient when traveling with a sag. Using such a device would have kept metal rings and fittings on my tent from punching holes in the fabric. I'd have a few repairs to make when I finished the trip.

Ft. Clinch State Park, Sunday, May 10

I heard Sam pack in the dark and ride out at dawn. Today I intended to see the fort. When hunger finally drove me to get up, I began chatting with the man at the next site. He was a fisherman who planned to take his boat out "just for a ride." He said he would be glad to take me to St. Marys, but when he went off to discuss weather conditions with the game warden, he changed his mind. "See those white caps? It's too rough for my type of boat. Small craft warnings are up, and I can't cross that open water. Sorry." I continued packing, thanked him anyway, and rode over to Fort Clinch.

The fort overlooked the strait at the north end of Amelia Island, and provided a view across the St. Marys River toward Cumberland Island, which marks the seacoast border with Georgia. Fort Clinch is located in a park of over a thousand untouched acres. There is swimming along the eastern shore, camping on the protected western side, and fishing from everywhere on the island.

As I approached the town, a pileated woodpecker seemed to be yelling at me from the top of a utility pole. I stopped to look at it through my binoculars. The sun glittered from its feathers as we eyed each other. Then, the huge bird turned his attention to destroying the utility pole, and I turned mine to pedaling.

After a pancake breakfast, I looked at the water, the harbor, the road, and the map. The wind was blowing hard, creating a fine tailwind. It was silly to hang around hoping for a boat ride when I could sail on my bike. In no time at all, I reached U.S. 17 and turned north, telling myself, "I probably would have been seasick on a boat anyway." Georgia welcomed me to "The State of Adventure."

"Heck, I was born here," I said back to the signboard.

South of Kingsland, the blackberries were ripe. I entered Steffen's Restaurant for beans, cole slaw, fish, and lemon pudding.

Several hot miles farther along, I stopped at the motel in Woodbine, Georgia. The barbecue place in Woodbine closed at six and I didn't get hungry until two hours later. Dinner consisted of lemon sherbet and oatmeal cookies while I watched "60 Minutes."

DISCOVERING THE THIRTEEN COLONIES

CHAPTER EIGHTEEN

Atlantic Marshscapes

Woodbine, Georgia, Monday, May 11

The Highway 17 bridge into Brunswick had been hit by a barge the week before and was closed. I would have to detour north of Brunswick and miss my intended turnoff to Jekyll and St. Simons Islands.

An hour of quiet pedaling, inland from the marsh, revealed slash pine, live oak, palmetto, and cactus. Interstate 95 paralleled my road closely enough for me to see the bridges and, sometimes, to hear the traffic thundering. Everyone in a hurry was on the interstate, and I shared my road with local people.When a red-winged blackbird sitting on a sign fussed at me, I stopped pedaling and coasted. The sweetness of unseen honeysuckle wafted like warm fog through the morning air. I passed New Hope Plantation, where young pine trees about a dozen feet high were growing, and Hofwyl-Broadfield Historic Site Plantation, and rode through a waterfowl preserve. Soon, I crossed the Altamaha River, the largest river system east of the Mississippi, whose fertile delta supported the most productive rice plantations in the South.

When I came to Butler Island Plantation, I read its historical marker. It had been a renowned nineteenth century rice plantation. Dikes and a canal system for rice cultivation had been installed by Dutch engineers. The owner, Pierce Butler, was married to Fanny Kemble, an English actress who wrote *Journal of a Residence on a Georgia Plantation*. Her book influenced the English against the Confederacy and slavery, and her political activism resulted in a divorce. Her husband was awarded custody of the children! I pedaled across Butler River and stopped in Darien on a bluff overlooking the waters of the delta meandering through marsh grass. I was now in McIntosh County.

The Altamaha delta region was settled in 1736 by Scottish highlanders under John McIntosh Mohr, and Georgia's first military parade occurred in Darien in 1736 when General James Edward Oglethorpe reviewed highland troops in full regalia.

Although a city park on the bluff offered attractive benches, I asked where local people preferred to eat and followed directions to Archies Restaurant. After I ordered, a gentleman approached my table and said, "May I ask you a question?"

"Yes." I wondered which one it would be.

"Where did you get your helmet rear view mirror?" That was a new question. "My son is a runner. He is moving to Washington to work. I thought with all the traffic, he would need a rear view mirror to run there." Although I didn't think his son would need one, I told him where it could be bought and invited him to join me for lunch.

"Thank you, I just came to pick up the mail. My wife will have lunch ready at home." He talked while I ate fresh vegetables.

Talbort Harding, a native of Cleveland where he had worked occasionally for *The Plain Dealer*, knew Marion Colson, the enamelist I met at Wesley Manor. Although he wanted to be an organic chemist, his required study of German proved so interesting that he majored in it. In 1933, unable to find a job, he went to Heidelburg University for an advanced degree in the German language. His knowledge and fluency had led to a career in government.

"Why did you retire here if you're neither a fisherman nor a golfer?"

"My wife and I spent two years driving around looking, and we liked it here. Have you seen Ashentilly?"

"No, but I've heard about it. How do I find it?"

"I'll show you."

I followed his car a mile out of town to Route 99. He said Darien had been prettier until they cut down the old trees to widen Main Street, Highway 17. At Ashentilly, Mr. Harding stopped, stuck his head out of the window, and told me, the house was restored by the W. G. Haynes family, who have owned it since 1918. The house was built in 1830, and is made of tabby.

Tabby is composed of equal parts of sand, lime, and

oyster shells mixed into a mortar and poured to forms like cement. The method of tabby construction was imported to Florida from Africa by the Spanish. In St. Augustine, it was replaced by coquina, but coastal Georgia, having no coquina quarries, continued to use tabby as late as the 1890s.

In Ridgeville, I stopped to look at the lovely homes and trees, still chuckling at Mr. Harding's comment when he had told me his address, "There are no house numbers in this county, and few street names, but we *do* have nine digit zip codes!"

I rolled through Crescent, Georgia, to Eulonia where I entered Jiffy Foods, drank a V8, and asked Jo Bell, who was minding the store, "Do many bicyclists come through here?"

"Yes, earlier today, a man I'd been expecting to return came back from Orlando. His doctor told him to sit, so he sat on his bike and rode it every day. When he went back to the doctor he was told, 'You're doing fine. I'm glad you've been sitting like I told you.' The man said, 'Lemme tell you what I've been doing. Been riding my bicycle. I rode down to Orlando and came back to Savannah.' The doctor didn't believe him. He just came through here again this morning, and he looked fine. Mostly, the bikers are men, or groups. Aren't you afraid? Isn't it dangerous alone?"

It was my least favorite question. Could I help her understand? "I'm a lot safer on my bike alone than you are minding this store. Who would expect a bicyclist to have any money, but you've got a lot to steal here. You're not afraid to tend this store alone."

Refreshed, I traveled on, accompanied occasionally by kingbirds or cardinals. Pineland Campground looked like a good place to end the day after sixty-seven hot miles. Although its store was closed for renovations, the owner charged me a dollar more for my tent site and provided what she had — an orange, apple, banana, and two pieces of bread with peanut butter. I got a site with an electrical outlet at no extra charge.

I was the only afternoon tenter. I lay on my back under a pine tree reading and watching an orchard oriole. I had eaten all my food and was still hungry when I heard the quiet put-put of a motorcycle coming to a stop. My motorcyclist neighbor was also a woman alone. Kay McGary introduced herself and invited me over to her table. She said, "I travel alone writing magazine articles, but when I get tired of that or run out of money, I get another job." She recounted meeting lost children, wandering the country to escape the social pressures of conformity. "Like us," she giggled. Kay prepared a Lipton's ten-minute noodle dish, and offered me her leftovers. I accepted.

She told of swerving her motorcycle to avoid a bear in Alaska, hitting a boulder, flipping herself off, and landing unconscious. "I don't remember anything between seeing the boulder, when I was almost back on the road after missing the bear, and having a truck driver lift my face mask and ask if I was all right."

"Were you?"

"Yes, except for a broken collar bone and a totaled motorcycle. Recovery took a long time, but I'm O.K. now. The motorcycle probably saved my life."

"How so?"

"Its motor never stopped running, they told me later. The truck driver thought the noise probably frightened the bear away from me between the time I flipped and when he arrived." Kay wanted to bicycle through Europe and Spain. "Do you want to go together?" she asked. "I can't imagine bicycling alone though I enjoy travel alone on the motorcycle."

"Thanks, I can't make any plans until I complete this trip. I guess I'll have to say not this year."

Although we had sprayed ourselves with Off, the bugs became bothersome. We retired to our tents.

South Newport, Tuesday, May 12

Up with the sun, Kay and I talked while she fixed breakfast and coffee. Since it was fewer than fifty flat miles to Courtney Gaines' house, and she wasn't expecting me until late afternoon, I wasn't in a hurry.

"I'll probably pass you soon," Kay laughed as I left the campground. About a mile later, just as I was leaving a noisy dog behind, Kay approached on her Honda 650, raised her face mask, smiled, tooted the horn, and disappeared up the Interstate 95 ramp.

I had been told to be sure to stop and see the "smallest church in America." Situated under old live oaks near South Newport, it was erected in 1950 by Mrs. Agnes C. Harper who, in 1967, deeded it to Jesus Christ in her will. I was more stunned that anyone would deed a building to Jesus than by the size of the place. The ten-by-fifteen-foot structure seats a dozen people. The stained-glass windows were imported from England, and a glass star in the roof lets the midday sun beam the interior with light.

In Riceboro, I found an old bridge with a new purpose. Its middle removed, each side was enlarged with a deck and a railing, making it suitable for fishing or picnicking. Midway contained a treasure-trove of historical markers, a church, a cemetery, and a museum. One marker pointed along a side road to Sunbury, an important colonial port of entry, where the first Masonic Lodge meeting in Georgia was believed to have been held with Oglethorpe as master.

Inside the Midway Museum, I discovered the road I was traveling is one of the oldest in the state. It was laid out by General Oglethorpe to connect Savannah with the Scottish settlement at Darien. Indians guided trail-blazers over the marshes and through the dense swamps. "Well," I thought, "I'm really on the road through the Colonies now."

The museum is a raised, cottage-style house typical of eighteenth century coastal homes. Thomas Little, the builder, turned one of the bannister posts upside down as his hallmark and for luck. There was a "coffin window" on the stairs. Since most people died at home, space was required to turn the coffin to take it downstairs — hence, a coffin window.

I wasn't interested in the portrait of Nathanial Steuart until the guide told us the famous Georgia Steuart pecan carried his name. My favorite item in the museum was the set of musical glasses, popular instruments in the eighteenth and nineteenth centuries. Played by wetting the fingertips with wine or vinegar and circling them rapidly around the rims, musical glasses apparently went out of style when a doctor decreed that the constant vibration of the players' fingertips affected the mind adversely.

Our guide explained that while Sherman's troops occupied Savannah, part of his cavalry came to Midway to forage for supplies. They stayed a month, forcing departure of many residents and destroying the plantations. The county has never recovered. I thought Sherman got modern help when the construction of Interstate 95 turned Route 17 into a concrete ribbon connecting derelict towns.

In Richmond Hill, I reentered the twentieth century along a fast-food highway strip. Although light rain began to sprinkle me for the first time since McAllen, Texas, I paused long enough to read signs and didn't bother putting on my raincoat.

I reached Courtney Gaines' home overlooking the marsh and found the key just before two. By the time the sky opened up, I was fast asleep on the sofa. How happy I was to be in a home, especially the home of an old friend!

Although it was dark when I awoke, Courtney still hadn't returned from her North Carolina mountain trip. Hungry, I microwaved some vegetables and began reading one of her many books about Savannah, *Eden on the Marsh* by Edward Chan Sieg. In discussing nicknames for Georgians, the author said the origin of "Georgia peach" was obviously a reference to the state's superior peach production, but the term "Georgia cracker" was more complex. Sieg's book explained that, when a new element, the feisty, rough-and-ready, barely-literate backwoods Scotch-Irish, drove wagons on Savannah's dirt streets, the cultivated English residents dubbed the whip-wielding intruders "crackers." I also learned the ancient Indian trail I rode through coastal Georgia was the invasion route to protect the Colonies from the Spanish in Florida and from the English during the Revolution.

My reading was interrupted when Courtney entered the front door. I was glad to see her and appreciated her returning a day early to meet me. Since she had never been to Sapelo Island or the Hofwyl-Broadfield Plantation, we decided to retrace my route by car in the morning.

Savannah, Wednesday, May 13

Most of Sapelo Island now belongs to the State of Georgia. It is home to the R. J. Reynolds State Wildlife Refuge, The University of Georgia's Marine Institute, and The Sapelo Island National Estuarine Sanctuary. Most residents of the four-hundred-acre, privately-owned Hog Hammock community trace their American ancestry to the early eighteenth century, to the days of slavery.

The upland area of Sapelo Island National Estuarine Sanctuary is a land of live oaks, loblolly pine, turkey, and deer. Ninety percent of the marsh consists of smooth cordgrass and black needlerush. At low tide, abundant crabs, mussels, fish, oysters, shrimp, minks, and raccoons are joined from the skies by osprey, egrets, rails, and herons. I was pleased to have seen whimbrels, clapper rails, and a ruddy turnstone among more common shoreside creatures.

Sapelo's was a mini-history of the southeastern coast. Indians were there over three thousand years before Europeans arrived in 1520. In 1800, Thomas Spalding purchased most of the island and turned it into a thriving plantation. After the Civil War, the island was abandoned to weeds until interest in Sapelo's residents, ecology, and wildlife revived it during the twentieth century. Our guide, Noel Holcomb, taught us about American and Georgian history and the characteristics of a salt marsh environment.

Courtney and I spent the afternoon near Darien visiting the Hofwyl-Broadfield Plantation which began about 1807. It ceased rice production in 1915 when war, hurricanes, and labor shortages made the crop unprofitable. Rice, I discovered, requires three times as much land as cotton and more labor.

Before falling asleep the second night at Courtney's lovely home, I chuckled as I read that Oglethorpe's original charter for Georgia did not permit Catholics, Lutherans, slaves, or lawyers to settle in the colony. Perhaps Oglethorpe had agreed with Lao-tzu that the more restrictive the law, the poorer the people and the more compassionate the government, the richer the populace.

Savannah, Thursday, May 14

A second rest day found me touring Savannah after watching a filmed reenactment of the siege of Savannah at the Visitors' Center. At Juliette Gordon Low's Girl Scouts National Center, I learned Juliette "Daisy" Low met Robert Baden Powell, founder of the Boy Scouts, in England in 1911. His sister, Agnes, founded the Girl Guides, and they persuaded Daisy to organize a group of Guides in Scotland. Daisy promoted the idea of Girl Scouts across America with help of prominent women who included the wives of Woodrow Wilson, Calvin Coolidge, and Thomas Edison. By 1915, the Girl Scouts of America was incorporated. I was a Girl Scout. I still have my badges and pins.

Savannah's river-bluff historical district, covering over two square miles, is larger than any other restored city area in America. High ground ideal for town development was rare along the East Coast marsh. Our group visited the Owen Thomas House, where Lafayette once delivered a two-hour speech in French from the balcony. Southern hospitality and the speaker's charisma caused the crowd to listen and applaud, although no one understood French.

Courtney drove me to Fort Pulaski National Monument where we marvelled at the brickwork and inhaled marsh breezes while gazing upon river views. The fort was named for Count Casimir Pulaski, a Polish soldier of fortune who died during the siege of Savannah in 1779. It was part of coastal fortifications established after the War of 1812. Second Lieutenant Robert E. Lee worked on the drainage system, and its builders took eighteen years to lay the twenty-five million bricks.

Courtney, also a bicyclist, had no difficulty convincing me to return in June to participate in the Bicycle Ride Across Georgia. I could ride an empty bike with plenty of company and learn more about Georgia over the three-hundred-fifty-mile route.

Savannah, Friday, May 15

Courtney drove me through the city to the other side of the Eugene Talmage Memorial Bridge over the Savannah River. As I hauled my bike out of the car, I noticed her bumper sticker: "Misery is Optional." I set my wheels down in South Carolina at eight a.m. and wobbled down the road. Two baby rabbits fled into high grass at my approach. In the first hour, I rode thirteen miles and kept rolling past the turnoff to Hilton Head Island. I was headed for my cousin Bill McCullough's home on Kiawah Island, twenty miles southeast of Charleston.

Since a hundred miles of pedaling lay ahead, I kept moving, hoping to cover as much ground as I could before afternoon heat began to debilitate me. I hoped to reach Highway 17 in time for my aunt and uncle to pick me up on their way to Kiawah. If we missed each other, I could ride into downtown Charleston and come back with my cousin after work or pedal to Kiawah. Either way, the mileage pedaled would be the same.

I gazed seaward across the water toward the place where General William Moultrie defeated the British attempt to capture Port Royal Island early in 1779. In this century, the island had been captured by developers.

After three hours, I rested a few minutes, ate a mango, and drank the rest of the now-hot water from my largest bottle. Another ten miles brought me to Gardens Corner — hungry. Next to the filling station was a small fish market. It was the only fish market I'd visited where you could select a fish and have it cooked for you. I received two whiting fillets, deep-fried with corn meal, served with homemade cole slaw — an excellent meal!

After refilling my water bottles, I was ready to face the next fifty miles. The upcoming stretch of Route 17 consisted of only two lanes, without paved shoulders and heavy with traffic. The roadside grass was packed hard and would be safe to use in emergencies unless the paving dropoff was more than a couple of inches. Since trucks and cars flew past frequently, I consulted my rear view constantly and remained alert.

Twenty miles of riding through lush green vegetation, mostly pine trees with palmetto undergrowth, brought me to a campground store where I stopped for a snack and refilled my water bottles. I sat outside in the shade to avoid the overly-cold air conditioning inside. Iced water and iced air tended to make me sick. As I ambled toward my bike, a truck driver striding toward the store asked where I was going. I, in turn, asked about his route.

He drove two Savannah-to-Charleston trips daily, hauling containerized shipping trailers, often without knowing their contents. He told me a story of an innocent driver who unwittingly delivered a load of drugs and was detained by agents who had traced his shipment from South America. The drug-smuggling recipients were arrested, and the driver was soon free.

"Do you see many bicyclists along your route?"

"About three or four a week, except in December and January, and many more than that during the summer."

"I've found truck drivers to be the most considerate drivers on the road. They always give me as much room as conditions permit. How do you feel about the bicyclists you see?"

"Most of the touring bikers ride straight and stay on the white line. But I hope they realize when two large trucks pass, the bikes have to move to the shoulder. My trailer weighs over seventy tons and the cabs have from ten to sixteen gears. We can't make snap decisions like bicyclists. If I put a wheel over a three-inch drop, I could flip my whole rig. I'm not sure bicyclists realize how heavy we are, how much momentum we have, and that we have to drive according to conditions as far ahead as we can see."

"How do you feel about being on the road all day, every day?"

"I like it. Of course, you don't get to know anyone on the

road. You just meet a lot of people and share a lunch or cold drink. We talk when we've done our hours. I don't overdo, but many drivers do. They're the ones who have accidents."

A few minutes later, he passed me and tooted his airhorn. Hours later, shortly before my turnoff, he tooted again on his way back to Savannah.

I saw my aunt and uncle, Sarah and Francis McCullough, go by. I knew they hadn't seen me because a panel truck they were passing blocked their view of my bike. Afraid of missing connections at my cousin's office in Charleston, I turned toward Kiawah Island. It was late in the day, and I immediately felt cooler on the little road canopied by live oaks and Spanish moss. Pickup trucks and small cars were replaced by luxury sedans as Charleston commuters passed me. Ever more slowly I rolled, propelled only by the knowledge that, when I finished today, I wouldn't turn a pedal for almost a week.

From the Kiawah Island Resort entrance, I saw a few American oyster catchers and some sandpiper-like shore birds out on the mud flats. When I turned at Bill and Betty's driveway, I had ticked off one-hundred-sixteen miles.

Kiawah Island, South Carolina, Saturday, May 16

After breakfast, Bill and Francis went to the golf course and Betty, Aunt Sarah, and I drove to Charleston where we wandered the market, watching women make and sell sweet grass baskets. We had lunch at the Cotton Exchange Restaurant and returned to Kiawah for dinner with Bill and Francis. Although I awakened with aching legs and had been groggy all day, I was happy to follow their plans and grateful to be surrounded by family.

Kiawah Island, Sunday, May 17

After Sarah and Francis left for home, and Bill and I puttered with his bicycle, I drove into Charleston to see the famous Visitors' Center movie, *Dear Charleston*.

In its early history, Charleston's divergent populace included pirates, representatives of the Church of England, Scotch-Irish immigrants, and slaves. Especially during the social season from November through May, formal dinners and lavish entertainment were a way of life. Colonial low-country life was neither unique nor isolated; it reflected seventeenth and eighteenth century worldwide trends.

By 1740, forty thousand slaves worked the rice fields in the Carolina low country. Four Charlestonians signed the Declaration of Independence in 1776; many, however, remained loyal to the British and one-fifth of the white male population of South Carolina died during that war. Devastation in the South after the Civil War was more severe than it was in Europe after the World Wars. Only one grand home remained. Drayton Hall escaped destruction because Dr. Drayton sent his slaves out to the road with yellow flags, signifying the presence of smallpox, as Sherman's army marched past.

It was the military, not agriculture, that finally brought prosperity back during World War II. The city has survived not only wars, economic and health woes, but also hurricanes, earthquakes, and five fires. "Now it must survive tourists," I smiled, "and even a bicyclist."

I went to Patriot's Point to fulfill my life-long wish to visit a submarine. On the ramp leading to the ships, I noticed a naval officer standing at parade rest, his head tilted back, looking up reverently at the bridge of the aircraft carrier *Yorktown*. His uniform looked so neat that he must have driven his car standing up, and his shoes glittered. He was alone. Under his cap, gray hair ridged the back of his head. He began to walk, slowly, still looking.

"Did you serve on her?" I asked quietly.

"Yes, I did. I've been a long time getting back to see her." I felt goosebumps on my arms when he spoke. "I was very young," he continued, half aloud.

I noted an unusually large collection of service ribbons on his uniform, gold wings and other insignia shining in the sun. I wondered if he dressed up for this reunion with his ship. "Where were you aboard her?"

"Okinawa and Iwo Jima," he responded without taking his eyes off the ship. "I have to leave the Navy soon." There was a catch in his voice. "Over thirty years service, and they won't let me fly jets. They want young people now. It's time for me to get out."

"It's the same everywhere. I left the CIA. They want Ph.D.s more than they want experience. I know how you feel. Now that I've retired, I'm really glad I left. I'm sure you will be, too. Don't forget to look ahead more than you look back."

"Thanks." He shook my hand in both of his, then stepped back one pace. I felt as though he saluted me. He turned and walked into his ship full of memories as I headed for the submarine.

I had been on destroyers and carriers in Singapore when they were full of officers, men, and planes. The ships clanked. Steam rattled and water gurgled through pipes. Metal clanged metal. They were alive. Walking inside the submarine and the *Yorktown* was like looking at skeletons and trying to visualize the people.

I drove quietly back to Kiawah Island and spent the next four days with family in North Carolina and North Georgia, where I visited my mother. The vacation from bicycling was welcome. Traveling on a bicycle had become a routine way of life, but it had not become work.

Kiawah Island, Friday, May 22

Bill assured me I could not bicycle from Charleston to Mt. Pleasant across the bridge, and he drove me to the other side. Set down at a filling station on Highway 17 in Mt. Pleasant, I waved my cousin goodbye. I pedaled north past sweet grass basket vendors hanging up their wares for the day. I might have some sun, and I'd probably have headwind all day with cross-wind relief when the road curved.

At a dirt drive, I turned off and leaned my bike against a fence while I adjusted the tilt of the seat. A pickup truck stopped. The driver stuck his head and elbow out the window and said, "Got a problem? Need any help?"

"Thanks. I just needed to adjust the seat. I hope I got it right this time." I took so much time answering William J. Shepard's questions about my trip that I realized I wasn't interest in pedaling today. When Bill Shepard asked my name and address, I opened my wallet and handed him a card. "You'll be in our prayers. Meeting you made my whole day!" he sang out as he drove away. Before I could push my bike through the sand back to the road, he reappeared and extended his hand with my card, "Please autograph the back. You might be famous some day, and I want that signature just in case." I laughed and signed.

As he drove away again, I realized that earlier in the trip, I had wanted to ride; it was bicycling that was appealing.

Now, I wanted to tarry with people.

But for the next week my goal was to get home. Ahead lay long stretches of road, marsh, seacoast, and a few special friends. There would be new people to meet and unexpected experiences, I promised myself. Today I hoped to cover the miles to Myrtle Beach State Park. I pushed into a slight headwind. Red clover in bloom along the roadside filled the sticky air with sweetness. I plugged away for a couple of hours.

Ahead, I noticed a small car pull off on the grassy shoulder. The young driver stood watching traffic. Did he have car trouble? Was he expecting a tow truck? He was watching me. As I approached, he unfolded his arms, stepped back, and smiled. I bounced the bike off the white line, through the grass, and over some gravel to a stop.

He greeted me, "Hi. Thanks for stopping. I've always wanted to do what you're doing and just *had* to talk with you. My name is Mike Roycroft. I study horticulture in Charleston but live in Georgetown where I'm headed for the weekend to work at my dad's nursery. Where are you going? Where have you been?"

When he stopped for breath, I replied. By the time I got to Georgetown, he would have finished work for the day. We planned that he would then bike with me about fifteen miles up to Litchfield. My spirits soared at the prospect of a new adventure. By the end of our chat, with instructions to his house in my pocket, I decided to give him all my panniers. I could ride forty miles without my load!

I was getting to know people up and down the road. Like the High Line in Montana, Route 17 tied the low country together. On a bare bike, I cut through the headwind three miles an hour faster. Though encouraged, I was still out of sorts. My knees, back, and arms hurt. Even wearing a hundred-percent cotton, loose, wet, cooling T-shirt, I was hot. Last summer, I had avoided moist heat. May humidity wilted my body as well as my will.

At quarter to four, less than a mile before the turnoff, Mike came in his car to meet me. "I couldn't wait any longer to get on my bike, too," he said, as we stowed my bike for the short trip to his house on Belle Isle.

At his home, Mike treated me like a colleague, although I am older than his parents. We looked at maps and talked routes while I drank water and depleted the family fruit bowl. Once we took to our bikes with Mike carrying two of my panniers, the talking ceased, and he rode like the wind. We stayed together through Georgetown before I said, "You're fresh, and I'm tired. Go your own pace, and I'll meet you at Litchfield." It was clear I couldn't have kept up; Mike was a strong rider. I concentrated on pedaling and tried to miss the caterpillars crawling on the road as well as debris, holes, and cracks.

At Litchfield, I met Mike's sister Susan. He put my bike in her car and drove me twenty miles to Myrtle Beach State Park, where he plied me with camping questions while I set up the tent. During dinner at a Chinese restaurant, I asked, "How did you get to be such a strong rider?"

Mike grinned. "I've been riding a stationary bike several hours two or three times a week. Can you tell? It's the type with a computer that tells how much hill grade you're riding and how fast. I like to work hard on it."

It was dark when Mike dropped me back at my tent. His companionship made a great day for me. I didn't tell him he was my first riding companion since I set off alone from Tucson.

Myrtle Beach, Saturday, May 23

At six a.m., it was too early to "slide, ride, or catch a tide" at the Myrtle Beach Water Park, or get a Klassy Kut Hair Design, or eat at the Crepe Myrtle. It was the best time to travel along the part of Highway 17 called Kings Highway, the Myrtle Beach tourist strip. Since grocery stores weren't open, I ate a couple of doughnuts that sat like lead in my stomach. After nearly two hours, I crossed into North Carolina and learned from a historical marker that I was on the First Post Road. In 1738, mail was carried along this route from New England through North Carolina to Charleston. Nearby was Boundary House, where the dividing line between North and South Carolina was agreed upon in 1764.

My destination for the day was Wilmington; my goal was eighty-one miles. It was a fine day. Whenever my cotton shirt got too dry, I entered a filling station restroom and wet it thoroughly. By midafternoon, it was so hot I stopped to eat a cherry Frozfruit. I couldn't help thinking how nice it would be if I were home reading a book, not having to go anywhere.

At Motel 6 in Wilmington, I watched Saturday afternoon sports on television, read, and went to sleep early.

Wilmington, North Carolina, Sunday, May 24

On the road before eight, I pedaled for two hours before stopping for a pancake breakfast. My dietary resolutions had weakened and faded, victims of excellent meals provided by my hosts, restaurant menus, and my lack of incentive. Tired of being on the road, I amused myself by reading signs: hair salons named Kuntry Kurl, Yankee Klipper, and Cutting Corner. The terrain was slightly rolling, not difficult for biking.

I cruised along just under fifteen miles an hour, accompanied by bluebirds, cardinals, finches, and swallows. Ready for a short rest, I stopped at Holly Ridge Fire Department and Rescue Squad's tent. The Radio Emergency Assistance Communications Team (REACT) was encouraging motorists to take a break to refresh themselves with cold juice or water. I drank a quart of water and refilled my bottles while talking with Jerry and Linda Krauske and other volunteers in the tent. Linda showed me a week-old pigeon and a week-old crow she found and was caring for. She feeds the birds wet high-protein dog food every hour. As her pets get older, she can feed them every four hours. "Nights are no problem. Even their parents don't feed them at night," Linda told me. As we talked, I ate a doughnut and contributed a couple of dollars to the fire department.

Soon, pedaling through Camp Lejeune Marine Base, I met two bicyclists, recent college graduates. They were headed from Ohio to Orlando, following the Bikecentennial Trail at the rate of about a hundred miles a day. The boys would take the trail south, passing along Topsail Beach before returning to Route 17. They told me I'd be on the Bikecentennial route they just took until I reached the Currituck Ferry.

On the north side of the military reservation, I stopped at a pizza place for an order of garlic bread and salad. A young marine studying communications told me that he joined the service because he couldn't afford college.

"You're smart to join the service." I told him, "You're creating opportunities for yourself." I wished him good luck and pedaled into the wind again. I noted a church sign that said, "It is never the wrong time to do the right thing." Then came signs for Classic Kuts, 4 Sea Suns tanning salon, and a Marine Corps sign adorned with red, white, and blue ribbons that proclaimed, "Pardon our noise, it is the sound of freedom."

I was reminded of highway dangers by dead opossums,

raccoons, snakes, and one turtle, but the most frightening sight was four kids on a moped. One was driving, and two others were on the seat behind. It was the kid sitting between the driver's knees and leaning backward against the handlebars as they bounced along the highway shoulder that gave me pause.

At last, I glided into Morehead City where the smell of boiling shrimp filled the air. Every now and then, I felt a waft of cool, fresh ocean breeze with a twang of salt. I crossed a bridge into Beaufort and rode along a few blocks back from the waterfront. One whole block smelled like fried fish.

On the waterfront, I entered Mike's and ordered broiled fillet of trout, cole slaw, hush puppies, and a pitcher of water. I'd traveled ninety-five miles. As I ate, I studied the map. The ferry appeared to be forty miles ahead — too far. If I wanted to catch the first ferry in the morning, I would have to bike another twenty miles to the only campground on my route. When I phoned the camp, they gave me directions and said there would be space for me.

"No problem," they said.

"That's what you think," I said to myself, hanging up the phone and glancing at the sun. It would be dark in an hour or less. Fortunately there wouldn't be any traffic on the ferry road. I'd just go for it.

I bundled up the rest of the hush puppies and pedaled out of town. The setting sun over the marsh was beautiful. I just couldn't go very fast. Knowing I'd never make it before dark, I slackened the pace. I turned on the flasher at the rear of the bike. The marsh hummed with evening and night sounds. When I had three miles to go, all the bugs emerged, providing motivation. I had to pedal fast to create enough wind to keep them out of my nose and ears.

Dusk turned black. I missed the campground entrance and wandered up and down the road looking for it. When I finally entered the campground office, I mentioned getting lost. "Didn't you see our big reflective sign?"

I laughed. I had no source of light to cause a reflection. After my hundred-twenty-five-mile trek, the hot shower felt wonderful, and I was soon asleep in my tent. Fifteen miles ahead floated the ferry which would depart at seven o'clock.

Sealevel, Monday, May 25

I began pedaling by five thirty. There were wonderful sunrise pictures; I took them only with my eyes, since I didn't want to miss the ferry. Crossing the water to the Outer Banks would take over two hours; I could rest on the boat. It was fun to ride through ground fog, which hovered four or five inches above the road and obscured its surface. Although I reached the ferry with about seven minutes to spare, the eatery was closed, and I couldn't satisfy my growling stomach. It would be a hungry morning, I told myself as I ate the last hush puppy.

Two bicyclists, a Marine and I, rolled our bikes up the ramp and leaned them against the bulkhead. We began talking, walked upstairs, sat on the deck, and introduced ourselves. Bruce Nicholson was from Maine. I was amused at the pair we made in our brilliant jerseys and black tights — an old lady and a Marine triathlete! His plan was to ride as far north as fast as possible and turn around in time to catch the three o'clock ferry back. I intended to go only far enough to reach Virginia's Eastern Shore two days from now.

Realizing I'd missed breakfast, Bruce shared the pork chops and boiled shrimp he prepared. "You're a good cook," I told him, between bites.

"It's just the leftovers from last night. Better eat it before the sun gets too hot," he grinned. "Do you have a sponsor?" he asked.

"No, I wanted no razzle-dazzle or pressure." Toward the end of our conversation, Bruce suggested I call his parents when I reached Waterford, Maine.

It had been a delightful crossing. At sea, the water was clear green, not murky like it was near shore. We arrived a few minutes after nine and were welcomed by a puff of orange smoke as a parachute flare landed on deck and exploded at my feet. Men were running up and down the beach looking for it. Someone yelled, and the Coast Guardsmen came to retrieve their flare.

Bruce and I rolled down the ferry ramp. He took off at twice my speed. Hours later, he waved as he returned, headed for the ferry and back to his base.

I wobbled along from one water bottle refill to the next among the sand dunes to the end of Okracoke Island. On the ferry ride across Hatteras Inlet, Bob Harland and Liz, from Durham, and I discussed bicycling the San Juan Islands where they had planned a summer trip. I encouraged them to go and was delighted to hear from them during their vacation. Enjoying the views and surf sounds, I headed north on the Outer Banks which stretched toward the mainland from fifty miles at sea.

At a market in Avon, I bought two Frozfruit bars. When it was extremely hot and I was exhausted, a Frozfruit could be counted on to get another ten miles out of my legs. While I was eating, Stanley and Edith Benjamin from Ohio arrived on their bicycles. They were the first cyclists anywhere near my age that I had seen, and I was delighted to meet them. The Benjamins biked at home in North Canton, Ohio, and they had been coming to the Outer Banks on vacation for about thirty years. When we parted, I rode north.

By the time I reached the Salvo Campground, my spokes had twinkled more than sixty miles. I was trying to convince myself that I shouldn't be so lazy but should go on to the next campground when two bicyclists arrived at the site next to mine. Their covered pickup and tent were already in place.

Joel and Wendy Goodwin asked questions and were so interested in my trip that they invited me to eat supper with them. "I don't have anything to share," I apologized, "I've got to find a store."

"We don't have anything either, but we're going in the truck to get some shrimp to boil. Please join us."

"I'd love to if you'll let me buy the shrimp."

Joel and Wendy were grad students at Chapel Hill, had been married a couple of years, and had come to the Outer Banks for a long weekend. We drank beer, peeled and ate shrimp, and talked about bicycling, camping, and hiking.

Salvo, Tuesday, May 26

I was lying still in my tent, listening to the surf, peeking out at the stormy sky, and smelling rain in the air. By seven o'clock, I was on the road in spite of aches in my arms and legs. I felt the wind pushing me backward as I moved forward under increasingly black clouds. Three miles brought me to a restaurant open for breakfast. Before I could order, drizzle changed to a tropical storm. Glad I left my bike on the porch under a roof, I ordered a big breakfast and settled into my chair. Outside, it was raining so hard that it couldn't last long — I hoped.

An hour later, I was pedaling again and feeling chilly under a heavy gray sky. The rain had blown away, and the road was dry in spots. Trucks and other service vehicles passed me headed south toward the end of the Outer Banks road. Through the gray morning I watched herons, cranes, and snowy egrets feeding, smelled damp honeysuckle, and could barely distinguish the outline of the lighthouse as I approached Bodies Inlet. The Goodwins passed me with honks and waves a little after ten o'clock. There were stretches when no one was on the highway but me. Trundling along, I paralleled the gray, churning surf. The past few days had been so hot and humid that I welcomed the clouds and chilly air.

Shortly after I turned inland, four cyclists went by on loaded touring bicycles. We didn't stop to talk. Bicyclists were so numerous that they stirred little interest, even in each other.

While waiting at a red light, I spoke to four people who flew from Michigan to bicycle out of Wilmington in a circle that included the Outer Banks. One rider told me that the Bikecentennial route was the only way to get through Cleveland without killing yourself. I said I'd come to the conclusion that if a city had more than twenty-five hundred people, it was too big. They laughed, nodding in agreement.

As the sun came out, I saw a man in a truck from Kentucky waiting at the end of the bridge. He had already stopped in front of me twice, saying he just wanted to talk. He claimed to be on a delivery run from Kentucky to Okracoke. If he was going back, he'd better get moving. He was dirty and unpleasant looking, and I didn't want to talk to him or make him angry.

"Hey, wait a minute!" the man yelled.

"I've ridden this bike over eight thousand miles. Someone is waiting for me up the road, and I'm late. Sorry, I have to keep moving."

"Well, I'll take you there."

"It's not that far. Have a good trip to Kentucky!" I yelled. I hoped never to see him again, and I didn't.

After passing a custom stained-glass works and an antiques shop, I asked at the North River Restaurant how big the town of Currituck was.

"Oh, they don't have no town. There's just the county court house and the jail. This is Currituck right here!" was the reply. I ate crab soup, continued riding, almost hit a baby rabbit, and dodged new frogs about an inch long.

It was funny how suddenly I got tired when I almost reached my goal. I traveled over seventy-five miles in order to reach the ferry by six p.m. I stopped just long enough to buy food. At the ferry there was time to phone Mary Eyre Peacock to confirm my next day's arrival.

The ferry ride was a quiet float across the inland waterway to Knotts Island. I found Barnes Campground and Marina less than a mile from the ferry dock. The camp was empty until dusk when a few fishing boats returned to shore.

At twilight, I lay in my tent reading, occasionally hearing distant laughter splashed with beer and fish stories. A pine cone dropped on my tent and slid down to the ground as the wind howled.

Knotts Island, Wednesday, May 27

By six, I was putting the tent away, and fishermen were gunning their engines over a sandbar toward the Back Bay fishing grounds. It was low tide, and their challenge was to hit the engines just right and clear the sand bars. My challenge would be getting through the Chesapeake Bay Bridge Tunnel, once I reached its entrance forty miles north. On the way, I took my time listening to marsh wrens sing. I soon passed near the place where the stake for the Carolina-Virginia boundary was driven in 1728.

Some miles later, as I walked into a country store, a man was coming out carrying three bags of ice. "Looks like you're all ready to catch that big one," I said.

He laughed, "They don't seem to bite too well. They just jump up and smile at you!"

I continued riding through marshlands, sharing space with warblers flashing yellow, blackbirds flashing red, robins flashing white tail tips, sparrows, and kids who rode the ferry to school. There were few houses; several had former owners planted under stones in the front yard.

By late morning, I spotted a billboard announcing, "Welcome to Virginia Beach, the World's Largest Resort City." Heavily populated suburban areas were separated by shopping centers. At last I found exactly what I was looking for — a pizza parlor advertising spaghetti. The women working at Ferro's talked while I ate. They came outside to see the bicycle and waved me cheerfully on my way.

At the toll entrance to the Chesapeake Bay Bridge

Tunnel, a police officer said, "We've been looking for you. We received a letter about you and don't know what to do." I momentarily forgot I'd written a query. I was invited into the office where Corporal Mike Flanagan summarized, "Insurance won't permit us to take you over. It's against the law to hitchhike. We're sorry. You may call public relations if you wish, but they don't know what to do either. I suggest you go back a few hundred feet, off the Bridge Tunnel property, and wait. We feel sure someone will offer you a ride. But you must not hitchhike! Just wait." His tone was kind.

"Did you really ride here from California?" another officer asked as I went out the door.

More than a little discouraged, I followed Mike's advice *exactly*. At the place where I had been told to wait, I noticed a man slam the door of his pickup and lean forward to start his engine. He was hauling a forty-foot Hawk power boat with a smaller boat inside. There was room in his pickup for my bike. "Hello," I said, tentatively stopping beside his window. The man had tired, kindly eyes. "Could you fit my bike in your pickup? I'll gladly pay the toll."

He looked at me, but he didn't say anything. He was having a problem with my request, but his face was reassuring. He smiled, "I'd be glad to take you, but I really can't. You see, I have a heart condition, and I wouldn't be able to lift your bike into the truck."

"I can lift it in the truck by myself. The bike comes apart. Piecemeal, it isn't heavy." I hesitated, to give him time to think. "It would be easier if you could lower the tailgate, but I could get it in anyway." He turned off the engine and my heart leaped.

Climbing down from the truck, Robert Goldsborough introduced himself. He was from Chrisfield, Maryland. "I'd really like to have some company. I've been driving by myself since before light this morning. Since I'm over seventy, I'm a little tired. I'd enjoy your company." He lowered the tailgate. I stowed everything away, and he closed the gate. I explained my trip and how pleased I was to get a ride.

Throughout the forty-mile drive through the tunnel and up the road to the Peacocks' gate at Eyre Hall, Robert pointed out buildings he constructed as a brick mason before he began a marina and boat business at Chrisfield. He had lived his entire life along the isolated spine of land surrounded by the sea and Chesapeake Bay.

"I've turned everything over to my three sons now, and

I'm the delivery boy for the marina. I even delivered two boats in the Pocono Mountains. People up there buy them from us because we give the best deal."

"How do you do that? Do you take a smaller markup?"

"No, I have what I need. I built the business, first started fourteen years ago. I was a bricklayer, then a builder, then a contractor. Now I have enough money."

He wouldn't let me pay the toll and when I thanked him he laughed, "It's my good deed for the day. You saw my soft spot, didn't you?"

"Yeah, I saw a pickup and a boat and thought there would be plenty of room for me to ride to Cape Charles."

On land again, we passed the turnoff to Cape Charles. We passed fields of potato blossoms and irrigation pipes on wheels. Robert said, "I want to see where you're going and be sure your people are home." He turned down the lane to Eyre Hall and rumbled his rig over crushed clam shells. (Clam shells are used on roads now because oyster shells are redeposited in the bay to encourage breeding.) At the lovely old house, the owner's son directed us to the original overseer's cottage which Mary and David Peacock restored and expanded for their retirement home, Golden Quarter.

I waved goodbye to Robert and pushed my bike along the drive cut through a former tobacco field. Mary and David showed me their new home. David encouraged me to get a word processor as he demonstrated his. We compared thoughts on current international and domestic news.

I agreed to stay a second night so that we could spend a whole day together. Mary secured my permission to be interviewed by the local paper and offered a tour of her family home. David suggested a boat ride to the barrier islands.

I reveled in my first hot shower since Wilmington.

Cheriton, Virginia, Thursday, May 28

The most authentically restored home on the shore, Eyre Hall is approached along a mile of cedars and large, old crape myrtles. The house is surrounded by an old-time picket fence. At the west end of the mansion is a wide cross-hall with doors leading to the oldest part of the boxwood garden. Mary Eyre Peacock is a descendant of the original owners.

As we stood in the hall and looked beyond a graceful

arch, Mary called my attention to the block-print paper pattern, Rives' "The Banks of the Bosphorus," produced by Dufor about 1816. "There are no repeats in this wallpaper," she showed me. There were stories about each room. After wandering in the boxwood gardens, we went down to the water's edge where a sailboat rode at anchor. We returned past fields planted with wheat and barley.

I learned from Mary that the main village of the largest Indian tribe on the shore was on Pocahontas Farm, and survivors of the tribe were found in Northhampton County as late as 1860. A cabin boy named Savage had been left with the Indians in exchange for Pocahontas but when she died, he was released. The Indians gave him some land, and he established a family. His descendant, Thomas Savage, a friend of the Peacocks, lives on the original land grant.

David took us over to the seaside to see the town of Oyster. We water-taxied to Cobb Island, one of Virginia's thirteen barrier islands. Ten miles seaward, Cobb Island has no inhabitants, no trees, and few bushes to hold the shifting sand. David cut the engine, and our boat rocked gently among the Atlantic waves while we listened to the marsh sounds and watched the oystercatchers and gulls. I felt I reached the real perimeter of the U.S.A., not just the highway perimeter where I usually traveled.

Cheriton, Friday, May 29

I cycled north along the seaside road past stands of thick trees and spacious fields of potatoes. Soon wheat and barley joined the potatoes, and squealing, squawking gulls kept me company. Across plowed fields, I saw vehicles racing along the Ocean Highway a half-mile away, but there was no traffic on my road.

Not long after I crossed the Maryland border, potato fields gave way to chicken houses. I stopped once for water and later at a market in Stockton. I told the woman making me a sandwich, "I came here a year and a half ago with a bunch of bicyclists. We particularly liked your sandwiches." The thermometer outside the store in the shade read ninety-four. No wonder I felt tired. After eating the sandwich and delicious raw peas Mary picked for me, I rubbed Tiger Balm on my knees. The sun would cause it to penetrate while I pedaled.

The day's ride was eighty miles of potatoes, a little corn, and lots of white clapboard houses. Some homes were being scraped and painted, and people on front porches waved.

After six o'clock, when I entered Delaware, my progress became slower. I'd wheeled a hundred-ten miles in about twelve hours, including stops — no small accomplishment in the heat. I was still too far away to reach the ferry before dark, so I went to the only motel within miles. Although it wasn't a pleasant place the shower was hot, the TV operable, and I had a place to sleep.

Millsboro, Delaware, Saturday, May 30

About five miles along my morning route, I discovered a campground which would have been much more comfortable than my no-stars motel. At Lewes Ferry, where Linda and I would resume the trip in July, I turned around and headed for Milton to catch a bus to Annapolis. It was ninety-eight degrees when I went into a store for a cold drink. An old man took a dim view of my question about where to catch the bus. He told me, "If you rode it this far, why don't you ride it back? If I walked five miles, I'd walk my five miles back." I didn't bother to explain that I'd completed over nine thousand miles and "riding it back" wouldn't get me home.

In another store, as I was buying oranges and V8, a woman told me I could wait for the bus across the road in her shady yard. Instead I waited in front of the ice cream shop, licking a cone as I sat on the curb in the shade.

When the bus driver stopped along the highway, I phoned my mother to meet me at a shopping center in Annapolis. We arrived at the same time, and I don't know who was happier.

CHAPTER NINETEEN

Skylines to Treelines

Lewes, Delaware, Sunday, July 12

Six weeks later, I returned to Delaware, stopping the car in the parking lot at the Lewes-Cape May Ferry. Linda Bell and I took our bikes out and pumped the tires while my mother and Betty Woodsend, on vacation from her retirement life in Kathmandu, Nepal, handed us tools, took pictures, and provided moral support. Betty was thrilled to participate in my great American adventure while she visited her native land.

The morning was hot, humid, and as sunny as the smiles of our send-off. Linda and I rolled our bikes on the ferry and walked upstairs to the top deck. As the moorings were loosed and the whistle blew, we waved to Mom and Betty from the rail. We were soon at sea among noises of gulls, sights of water, and smells of fresh salt air. The prow of the ferry disappeared into a fogbank, and our world turned cool, damp, and gray. About two hours later, we emerged into the sun again as the ferry nudged its landing dock in New Jersey.

During much of the ferry ride, Linda and I talked with Chris Proctor from Chapel Hill, the only other bicyclist on board. Chris rode to the ferry from Aiken, South Carolina. He told us stories about his bicycling adventures. We thought his most imaginative accommodations had been with lifeguards at beach resorts. The guards, who often shared houses or barracks-type accommodations, invited him to fling his sleeping bag at their places.

We three took the same road north from the ferry and Chris continued with us for the rest of the day. After a leisurely thirty-three miles, we pitched three tents at Ocean View Campground. The campground with 1,175 sites, few of them empty, was more populated than many towns. Many campers were Canadians. After cruising around, Chris announced that everyone appeared to be under thirteen years old. Linda quipped, "He only saw the girls!"

Ocean View, New Jersey, Monday, July 13

Continuing up the coast, we stopped briefly on the Atlantic City Boardwalk to throw a few quarters into the Golden Nugget slots. We pedaled on along roads that were causeways through the marsh with "Turtle Crossing" signs. Near midday, Chris turned toward Princeton.

Crossing each bridge cost a bicyclist forty cents, the same fee as for a car. We argued. "I don't make the rules. I just collect the money," one toll-booth operator told us. The grumbling was mine, for Linda laughs at everything. I couldn't have had a better companion. Floyd Hartman, friend and bicycle advisor to us both, had told me Linda worried about keeping up with me. "Ridiculous," I had replied. There was no contest — Linda was a far stronger rider. Linda rode a mountain bicycle, heavier than my bicycle, twenty hilly miles a day to work. She probably doubled her cycling mileage on weekends. She was also twenty years younger and thirty pounds lighter than I. My advantage was the experience of being on the road day in and day out, but my six-week hiatus had included little cycling. Less than a week off a bike weakens conditioning gained from daily riding. I rode about twice a week and, while in Georgia, joined the first three days of the annual Bicycle Ride Across Georgia (BRAG), but it wasn't enough.

Unable to penetrate the summer haze, the morning sun hung over the New Jersey marsh like a harvest moon. The temperature was in the nineties and the humidity weighed a ton. At the entry to the Garden State Parkway, which we had to use for about five miles to cross a bridge, a large sign announced, "No Bicycles." We waited under the sign until a man in a van stopped and told us, "I've ridden my bike across twice. I can take you in the van, but riding is no problem. You'll be seeing a lot of 'no bicycles' signs. You just have to go anyway. That's what we do, especially in New York." We thanked him for his advice, but accepted the lift.

When we were on the road again, Linda, whose name was on the back of her T-shirt, was followed by a car. An occupant yelled, "Hey, Linda, how far have you come?"

"From Washington, D.C."

"All *right!*" He waved, and the car sped on. Linda looked at me, grinning. She was catching the spirit of the trip. As we leaned our bikes against a diner, she said, "It's no wonder you can't do hills, you're always eating!"

"But there are no hills between here and Maine!" I replied. After soup and sandwiches we enjoyed being pushed by a helpful tailwind for a while. We stopped at a vegetable stand where Lillie B. Cranmer, the owner, told us she was eighty and had been selling fruit and vegetables there for over forty years. Most of her customers are commuters. "The town people don't buy," Lillie told us. She said she receives letters from all over the world. "Lots of foreigners ask me how I grow stuff without all the chemicals and everything." We bought and ate fruit while we talked.

Linda and I decided not to carry food or a stove because we would be riding through populated areas. We also felt we could eat most of the foods we liked raw. We came to a campground at Barnegat after traveling about sixty-five miles. The Oak Grove A&P was less than a mile away. We refueled with a supper of fruits and vegetables, some cheese, and a corn muffin. For dessert, snacks, and breakfast, we ate grapes, lots of grapes.

Barnegat, Tuesday, July 14

At five o'clock, a whippoorwill's call stirred me out of bed. By six-thirty, we were churning through the humidity. It wasn't long before our cool damp shirts were sweaty, clammy, and hot. Again, the temperature and humidity were in the high nineties. We stopped in the shade of the Nash Fashion Mart in Howell where we ate the last of our grapes and drained and refilled our water bottles. I bought some white cotton pants from Doris Nash's shop.

Our next stop, also on Route 9, was The Bagel World at Gordon's Corner. The workers told me the hand-rolling and the water used in the dough made the bagels especially good. I ate three of them during the day and wished I'd bought more. Linda ate none, claiming, "Bagels are too heavy." By the time we reached a shopping center near our destination, we were ready for a spaghetti lunch. We pedaled into Cheesequake State

Park about two o'clock, concluding fifty-three miles of travel. Fortunately, we pitched our tents and took showers without delay. The temperature dropped suddenly; the sky blackened; the trees swirled overhead. By four o'clock, sheets of rain had driven us into our tents.

A couple of hours later, the rain had stopped. After weeks of stultifying heat and humidity, the temperature was pleasant again. We ate our leftover vegetables, fruits, and cheese instead of riding into town for dinner.

Cheesequake State Park, Wednesday, July 15

I crawled out wearing cotton shorts and a T-shirt, chilly. The temperature had dropped over thirty degrees since the day before. I shook out my tent and upended it to dry while I packed up.

In downtown Perth Amboy, we resupplied our food pannier with fruit and vegetables. We drank a quart of orange juice in the store parking lot, then, passing the "I'm Not Here When My Wife Calls" Tavern, we rode over the Outerbridge Crossing Bridge. We were blind to a "Bicycles Prohibited" sign and glad that midmorning traffic wasn't heavy. The toll-gate-keeper yelled, "You're not supposed to be here. Get going — quick!"

We disappeared at top speed down a ramp into Staten Island, and crossed to Hyland Avenue. I expected Staten Island to be busy and congested with heavy industry. Instead, we wheeled along a broad boulevard with fields, homes, and parks on both sides. Just as the city crept upon us, we found a bike path and continued along the shore past beach, flatlands, and marsh. We cycled under the Verrazano Narrows Bridge along Bay Street to the ferry which carried us to Battery Park in Manhattan.

We leaned our bikes against a park bench and ate lunch among members of the Wall Street working class, enjoying the warm sun and pleasant breeze. Police officers, bike messengers, parking lot attendants, and park rangers advised against leaving our bikes anywhere. This advice was underscored at a stoplight in Manhattan, when Linda noticed a man·carrying a heavy-duty guaranteed bicycle lock. "Looking for your bicycle?" she asked him.

"Yes, it was *just* stolen. I wasn't gone twenty minutes. I

think they froze the lock, then hit it with a hammer, and took my brand new eight-hundred-fifty-dollar bike. I'd only had it a week."

We pedaled up West Street and 10th Avenue to Broadway and as far as the Eighties before continuing up West End Avenue to 99th Street where Rob Fisher, a music director and expert on Gershwin, welcomed us to his apartment.

With Rob, we bought barbecued chicken and salad bar carry-out. Showered and changed, we spent a grand evening with my cousins Sam and Babs Folsom who brought home-made potato salad, wine, and laughter.

New York City, New York, Thursday, July 16

During the morning, we ventured into the subway and toured the Statue of Liberty. We read everything and looked at all the exhibits, enjoying the glorious feeling of being at sea in the Hudson River. After returning on the subway, I napped away the afternoon and Linda walked to Grant's Tomb.

New York City, Friday, July 17

By six in the morning, Linda and I were speeding down Broadway. The city was not yet awake; even the street people slept soundly as we passed. A taxi driver shouted "Where're ya going?"

"Maine," we chorused without missing a turn of the pedals. He responded with thumbs up. We headed west to Lexington Avenue, continuing downtown to Third Avenue, the Bowery, and, finally, across the Brooklyn Bridge to head out Lafayette Street. There, glass penetrated one of my tires. While I sat on the curb repairing the flat, a woman escorted her children to the school bus. As it drove away, she turned, introduced herself as Holly and asked, "Do you need any help?"

I responded quickly, "Could I use your bathroom?" Although I had stopped at two fast food places and one filling station, I had not found a public restroom.

"Oh, sure," said Holly, "straight up the stairs. We're at the ninth mile of the New York Marathon, and my brother stops when he races."

Having repaired my first flat tire since Louisiana, we continued through Brooklyn on Myrtle Street and out Long Island on Union Turnpike where we stopped for lunch in a shady school yard. At the Hot Bagel Shop in Syosset, we saw Maggie Clark, Irv Weissman, and several other bicyclists I met the year before at GEAR in Buffalo and saw during the Erie Canal ride that followed. I introduced them to Linda, and we rode together along Vanderbilt and Motorway until Linda and I stopped for pizza.

When we rolled into State University of New York at Stony Brook, Linda and I took up residence in a dormitory room and found Floyd Hartman, who had just arrived in his small truck. The next day was the first day of GEAR. Floyd, Linda, and I took the four-village ride of about forty miles, and the following day we drove to Sag Harbor to join another ride. The rest of the time, we looked at the GEAR exhibits, attended lectures, and fingered new bicycles and equipment. Most of all, we ate and visited with friends. I was delighted by the people who came when I gave a talk about my perimeter trip: Sue Haffey from Buffalo, Mary Ann Brame, my last year's room-mate at GEAR, and several people from the Erie Canal ride, including Don Moffet and Al Kelly. Al asked me to ride with him at NEAR, another rally, which would be held soon in New Hampshire. I hadn't planned to go, but a look at the map and the calendar was encouraging. Even Slim, the bicyclist I met in Michigan at Wandering Wheels Campground, came to greet me. Rose Eicken, from Baltimore and the Erie Canal trip, told me how much she had enjoyed my *Pedalgram*.

"How did you get it?" I wondered.

"Easy," she said, "A friend of yours in Peru sent it to someone in my office who showed it to me without knowing I knew you. Could we get it more directly from now on?"

I said hello to Fran and Mo Christopher from Miami who were selling Fran's marvelous bicycling clothes and were also going to NEAR. I took some time to try out a Terry bicycle and talked with Georgena Terry when I attended her workshop about fitting bikes to people.

Stony Brook, Long Island, Monday, July 20

After breakfast, Linda and Floyd presented me with a no-cal birthday cake: fifty-seven candles set in a plastic butter dish filled with concrete. I waved goodbye to Floyd, Linda, and other friends and headed for Greenport at the eastern end of Long Island. I found the village campground early in the afternoon. The campground keeper was a former chemist. He and his wife live on Long Island in their motorhome four months each year and in Florida the rest of the time.

In Greenport, I bought tent sealer and sealed the edges of my tent to avoid future leaks. Before it rained, I'd never bothered to follow the water seal instructions. For my bike, I got a plastic cover off a new twin-size mattress. I could easily roll the whole bicycle inside this new garage, and it was completely enclosed. There were a few small holes, which prevented sweating and wouldn't admit significant amounts of rain. After the storm at Cheesequake State Park, I was convinced it was worth carrying a bike shelter. When a really pounding rain hits the ground around a tarp-covered bike, mud and water splatter the chain and moving parts as well as the wheels. Protecting the drive train, especially the chain, was a priority. After completing my chores, I caught a ferry to Shelter Island and explored it, returning to camp for supper and sleep before dark.

Greenport, Long Island, Tuesday, July 21

A nine-mile ride in the cool morning air brought me to the Long Island-New London ferry. While crossing, I ate my fresh fruit breakfast and wondered, as I looked through surface fog, why there were two light houses so close together. Then, I realized one was moving. Through my binoculars, I discovered it was a submarine! Ashore, I found the bike path toward Old Mystic Seaport, where I spent three hours on the ship *Joseph Conrad* and wandering the streets of the colonial-era, seaport town.

I had left my bicycle unattended, and I prayed that it be protected. When I returned, the bicycle had fallen over, but no one had bothered it. A quiet thank-you was in order. Although I'd barely sampled Connecticut, I picked up my bike and headed for Newport, Rhode Island.

The hot, humid afternoon melted my will power and by three-thirty, I turned off of Old Boston Neck Road at the Vanilla Bean Ice Cream Parlor. As I slowly licked homemade raspberry ice, I met Sheila Falconer and Julie Norbert. They heard about my travels and invited me to stay overnight with them. They would take me over the bridge in the morning, they said, insisting bicycles were forbidden to cross. My day looked brighter with only five miles to Sheila's house and company!

It turned out to be a relaxed evening of talk and carry-out Chinese food for a dozen-and-a-half people. When I got too tired, I zipped myself into my tent in the back yard.

I certainly liked having company. Bicycling with Linda had spoiled me.

Saunderstown, Rhode Island, Wednesday, July 22

While waiting for my hosts to stir, I planned how to reach Falmouth, Massachusetts from Saunderstown, Rhode Island in one day. Bridges that prohibited bicycles presented problems. If I caught all the ferries on time, I would reach Bland Keith's home when she expected me in the evening.

I needed to catch the New Bedford ferry on which the next three days depended, so I woke Sheila. We had a nice chat during the ten-mile drive over the bridges. Her parting words were, "You deserve a lot of credit." Lots of people said that to me, but no one ever said what it was I deserved credit for.

I pushed my pedals through Portsmouth, Tiverton, and North Dartmouth into New Bedford, where I halted at Lillian London Bakery Shop for a scone with raisins, a lemon custard bar, and a lemon tart with meringue. Linda suggested that I list all the bakeries I visited on my trip and award them cream puffs! This would be a five-cream-puff bakery, among the very best.

Riding through the historic district of New Bedford told me I needed to spend days, not hours, there. A look at my watch indicated that, if I chanced finding the ferry without a hitch, I could visit the Whaling Museum. Inside, volunteer guides suggested what I should see. Perhaps my favorite exhibit was the largest ship model in the world, the Bark Lagoda, built to half-scale. It made me feel like Gulliver among the Lilliputians. I can't resist climbing aboard anything that floats, often wondering how many incarnations I spent as a sailor! Volunteer Marilyn Poulos and I talked as I headed out the door. "Come and visit us, have a lunch on me. I'm Irish. My husband's Greek, and we run a Jewish deli on Pleasant Street."

"Thanks, but I've got to catch the ferry, and I'm not sure I have enough time."

I turned to my bicycle which was leaning against a bench. A woman with a bunch of kids was sitting near it, and a small boy asked, "Why didn't you lock your bike?"

"I knew you were going to come along and watch it for me, so I didn't need to worry. Thanks." I smiled.

The ferry was further than I expected. Once aboard, I took off my sunglasses and turned my face up in hopes of adding color to my white eyesockets. Engine vibrations massaged my back. Later, passing between Woods Hole and Martha's Vineyard, I watched the water and compared the land forms with the map. From the dock at Vineyard Haven, I bicycled along Beach Road to Oak Bluffs. The shingle designs on houses and the Carpenter Gothic gingerbread cottages fascinated me. A short ferry trip carried me to Falmouth where pedaling briefly took me up the drive to shouts of welcome at Bland Keith's house.

With catch-up talk running full speed, especially about Bland's recent trip to Kathmandu to visit Betty Woodsend, we walked to the beach. The air was in the seventies, and the water was sixty-eight. Bland swam. I got my legs blue up to the knees.

We ate macrobiotic food for dinner while Sho Fu, Bland's Lhasa Apso dog, danced around our feet. The food was delicious and a new experience for me. It would be wise for me to adopt such a healthy diet.

Falmouth, Massachusetts, Thursday, July 23

Fortunately, Bland wasn't on a schedule. I felt as if I'd been on deadline since resuming the trip. Today, I hoped Bland wouldn't notice if my anchor was dragging. We went to Woods Hole for lunch overlooking the water.

Hazel Keith and Fran Moore, who joined us for supper, wanted to see my bike and mini-stove. I thought their lives much more interesting than mine. They had raised kids, supported high-achiever husbands, and launched successful careers. All I had done was march to the government tune and ride a bicycle. Perhaps the grass is always greener in someone else's yard.

Falmouth, Friday, July 24

At our before-breakfast swim in the sea, I managed to dip my arms to the elbows and turn my legs blue again. Ever since living in Singapore, where the ocean water is eighty-six degrees all year long, cold water had been anathema to my body. My old joints and biking muscles preferred a warm shower to the cool July salt sea.

After breakfast, I spun my wheels unhurriedly from Falmouth to the Cape Cod Canal along a road that paralleled Buzzards Bay. Then riding across a bridge, along Highway 3A, I unexpectedly came upon a "Welcome to Plymouth" sign far south of the city. Plymouth, with seventeen miles of shore, calls itself America's hometown.

I arrived at the Fehlows' home before lunch. We sat around the picnic table in the garden with my friend Susan Fehlow's parents, Marie and Otto, younger sister Christina, home from college, and Jane and her baby, Sarah, visiting from Virginia. On our hilltop, trees fluttered in the sea breezes. For an hour we went to the beach where I got another case of blue legs. Cape Cod Bay was colder than Buzzards Bay had been.

Susan's Aunt Alba Thompson, a graduate of Stanford and the wartime military, a scholar's widow, and the first woman to serve as Plymouth Selectman, joined us for a lobster and clam boil. I watched to see how the food was layered for cooking. Potatoes on the bottom were topped by other vegetables, then the lobsters, and then the clams.

Plymouth, Saturday, July 25

Aunt Alba escorted me to Plimouth Plantation, a recreated 1727 village. Except for its modern cleanliness and lack of smells, Plymouth reminded me of my walks in the Himalayan villages.

We went to look at the famous rock and behind it, Burial Hill, where the first Plymouth fort was built near fresh water in 1621. Today there was a salon nearby: Hairloom.

When we reached the cranberry bogs, and Alba told me, "Since the berries float, the workers knock them off the bushes and lift them out of the water. Equipment and tools have been changed over the years, but the method of harvest remains the same."

I loved the visit, being in a home, and learning about old and new Plymouth. I wrote and typed my *Pedalgram*, enjoyed dinner guest Andy Dietlin's stories, and was interviewed by Christine Howard for the Old Colony Memorial paper.

My disk was full; I was on overload. I needed time assimilate my experiences. There was no more space for impressions, information, humor, anybody, or anything. I would leave early in the morning for Boston. I was ready for the open road and small towns.

Plymouth, Tuesday, July 28

I rolled out of Plymouth and ambled along Route 3A observing the homes, gardens, and gently rolling terrain. Even the little inclines were welcome after my long tour of coastal flatland. I arrived seconds too late for the nine-thirty commuters' ferry to Boston. I found a grocery, ate lunch in the sun by the Hingham Dock, and caught *Capt. Red*, the eleven o'clock boat.

The water glistened, the sky was clear. It was the sort of day when nothing could make me angry. I was gazing toward Bumpkin Island and World's End, when I heard a woman's voice say, "Somebody put this bicycle in the way so there aren't enough seats for all of us." I walked over to the bike and moved it, then turned to sit down myself. The woman and her grandchildren were taking up all the space. "Look," I told her, "I moved the bike for you. The least you could do is permit me to sit down, also." For the rest of the trip, the woman stumbled over herself trying to be nice to me.

I rolled the bike ashore in downtown Boston, looked up at the high-rise buildings everywhere, and decided to keep moving. Right through town, across a bridge to the end of Bunker Hill Street, over another bridge, on to Lynn, and through Salem I went. Then I took a side road to Palmer State Park, which was only for day use. I was hot and tired and had no idea where to spend the night.

In the park, a woman with three children suggested, "The Ipswich River Wildlife Sanctuary in Topsfield isn't far, and they may allow camping." We tried to phone, but neither the book nor the operator could produce a number. The woman's thrice-repeated directions and many assurances encouraged me to search on my bike. Her help was splendid, and I wish I had asked her name.

At the Wildlife Sanctuary, David Thurlow showed me a small cabin which rented in the spring and fall for thirty dollars, but it was stuffy now in midsummer. He suggested camping outside nearby. It was late afternoon when I pitched the tent, unloaded my bike, and rode into Topsfield for food.

At the sanctuary, high on a windblown hilltop, are a rambling two-hundred-year-old house and outbuildings that include a public restroom, library, and research area. I wandered along the open field and, in the last rays of the sun, lay down to sleep.

Topsfield, Wednesday, July 29

The warmth of the sun on my tent forced me outside, and the cabin's breezy front porch provided a comfortable place to read. About nine-thirty, Dave and his team of workers came to check on me, tell me about the walk to the rockery, and invite me to their kitchen for lunch.

They went to work building a walkway, and I took to my feet to look around the estate. I ambled to the rockery, then to the house to share peanut butter sandwiches. We sang for Dave's birthday. They went back to work and sent me off after lunch with a canoe key, a paddle, and a life jacket. I spent two hours on the narrow Ipswich River. The half-size canoe was easy to paddle and light enough for one person to lift. Dreaming of dinner, I selected a half-dozen mussels from the mud, washed them and dropped them into the canoe before realizing they qualified as protected wildlife. I replaced them on the mud bank.

As I was about to take the canoe out of the water, a man and his son appeared and helped me carry it. I carried the dripping paddle and life preserver back up to the house. I identified a man walking through the parking lot with a mosquito net over his head, a backpack, and heavy boots as a bird watcher. His binoculars and the book hanging in its special bag identified him. About five, when Dave finished an impromptu game of basketball, he offered to let me shower in the house, where there was hot water.

Topsfield, Thursday, July 30

I got lost in Haverhill, but not so lost I missed Joseph's Italian Bakery! In Exeter, after consulting with the driver of a telephone utility truck, I found the road I needed.

Late in the afternoon, I discovered the cause of the persistent itch on my forehead. A hungry bug was hiding under the sweat sponge of my helmet and nibbling on my skin at the hairline. I dumped the critter out, and the itch subsided.

At Durham, New Hampshire, I registered in midafternoon at the university for NEAR (New England Area Rally). I was issued a tenth floor dorm room with cross ventilation and a bat! I shepherded the bat out into the hall near an open window, closed my door, and sat down to read the ride and exhibit schedules, two-days' plans for about a thousand bikers. I decided to ride inland one day and seaward the next to see more New Hampshire and Maine countryside without carrying my heavy load.

On Friday, I rode northwest with Al Kelly and others to Milton Mills, Maine. The seventy-five-mile tour filled up most of the day. Al and I had become acquainted on the Erie Canal ride the year before. Now, he rode a new bike and was such an excellent bicyclist I had trouble keeping up with him. He was good company and said he didn't mind a relaxed pace. There were few towns and no people. Sometimes we talked, but mostly we pedaled.

I spent the late afternoon and evening visiting exhibits and talking with Ruth Huking who handcrafts bicycle-motif items in stained glass, and with Georgena Terry and Mo and Fran Christopher, whom I'd seen at GEAR.

Durham, New Hampshire, Saturday, August 1

August dawned clear, crisp, and breezy. Georgena offered me one of her bicycles for the day, and I rode it seventy-seven miles, traveling at my own pace along the coast, and returned less tired than I felt the day before on my own bicycle. An engineer, she designs Terry bicycles to fit women's frames, and they do. Terry's influence has changed the bicycle industry.

Along the coast were Maine's typical rocks, inlets, small harbors, and towns, including the state's oldest, Kittery. At

York Beach, a parade included a dozen antique bicycles with costumed riders. For the first time I watched riders mount an ordinary, the antique bike with a high front wheel. The difficult part seemed to be getting off without falling on your nose. When ordinaries were common, so were wicker nose guards!

At a workshop that evening, I learned about the Women's Cycling Network from Susan Notorangelo, winner of the Race Across America (RAAM). Her husband, Lon Haldeman, had won RAAM several times in the 1980s. I learned that more American women than men participate in bicycling as a recreational sport, and I marveled at the number of women who said they wished to jump on their bicycles and accompany me.

Durham, Sunday, August 2

As I packed, I thought how nice it was to be going somewhere instead of riding in a circle or out and back. Rally cyclists lack the touring biker's sense of destination. Out of New Hampshire and into Maine, I rolled along the numbered highways which are graded better than the country roads we used during the rallies. There was more traffic, too. Entering Maine, I headed north and later east toward Cape Cottage and Cape Elizabeth near Portland. I planned to stop late in the afternoon at one of two state parks, but both turned out to be for day use only. There were no motels, and I had nowhere to camp. I put aside worries about where to spend the night and concentrated on the mission my mother assigned me for Cape Cottage — finding out what had happened to a high school friend whose phone had been disconnected.

It was late afternoon when I reached the correct street in an old, elegant community along the shore. Talking with neighbors, I discovered Sally was temporarily in a nursing home because her daughter was moving. My mission was accomplished.

I returned to the yard where my bike was parked. I thanked Arthur, the owner, for his help, and he graciously inquired if there was anything else he could do. I asked if I could camp in his back yard, since there weren't any available campgrounds. Arthur invited me into the house for a cold drink and, when I was on my third glass of water, he offered me his daughter's room.

"Thanks. I accept, but I'll use my sleeping bag so there won't be any sheets to launder."

Arthur, a lawyer, told me about Cape Cottage while he fixed us supper. In the twenties, it was at the end of the streetcar line and people from Portland came out for a day at the shore. All the land on this street belonged to the streetcar company. The big house at the end of the street was the casino, and Sally's house might have been a caretaker's place for the car company or the casino.

Cape Cottage, Maine, Monday, August 3

The next morning it was raining and the foghorn was blowing. It sounded dismal. I didn't hurry. When I reached the kitchen with gear in hand, rain was pounding on the roof and running down the sides of the house.

"I'm going to work," Arthur said. "Why don't you stay over a day, make yourself at home, and leave in the morning? The rain is supposed to continue until late afternoon, but it should be fine tomorrow."

After thanking him, I marched my sleeping bag upstairs and returned for bacon and eggs. It felt strange to have a man cook for me. I wondered what happened to his wife. He was a kind person, sensible and balanced. I always heard people in Maine were quite reserved, and I behaved rather formally, for me.

I spent the day typing the *Pedalgram* on his daughter's typewriter and I mailed a few things at the branch post office, presided over by Annie Burke, who had run it for forty-six years. Informed of my mission, Annie told me, "Sally isn't ill as far as I knew, just a bit absentminded with age. Her husband grew up right here."

Late in the afternoon, when I had returned from photographing the famous Portland Head Light at Fort Williams, Arthur came home and, for dinner, prepared the best swordfish I ever ate.

Cape Cottage, Tuesday, August 4

Before sunup I was in the garage packing my bike. The sky was clear, cleaned of haze and humidity, and the foghorns were quiet. While we ate breakfast, Arthur talked about being a top gunner on a B25 at the end of World War II. "Getting ready to go to Japan, we were told to expect fifty-percent casualties. Naturally, at that age, I expected to be among the survivors. Then they dropped the bomb, and we came home instead."

With a stomach full of pancakes, I pedaled along Shore Road into Portland, and out of town on U.S. 1. I was ahead of the working crowd and enjoyed the city shining in the morning sun. Headmasters Haircare and the outlet stores caught my eye, and I was making good time on the open road until I reached L. L. Bean in Freeport, Maine's most popular institution. I bought some clothes, sent them home, and crawled in and out of every small tent as I talked with Eric, a salesman, about them.

I pointed my front wheel toward Bath. I hadn't gone far before I passed The Cutting Room and then turned at Yankee Pedalers Bike Shop. Lorraine Barte, one of the owners, was truing a wheel. She advised that I rotate my tires instead of buying a new K-4 for the rear. My tires could last longer. With a hand pump, I got tired before I inflated them to optimal pressure.

In Bath, at the Maine Maritime Museum ticket window, I met Jeff Sibley mounting his bicycle. "Spend as much time here as you can. It's worth every minute."

"Where are you from?"

"I flew up here from Louisiana for a two-week biking vacation. Most of the time I rode through Nova Scotia, a great place for bicycling, not to be missed!" I spent three hours in the museum buildings and on the tourist boat ride along the river. The museum contained a wonderful children's room with a ship's wheel to turn and rigging to climb. Displays about lobsters filled an entire building.

The Bath waterfront was dominated by the Iron Works, which employs about six thousand people. Bath was a shipbuilding town for two hundred years before the Iron Works was founded, and shipbuilding remains the reason for the town's existence. The most unusual job in town was that of Susan Quick Cahoon, who decorates champagne bottles with satin ribbons. They've been smashed at every ship launching for more than thirty-five years!

At Yankee Pedalers I had seen a notice advertising a camp for bicyclists at Swango Farm on the Kennebeck River ten miles from Bath and eight miles north of Route 1. The eight-mile detour from my route led me up and down hilly back roads along the river. Negotiating the farm entrance road, a mile of steep, unpaved surface, with my heavily-loaded bike wasn't fun. I was hungry and tired.

The farm consisted of a house, a barn, and a greenhouse. The crops needed tending. The campsite on the bank of the Kennebeck River consisted of a ring of stones around some old ashes. The shower was at the barn two hundred yards away. It needed cleaning.

Jim, the owner, returned from delivering vegetables and asked if I'd like to ride in his station wagon to Wiscassett for his final delivery. Assured we would return in an hour or less, I decided to go. He told me about coming from California to Maine in the Air Force and his decision to become a farmer.

At dusk, we returned to the farm and Jim suggested I shower in the house. Afterwards, he took me to the cooler in the barn to find something to eat. I could have eaten all of it! I bought peas, grapes, nectarines, and an ear of corn. He gave me some bruised peaches.

Kennebeck Riverside, Wednesday, August 5

I slept well in the pine and fir grove. Pushing the bike and slipping on the gravel until I reached the paved road, I began to ride at sunup. A mile later, I hit something sharp and pinched both tubes in two places. Doggedly, I applied four patches. It was not an auspicious beginning to a long day of pedaling steep back roads in order to come out on Route 1 further up the coast.

In midafternoon, a "Wild Blueberries" sign in front of barn a halted me. I bought a heaping quart for two dollars and began to eat the sweet berries by the handful. Accustomed as I was to the commercial product from New Jersey, these tiny sweet wild berries tasted like a different fruit. I watched a machine blow leaves out of the berries before they rolled along a conveyor belt. Two women inspected and removed discolored berries and stems before the fruit was boxed.

"Do you do anything besides pick them?" I asked.

"Oh, yes, we fertilize, but the bushes all grow wild," Lois M. Hart told me. I had seen them on the hillsides all day.

After passing Yankey Stripper, a furniture restoration center, I stopped at the Moss Tent Outlet. I liked their tents so well I decided to visit the factory. Eventually, unable to decide what I needed, I bought two tents. The one-man was sent to Milo, Maine and the two-man was sent to Spencerport, New

York. By the end of the trip, I had decided there is no such thing as a perfect tent, but the Moss two-man Starlet suited me.

Riding from the factory back to Route 1, through Camden, I decided, based on the morning's double-flat-tire experience, to rotate the most-used tire into the trash. I bought a new one-and-an-eighth-inch tire for the front and would rotate the one-and-a-quarter-inch front tire to the rear.

With the new tire tied to my bike, I soon reached the state park on the outskirts of Camden. It had been full since noon. It was after five, and the next campground, Homestead, was seven hilly miles away.

A young man behind me in line offered to take my panniers in his car and leave them at the Homestead Campground office for my arrival. I was so delighted and so tired that I gave him everything except the bicycle. As he and his companion drove off, I realized I didn't know their names. I quickly noted the BMW had a New Jersey license plate. The numbers were a blur.

I covered the remaining miles to Homestead Campground rapidly. My possessions lay there on the office floor and the proprietor welcomed me with a big smile, "You must be the bicyclist." He told me my benefactor was Andrew Schenkel.

Camden, Thursday, August 6

After eating blueberries in bed and refreshing myself with a shower and shampoo, I turned my attention to the tires. The Specialized K-4 rear tire made its final roll from New Orleans into the trash barrel. Using a wash basin to find tiny leaks, I inspected and patched the tubes and then put the front K-4 on the rear and the new, narrower Cyclepro Kevlar-Taffeta tire on the front. I remembered to recalibrate my Avocet for the front tire size change. Putting everything back together, cleaning the bike, and packing consumed the morning. I was rolling toward Belfast before noon.

A toasted hot dog roll filled with lobster salad made a fine lunch before I cycled through Searsport, a town of antique shops. I admired homes, gardens, and antique displays from the road. Later, in a cafe, someone asked whether I was a blueberry raker or a bicyclist. "It's because of the gloves—blueberry rakers wear bicyclists' gloves," he explained. I continued to a campground at Ellsworth.

On the advice of Debbie Calder who plays cards with

my mother, I called Jim and Ruth Bunker. Jim said the road through their town was too hilly for me and offered to bring me a letter I'd received at their address. I told them where I was, put up my tent, and walked over to The Captain's Mate for a seafood dinner. I remembered David and Mary Peacock said the biggest market for Virginia clams was in Maine.

I had just returned to my tent when the Bunkers arrived with Debbie Calder and her three sons who live in Maryland. What a surprise! Debbie had supplied me with names and addresses of her friends and relatives all over Maine. In addition, she read all my *Pedalgrams* and wrote to me during the trip. We had a grand visit punctuated by the boys' climbing into my tent and throwing rocks at my laundry. Debbie briefed me on her friends who lived along my route and insisted I look up all of them. "I just feel you are so much safer when you have local people to call 'just in case,' but you should call them anyway. They will want to meet you."

I was sorry when their car disappeared over the hill. So many people helped me in so many different ways! I had heard much about reticence and reserve among Maine natives, though I hadn't noticed any, so I was particularly grateful for Debbie's list of friends. As I zipped myself into the tent, I thought again, "Everytime I unzip this thing an adventure is waiting. Life is so much fun!"

If I stayed two nights at this campsite, I could ride without baggage for a day in Acadia National Park. On Friday, implementing Arthur's suggestion, I explored the non-park area of Mt. Desert Island including Somes Sound, the largest natural fjord on the East Coast.

Trenton, Saturday, August 8

Some mornings it was hard to get moving. Damp gray clouds hung over camp, and, by the time I left, there was mist. Rain, thunder, and lightning pursued me as I splashed along the shoulder of U.S. 1, mumbling to myself, "I can't get wetter than wet." The crashing and flashing intensified and the rain-drops got bigger and closer together. The storm was right overhead. I felt little danger from lightning, because in a forest I was the shortest thing around.

About the time I began to feel chilly, I came to a store with a porch which could shield my bike. I turned in, pulled the bike up a few steps, and removed my dripping helmet. A couple with two kids ran from a mobile home through the rain and shook themselves on the porch. The woman announced, "When the trailer started shaking, we left!" After toweling off, I took out my warm, dry sweatshirt to replace my sodden T-shirt and windbreaker. I again bemoaned the loss of my rain jacket on that plane in Texas. I ordered coffee and a "sunrise," an English muffin with Canadian bacon. This was my first severe rain encounter since the day I ended up with my muddy bike in the shower in McAllen, Texas.

A man on the next stool asked, "Where are you going?"

"North on Route 1."

"You mean east," he corrected flatly.

"The sign said north," I maintained.

"Well, you're 'down east' now — headed east."

Half-an-hour later, in dry air, I left the Gouldsboro store for the open road and in early afternoon, I concluded a fifty-four mile day at Jonesboro.

A whole "free" afternoon melted away as I cleaned and cooked the chain, put up the tent, wrote a *Pedalgram*, and dried my sleeping bag in a dryer at the owner's house. Its sack was so worn it wasn't waterproof anymore. I stored the dry bike with its freshly waxed chain in its plastic garage. Fair weather was predicted for morning.

Jonesboro, Sunday, August 9

As I began rolling my bike out of camp, Marion and Carl Apsley intercepted me. He was from Rock Hall on Maryland's Eastern Shore where I raced my sailboat, and she was from Plainfield, New Jersey, where a college friend lived. They were my age, and her dream, to travel on a long walk, was shelved while they raised five children. Marion said, "When one daughter wanted to go to Scotland on a walking tour, I told her to go. Go now before she was too old. My legs won't walk very far any more, but I hope Carl and I can keep on camping for a few more years." They made me feel fortunate to be so active. It was an encouraging send-off.

Headed for Campobello, I was satisfied to speed through Lubeck, the eastern-most city in the United States, and bypass Quoddy Head State Park, the eastern-most point of land, to spend more time at The Roosevelt Cottage. I decided to concentrate on Campobello because I grew up when Roosevelt was president. He was inaugurated when I was three and died when I was fifteen. The words President and Roosevelt were synonymous to me for many years.

At Campobello, he collapsed with polio. I learned about his family vacations there during more than thirty summers on his "beloved island." I remembered the Warm Springs White House in Georgia, built much later, had a similar floor plan, perhaps intentionally.

I pedaled to the ferry, crossed to Deer Island, and took another ferry to Eastport, where the Roosevelts arrived on the train and stepped into boats for Campobello. I pedaled until I reached a campground overlooking Passamaquoddy Bay.

Perry, Monday, August 10

From my tent, I watched the sun rise right into overcast clouds. I decided to pump my tires ten strokes every morning whether they needed it or not. That morning, they seemed to need twelve hefty squirts before I left. Gin Cove Road took me back to the highway. I took my time pedaling to Princeton, Debbie Calder's husband's hometown, and my day's destination.

Traveling upstream along the St. Croix River, I passed several original milestones — twelve miles to Calais, nine miles to Calais. On top of one stone was a ring, perhaps for tethering a horse. Along the route Champlain had taken by boat, I passed a park located where he once camped for the winter. When I stopped for a rest, I phoned Debbie's friends in Milo.

Road construction was converting my three-lane road to a two-lane road with wider lanes. They were taking the dipsy-doodles out of it by smoothing off the tops of rises and sliding the dippy out of them. As I picked my way along the uneven surface, I chuckled, remembering the lady who had asked me yesterday as I was getting on the ferry, "Is that wet suit you're wearing comfortable?" People sometimes don't know what to make of bicyclists' clothing!

In Princeton by one p.m., I was camped behind a hundred-year-old house a few feet from a lake's rocky shoreline. With Route 1 at their front door, Joeline and Bruce Cochran ran a campground and marina in their back yard.

"We have more purple martins in residence that any

other private home in America," Joeline told me. "Bruce built each bird-apartment house — the largest has fifty nesting compartments.

"Condos are everywhere," I thought.

Joeline continued, "Last year the Audubon Society recorded one-hundred-ten pairs of martins and we estimate five-hundred to six-hundred birds living here now." While she was talking, a loon flew over, and Joeline looked up. "They might keep you awake tonight."

Princeton, Tuesday, August 11

At the edge of the town of Princeton, Route 1 crossed a tiny bridge and entered an Indian reservation. I pedaled until I came to a left turn off Route 1 into the Trans-Maine Trail at Topsfield. I turned west! The wind was no longer in my face and the road seemed flatter. Blackberries were ripe, and potato plants were in blossom. Springing from among the berry bushes, a red fox ran across the road ahead of me.

By midafternoon, I passed Lincoln and turned into Lakeside Campground. The owner, Gil Martin, from Frederick, Maryland, retired "from his wife and work" and bought this land cheap because it was swampy. He filled in the wet areas and built a marvelous small campground in a hidden ravine. For recreation, he rides his bike eighteen miles a day as fast as he can. In winter, he closes the campground and skis. "Long before winter," I thought, "I'll be home."

BACK
TO THE
BEGINNING

CHAPTER TWENTY

To Square One

Lincoln, Maine, Wednesday, August 12

I packed away my Eureka Crescent tent for the last time. A Moss Solet was in the mail. I washed my hands one last time, filled the empty water bottle, and departed. When I passed Howland, resplendent with fast food restaurants, I wasn't hungry. But twelve miles later, at Lagrange, I was starving, and there was no place to eat. After buying a lemon pie at a filling station, I pedaled on past the James River Corporation chip plant, right into Milo.

At the Merritt Trust Company, I found Debbie's friend, Frances Hamlin, but my tent had not arrived. I phoned Moss Tent and they said the Solet should arrive the next morning. The Hamlins already had invited me to spend the night at their house. I certainly hadn't seen any of that Maine reserve I'd heard about.

Phil Gerow, a next door neighbor, was a correspondent for the *Bangor Daily News*. I thought he was teasing and agreed to an interview to call his bluff. My mistake. I was interviewed and photographed.

Frances returned to work while her daughter, Georgia, showed me the town — the old railroad roundhouse, the former American Thread Company, last spring's flood damage, and the slate quarries. We walked among the abandoned quarries, now deep pools. She told me when she was in high school, a couple came to the quarry to park, took off their clothes, and when the car began to roll toward the pool, they jumped out just in time. The car and clothes disappeared under water!

Frances and Georgia took me to the Lakeside Restaurant for broiled fish dinner, and then we drove to Lake View on

Schoodic Lake where they had a cottage. Only when I asked, did Georgia explain that she teaches the blind and partially blind in special education sections of a public school.

Milo, Thursday, August 13

After I retrieved my new tent at the Milo Post Office, I mailed the old one home. I set up the Solet on the Hamlins' front lawn before departing. I wanted to stay, but I will finish pounded in my head. The Hamlins told me it would be a hilly route; the toughest hill was leaving such kind company.

Before rolling into Dover-Foxcroft, I passed an old barn where there was a sign, "No two people are alike and both are glad of it." In town, I stopped to consult a druggist who recommended hydrocortisone cream for my itchy forehead. The road was free of traffic and I decided to ride without my helmet for a while. A man digging a hole for a new utility pole looked up and smiled as I puffed up another hill. "You've got courage," he yelled. I waved and wobbled up along the Moosehead and Trans-Maine Trails. The landscape was quiet except for the wind in the trees and an occasional bird. Once in a while, there was the faint sound of a distant chainsaw.

I stopped for half an hour at a Kingsbury Pond rest area and looked at the water while I sat on a picnic table eating a nectarine. My route around the water appeared fairly flat, but the road seemed entirely too long to encircle something called a pond. At the pond's far end, the climb was steep and I had to get off and push the bike. A man in a blue truck passed me, returned, and stopped just as I was climbing back on the bike. "Oh, I was afraid your bike was broke and didn't want you to be stuck out here," he said.

"Thanks, I was just tired, and the hill was steep."

"Glad it's not broke. It's nine miles to town but this is the last big hill. Now its mostly down." At the crest I saw that wonderful caution sign: "Continuous ten-percent downgrade next three miles." I passed through Bingham with its church-tower bell made by Paul Revere and continued along the river in the same direction as the water. Near Solon, I saw a sign: "Gateway to Maine Forest halfway between the North Pole 3107 miles and the Equator 3107 miles. Altitude 325 feet. Welcome to God's Country."

I camped at The Evergreens where Bill Perry, the owner,

told me the site had been used by Norse, Indians, Benedict Arnold's troops, and for the last twenty-six years, campers like me. It consisted of cabins, campsites, and a restaurant beside the Kennebec River. I set up my new tent under a tall evergreen, sealed the seams twice, and let it dry while I went to the restaurant. Bill fixed me a big plate with mashed potatoes, peas, and a pork chop and spiced the dinner with historical tales.

Bill Perry told of how mad he got with the president of Scott Paper Company, who asked, "What is your little problem?" The problem was bark and wood trash that washed up on Bill's property from logs Scott Paper floated down the Kennebec River. Bill hired an attorney and sued. The case went to the Supreme Court. It is now against the law to float logs in any navigable water in America. Bill's next project was to figure out how to require a passageway for spawning fish to be built into any dam across our rivers. Meanwhile, he is building an airplane he designed.

Solon, Friday, August 14

The sun was coming out, heralding a nice day for my ride through Kingfield and Rangeley toward my destination, Errol, New Hampshire. At Kingfield, I stopped at The Woodsman restaurant. While eating, I read a newspaper article about the history of the Appalachian Trail. I stuck two slices of bread and a bran muffin in my pocket for later.

About eleven o'clock, I glanced quickly at the map without my reading glasses, and headed away from Kingfield in what I thought was the direction of Phillips. The water in the river I paralleled was still and so clear the stones in the bottom were visible. After about twelve miles, I passed a suspension bridge built with Sheffield Steel cable which had been there since the 1800s. "Just like Nepal," I said aloud. Signs told me I was on the Arnold Trail Highway passing Reed Brook in the Carrabassett Valley. I had no idea this route would be so pleasant. "I should be coming to Phillips soon," I thought, looking at my watch.

Ski cottages along the river were all closed. There were ski runs up on the mountain, and I passed a sign about Sugarloaf. How in the world could I be seeing Sugarloaf Mountain ski runs? I stopped my bike, pulled out my granny glasses, and read the map that had been right in front of me all along.

I had taken the northern route into the mountains via Stratton instead of the southern route via Phillips. It was a pleasant ride, and I'd enjoyed every minute of it. Although the way I mistakenly chose was longer, it may have been less hilly because it ran next to streams. I wasn't going to turn around.

No sooner had I remounted the bike than I was passed by about fifteen cars, including several from the press. Beyond a bend, they turned into a dirt road where a man was directing traffic. The man's T-shirt announced today was the fiftieth birthday of the Appalachian Trail!

In Stratton, I inspected a replica of the type of bateau believed to have been used by Colonel Benedict Arnold in his expedition to Quebec between 1775 and 1776. The replica was constructed for the bicentennial reenactment of the expedition, and the Stratton-Eustis Chamber of Commerce purchased it for the town.

At the Gingerbread Bakery, the aroma of cinnamon buns led me inside. Just out of the oven, the buns were delicious. The baker said she uses less sugar because so many people are trying to lose weight or be health conscious. I awarded a six-cream-puff rating to Gingerbread Bakery!

The twenty-mile ride into Rangeley was mostly downhill and thoroughly enjoyable. The nearest campground was a state park on the other side of the lake, seven miles off my route. Remembering I often passed campgrounds that I hadn't known existed, I decided to ride until I found a place. There was plenty of forest to camp in if no campground appeared.

As I puffed up a hill two miles short of Oquossoc, a station wagon pulled off the road in front of me, and a woman and two children jumped out. All talking at once, they ran toward me. "I'm Brenda Piampiano and this is John Mark and Sarah. Where are you going? Where have you come from? How far have you come today? Where are you staying tonight? Our cottage is just eight miles down this road — will you stay with us?" I never memorized directions so fast. "How soon can you come?" they clamored.

"A lot sooner if you carry my stuff," I admitted. Sleeping bag, tent, panniers, and pump fairly flew into the station wagon. The Piampianos jumped in and were gone. I dictated the license plate number into my recorder as the car disappeared into the distance. I flew over the hills, past "Moose Next 4 Miles" signs, and eight miles melted away.

At the Piampianos', as dogs danced around me, I tried to sort out eleven names and faces. The fatigue of seventy-one miles disappeared as the family showed me the house. Its basic structure was over a hundred years old. Additional rooms and a porch overlooked Cupsuptic Lake.

Jeff and John Mark took Josephine, their grandmother of about my age, and me for a boat ride before supper. If you really want to see Maine, get a boat! As we sped across the water, I realized I hadn't seen the views for the trees. We whizzed right past three unconcerned loons. When I exclaimed over seeing them so close, Jeff circled the boat and they "looned" under water.

We talked of skiing on water and on snow, of bicycles and touring, of hiking, books, politics, Washington, lawyers, and Maine through dinner and dishwashing. In the quiet of my tent, their voices echoed in my head. I could hardly go to sleep.

Pleasant Island, Saturday, August 15

There was a lot of scuffling up and down the tree outside my tent. I silently inched the zipper open and looked right past a twitching nose into the eyes of a small red squirrel who responded by shaking his tail and fussing at me loudly. Over cantaloupe and coffee, Josephine told me the red squirrels are rare.

When we discussed my route, one of the boys said,"Too bad you can't put styrofoam tires on your bike and ride right across to the other end of this lake. You'd be right where you're going."

While I took my tent down, the squirrel ran up and down the tree and squawked at me. It had a white stomach, light auburn back, and red legs and was half the size of an eastern gray squirrel.

It was hard to leave. "I'm coming back to Maine," was getting to be a refrain. The mountains were not so dramatic as the Alps or spacious as the Himalayas and the Rockies. They were quiet, soft, subtle, and smooth like spruce velveteen, blue and green. It was quiet but not lonely.

I was getting close enough to see the end of my journey. Ready to go home, I hated thinking about the trip's end. I disagreed with the utility pole worker who told me I had courage, "No. I have no courage. Anybody could do what I am doing."

Brenda Piampiano talked about discipline. "It affects everything you want to accomplish in life. Life doesn't take courage so much as discipline. Freedom, unlike stress, is re-laxed control. You have to push everything else aside to do what you want."

Although the "Welcome to New Hampshire" sign was followed by moose-crossing warnings and hoof prints in the bog on either side of the road, I saw none of the animals. Every car that shared the road with me had New Hampshire tags, and almost every car carried a canoe.

The town of Errol, established in 1774, looked like a good place for lunch. After eating, I walked out into the parking lot where a woman asked me, "Didn't we pass you a few days ago in Dover-Foxcroft?"

"Yes."

"We owe you an apology."

"Whatever for?"

"We were worried because our trailer swayed and almost knocked you off the road."

"Not that I noticed!"

Bruce and Marion Carel and baby Melissa came from New Jersey. We shared a laugh about people in the New England mountains thinking it was hot and humid, although we found the weather pleasant for August.

Dixville Notch lay ahead. The Hamlins and Piampianos looked incredulous when I had said I thought I could ride over it. On the map, the peak was labeled 3,482 feet — not too bad a climb — and the road wouldn't go that high. I figured it would be my last real mountain of the trip. Since the slope was about ten miles long, I didn't think it would be too steep. It wasn't, but it was slow going.

My leg muscles were complaining. I drank half a bottle of water. I'd been stopping too much, and would have liked to stop again. The Piampianos told me I couldn't get over Dixville Notch without walking. Nothing is quite so motivating as somebody telling me I can't do something! Not much further. There was always a tough place just before the crest. Up and over! On the other side, one of those giant Victorian hotels appeared. How splendid! I descended into the Mohawk River Valley at forty-five miles an hour, tears of joy flying out of the corners of my eyes.

I made it, Errol to Colebrook, twenty-two miles in two hours for a day's total of fifty-two miles so far. I sang to myself until I crossed the Connecticut River into Vermont, having covered sixty-five miles by three o'clock. A glance at the map indicated another fifteen to Island Pond, my campsite for the night.

At five o'clock I leaned my bike against a picnic table and read the Avocet at eighty-and-a-half miles. In very slow motion I put up the tent, unpacked, took a shower, washed clothes, and hung them to dry. When rested, I jumped on the denuded bike and headed for food in town, reminding myself, "It's Saturday night, and I need food for tomorrow." In Island Pond, I came to the grocery before I saw a restaurant, and decided to eat in my tent. Rain threatened as I selected a ready-made chef's salad, no-salt potato chips, rice crackers which weigh nothing and don't get stale, fruit, baby carrots, and an avocado. The supplies could last through Sunday. When I came out of the grocery, it had begun to sprinkle. I sped back to camp.

The campground was quiet. While it rained, I enjoyed my supper in the tent, then read and went to sleep.

Island Pond, Vermont, Sunday, August 16

Whenever I awoke for a few minutes during the night, I ate fruit. Needing no breakfast for a while in the morning made riding easier. Some mornings, it took me at least ten miles or one terrible hill to warm up and loosen up from overnight stiffness. My clothes were dry enough to wear. I rode the mile-and-a-half to Island Pond and entered Common Sense, a health food store and restaurant apparently run by flower children who had taken root and grown older. The food was good, the people cordial. If they had known I was a retired CIA employee they might not have been so gracious.

Barn swallows swirled as I pedaled through Derby and Newport. As I crested a pass where the Long Trail crossed my route, I stopped to talk with a backpack-laden couple emerging from the trail. They started this morning and found the flies bothersome. I was very glad I was bicycling instead of hiking.

The afternoon slid by as I rolled through the Missisquoi River Valley. I had been wondering what birds I was seeing. When I noticed a dead one on the highway, I stopped to identify a male white-winged crossbill.

At Sheldon Junction, hot and tired, I decided seventy-four miles was enough and entered a motel in time for Sunday sports television. For two hours, I lay abed watching the tube, hurting from hunger, too tired to eat. Gradually becoming rested, I ate, showered, and slept.

Sheldon Junction, Monday, August 17

When I awoke, I felt as though I pedaled over every mountain in New England. In fact, I mostly traveled along rivers, streams, and around lakes where the terrain was pleasantly rolling. Consulting the map, I planned a sixty-five mile day with Lake Champlain first on the itinerary. The magnet of finishing the trip tugged me onward as the sun climbed in the sky and the wind blew more strongly in my face. Other interests and thoughts were blotted out by pedaling, pushing myself and the bike into the wind.

I traveled slowly. At midmorning, I stopped for water at a bar where the accents were so Irish I could hardly understand them. My water bottle was graciously refilled, and I went on, discouraged. In an hour, I covered six miles. Another hour brought me to a cemetery where freshly cut grass under large cedar trees offered peaceful shade. I leaned my bike against a headstone and lay under a tree as I listened to the birds.

I looked at the bent over grass, estimating the wind at twenty miles an hour. The headwind along the road would continue right down my throat. My campground destination was fifteen miles ahead, another two hours. I pushed the bike back to the road and began to turn the pedals.

Two miles brought me to Ranch Side Park Campground. The Avocet said I had covered fifty-seven miles; my watch announced two o'clock; my body cried, "Enough is enough!" I found a shady, spacious campsite and leaned Centurion against the picnic table. I had the whole afternoon to rest and would go to sleep early, leave at first light, and ride fast before the wind could blow me backward. Now, however, I'd do nothing.

"Doing nothing" meant putting up my tent, showering, washing my clothes, and hanging them to dry on the parachute-cord line. I was the only tent camper. The campground was inhabited by English-speaking Canadians. Soon, several neighborly trailer residents came over to make me welcome. Near me was a couple from Montreal, forty-seven miles away. The woman said they would never camp in Canada.

"Why?" I asked.

"The sites are close together." Her pause caught my attention. I would have to read between the lines. She continued, "You can hear your neighbor snore."

I smiled and, deciding to try a long shot, continued her

sentence for her, "And they are all French, aggressive, and noisy," allowing my eyes to twinkle.

Her eyes glittered back, and her smile broadened. There was a slight nod. "Well, I wouldn't have said that," she responded.

"Do the French come to this campground?" I asked, on safer ground.

"Occasionally, but not unless they speak English."

"Are there any Americans who come here to camp?"

"A few transients, but they don't stay long."

"These trailers look more like homes than campsites. They have gardens with vegetables and wonderful flowers. Does everyone live here full time?"

Again she laughed, "My husband and I live in an apartment in Montreal. We put our trailer here permanently so we can come on weekends for the season from May to October. Now that we are retired, we spend longer weekends here and a shorter time in the city. We go to Florida in the winter. Some people like this place so much they commute to work in Canada from here. It's like a small town." Her husband called, and she excused herself, wishing me a comfortable visit.

Even though I lived in the open, people treated my space as though it were a home, asking from a respectable distance if they could disturb me for a chat. One woman loaned me a chair, another a couple of magazines. I passed the afternoon lounging comfortably. I even strolled around briefly, an invitation to chat I learned in other campgrounds.

For supper I cooked a package of Lipton's noodles with beef sauce and added mozzarella cheese. While it melted and I stirred, I munched raw carrots. At the store near the campground, I also bought Oreo cookies with green mint filling. (I seldom bought cookies except in single serving packages.) For the next day, I had reserved fruit and a quart of juice for breakfast, granola and a can of V8 for lunch, and grits and a can of chicken for supper.

Other campers thought the upper-eighties temperature horridly hot, but I thought it lovely. The humidity was low, and there was a slight breeze. By evening I felt relaxed and content. I liked my Moss tent. It was grand to lie inside shielded from the bugs and look through a whole tent of mesh at the trees, birds, and sky with the breeze to keep me cool.

Before I went to sleep, I stretched the fly over the tent and, thinking how I adore the French language, songs, and razzle-dazzle, listened to a French station on the radio.

Ellenburg, New York, Tuesday, August 18

My body felt like a lead weight. I'd had a few days with short mileage but not a whole day off the bike since rain had kept me indoors south of Portland. The last five days had been long, hilly, windy, and hard, and I'd earned a day off in a splendid, quiet place.

I studied the maps and planned the campsites and routes to Rochester where, in four days, I would visit the Thomases. Then, after visiting people I had met the year before in Buffalo, I would push on to Detroit. I wanted to complete the journey and be off the road before Labor Day.

One neighbor brought wild blackberries, another recommended seeing the owner's pets, spotted deer from Germany. The closest neighbors, Flo and Ernie Trussler, invited me to come and see their craft projects. Flo blows out eggs and decorates the shells. Ernie designs and builds miniature bird houses on sticks for use in floral arrangements.

After our conversation, Ernie invited me to return and Flo followed up, "We've enjoyed hearing about your trip. Please come back about seven o'clock and eat with us."

I liked their company even more the second time. When I thanked them for the meal, they thanked me for bringing "a breath of fresh air." Flo sent me off with Canadian peaches and suggestions about the route ahead.

Ellenburg, Wednesday, August 19

In spite of the headwind that began early and blew ever stronger, I set out shortly after first light. By using willpower and never pausing, I was able to average ten miles an hour. I rolled right between two women yelling across the highway from their front porches, "Your cat got in a fight with my cat last night!" A passing truck blotted out the rest. I'd traveled so much more in other countries than in my own it was a special joy to understand scraps of language my ears picked up.

At the Bear's Den Trading Post Truck Stop on the Mohawk reservation, two bowls of corn soup thick with hominy and kidney beans refueled my legs. An eastern kingbird hippity-hopped along the guard rail beside me as I continued, battling the wind. I passed huge piles of aluminum ingots at the Reynolds St. Lawrence reduction plant before stopping at a marker to read my New York history lesson. The motto of the Empire State, *excelsior*, means "ever upward." It seemed to apply to my cycling struggles.

By early afternoon, I checked into Cole Creek State Park just in time to sprint my bike from the entrance to shelter in the women's room. The door shut on my back wheel as a storm deluged the park. I showered my tired muscles in water that was blissfully warm.

When the rain stopped, I pitched the tent and went in search of food at the snack bar, then read as the setting sun winked out. The temperature had plunged, and I put on all my shirts and pants in layers. The Solet tent, great for hot weather, was so well ventilated it didn't hold body heat. Perhaps no perfect tent exists.

Nearby, along the St. Lawrence Seaway, foghorns blew and heavy diesel engines thumped the ships upstream at ten miles an hour, my average biking speed.

Cole Creek State Park, Thursday, August 20

In the restroom, I noticed black circles under my eyes. I walked out and pedaled into a clear, cool morning, saying to myself, "I gotta do it. I gotta do it. I gotta finish."

The Seaway Trail was beautiful, and I paused at every overlook to read historical markers and feast on views of fields and the St. Lawrence Seaway. During the morning, the cloudless sky was spectacular; by afternoon, the intense blue was full of popcorn clouds. I decided to aim for maximum mileage, knowing if I went far enough, the next day would bring me to the Thomases in Rochester.

While passing not far from Philadelphia, New York, where cream cheese originated in the mid-1800s, I admired the Thousand Islands the Iroquois called the "Garden of the Great Spirit." I turned south and rolled through the Golden Crescent of fishing rivers that flow into Lake Ontario. Muskie, northern and walleye pike, large- and small-mouth bass, lake, brown, and steelhead trout, and coho, Atlantic, and chinook salmon inhabit the rivers.

At Phillips Corner stood a monument commemorating the men who carried a several-ton cable twenty miles during the War of 1812. Wars certainly create strange problems!

On and on I rolled, past stone houses in farming country filled with butterflies and wildflowers. I must have seen every wildflower that grows along an American highway! Perhaps on my next trip I'd take along a wildflower book.

The Stonehill Museum called me to halt. I prowled among harvesting machines and machines that cut corn off cobs. The fully-equipped schoolroom had desks like those I'd used in elementary school, the same picture of George Washington, and the same map case and maps. Maybe I'm an antique, too! I didn't feel like one.

Ten hours on the road, ninety-five miles, brought me to rest at Westcott Beach State Park on Lake Ontario. I had forgotten my tarp. That morning I left it drying on the picnic table. I improvised, putting the "bicycle garage" under the tent floor.

Then I phoned the Thomases who, instead of being at home in Spencerport, were at their Finger Lake cottage. They preferred to pick me up on the road and take me to the lake before we all went to Spencerport on Sunday. Riding only half the expected distance was most appealing. On the Erie Canal tour, I'd already covered the same area by bicycle.

Westcott Beach State Park, Friday, August 21

I was headed for the highway before there was enough light for safety but rationalized the shoulder was broad and cars were few. Rabbits and deer and I were the only creatures stirring.

I almost had left Oswego behind when I noted a laden touring bicycle leaning on a tree outside the tourist information office. When a young woman bounded down the stairs and headed for her bicycle, I swerved across the highway, and we introduced ourselves. Neither of us had met a lone female cyclist before. Cindy Gagnon had traveled from the West Coast and hoped to be in Bar Harbor before Labor Day. We talked about chains, tents, routes, and our mutual wish to be home and finished, yet not miss anything along the way.

"Too bad we didn't meet in a campground so we could talk longer," Cindy said, expressing my feelings exactly.

On the road again, I could expect to see Woody and Merrillan Thomas anytime. Woody, a cousin, had married Merrillan, my roommate in Switzerland, before we went to college. Retired from Eastman Kodak, Woody began new career making travel films. He took the pictures, and Merrillan recorded the sound. They both edited and wrote commentary which Woody delivered while Merrillan engineered sound during each performance. They were traveling America and Canada showing their film on Yellowstone. Films on Japan and France were next.

Their timing was perfect. We met at the bottom of a long, hot hill, before I'd puffed to the top. We drove to their Finger Lakes cottage and swapped travel stories for two days.

Spencerport, Tuesday, August 25

After my stay with the Thomases, my route was plotted and friends were alerted. The bicycle and I were clean and rested. They waved as I pedaled north from Spencerport and headed to Lake Ontario.

Goldfinches scattered from their feeding perches on roadside wildflowers as I passed. They surrounded me all day, and I saw them just often enough to be delighted by each unexpected appearance.

Although late-morning and early-afternoon headwinds slowed me, I entered Four Mile State Campground near the Canadian border about four o'clock. The second Moss tent arrived while I was at Spencerport, and I had mailed the other one home. I popped the new tent up under a small willow tree. The Starlet, larger and heavier by two pounds, had been my preference all along. Campsites often required a tent that would stand up without being staked, and, for that purpose, the Starlet was the best small tent I'd seen. It provided good ventilation and privacy with or without the fly covering it. The Solet would be the tent choice for hiking the Appalachian Trail or camping in hot, still weather such as I experienced in Florida and along the Southeastern coast. The Solet, almost a whole tent of net, proved too drafty for me in cool weather and, for the first time during the whole trip, I had the early signs of a head cold. When I was younger, I had laughed at old ladies who complained about drafts, but I didn't laugh anymore.

I phoned and arranged a visit with Sue Haffey, whom I had met at GEAR in Buffalo and seen again at GEAR on Long Island. She drove to a stop at my tent with other bicyclists whom she introduced as Raleigh Spinks, Irwin Lauv, and Suzanne Toomey.

Suzanne brought her new Cannondale bicycle, her tent, and gear so that she could ride and camp with me the following day and night before returning to Buffalo. This evening, Sue would drive us to the Riverview Inn at Lewiston where we would meet Marlene McCumber, one of our leaders on the Erie Canal trip. Not expecting a banquet, I was overwhelmed and delighted.

We helped Suzanne set up her tent, locked the bicycles, and piled into Sue's car. At a vegetable stand, we bought cantaloupes for breakfast, and we left to take a quick look at Fort Niagara.

We met Marlene and took our seats at the restaurant. High on a bluff overlooking the Niagara River, we chatted about bicycling and mutual friends and acquaintances. All of them wanted to share my trip. Any one of them could have done the bicycling better than I. The banquet celebrated the mental beginning and completion of my journey, because Buffalo had been my first choice for a starting point. Bea's prepaid bicycle tour of England had delayed the start of our tour. To beat Rocky Mountain snow, we moved our starting point to Detroit.

Four Mile Creek State Park, Wednesday, August 26

Suzanne and I became further acquainted during breakfast as we spooned out vine-ripened melon and discussed the route. The cantaloupes, too heavy to carry, were a treat.

"The Canadian side is a much nicer ride — less congested, better views," Suzanne advised.

I rode the American side three times last year during GEAR, and, since the river is the border, both routes parallel the river. But I would not take the short cut to Detroit through Canada.

As Suzanne folded up a luxuriously large towel, I asked her about it. Mine was a one-by-two-foot cotton and nylon Turkish weave which dried fast.

"It's just baby diaper material. The weave that makes it absorbent also makes it dry fast," she explained. "It's big enough to wrap up in and no heavier than your towel. Cotton dish towels are good, too, but awfully small, or you could use a long, thin roller-towel that's supposed to go in a machine."

The sun was fully up now, but the sky was overcast. Suzanne guided me right down Main Street through the city of Niagara Falls, across the Rainbow Bridge, and along the river on the Canadian side. We stopped at her favorite spot for breakfast, Beachwater Place Coffee Shop. It was a grand meal, with Norma, one of the owners, and several others making a fuss over us. Suzanne made a trip alone from New England to Buffalo the year before and bicycled down the Pacific Coast in California.

The American side of the river is cluttered with industry and rail yards, but on the Canadian side, a narrow park parallels the road along the river almost the whole way to Buffalo. The park was resplendent with groomed grass and flowers. Canada, with no bottle, law was among the cleanest places of the whole trip. We enjoyed the calla lilies, geraniums, impatiens, and marigolds planted in patterns along the park and in private yards. We rode over the Peace Bridge into Buffalo, past grain silos. "General Mills — where they make Cheerios," Suzanne said, "and that's Pillsbury." We pedaled along and over the rail yards, avoiding the Skyway Bridge. Suzanne described it, saying, "It's so windy that one man who was repairing a flat tire was blown off."

It was curious to ride with another person again. The relaxation in following someone who knew the route surprised me. I hadn't realized how much energy I'd expended pathfinding. I was grateful to have a guide. We pedaled through swarms of gnats and arrived at the Botanical Gardens at Lackawanna, where we stopped for a brief rest and talked to an old man who said he pedaled his three-speed bicycle twenty miles a day. As we were leaving, a garden employee stopped us to talk. She was an aunt of Pete Penseyres, who won the Race Across America on a single bike and with Lon Haldeman on a tandem. She and the man waved us on as we pedaled away.

We were reveling in a social day a-wheel, talking with each other and with people along the way. When mist changed to intermittent rain, we concentrated on getting to Evangola State Park. Suzanne led me along roads I never would have found using my maps.

Not wishing to cook in the rain, we stopped three miles short of the state park for spaghetti at Captain Kidd's Restaurant. After ordering, we disappeared into the restroom to replace our wet shirts with dry, warm clothes. It rained hard while we ate but was only misting when we were ready to leave. Deciding not to risk our last dry clothes, we changed again into clammy, cold shirts, taking a long time to get ready. We weren't eager to depart for an evening of camping in the rain. Finally, we got on our bikes and began bumping around puddles in the parking lot.

In the town park across the road, I spotted three-sided wooden shelters. "One of those would make a nicer umbrella for our tents than anything the state park is likely to have. What do you think?" I asked Suzanne.

She summarized a sign. "It closes at ten p.m. and is for town residents only," she replied. I had read the sign, too. I asked, "Is your tent self-supporting or do you anchor it in the ground?"

"Self-supporting."

"Are you willing to spend five minutes on a few questions? You've been to the state park, would this be better?"

"Much better — let's try. They couldn't say anything worse than no."

We went to the entrance to plead with two people on duty. We explained our journey and our plight, suggesting that, in such weather, we wouldn't interfere with townspeople using the park. We hoped to put our tents inside one of their shelters, just for the night. They agreed to admit us.

We were warm and comfortable under the shelter. Even with our tents up, we had space to walk around — dry. There were no showers, but the restroom wash basin spewed hot water as well as cold. Settled in for the evening, we cleaned and prepared our bikes and swapped travel stories. When we tired of sitting, we reclined in our tents and sleeping bags and continued yarning in the dark.

Evans, Thursday, August 27

Since it was still raining, we were in no great hurry to get up. After our hot Ovaltine helped us get moving, we discovered the park snack bar had opened as usual but was closing soon because of the weather. We ran through the rain for hot tea and doughnuts. By nine o'clock, we were packed, and the rain had stopped.

At the Evans Town Park gate, we paused and stood over our bicycles before going in opposite directions. I hated to see Suzanne head home, particularly with the rain. As we put our feet to the pedals, she said, "You'll be riding out of it. We get our weather from the west, you know."

All day under a cloudy sky with Lake Erie and the goldfinches and vineyards for company, I remembered the friendliness of the Buffalo bicyclists and kept my feet turning effortlessly. I felt I had five extra pairs of feet. I put seventy-five miles under my wheels before I stopped at a motel on the west side of Erie for a hot shower and a dry bed during another night of rain. The motel owner brought me two peaches from his tree and a couple of tomatoes.

Erie, Pennsylvania, Friday, August 28

Just as I opened the door, rain descended again. Twice, I wheeled the bike outside under the overhang, then came back. By the time I got going, I had a misty view of orchards, vineyards, goldfinches, mourning doves, and roadside fruit stands in Ohio. I brunched at the Bakery in Conneaut, Ohio, and bumped along miles of road without a shoulder. A state trooper invited me to leave a freeway after twelve miles of smooth, graded shoulder. By midafternoon, light steady rain replaced the mist.

Rain continued for the three hours it took me to struggle through Cleveland at rush hour. The streets were slick and full of people. Umbrellas blew backwards, and cars and busses splashed me while I tried to distinguish puddles from potholes. When I rode by, I looked longingly at the Cleveland Museum — I didn't dare enter dripping wet.

I'd been assisted much of the afternoon by a slight tailwind, had stopped for more traffic lights than during the rest of my journey, and pedaled through water running toward Lake Erie. By the time I reached the west side of Cleveland, after one-hundred-eleven miles, I wasn't sure whether I'd ridden along Lake Erie or through it! "I'm hungry too," I moaned. Just then, I saw the bright lights of a Pepperidge Farm Outlet and stopped.

I stuck my head in the door. "Will you let me in? I'm awfully wet."

"Sure," the woman laughed. I could only carry and keep dry a few packages of Irish oatmeal cookies. The assistant manager told me where to find the nearest motel, and I arrived just before dark.

That night I asked for a rag from the motel clerk and cleaned the bike. I'd also cooked the chain, lighting the stove on the shower stall floor. It was raining again when, unable to find a phone elsewhere, I squished into the lobby of a nearby inn. In dripping bicycle clothes, with wet hair, I stood making calls while dressed-up people walked past me to a wedding reception in the next room.

Westlake, Ohio, Saturday, August 29

A look outside about five-thirty a.m. revealed a cloudy but dry morning. About eight o'clock, I pushed the bike outside into a sunny, warm day. Yesterday's landscape contained apple, peach, pear, and plum orchards separated by fruit stands. At one, there was no one to take my money. I left a dime and the banana skin on the table.

Now, I pedaled past fields of corn and Blue Lake string beans until I reached Milan where a side street led me to the small brick house where Thomas A. Edison was born. Once a prosperous inland shipping center, the town had fewer than two thousand people. I found it a vibrant, interesting place built around a square.

The Milan Historical Museum boasts the sixth-largest collection of fine glass in our nation, reposing on well-lit shelves. There were over fifteen hundred pieces, including a whole case of Sandwich glass. The museum also contained guns, dolls and doll houses, shoes, clothes, hats, a store, and a blacksmith shop. A vacuum cleaner that pre-dated electricity caught my eye. As it rolled, suction was created by a series of wheels and belts. A ladder resembling a pole when folded stood open to show carefully-carved rungs. Said to be an invention of Thomas Jefferson, the pole ladder was used on ships and by chimney sweeps in Europe. I returned to the town square for lunch at The Invention, a splendid family restaurant.

Ohio is a tidy state: in the afternoon I passed a farmer riding his lawn mower up and down the road beside his fields; the right-of-way grass looked like his front lawn. I adored riding beside orderly corn fields where the dried stalks rustled and crackled in the wind.

I passed a house where about ten boys were sitting on a front porch. One of them said, "Ah ha! A voyager!" He began to clap, and then they all clapped as I waved and continued pedaling.

In Clyde, I wandered through the Mad River Nickel Plate Railroad Society Museum. I walked through the Silver Dome passenger coach like the one I'd ridden to college, the diner, the caboose, and two engines. There was another coach like the one my mother and I had ridden home from my first trip to New York City where we left my dad, who boarded a troop ship for war in Europe. In freight cars transformed into mini-museums, I found a program and photographs of The American Freedom Train Spirit of 1776-1976 that my college friend, Joanne Noreen, helped create. I paused over old telegraphs, ticket stamps, oil cans, flags, and tools.

Sightseeing fatigue, unwilling legs, and a slight head-wind dampened my zeal early that afternoon and sent me into a motel after sixty-two miles.

Clyde, Sunday, August 30

In the morning, I was blessed with a clear sunny sky and a light tailwind. If it held all day and increased, the tailwind could give me ten effortless miles during the day. It might be possible to catch a plane home today! I folded the map and took to the pedals to see how soon I could reach Toledo. Since it was Sunday, I sped along roads that would have been clogged by commuters on a weekday.

After a McDonald's breakfast, the tailwind was holding! Over a bridge and into Toledo, an All-American City, winds and exuberance carried me. The pavement on Route 51 was six lanes wide — new, smooth, and free of cars. Cherry Street led me to Route 24 where, forty-six miles into my day, I crossed the state line.

"Whoopee! I'm in Michigan again!" I shouted to no one. The wind shoved more insistently on my left elbow. A few miles further, I entered a highway police station and requested a map showing detail near the airport. The officer on duty estimated the airport was sixty miles away, but my calculations from the map indicated thirty or forty miles, which I could cover before sunset. I continued rolling at seventeen to nineteen miles an hour. Cornstalks stood like sentinels on both sides of the road.

After buying a couple of bananas, I called *The Detroit News*. The operator had never heard of the person I asked for, and connected me with the news desk. I explained from the beginning who I was and what I was doing, and inquired whether they wanted the story when I arrived at the airport two hours hence. I was told to call again from the airport, and a photographer would be sent. Three days later, I realized I originally called the other Detroit newspaper. I copied the phone numbers on a scrap of paper a few days before, hoping to record my finish in a photograph for my mother. It was the first and only time I took the initiative to get publicity.

When my route crossed Monroe Pike, I paused to rest and read the historical marker. From Monroe, pioneer families traveled by covered wagons over the Monroe Pike and the Chicago Pike. When stagecoach routes began in 1826, taverns were built along the road to shelter the growing number of travelers.

As I got closer to the Wayne County Detroit Metropolitan Airport, the tailwind blew me forward, and my feet whirred of their own accord. The distant whiff of kerosene fueled my progress as planes passed closer and closer overhead. At two-twenty-nine, I rolled right into the terminal building.

Susan Tusa, a photographer from *The Detroit News*, took me out of the ticket line to capture the grandest smile ever seen on my face. A baggage handler came to get my bike and rolled it away. A ticket was thrust into my hand, and I ran toward the plane to claim a seat. On board, we waited almost an hour for thirty passengers from Japan. I breathed a big sigh and unwound enough to realize how hungry I was. Returning to the terminal, I found a sandwich and phoned Linda Bell, who offered to meet the Northwest Airlines flight which would carry me home to Washington.

EPILOGUE

I stepped out on my porch, inhaled the fresh air and looked up a crystal sky, unusual for Washington, D.C. The air was unseasonably cool, more like October than the last day of June. Restless, I decided to pedal down a bike path along the Potomac River. The path led me through Old Town Alexandria where the aroma of baking bread drew me to a halt.

I leaned my bike against a ramp to the deck outside a deli-bakery. A woman and a boy came out, sat down on a bench, and shared a sandwich made of the rolls I'd smelled baking. I drank a soft drink, dropped the can in a trash bin, glanced at the sandwich the woman almost had finished, and headed toward my bike.

As I walked down the ramp, they followed a few steps behind, and the woman said pleasantly, "Excuse me, could I have seen you in Montana?"

"When?" I replied absently, knowing she could have.

"I've been watching you, and I feel sure I saw you pedaling up the mountain road in Glacier National Park."

"Yes, I did that once," I said.

"It was quite a while ago. You were riding up the mountain with another woman. We passed you in a car — I remember because we waved, yelled, and acted silly. I just couldn't believe a woman about my size was really riding a bicycle up that mountain. When I got home and was still wondering who you were, I even told my son here about you. It *was* you wasn't it?"

Smiling, I asked, "Could it have been in August, almost two years ago?" I knew she was right, but I didn't remember seeing her, though I hoped to meet some of the people who had waved and encouraged me. My smile grew bigger and bigger. My wish had come true. All three of us stood smiling at each other in the parking lot, my wish and hers confronting each other.

Finally, I asked, "May I please have your name and address? I like to collect them from people I met on the trip."

Norma de Freitas lives in Alexandria. Two years ago, she was on a business trip as a conference coordinator when she and her colleagues had passed me in their car.

"It was a wonderful place on top of the Going-to-the-Sun Road, wasn't it?" she asked.

"Yes — a day like this. I spent a lot of time up there."

"I think it's marvelous that you could ride a bicycle on that road. My house isn't far from here. Please come and have a cup of tea next time you ride this way."

"I will, thank you."

They watched and waved as I mounted my bike and headed for home.

APPENDIX

Information about organizations mentioned in *Changing Gears*

League of American Wheelmen (LAW)
6707 Whitestone Road, Suite 209
Baltimore, MD 21207
(301) 944-3399
Executive Director: John Cornelison

A national organization of bicyclist volunteers that sponsors advocacy, educational, and recreational programs. Members receive a comprehensive annual directory *(Bicycle USA Almanac)* of bicycle clubs and activities and the magazine *Bicycle USA*. LAW sponsors a number of gatherings and rides, including the Pedal for Power tours that raise money for charity. For information on Pedal for Power, call 1-800-762-BIKE.

Bikecentennial
P.O. Box 8308
Missoula, MT 59807
(406) 721-1776
Executive Director: Gary McFadden

Organization that sells maps and bicycle touring information. Publishes the magazine *Bike Report* and the annual *Cyclists' Yellow Pages*. Bikecentennial trains tour directors, runs tours, and makes maps for bicyclists.

Race Across America (RAAM) is the longest non-stop bicycle race in the world. Its sanctioning organization is:
Ultra-Marathon Cycling Association (UMCA)
4790 Irvine Blvd. #105-111
Irvine, CA 92720
(714) 544-1701

RAAM founders: John Marino, Michael Shermer, Lon Haldeman

Women's Cycling Network
P.O. Box 73
Harvard, IL 60033
Executive Director: Susan Notorangelo

Promotes women's participation in the cycling sport and industry.

Many organizations and publications are listed in *The Woman Cyclist* by Elaine Mariolle and Michael Shermer, published by Contemporary Books, Chicago, IL.

INDEX

Abrams, Gene 162
Abrahamson, Gloria 50, 51
Adobe 245
Alabama
  Bayou La Batre 302
  Dauphin Island 303
  Grand Bay 302
  Gulf Shores 303
Albeni Falls Dam 103
Alex 165
Algonquian Indians 22
All American Canal 209
Alma 58
Animals
  antelope 77-78, 238
  bear 36, 83, 89, 111
  beechy ground squirrels 177
  bobcat 262-63
  black-tailed deer 140
  buffalo 18, 72
  cat 280
  caterpillars 339
  cattle 132
  chickens 67
  chipmunks 22, 114, 115
  Columbian ground squirrels 87
  cows 151, 284
  coyotes 113, 141, 247
  deer 38, 67, 116, 251
  dogs 143, 180
  fox 77, 78, 371
  frogs 344
  goat 252
  grasshoppers 58, 62
  harbor seal 153
  horse 210, 248
  javelina 219, 221, 244
  marmots 88
  moose 30
  mountain goat 88
  mule deer 132, 237
  peccary. see javelina
  ponies 66
  prairie dog 234, 237
  rabbit 30, 312, 344
  raccoon 133, 135, 305, 312, 341
  sea lions 152, 176
  sea otters 176, 177
  squirrel 87, 312, 378

  skunk 97
  whale 130, 152
  wood rat 177
  zebra 179
Ankney, Sam 322, 323
Appalachian Trail 376, 377
Appendicitis 182
Apple, eating with dentures 263
Apsley, Carl 369
Apsley, Marion 369
Archer, Vicki 121, 122, 124
Arizona
  Apache 229
  Bisbee 227
  Dateland 212-213
  Douglas 227-29
  Gila Bend 214, 215
  Huachuca City 224
  Organ Pipe 218
  Portal 229-30
  Sierra Vista 225-26
  Sonoita 224
  Tucson 220, 221, 222
  Why 216, 217, 218
  Yuma 210, 211
Armando 247-48
Arthur 363-64
Ashentilly 327
Ashford, John B. 239
Assiniboin Indians 60, 68, 69
Association for Mutual American/
    Soviet Understanding 195
Aston Villa 284

Bagel World, The 352
Bailey, Peggy 305
Baker, Gay 284
Bangor Daily News 374
Barte, Lorraine 365
Barth, Pat 55, 56, 57, 58, 137
Bassett, Fred 148
Bates, Sandi 49
Baty, Lou Ann 148
Bean, Judge Roy Visitors Center 252
Bean, L.L. 365
Bean, Mr. 286
Bear's Den Trading Post
    Truck Stop 383
Bell, Jo 328

Bell, Linda 349, 350-56, 393
Bellingham Barker 160
Ben Gay 62
Benjamin, Edith 343
Benjamin, Dr. Stanley 343
Bernstein, Carl 288
Betty 253
Bicycle USA 105
Bicycle
    Avocet cyclometer 61, 64, 68, 92,
      367
    belt beacon 203, 205-6
    bottom bracket 86, 89
    butyl tube 108
    Cat Eye cyclometer 193
    Centurion 6
    chain 201, 203
    chain rings 203
    derailleur 64
    drafting 40
    Fuji 6
    flat tire 38, 92, 95, 102, 109, 354
    gears 36
    generator 136
    handlebars 70, 86
    helmet 65
    lights 136
    paraffin 9, 64
    panniers 104
    patch kit 109
    presta valve 108
    pump 24, 86
    racing rims 109
    rim tape 108
    stove fuel, for cleaning 64
    Tailwind panniers 77
    tire irons 86, 102
    tires 123, 204, 365, 367
    toe clips 63, 66
    tour questions 123
    weight of 4, 185, 311
    wheels trued 92
Bicycle clothing 77, 91, 145, 370
    glacier glasses 213
    gloves 76, 91
    rain gear 121, 123
    shorts 147, 148
    shoes 38, 63
Bicycling the Pacific Coast 146
Bicycle Ride Across Georgia 333, 351
Bicycle shops

Bikesmith 298
Cascade Sports 136
Clarke's All-Sport Shop 108
Glacier Cycle 93
Spokes and Sprockets 288
Wheels 'n Things 203
World Bicycles 6
Yankee Pedalers 365
Bicyclists
    fatigue 201
    hands 65, 201
    cartoonist 240
Bikecentennial 18, 45, 68, 340, 344
Bingo 51, 54, 265
Binoculars 34
Birds
    acorn woodpecker 180, 205
    American coots 202, 285
    American egret 199
    American oyster catchers 335
    American redstart 24
    American widgeons 202
    anhingas 302
    Anna's humming 166
    Audubon's yellow rumped
      warblers 204, 205
    avocet 199
    barn swallows 380
    barred owl 113
    black and surf scoters 138
    black and white sparrows 230
    black and white warbler 22
    black phoebe 243
    black-bellied whistling ducks 258
    blacked-capped phoebe 246
    black-headed gulls 199
    black-necked stilt 258
    black-throated blue warbler 320
    black-throated sparrows 230
    blue grosbeak 289
    blue-winged teal 270, 292
    Brandt's cormorants 177
    Brewer's blackbirds 205, 258
    bridled titmice 234
    broad-winged hawk 270
    bronzed cowbirds 258
    brown towhees 205
    brown-headed cowbird 258
    cactus wren 217
    Canada geese 24, 41, 292
    canyon wrens 246

cardinals 230, 301, 340
Carolina wrens 302
cedar waxwings 24
cinnamon teal 199
clapper rails 331
Clark's jay 118
cliff swallows 246
cormorants 131, 153
crow 340
ducks 166, 231, 241
egret, great 262
evening grosbeaks 20, 24
gallinules 285
Gambel's quail 219
gila woodpecker 217
glaucous gulls 131
goldfinches 10, 390
great-horned owl 279
grebes 24, 30, 131
great-tailed grackles 243, 258
green jay 270
grey and yellow warblers 230
grey jay 114, 118
grinkos 230
harlequin ducks 150
Harris hawk 270
herons 18, 289, 331, 344
herring gulls 131
house finches 204
Inca dove 270
indigo bunting 289, 302
juncos 113, 114
killdeer 11, 240, 258
kingbirds 10, 289, 302
kinglets 37
kingfisher 263
ladder-backed woodpecker 270
least grebe 270
loon 24, 29, 30, 378
magnolia warblers 30
marsh hawks 199, 279
marsh wrens 345
meadowlarks 97, 230, 279
moorhens 285
murres 177
myrtle warbler 22
northern pintails 199
northern shoveler 270
orchard oriole 293
oriole 302
osprey 41, 302, 331

pelicans 176, 177
phainopepla 219
pigeon 340
pileated woodpecker 323
plain chachalaca 270
purple martins 371
purple finches 22
red-bellied woodpecker 320
red-headed woodpecker 12, 302
red-winged blackbirds 10, 59, 258,
    284, 326
red-tailed hawk 58, 217
roadrunners 232
robins 10, 345
ruddy turnstone 331
ruff-legged hawk 20
sanderlings 279
scarlet tanager 302
scissor-tailed flycatcher 240, 259,
    274, 279
scrub jay 205
sea gulls 177, 279
snow geese 41
snowy egrets 344
sora 270
Steller's jay 113, 143, 201
stilts 199
summer tanagers 289, 292
Swainson's hawk 67
swallows 340
terns 279, 292
titmice 230
tri-color (Louisiana) heron 270
turkey buzzard 244
vermilion flycatcher 243
western bluebirds 204
western grebes 147, 199
whimbrels 331
white-breasted nuthatch 24, 206
white-tailed hawk 262
white-winged and sea scoters 145
white-winged crossbill 380
white-winged scoter 138
whooping cranes 281
widgeons 199
Wilson's warblers 41
yellow-headed blackbirds 41, 59
Birds of North America (Golden) 217,
    257
Bisbee Observer, The 228
Bishop, Maureen 90, 91

Bishop, Russ 90
Blanche, Mattilda 37
Blackberries 145, 323, 383
Blade, Robert 320
Blanton, Muriel 287
Bob's Bargain Barn 220
Boon, Harry 199, 200
Boon, Hunter 200
Boussard, Teddy 291
Bowman, Ben 257-58
Bowman, Bev 257
Brackelsberg, Carolyn 51
Brackelsberg, Marlo 51, 52, 53, 59
Brame, Mary Ann 355
Brendel, Ann 107
Brendel, Frank 107
Brooke, Kevin 60
Brussels sprouts 174
Budget-Rent-a-Car 139, 276
Bullock's Wilshire 198
Bunker, Jim 368
Bunker, Ruth 368
Burke, Annie 364
Burlington Northern Railroad 69
Butler Island Plantation 326

Cafe ritual 76
Cahoon, Susan Quick 365
Cajun 295
Calder, Debbie 368, 370
California
    Albion 166-67
    Aptos 176
    Big Sur 178
    Bodega 169
    Campo 206
    Capitola 176
    Carmel 177, 178
    Claremont 195, 199
    Crescent City 155-57
    Daly City 174
    Del Rio 160
    Dogpatch U.S.A. 206
    El Cajon 202, 204
    El Centro 207, 208
    Elijo Beach 201
    Elk 167
    Eureka 159
    Fort Bragg 166
    Fortuna 159
    Garberville 161-62

Gualala 168
Half Moon Bay 174
Jacumba 207
Jamul 204
Jenner 169
La Jolla 202
Leggett 162
Leggett Hill 164
Leucadia 201
Los Angeles 184, 194, 198
Los Olives 180
Mendocino 166
Montara 174
Monterey 176
Monterey Bay 176
Newport Beach 199-200
Northridge 182-84
Orick 158
Pepperwood 161
Point Arena 167, 168
Point Lobos State Reserve 177
Point Loma 203
Point Sur 178
Potrero 206
San Diego 184, 203
San Francisco 171
San Luis Obispo 179
San Simeon 178, 179
Santa Barbara 180-81, 192
Santa Cruz 174
Santa Maria 179-80
Sausalito 170
Scotia 159
Sea Ranch 169
Seaside 176
Simi 194
Trinidad 158-59
Ventura 193
Westport 164-66
Wydell 206
Camping gear
    bivy sack 207
    fuel bottle 121
    stove fuel 82, 92
    tents
        Eureka Crescent 203, 243, 374
        Moss Solet 374, 375, 382, 384, 386
        Moss Starlet 367, 386
        Sierra Designs Divine Light 322
Whisperlight stove 121, 142
Camp Lejeune Marine Base 340

Camp Pendleton 200
Campgrounds
  Barnes 345
  Bass Lake RV Park 264
  Beaver 108
  Bowman Village 257-59
  Cottonwood 247, 248
  Crazy Horse 218, 222, 223
  Daisy Farm 30
  Double Adobe 227-28
  Evergreens, The 375-76
  Flats 9
  Four Mile State 386, 387
  Goose Island State Recreation Area
    279-80
  Holiday 307
  Homestead 367
  Hoo Doo 37
  Housetop Mountain 251
  Kalaloch 142
  Klipchuck 115-16
  Lake End Park 294-97
  Lake Leo 106, 107
  Lakedale 129
  Lakeside 371
  Loop Loop 113
  Newport Springs 308-9
  Ocean View 350-51
  Outdoor World 206
  Pete Creek 97-100
  Pineland 328
  Pio Pico 204
  Ranch Side Park 381
  Rolla City Park 46
  Roosevelt Lake 109
  Salvo 343
  Sherman Pass 111
  Sprague Creek 90
  Swango Farm 365-66
  Thousand Trails, Pio Pico 204-5
  Wandering Wheels 20
  Wildhurst 35
Canada
  Campobello 369-70
  Sidney 136
  Victoria 136, 137, 139
Candelilla 249
Cannondale bicycle 386
Carel, Bruce and Marion 379
Castillo San Marcos 317
Chamberlain, Joe 88

Chandler, Anne 121, 124
Chandler, Celia 82, 120, 124
Chandler, Jerome 120, 124
Chandler, Paul 121, 124
Chapin General Store 7
Charlie 149
Chavez, Nick 254-55
Chenoweth, Eunice 244-45
Chesapeake Bay Bridge Tunnel
  345-46
Chippewa 41
Cholla 213
Christopher, Fran 355, 362
Christophner, Mo 355, 362
CIA 34, 162, 192, 222, 234, 287-88, 310,
  336, 380
Cindy 247-48
Civilian Conservation Corps 48
Clancy 286, 287, 289
Clatsop Indians 148
Clark, Maggie 355
Clark, Malcolm L. 287
Cliff May house 196
Cobwebs 169
Cochran, Bruce 370-71
Cochran, Joeline 370-71
Cold Springs Deer Farm 38
Colson, Marion 314, 317, 318, 327
Connecticut
  New London 356
  Old Mystic Seaport 356
Continental Divide 231
Coronado National Memorial 227
Cranberries 144, 359
Crankshaw, Ruby 321
Cranmer, Lillie B. 352
Crawfish 291, 297
Crazy Angie's Store 243
Creeks
  Bonaparte 112
  Cutthroat 117
  Early Winters 115
  Julington 314
  McDonald 89
  Sherman 110
  Silver Star 117
Cruz, David 286

Dakota 37
Debault, Debra 289
De Freitas, Norma 394

De Grazias studio 221
Delaware
    Lewes 350
    Lewes Ferry 350
    Millsboro 349
    Milton 349
Delorme, Dave 264
Delorme, Sonia 265
Detroit News, The 392-93
Dietlin, Andy 360
Dirty Shame Saloon 97
Drew 31
Dungeness Bay 138
Durand, Tom 78-80
Durinda Flinn 249, 251

Ebb Tide 128
Eicken, Rose 355
El Paso Bicycle Club 232
Elsie 181, 182-84, 194
Eric 365
Eyre Hall 346

Falconer, Sheila 356, 357
Fehlow family 359
Fiege, Gale 124
Fisher, Rob 354
Fit for Life 278, 281
Flanagan, Mike 346
Flax 45
Florida
    Amelia Island 321, 323
    Apalachicola 306-7
    Bradford 311
    Carrabelle Beach 307
    Coquina Village 304
    Destin 305-6
    Fernandina Beach 321
    Fort White 311
    Ft. George Island 321
    Jacksonville 320-21
    Jax Beach 316
    Lake Butler 312
    Mandarin 314
    Mayo 311
    Mayport 321
    Mexico Beach 306
    Orangedale 314
    Panacea 307
    Panama City 306
    Penny Farms 313

    Perry 310
    Port St. Joe 306
    St. Augustine 319, 320
    Starke 313
    Tyndall Air Force Base 306
    Wakulla Springs 308
    Wesley Manor 314-20
Floyd in Conway 122
Floyd, Jack 150
Folsom, Babs 354
Folsom, Sam 354
Fort Columbia 145
Fort Mackinac 15
Fort Niagara 387
Fort Pulaski National Monument 333
Fort Wilkins 28
Fort Williams 364
Fowler, Sheila 319
Fox, Annamarie 267
Fox, Ray 267, 268
Frank 298
Fredrickson, Angie 37
Frozfruit 339, 343
Fuji film 267

Gadsden Hotel 228-29
Gage Hotel 251
Gagnon, Cindy 385
Gaines, Courtney 329, 330-31, 333
Gallery in the Sun 221
Garcia, Beth 242, 245
Gardner, Jack 131, 132, 134, 136
Gardner, Jane 134, 136
GEAR (sponsored by LAW) 5, 355-56
Georgia
    Brunswick 326
    Crescent 328
    Darien 326
    Eulonia 328
    Hog Hammock 331
    Midway 330
    Riceboro 330
    Richmond Hill 330
    Ridgeville 328
    Sapelo Island 331-32
    Savannah 330-33
    South Newport 329
    Woodbine 323, 326
General Mills 388
Georgia-Pacific 166
Geronimo 229, 230

Gerow, Phil 374
Gingerbread Bakery 377
Girl Scouts National Center 332
Going-to-the-Sun Road 75, 81, 84, 394
Golden Gate Bridge 170
Golden Nugget 351
Goldman, Carl 8
Goldman, Mary 8
Goldsborough, Robert 346-47
Gomez, Elizabeth 274, 275
Gonzales, Cynthia 274, 275
Gonzales-Alvarez House 316
Goodwin, Joel 343
Goodwin, Wendy 343
Greenhouse, Solar Prism 161
Griffin, Norwood 121
Grouch, Official 110
Guerin, Eleanor 86, 87
Grumdahl, Marion 263
Grumdahl, Olaf 263
Gwen's Shop 161

Haffey, Sue 355, 386-87
Haldeman, Lon 363, 388
Halt 143, 260, 267
Hamlin, Frances 374, 379
Hamlin, Georgia 374-75, 379
Handi-Dogs, Inc. 221
Hang glider 174
Harding, Talbort 327
Harland, Bob 342
Harper, Susan 190
Hart, Lois M. 366
Hartman, Floyd 6, 351, 355, 356
Harvey, Roy 319
Hathaway, Jane 129
Hebert, Harold 295
Hebert, Joyce 295
Herrero, Stephen 83
Hi-Line Road 78, 79
Hilmes, Jan 99, 100
Hoffpauer, Clark Sr. 292
Hofwyl-Broadfield Historic Site
        Plantation 326, 332
Holcomb, Jerry 315
Holcomb, Noel 332
Holly 354
Holt, Lil 298, 300
Horne, Bill 238, 241
Hot Bagel Shop 355
Howard, Christine 360

Howard, Elizabeth 200
Howard, Lee 166
Howard, Virginia, 166
Huckleberries 99, 100
Huking, Ruth 362
Hull, Dottie 55, 56, 57, 58, 137, 227,
        228
Hull, Hank 55, 56, 57, 58, 137, 227, 228
Huntington Desert Garden 196
Huntington Library 196

Idaho
    Priest River 102, 103
    Sandpoint 102
Indian reservations
    Blackfeet 78
    Fort Peck 68
    L'Anse 25
    Mohawk 383
    Turtle Mountain 47
International House of Pancakes 320
International Peace Garden 47-48
Ipswich River Wildlife Sanctuary
        360-61
Ironwood 218
Iroquois Indians 384

Jackie 290
Jackson, Sally 363
Jacobsen, Joel 104
Jam Lady 27
Johns, Bobby 37
Johnson Family 82, 85
Johnson, Pat & Bill 49
Johnson, Paul 161
Johnson, Worth and Walter 28
Johnson's Bayou Store 290
Jojoba 197, 218
Joseph's Italian Bakery 362

Kauczka, Slim 20, 355
Keith, Bland 358
Keith, Hazel 358
Kelly, Al 355, 362
Ketchum, Larry 228
Keweenaw Peninsula 25
Kirkendall, Tom 146
Kootenai National Forest 95
Krauske, Jerry 340
Krauske, Linda 340
Kummholz 87

LAW. *see* League of American
    Wheelmen
Laguna Atacosta National Wildlife
    Refuge 274
Lakes
    alkali 61
    Amistad 255
    Cachuma 180
    Cascade 132
    Champlain 381
    Cupsuptic 378
    Diablo 119
    Erie 389, 390
    Hidden 88
    Higgins 10
    Houghton 10
    Huron 13
    Koocanusa 94
    Leo 107
    McDonald 91
    Michigan 13
    North Manistique 19
    Ontario 384, 385
    Otay 205
    Roosevelt 110
    Ross 118
    Sanford 9
    Schoodic 375
    St. Mary 86-7
    Superior 27, 29
    Three 23
    Vermilion 37
    Whitefish 93
    Woods, Lake of the 41, 43
Lauv, Irwin 386
League of American Wheelmen 105
Leeper, Arthur 171, 172, 173
Leeper, Cynthia 171, 172, 173
Lee's Highway Service Station 61
Leech, Janet 24
Leech, Ronnie 25
Levesque family 243
Lewis and Clark Expedition 70,
    103, 145
Lillian London Bakery 357
Lindgren, Axel 158
Linebough, David 245-47
Liz 342
Loners on Wheels 55, 57
Long Trail 380

Louisiana
    Abbeville 293
    Avery Island 294
    Boutte 298
    Cameron 290
    Creole 290
    Franklin 294
    Garden City 294
    Grand Chenier 292
    Gretna 298
    Johnson's Bayou 290
    Morgan City 294, 296-297
    New Iberia 294
    New Orleans 289-300
    Oak Grove 290, 292
    Pecan Island 292
    Raceland 297
    Tribodaux 297
    Westwego 298
Luke family 294

Maine
    Bath 365
    Belfast 367
    Bingham 375
    Calais 370
    Camden 367
    Cape Cottage 363-65
    Dover-Foxcroft 375
    Eastport 370
    Ellsworth 367
    Freeport 365
    Gouldsboro 369
    Howland 374
    Jonesboro 369
    Kingfield 376
    Kingsbury Pond 375
    Kittery 362
    Lagrange 374
    Lake View 374
    Lincoln 371, 374
    Lubeck 369
    Milo 370, 374
    Milton Mills 362
    Mt. Desert Island 368
    Oquossoc 377
    Perry 370
    Pleasant Island 378
    Portland 364
    Princeton 370, 371
    Rangeley 376, 377

Searsport 367
Solon 375, 376
Stratton 377
Topsfield 371
Trenton 368
Wiscassett 366
York Beach 363
Mandarin News 318
Marion Springs Country Store 8
Mark Slann 247
Martin, Gil 371
Maryland
   Annapolis 349
   Baltimore 235
   Stockton 348
Massachusetts
   Boston 360
   Bumpkin Island 360
   Cape Cod Canal 359
   Falmouth 358, 359
   Haverhill 362
   Lynn 360
   Martha's Vineyard 358
   New Bedford 357
   Plymouth 359-60
   Salem 360
   Topsfield 360-62
   Woods Hole 358
   World's End 360
McCullough, Betty 335
McCullough, Bill 333, 335, 337
McCullough, Francis 335
McCullough, Sarah 335
McCumber, Marlene 387
McDonald, Dot 241
McDonald, John 241
McDonald's 392
McFarlin, Karen 60
McGary, Kay 328-29
McIntosh, Joan 174, 175, 176, 186, 202,
   204-5, 207
McIntosh, Mac 174, 175, 176, 186, 292,
   204-5, 207
McRantalr, Lois 254
Mesick, Charlotte 218, 220
Mildred 182, 183
Melby, Herb 31, 33
Menominee Indians 22
Miami Indians 22
Michigan

Ann Arbor 5
Baraga 25
Beaverton 9
Boyne City 12
Brevort 18
Calumet 26
Champion 22-23
Cliff 27
Copper Harbor 28
Curtis 18
Detroit 2-4, 393
Eagle Harbor 27
Epoufette 18
Gaylord 10-11
Gladwin 9
Good Hart 13
Gould City 18
Harbor Springs 13
Harvey 21
Helmer 18, 19
L'Anse 24
Mackinac Island 15
Mackinaw City 13
Marquette 21
McMillan 19
Mohawk 26
Monroe 393
Moran 17
Naubinway 18
Owosso 7
Petroskey 12
Phoenix 27
Prudenville 10
Rock Harbor 29
Sanford Lake 9
Seney 20
Skeels 9
St. Ignace 14, 17
Vanderbilt 11
Wayne County Detroit
   Metropolitan Airport 2, 393
Wetmore 20
Whitmore Lake 5, 6
Mihelcich, Florence 27
Minnesota
   Baudette 40
   Ely 36
   Finland 35
   Finland State Forest 36
   Grand Portage 31, 33
   Greenbush 43

Hallock 43
Hat Point 31
International Falls 39
Isabella 36
Lake Bronson 43
Lutsen 34
Northwest Angle 42
Old Vermilion Trail 37
Orr 38
Schroeder 34
Tofte 34
Tower 37
Warroad 40, 42, 43
Winston City 37
Minor, Barbara 132-36, 137
Minor, Mike 132-36, 137
Mischiganong 22
Mississippi
  Biloxi 301
  Gulfport 301
Moffet, Don 355
Montana
  Apgar 90
  Brockton 68
  Browning 79
  Chester 76-77
  Columbia Falls 92
  Culbertson 67
  Cut Bank 78-79
  Eureka 94
  Frazer 70
  Glasgow 71-73
  Harlem 75
  Havre 76
  Hinsdale 73
  Hungry Horse 92
  Inverness 79
  Logan Pass 88
  Malta 74-75
  Medicine Lake 66
  Nashua 70
  Plentywood 62-66
  Poplar 69
  Rexford 94-5
  Saco 73
  Shelby 78
  St. Mary 78, 80-83, 85
  Sylvanite 100
  West Glacier 92
  Westby 61
  Whitefish 92-4

Wolf Point 69-70
Yaak 97
Montana Magazine 81, 83
Monterey cypress 177
Moore, Bud 122
Moore, Fran 358
Moss Tent Outlet 366
Motels
  Albion River Inn 166
  Alexander 38
  Balia Inn 239
  Baudette 40
  Brockway Inn 28
  Downtowner 99
  Exxon Station 252
  Fawn 10
  International Falls Motor
    Lodge 39
  Johnson's Red Eagle 80
  Klondike 112
  Lakes 5
  Mann's 75
  Motel 6
    Brownsville 271
    Clute 282-83
    Corpus Christi 277
    Del Rio 255
    Deming 231
    Douglas 227
    El Paso 232
    McAllen 269
    Santa Maria 179
    Simi 194
    Wilmington 339
  MX 77
  Newport 152
  Okanogan 112
  Plains 63
  Portal 229
  R&R 76
  Raymondville Motor Inn 275
  Rustic Lodge 70
  Sea View 178
  Sherman Motor Inn 69
  Smuggler's Inn 141
  Sundowner 138
  Thunderbird 239
  Voyageur Marina 31
  Welcome Inn 7
  Western 225
  Westport Inn and Bakery 165

Mountains
  Ajo 217
  Bear Claw 76
  Cascades 114
  Huachuca 226, 227
  Liberty Bell 116
  Mule 226
  Needles 117
  Olympic 138
  Rocky 80, 85
  Santa Lucia 178
  Sawtooth 34
  Silver Star 116
  Sugarloaf 376
  Turtle 47
Museums
  Arizona-Sonora Desert 221
  Cochise County Historical 228
  Desert 219, 222
  in Plentywood 65
  Indian Arts and Crafts 69
  Koochiching County 39
  Lajitas 244-45
  Los Angeles County 198
  Mad River Nickel Plate Railroad
    Society 391
  Maine Maritime 365
  Makah 141
  Midway 330
  Milan Historical 391
  Pima Air 220
  Pioneer 71-73
  Provincial (Canada) 136
  Seattle Science Center 125
  Seafood Industry 301
  Stonehill 385
  Tar Pits 198
  Wells Fargo 172
  Whale 129, 130
  Whaling 357
  Wolf Point 70
Musical glasses 330
Myrtlewood 154

Nash, Doris 352
National Parks
  Big Bend 247-50
  Glacier 80-81, 85-87, 394
  Isle Royale 28-31
  Olympic 140
  Voyageurs 38

NEAR (New England Area
    Rally) 355, 362
New Hampshire
  Colebrook 379
  Dixville Notch 379
  Durham 362-63
  Errol 379
  Exeter 362
New Hope Plantation 326
New Jersey
  Atlantic City 351
  Barnegat 352
  Gordon's Corner 352
  Howell 352
  Ocean View 350-51
  Perth Amboy 353
New Mexico
  Anthony 232
  Berino 232
  Deming 231-32
  East Deming 232
  Las Cruces 232
  Lordsburg 231
  Mesilla 232
  Road Forks 230
  Rodeo 229
  Vado 232
New York
  Brooklyn 355
  Buffalo 388
  Ellenburg 383
  Evans 389
  Greenport 356
  Lackawanna 388
  Lewiston 387
  Manhattan 353
  New York 353-54
  Niagara Falls 388
  Oswego 385
  Philadelphia 384
  Phillips Corner 384
  Sag Harbor 355
  Shelter Island 356
  Spencerport 385, 386
  St. Lawrence Seaway 384
  Staten Island 353
  Stony Brook 355
  Syosset 355
Nicholson, Bruce 342
Norbert, Julie 356
Noreen, Joanne 392

Norma 388
Norman, Arlan 49
Norman, Diane 49
North Carolina
    Avon 343
    Beaufort 341
    Currituck 344
    Holly Ridge 340
    Knotts Island 345
    Morehead City 341
    Okracoke Island 342
    Outer Banks 343-44
    Salvo 343
    Sealevel 342
    Wilmington 339
North Dakota
    Belcourt 47
    Bottineau 49
    Bowbells 54, 58
    Cavalier 44
    Clyde 45
    Columbus 58
    Crosby 59-60
    Dunseith 49
    Fortuna 61
    Langdon 44, 45
    Mohall 50
    Rock Lake 45
    Rolla 46
Notorangelo, Susan 363

Oaklawn Manor 294
Oaks family 307
Ocotillo 213
Ohio
    Cleveland 390
    Clyde 391, 392
    Conneaut 390
    Milan 391
    Toledo 392
    Westlake 391
Ojibwa Indians 34
Olsen, Gary 34
Oregon
    Arch Cape 150
    Astoria 146
    Boiler Bay 152
    Brandon 153
    Coos Bay 153
    Florence 152
    Gardiner 153

Gold Beach 154
Lincoln City 151
Manzanita 150
Newport 152
Port Orford 154
Seaside 147-49
Tillamook 150
Organ Pipe Cactus National
    Monument 217
Oregon Trail 45
Ottawa Indians 22
Otter Lake Conservation School 86

Pacific Crest Trail 117
Pacific Lumber Company 159, 161
Page and Palette, Inc. 304
Palo-verde 217
Paper Clip, The 226
Parker, Mary Lou 232-33, 235
Parkers 235-36
Paul 242
Peacock, David 347, 348
Peacock, Mary 345, 347, 348
Pedalgrams 203, 226, 299, 305, 316,
    319, 355, 360, 364, 368, 369
Pennsylvania, Erie 390
Penseyres, Pete's aunt 388
Pepperidge Farm Outlet 390
Performance cycling shoes 63
Perry, Bill 375, 376
Peters, Jean 97, 98
Peters, Jim 98
Peterson, Axel 35
Peterson, Joyce 35
Pham family 200, 281
Piampiano family 377-78, 379
Pig War 129
Pillsbury 388
Plank Road 209
Potawatomi Indians 22
Poulos, Marilyn 357
Price, Angie 243-44
Proctor, Chris 350-51
Pull Tabs 51, 54

RAAM 22, 363, 388
Rainey, Don 283
Randolph-Macon Woman's
    College 221
Reaves, Bitsy 221
Reddy, Carol 37

Redwoods 157-58
REI 121
Restaurants
    Albion River Inn 166
    Archies 327
    A&W 21
    Bakkes Chat and Chew 59, 60, 61
    Bamboo 322
    Beachwater Place Coffee Shop 388
    Border Cowboy Truck Stop 231
    Buffalo Cafe 93
    Cajun Crawfish House 293
    Calico Cupboard Bakery and
        Cafe 122
    Captain Kidd's 388
    Captain's Mate, The 368
    Cats Incredible Cafe 176
    Cedar River Seafood and Oyster
        Bar 318
    City Cafe 281
    Coffee Mug, The 147, 149
    Common Sense 380
    Community Coffee Shop 46
    Cotton Exchange 335
    Cove, The 176
    Dairy Freeze 264
    Dairy Queen 74
    Debbies Donut 159
    Deb's Diner 75
    Denny's 155
    Donut Shop, The 137
    Double D 73
    Duck Brand 114
    Downrigger's 128
    Eat'n Station 154
    Eel River Cafe 162
    Egghead Omelettes 166
    Ferro's 345
    Gourmet Bakery 225, 226
    Hilltop 24
    Hungry Hutch 159
    Hut, The 10
    Imperial China 210
    Irene's Pizza 24
    Isabella 36
    John's Family 26
    Johnson's 82
    Juleps 261
    Lakeside 374
    Mary's Cafe 256
    Mike's 341
    Moby Dick 181
    Nettelon's 22
    Nick and Helen's Bar 45
    North 40 47, 75
    Northern Lights 14, 17
    North River 344
    Oaks, The 307
    Oasis 252
    Olga 134
    Outpost Cafe 106
    Paragon Cafe 53
    Portal Cafe 229
    Post Cafe 80
    Ranch House 39
    Red's Donut Shop 176
    Red's Family 144
    Reed's Landing 43
    Riverview Inn 387
    Rolland's 283
    Rustic Inn 108
    Saguaro Corners 221
    Sartin's Seafood 288
    Sawtooth Cafe 113
    Smithy's Pancake House 139
    Steamboat 311
    Steffen's 323
    Stockman's Cafe 70
    Tanque Verde Ranch 221
    Tower Cafe 38
    Wild West Diner 67
    Woodsman 376
    Yakitori II 203
Reynolds, Dr. Bill 233
Reyno's Food Store 280
Rhea, Ann 298
Rhea, Wendy 298-99
Rhode Island, Saunderstown 357
Riordan, John J. 19
Rivers
    Albion 167
    Altamaha 326
    Bayou Teche 294
    Big Muddy 67
    Butler 326
    Carmel 178
    Colorado 209
    Columbia 103, 145-46, 110
    Connecticut 379
    Eel 161, 162
    Gualala 168
    Hudson 354

Ipswich 361
Kalamath 158
Kennebec 365-66, 376
Milk 73
Missisquoi 380
Mississippi 60, 292, 297, 298
Missouri 60, 67, 69
Mohawk 379
Mouse 53
Niagara 387
Okanogan 112
Pearl 300
Pend Oreille 102, 105, 106
Potomac 394
Rainy 39
Red 41,44
Rio Grande 232, 239, 257
Rogue 154
Roseau 41, 44
San Diego 202
Santa Ana 199
Savannah 333
Skagit 119
St. Croix 370
St. Johns 313, 321
St. Lawrence 15
St. Mark's 308
St. Marys 323
Suwannee 310
Tobacco 94
Vermilion 293
Yaak 101
Robinson, Barb 27
Robinson, Ken 27
Rockefeller Wildlife Refuge 292-93
Rochette, Joyce 300
Rogers, John 295
Rogers, Yola 295
Rogger, Hans 195-96
Roosevelt Cottage 370
Rowlett, Dot 301, 314-16
Roycroft, Mike 338, 339
Roycroft, Susan 339
Ruoff, David 300
Russell, Margaret 137
Roosevelt County Fair 67

Sag 20, 202
Salmon 151, 161, 384
Sally 155
Samarkand 180-81

Samson, Julia 22
Santa Ana National Wildlife
   Refuge 270
Saunders, Peggy 318
San Fernando Mission 184
Save-the-Redwoods League 161
Schenkel, Andrew 367
Schnell, Frank 307
Schnell, Katie 183
Schwinn 77
Sea Lion Caves 152
Seaside Signal's Senior Magazine 148
Seattle World's Fair Center 121
Shaw, Don 140
Shaw, Dorothy 173, 185, 202, 204
Shaw, Ellen 245, 246
Shaw, Homer 173, 174, 185, 202, 204
Shaw, Janet 173
Shaw, John 245, 246
Shaw, John 173
Shepard, William J. 337
Sheridan, Alan 263
Sheridan, Jean 263
Shine, Sue 316-17, 319-20
Shreve, Mack 233
Sibley, Jeff 365
Sioux Indians 41, 60, 68, 69
Sirois, Lou 228
Skagit Valley Herald 124
Slaton, Dr. Roy F. 239
Smith, Jim 163
Sonora Desert 215
South Carolina
   Charleston 335
   Gardens Corner 333
   Georgetown 339
   Kiawah Island 335, 337
   Litchfield 339
   Mt. Pleasant 337
   Myrtle Beach 339
   Patriot's Point 336
South Texas Nuclear Project 282
Spinks, Raleigh 386
Spiro, Suenell 317
Spring, Vicky 146
Squires, Deborah 318
State Parks
   Baraga 24
   Big Lagoon 304
   Cheesequake 352-53
   Cole Creek 384

Del Norte Coast Redwood 157
Evangola 388
English Camp 129
Fort Ross 168
Fort Clinch 321-23
Four Mile Creek 386
F. J. McLain 26
Gulf 303
Gulf Shores 304
Humboldt Redwood 161
Lime Kiln Point 129
Moran 131
Myrtle Beach 339
O'Leno 312
Palmer 360
Rockport 120
Sea Rim 285
Seminole Canyon 254
Straits 13-14, 15
Torrey Pines 201
Van Riper 21
Westcott Beach 385
Young's 12
State University of New York 355
Steve Akers 247
Steve 298
Stowe, Harriet Beecher 315
Strait of Juan de Fuca 138
Straits of Mackinac 14
Sunflowers 45, 59

Tabby 327-28
Tanyhill, Jean 180, 181, 192
Terrell, Scott 124
Terry bicycle 362
Terry, Georgena 355, 362
Terwilliger, Katherine 317, 318
Texas
    Asherton 260
    Brazoria 282
    Brownsville 271, 274
    Carrizo Springs 260
    Chocolate Bayou 281
    Clute 282-83
    Comstock 254
    Corpus Christi 276, 277
    Del Rio 255-57
    Dryden 252
    Eagle Pass 260
    El Paso 232-34, 235
    Galveston 283

Goose Island 280
Hidalgo 270
Hog Bayou 281
Kingsville 276
Lajitas 242-45
Lake Jackson 282
Langtry 252-53
Laredo 261
Los Fresnos 274
Marathon 250-51
Marfa 239-40
McAllen 269
McNary 237
Mustang Island 278
Padre Island 278
Palacios 281
Point Comfort 281
Port Aransas 279
Port Arthur 284, 286, 287-288
Port Bolivar 284
Port Lavaca 281
Presidio 241
Quemado 259
Raymondville 275
Redford 241
Rio Hondo 275
Rockport 279
Rollover Fish Pass 284
Sabine Pass 286
San Ygnacio 263
Sanderson 252
Shafter 240
Sierra Blanca 237
Tornillo 236
Valentine 239
Van Horn 237
Wadsworth 282
Zapata 264-65
Texas Travel Handbook 237
Thelma 164-65
Theresa 24
Theriot, Betty 291
Theriot, Oberley 291-92
Thibodeaux, Phil 295, 297
Thibodeaux, Theresa 295-297
Thimbleberries 25
Thomas, Bob 52
Thomas, Jeanne 50, 53
Thomas, Merrillan 385-86
Thomas, Woody 385-86
Thompson, Alba 359

Thorntons 116
Thurlow, David 361
Tiger Balm 261, 348
Tom 90
Tomlinson, Gene 288
Tomlinson, Liz 288
Toomey, Suzanne 386-89
Travels with Charlie 147
Trout 99, 384
Trussler, Ernie 383
Trussler, Flo 383
Tusa, Susan 393

Upper Souris National Wildlife
    Refuge 53

Vanilla Bean Ice Cream Parlor 356
Vaughn, Jimmy 304-6
Vaughn, Vivian 304-6
Vawser, Edward T. 276
Vermont
    Derby 380
    Island Pond 379-80
    Newport 380
    Sheldon Junction 380-81
Vieg, Elizabeth 195, 196, 197, 198, 199
Vieg, John 195, 196, 197, 199
Virginia
    Cape Charles 347
    Cheriton 347-48
    Cobb Island 348
    Oyster 348
    Virginia Beach 345
Voss, Sister Anna 177-78

Wallace, Opal 284, 286-88, 289
Washington
    Aberdeen 144
    Amanda Park 143
    Anacortes 128
    Blueslide 106
    Cape Flattery 144
    Cascade Loop 117
    Clallam Bay 141
    Colville 110
    Conway 121, 124
    Diablo Dam 119
    Eastsound 131
    Forks 142
    Friday Harbor 128, 131
    Hoquiam 144

Humptulips 143
Ilwaco 144, 145
Kettle Falls 109, 110
Klipchuck 115-16
La Conner 121, 122, 140
Lake Leo 106, 107
Loop Loop Pass 113
Mt. Vernon 120-28, 137-38, 139
Neah Bay 140
Newport 104, 106
Okanogan 112, 113
Oldtown 105
Omak 112
Orcas Island 131
Ozette 141
Park Rapids 108
Port Angeles 138, 140
Rainy Pass 117
Raymond 144
Republic 111-12
Rockport 119
San Juan Island 128-36
Seattle 121, 125, 140
Seaview 144
Sedro Woolley 120
Sequim 138
Sherman Pass 110, 111
Skagit Valley 121
Tiger 106
Tonasket 112
Twisp 117
Washington Pass 115
Wauconda Pass 112
Winthrop 114
Washington, D.C. 140, 186-87,
    190, 394
Wavin Enterprises 37
WD40 9, 37, 64, 113
Weaver, Beth 149
Weissman, Irv 355
Wells, M. G. 289-90
Whiteley, Jo 137, 139
Wickliffe, Jackie 286
Wildflowers 18, 23, 59, 87, 88, 166,
    241, 386
Williams, Dick 90
Williams, Marilyn 90
Williams, Samuel May home 283
Wognum, Anne 37
Wolff, Betty Jo 304
Women's Cycling Network 363

Wood Merchant 139
Woodsend, Betty 80, 350
Wyandot Indians 22

Young, Delores 250
Young, Linda 249-50
Young, Noland 250
Young family 251
Yaak Mercantile 97
Yurok Indians 158
YWCA 136, 139

Zerc milestones
    Old Spanish Trail 319
    Trans-Canada Highway 139